Babylon to Jerusalem

WITH FIVE GREAT MEN

Robert E. Surgenor

BABYLON TO JERUSALEM

Published by Gospel Folio Press
304 Killaly Street West
Port Colborne, ON L3K 6A6
Canada

ISBN 1-882701-97-6

ORDERING INFORMATION
Gospel Folio Press
Phone: 1-800-952-2382
E-mail: orders@gospelfolio.com

Printed in the United States of America

Contents

Acknowledgements

At midnight, February 10th, 1952, my wife, Wilda, saved only six days, led me to Christ. In 1963, she took full responsibility of raising our two sons, as I went forth for His name's sake into the harvest field to win souls for Christ.

On many occasions I was absent from home for five months, only to return home for a week or two before leaving again. God gave my dear wife the grace to manage the home in a godly manner during my absence, raising our two sons in the nurture and admonition of the Lord.

In the writing of this book, once again I am deeply indebted to her, and also to my sister in the faith, Doris Ramsay, of the Newington Assembly in Connecticut, for their labor of love in correcting my grammatical errors prior to publication.

EASY TO READ

This book, brings five great men to life with exceedingly practical lessons for our Christian life today.

* Come with Zerubbabel and Jeshua on their journey from Babylon to Jerusalem, about 536 B.C..

* Observe their difficulties with the adversaries and enemies in the land, as they seek to build the temple for Jehovah.

* Read with interest the blunt prophesies of Haggai as he stirs the people to work.

* Read with awe the eight profound night visions of Zechariah, made simple to understand, as well as his final prophecies.

* Observe the visitors from Babylon and Bethel, and notice the contrast.

* Move on 58 more years and view the skillful movements of Ezra as he instructs the remnant of Israel back in the land, in 457 B.C.

Preface

Israel – the most unique and interesting nation on the face of planet earth! Elected and brought into existence to fulfill God's purposes, this nation was raised to a position of unsurpassed glory, only to be reduced to utter destruction and despair under the destructive power of Nebuchadnezzar. However, God's purposes were for the nation to revive after seventy years of servitude, and return to the land, and city where He had placed His name. The tracing of the return of the remnant, their purpose of heart, and their problems are most instructive for the Christian today. The path of separation and the maintaining of God's order seen in the remnant are most instructive for our behavior, as a remnant testimony, in a dark world that desires not the knowledge of God's ways. We trust that the consideration of the five great men in this book connected with this movement will instruct and inspire us all to endeavor to maintain a distinct testimony and a separated life for God.

CHAPTER ONE

Departure and Judgment

COME WITH ME back in time to the city of Jerusalem in its final days of testimony for Jehovah. The year is B.C. 605, and King Jehoiakim is on the throne. Like a floundering ship, the beloved city of God is rapidly sinking, ready for its final plunge into the depths of the Gentile sea. Never in the history of the nation of Israel were the days so dark. The longsuffering of God had now come to its end, and the severe judgment of God was about to follow. Darkness prevailed, and the hearts of many were permeated with fear. Time and time again, the prophets of God had faithfully warned the nation, only to be mocked and ridiculed by the leaders. The mournful account is indelibly written on the page of holy writ in 2 Chronicles 36.

King Jehoahaz

"Then the people of the land took Jehoahaz the son of Josiah, and made him king in his father's stead in Jerusalem." He was Judah's sixteenth king, the year being 608 B.C. "Jehoahaz was twenty and three years old when he began to reign, and he reigned three months in Jerusalem. And the king of Egypt put him down at Jerusalem, and condemned the land in an hundred talents of silver and a talent of gold. And the king of Egypt made Eliakim his brother king over Judah and Jerusalem, and turned his name to Jehoiakim. And Necho took Jehoahaz his brother, and carried him to Egypt."

King Jehoiakim

"Jehoiakim was twenty and five years old when he began to reign, and he reigned eleven years in Jerusalem: and he did that which was evil in the sight of the LORD his God." Made king by the king of Egypt in 608 B.C., this monarch's record was dark. He was the seventeenth king of Judah. He killed Urijah the prophet (Jer. 26:23), burned the word of God (Jer. 36:23), attempted to arrest Jeremiah and his secretary, Baruch, but the Lord hid them (Jer. 36:19). Jeremiah prophesied of his untimely end, "He shall be buried with the burial of an ass, drawn and cast forth beyond the gates of Jerusalem…Therefore thus saith the LORD of Jehoiakim king of Judah; He shall have none to sit upon the throne of David: and his dead body shall be cast out in the day to the heat, and in the night to the frost" (Jer. 22:19; 36:30). "Against him came up Nebuchadnezzar king of Babylon (605 B.C.), and bound him in fetters (chains of brass), to carry him to Babylon." However, this did not take place, for Nebuchadnezzar allowed him to stay. "Nebuchadnezzar also carried of the vessels of the house of the LORD to Babylon, and put them in his temple at Babylon. Now the rest of the acts of Jehoiakim, and his abominations which he did, and that which was found in him, behold, they are written in the book of the kings of Israel and Judah: and Jehoiachin his son reigned in his stead."

King Jehoiachin

"Jehoiachin was eight years old when he began to reign (597 B.C., the eighteenth king), and he reigned three months and ten days in Jerusalem: and he did that which was evil in the sight of the LORD. And when the year was expired, king Nebuchadnezzar sent, and brought him to Babylon, with the goodly vessels of the house of the LORD, and made Zedekiah his brother king over Judah and Jerusalem."

King Zedekiah

"Zedekiah (the nineteenth king) was one and twenty years old when he began to reign, and reigned eleven years in Jerusalem (597 to 586 B.C.). And he did that which was evil in the sight of the LORD his God, and humbled not himself before Jeremiah the prophet speaking from the mouth of the LORD. And he also rebelled against king Nebuchadnezzar, who had made him swear by God: but he stiffened his neck, and hardened his heart from turning unto the LORD God of Israel."

Judah – A terminal case

"Moreover all the chief of the priests, and the people, transgressed very much after all the abominations of the heathen; and polluted the house of the LORD which He had hallowed (to make clean) in Jerusalem. And the LORD God of their fathers sent to them by His messengers, rising up betimes (continually and carefully), and sending; because He had compassion on His people, and on His dwelling place: But they mocked (made jokes) the messengers of God, and despised (hold in contempt, count worthless) His words, and misused (scoffed at, ridiculed) His prophets, until the wrath of the LORD arose against His people, till there was no remedy" Thus we see the nation spiritually sick – a terminal case! "Therefore He brought upon them the king of the Chaldees, who slew their young men with the sword in the house of their sanctuary, and had no compassion upon young man or maiden, old man, or him that stooped for age: He gave them all into his hand. And all the vessels of the house of God, great and small, and the treasures of the house of the LORD, and the treasures of the king, and of his princes; all these he brought to Babylon. And they burnt the house of God, and brake down the wall of Jerusalem, and burnt all the palaces thereof with fire, and destroyed all the goodly vessels thereof. And them that had escaped from the sword carried he away to Babylon; where they were servants to him and his sons until the reign of the kingdom of Persia: To fulfill the word of the LORD by the mouth of Jeremiah, until the land had enjoyed her sabbaths: for as long as she lay desolate she kept sabbath, to fulfill threescore and ten years" (2 Chr. 36:6-21).

Jeremiah's Ministry

That word spoken by Jeremiah was as follows. "Therefore thus saith the LORD of hosts; Because ye have not heard My words, Behold, I will send and take all the families of the north, saith the LORD, and Nebuchadrezzar the king of Babylon, My servant, and will bring them against this land, and against the inhabitants thereof, and against all these nations round about, and will utterly destroy them, and make them an astonishment, and an hissing, and perpetual desolations. Moreover I will take from them the voice of mirth, and the voice of gladness, the voice of the bridegroom, and the voice of the bride, the sound of the millstones, and the light of the candle. And this whole land shall be a desolation, and an astonishment; and these nations shall serve the king of Babylon seventy years" (Jer. 25:8-11).

The result of Jeremiah's faithful ministry is very interesting and finds a parallel to faithful messengers of the word of God today in certain areas. Notice! "When the princes of Judah heard these things, then they came up from the king's house unto the house of the LORD, and sat down in the entry of the new gate of the LORD'S house. Then spake the priests and the prophets unto the princes and to all the people, saying, This man is worthy to die; for he hath prophesied against this city, as ye have heard with your ears." (Jer. 26:10,11). Where such an attitude prevails today against corrective, negative ministry, the method of silencing is not threatening with death, but by simply not inviting the faithful minister back, or supporting him in a material way to carry on his work. Another method also is to corner him after the meeting with critical remarks concerning his ministry. As one old Puritan exclaimed concerning the Bible, "Not every Christian can stand the glare of an open book." However, their threats did not hinder the faithful prophet, he continued with his faithful warnings, and with faithful men today, it is the same. In love to the Lord's people they seek to be true in handling the holy scriptures and have no concern about monetary gain, or popularity – they continue to preach the unvarnished truth, no matter what the consequences may be. As one faithful minister remarked, "My conscience is not for sale."

There are a few things worthy to notice about the old testament prophets: (1) They appeared on the scene primarily in days of sin and declension; (2) they walked primarily alone with the Lord in total separation from the apostasy surrounding them; (3) the corrupt religious system, composed of false prophets and wayward priests, certainly did not endorse them; (4) their messages were only heeded by an insignificant remnant.

The destruction of Jerusalem and the captivity of His people accomplished a number of things; one of them being that it cured the people of Judah of their persistent attraction to idolatry. Since the captivity the Jews have never been guilty of worshipping idols. During their captivity, God raised up men with a purpose of heart to restore worship to the true God, the God of their fathers, and to restore scriptural worship to the Lord in the place where it had pleased Him to place His name – Jerusalem.

CHAPTER TWO

Daniel - His Prayer

Cyrus - His Proclamation

AS THE ACCOUNT of Ezra opens, we are immediately drawn to the greatest king at that time, Cyrus, king of Persia. There has been much conjecture regarding this mighty monarch, whether he was saved or not, and just what prompted him to give a proclamation throughout his kingdom to build God a house at Jerusalem, which is in Judah (Ezra 1:3).

Daniel – The Saintly Man

However, before considering Cyrus, let us take note of another man, an old saintly man who had proved God all his days in Babylon. Taken there in his teens, he had been incorporated into a high governmental position by Nebuchadnezzar, and seemingly was still in a very influential position as Cyrus took the kingdom. His name? - Daniel! How beautiful is the God-given account. "In the first year of Darius the son of Ahasuerus, of the seed of the Medes, which was made king over the realm of the Chaldeans; In the first year of his reign I Daniel understood by books the number of the years, whereof the word of the LORD came to Jeremiah the prophet, that he would accomplish seventy years in the desolations of Jerusalem. And I set my face unto the Lord God, to seek by prayer and supplications, with fasting, and sackcloth, and ashes" (Dan. 9:1-3). The following verses reveal Daniel confessing the nation's sin, and then he prays that God will hear his prayer and cause His face to shine upon His sanctuary that is desolate, for His sake (Dan. 9:17).

Thus we see, at the very commencement of the great movement back to Jerusalem, a humble man studying the prophecy of Jeremiah and praying in regard to its fulfillment. The Puritans confessed that, *prayer moves the hand that holds the world.* The great revival of 1859, originating in Kells, Northern Ireland, commenced with a few saints bowed in earnest, humble prayer. It was Daniel who supplicated the face of his God, and it was God Who stirred up the spirit of Cyrus. Truly, "The king's heart is in the hand of the LORD, as the rivers of water: He turneth it whithersoever He will" (Prov. 21:1).

Cyrus – King of Persia

It seems highly improbable that Cyrus was a child of God. Seemingly he believed in a multiplicity of gods. A little cylinder of clay from his time reveals that he said, "the gods had deserted Nabonidas, the last king of Babylon, because he had neglected their service; and that the god named Merodach, of Babylon, had transferred his favor to Cyrus; who now honors him with many praises." When it came to various forms of religion, Cyrus was very liberal-minded.

Writers have been led to believe, through the historian Josephus, that Cyrus, through reading the prophecy of Isaiah, when he saw his name in the prophecy regarding the rebuilding of Jerusalem (44:28), written 200 years prior to his birth, immediately was possessed with a strong desire to fulfill the writing; thus his proclamation to return and rebuild the city. It all sounds very plausible. However, Josephus, by some historians is considered untrustworthy whenever he touches the relations between the Jews and Gentiles, especially in his recording of the Persian Period. If his report were true, would not Ezra have incorporated the event in his book? However, Ezra is silent. It has also been thought that the Jews approached Cyrus with Isaiah's prophetic statement and read it to him. This too is conjecture. There is no evidence to prove it. It is highly improbable that such a great monarch, glowing with victory, would bother himself to fulfill a prophecy from the deity of one of the conquered nations, especially considering that the prediction was totally in their favor.

There seem to be some other considerations on his part involving his proclamation. Cyrus was a man of real genius. Considering the fact of retaining a restless foreign people in his kingdom, he saw that a liberation of the Jews would be a very wise policy. However, even though his proclamation may not have been as a result of religious convictions, or even as a result of state policy, yet we see the amazing overruling of the providence of Almighty God – the God of Israel! How graphic are the words of God, as Ezra begins to pen the sacred writing. "Now in the first year of Cyrus king of Persia, that the word of the LORD by the mouth of Jeremiah might be fulfilled, the LORD stirred up the spirit of Cyrus king of Persia, that he made a proclamation throughout all his kingdom, and put it also in writing, saying" (Ezra 1:1). The God that always accurately foretells the future can also stir the spirits of men, independently of all outward influences and circumstances. The spirit of Cyrus was stirred up – God was working!

The word "stirred up" is very interesting. It is found seventy-nine times in the Old Testament, in sixty-five verses. It is always profitable to notice the first occurrence of a word in the Holy Scriptures. "Stirred up," is found in Deuteronomy 32:11. "As an eagle stirreth up her nest, fluttereth over her young, spreadeth abroad her wings, taketh them, beareth them on her wings." In this portion, God is referring to His people Israel. The first thing noticed is God awakening them. He then manifests His affection to them, metaphorically speaking, as fluttering over them. Finally, He takes them and bears them on His wings, just as an eagle takes her young and bears them on her wings, teaching them to fly. Through the stirring up of Cyrus, awakening him to activity, Israel was now going to be awakened to return to their land, by the king's proclamation. Not only this, there is a God-induced affection in the heart of Cyrus for God's people, and he was prepared to help them learn to "fly" by supplying them with the necessary essentials for their return and for the rebuilding of God's testimony in Jerusalem. Thus God was accomplishing His purposes, using a Gentile king.

"O the depth of the riches both of the wisdom and knowledge of God! how unsearchable are His judgments, and His ways past finding out!" Romans 11:33.

The same God Who mentioned Cyrus by name, was the same God Who stirred up his spirit and moved his heart. Thus we see the overruling providence of God. In using men, Nebuchadnezzar was portrayed as God's "servant," for even though unknown to him, he was a tool in the hand of God fulfilling His designs. In like manner, Cyrus was described as God's "shepherd," God creating within him a care for the people of God, to fulfill His designs.

The Royal Decree

"Thus saith Cyrus king of Persia, The LORD God of heaven hath given me all the kingdoms of the earth; and He hath charged me to build Him an house at Jerusalem, which is in Judah. Who is there among you of all His people? his God be with him, and let him go up to Jerusalem, which is in Judah, and build the house of the LORD God of Israel, (He is the God,) which is in Jerusalem. And whosoever remaineth in any place where he sojourneth, let the men of his place help him with silver, and with gold, and with goods, and with beasts, beside the freewill offering for the house of God that is in Jerusalem" (Ezra 1:2-4).

The statement in the king's decree, "(He is the God)" being in brackets tends to be misleading. The R.V. of 1881, and other translations, omit them. As it reads in the Authorized Version, one is led to believe that Cyrus believed that Jehovah was the *only* God. Let us remember that, as a polytheist, Cyrus acknowledged many gods. On the Cyrus Cylinder this benevolent king, upon taking possession of Babylon, acknowledged Merodach as his god. He even requested his subjects to beseech the gods Bel and Nebo in his behalf. However, Isaiah 45:5, when speaking of Cyrus, settles the question - "I am the LORD, and there is none else, there is no God beside Me: I girded thee, though thou hast not known Me." If his decree is read without the unwarranted brackets, we see that he is simply informing non-Jews who may read his decree, who Jehovah is, He is the God Who dwells in Jerusalem. In other words, there are many gods, but the God of the Jews dwells in Jerusalem.

In his decree, the king is quick to acknowledge the superiority of the God of the Jews, attributing his military success to Him. He also acknowledges that it was this God that stirred him up to build Him a house in Jerusalem. He speaks of Him as "the LORD God of heaven." This description of God is used eight times in Ezra and four times in Nehemiah. It indicates that God had withdrawn His throne from earth and had given His people into Gentile hands. He had left and returned to His place, thus He was then known as the God of heaven.

He also speaks of Him as, "the LORD God of Israel," indicating that He is the God of testimony. Certainly this diplomatic and highly intelligent king knew how to draw up a proclamation in language that would be very appealing to his Jewish subjects. His diplomacy was exceptional, catering to the prejudices of his subjects. Cyrus acknowledged the greatness of the Jew's God, thus he desired the favor of this God, which he believed could be obtained by helping to rebuild His sanctuary.

His edict is not a compulsory draft – it was voluntary. None were forced to go, but all were allowed. Jerusalem lay in ruins. The land had become unproductive, resting for seventy years. Rubble and rubbish abounded. Many in Babylon were well settled and living quite comfortably. Why leave a comfortable home and prosperity in exchange for desolation and hardship? The volunteers were few in comparison to the total Jewish population. However, when one hundred percent of the people are volunteers you have a good elevation of quality and spirit. Drafted men may grumble and shirk their duties, but volunteers are wholehearted in what they put their minds to do. Quality is of more value than quantity.

Cyrus was also quick to recognize the fact that materials would be needed for this holy venture; thus he enjoins those remaining to have fellowship in this mighty work by contributing their substance.

Bringing this up to our day, do we not see a divine parallel expounded in 1 Corinthians chapter nine? Paul, as an apostle and an evangelist, states, "Have we not power (the right) to eat and to drink? Have we not power (the right) to lead about a sister, a wife, as well as other apostles, and as the brethren of the Lord, and Cephas? Or I only and Barnabas, have not we power (the right) to forbear working? Who goeth a warfare any time at his own charges? who planteth a vineyard, and eateth not of the fruit thereof? or who feedeth a flock, and eateth not of the milk of the flock? Say I these things as a man? or saith not the law the same also? For it is written in the law of Moses, Thou shalt not muzzle the mouth of the ox that treadeth out the corn. Doth God take care for oxen? Or saith he it altogether for our sakes? For our sakes, no doubt, this is written: that he that ploweth should plow in hope; and that he that thresheth in hope should be partaker of his hope. If we have sown unto you spiritual things, is it a great thing if we shall reap your carnal things? …Do ye not know that they which minister about holy things live of the things of the temple? and they which wait at the altar are partakers with the altar? Even so hath the Lord ordained that they which preach the gospel should live of the gospel."

Evangelists and their Support

Leaving the comforts of home, the true evangelist goes to regions beyond in the great harvest field. He does not cater to any group for guaranteed funds to support his ministry. He sees no need to give repeated reports of his work throughout the land, skipping here and there, filling his purse. His hand is to the plow, his eyes are toward the throne, and his labors are among those who have never heard a true gospel. Occasionally, out of gratitude and exercise, he visits assemblies that have enabled him to carry on his work for God, through their temporal ministry, and in return, ministers unto them of spiritual things. Just because he is no longer employed in a secular way, should he be deprived of food, or the right to support a wife? He has gone to war, but not at his own expense. As God cares for the planter of a vineyard, a shepherd of sheep, an ox treading out the corn, or even the priests attending the altar, even so He has ordained that they which preach the gospel should live of the gospel.

Let us challenge ourselves: Do we support such men with our substance? How long has it been since you have personally written a faithful laborer away out in the harvest field, alone with God, and sent him some means to support himself, his wife, his children, his work for God? Our closets may be full of various clothes. Our automobiles may be late models with luxuries; our tables may be daily spread with fine food, our homes may be well decorated, and our little "toys" many, but let me ask you this, when it comes for you to leave it all behind, how much treasure will you experience in the glory? In other words, how much treasure have you laid up for yourself in heaven? Do we really need those fleshly-desired extras, while perhaps some faithful servant is in need? I am not speaking of men that are always around the saints preaching. Such have it quite comfortable. I am speaking of those who have sacrificed a normal marriage and a comfortable life for the sake of the gospel. Yes, such men are rare in our day, but let us be aware, there are some here and there, and we owe God our support of them. The remnant went forth, fully supported by those who remained behind. The decree of Cyrus was sensible, scriptural, and serviceable.

Another thing we may consider: Was the giving of those who remained entirely voluntary? "Let the men of his place help him with silver, and with gold, and with goods, and with beasts, beside the freewill offering for the house of God that is in Jerusalem" (Ezra 1:4).

You will notice that word, "beside the freewill offering…beside all that was willingly offered." There seems to be some indication that Cyrus directed contributions to be made toward the work. No doubt the rich were called upon to donate the gold, silver and other precious things. We also are called upon, enjoined, to support the work of God. "Now concerning the collection for the saints, as I have given order to the churches of Galatia, even so do ye. Upon the first day of the week let every one of you lay by him in store, as God hath prospered him, that there be no gatherings when I come" (1 Cor. 16:1,2).

The Response to the Decree

The response to the proclamation was immediate. "Then rose up the chief of the fathers of Judah and Benjamin, and the priests, and the Levites, with all them whose spirit God had raised, to go up to build the house of the LORD which is in Jerusalem. And all they that were about them strengthened their hands with vessels of silver, with gold, with goods, and with beasts, and with precious things, beside all that was willingly offered" (Ezra 1:5,6).

It was the same God which stirred up Cyrus, Who now stirs up the prominent men and the priests. They had become awakened, God had opened their eyes. How is our vision? Peter speaks of spiritual eyesight in his second epistle. "But he that lacketh these things is blind, and cannot see afar off, and hath forgotten that he was purged from his old sins" (2 Pet.1:9). *He is blind*, he lacks discernment of true spiritual values. *He cannot see afar off.* He lives for the present rather than for the future. He is preoccupied with the temporal things of this earth, to the neglect of things spiritual. *He has forgotten* the blessed truth of his redemption. Redemptive truths no longer have a grip on his soul, and more than likely he is now playing with the very sins that caused the Saviour's death. A very sad situation indeed. If it was seen in Peter's day, how much more is it observed in our day! The chief fathers and priests had their eyes opened.

The vessels of the house of the Lord that Nebuchadnezzar had brought from Jerusalem were carefully guarded and kept by Cyrus. Warriors of ancient times usually carried their gods (idols) with them into battle, to assure them of victory. Upon vanquishing their foes, they would capture their gods and take them back to their own land, keeping them safely to appease them and not occasion their anger. Israel had no idols, but when Nebuchadnezzar defeated them, he carefully took the vessels of God's sanctuary back to Babylon. These vessels in his mind would convey the same importance as the idols of his conquered nations. Nebuchadnezzar had placed them in the house of his gods. Now the time had come for their release, thus we read: "Even those did Cyrus king of Persia bring forth by the hand of Mithredath the treasurer, and numbered them unto Sheshbazzar, the prince of Judah." (Ezra 1:8.).

The treasurer's name is worthy of notice. "Mithredath," means "given by Mithra," or "devoted to Mithra." The Persian sun god was worshipped among the servants of Cyrus. However, in spite of the treasurer's false god, yet he is constrained to pay honor to the God of Israel.

The Holy Vessels of God's House

In the vessels of God being stolen and kept in Babylon, then returned to the rightful owner seventy years later, we find an analogy. During their confinement in a strange land, they were perverted in their use. Notice the testimony of Daniel 5:1–4. "Belshazzar the king made a great feast to a thousand of his lords, and drank wine before the thousand. Belshazzar, whiles he tasted the wine, commanded to bring the golden and silver vessels which his father Nebuchadnezzar had taken out of the temple which was in Jerusalem;

that the king, and his princes, his wives, and his concubines, might drink therein. Then they brought the golden vessels that were taken out of the temple of the house of God which was at Jerusalem; and the king, and his princes, his wives, and his concubines, drank in them. They drank wine, and praised the gods of gold, and of silver, of brass, of iron, of wood, and of stone." Thus in the returning of the vessels to their rightful Owner we see a restoration of perverted things to their God-ordained use. Consider now man, made in the image and likeness of God, that he might glorify God. The Creator gave him a tongue to praise Him; He gave him a mind to meditate upon Him; He imparted to him eyes to behold His wondrous works, and ears to hear His voice, but alas, sin entered into the world and man died spiritually. He was sold on the slave market into sin. Paul laments, "we have before proved both Jews and Gentiles, that they are all under sin" (Rom. 3:9). That is, under its power, dominion, and control. The "vessels" have been taken captive, and the tongue, designed by God to praise Him, now curses Him. The mind given to meditate upon divine things is now used to devise wicked devices, and every imagination of the thoughts of his heart is only evil continually (Gen. 6:5). "Even their mind and conscience is defiled" (Titus 1:15). His God-given eyes are perverted. Thus the scripture states, "Having eyes full of adultery, and that cannot cease from sin" (2 Pet. 2:14). His ears are tuned to the world's music, its diabolical teachings, and the laughter of the fool.

However, when the salvation of a soul takes place the vessel, as it were, is returned to its original Owner. Thus the injunction, "Ye are bought with a price: therefore glorify God in your body, and in your spirit, which are God's" (1 Cor. 6:20). "I beseech you therefore, brethren, by the mercies of God, that ye present your bodies a living sacrifice, holy, acceptable unto God, which is your reasonable service. And be not conformed to this world: but be ye transformed by the renewing of your mind, that ye may prove what is that good, and acceptable, and perfect, will of God" (Rom. 12:1-2).

With the vessel being returned to God, the believer exclaims, "My tongue shall speak of Thy righteousness and of Thy praise all the day long" (Psa. 35:28). His mind finds new employment. "My meditation of Him shall be sweet: I will be glad in the LORD" (Psa. 104:34). Regarding his eyes, the new believer exclaims, "Open Thou mine eyes, that I may behold wondrous things out of Thy law" (Psa. 119:18). Regarding his ears it can be said of them, "Blessed is the people that know the joyful sound: they shall walk, O LORD, in the light of Thy countenance" (Psa. 89:15). The vessels of gold and silver, restored to God and placed into the hand of Zerubbabel, is a graphic picture of a sinner being saved and brought back to God, to intelligently serve Him with reverence and with godly fear.

The Meanings of Names.

The question now arises, who was Sheshbazzar? Some think that he was Zerubbabel's uncle and that Zerubbabel, upon his uncle's sudden death, was elevated to his position. Another theory is that Sheshbazzar was the officially appointed leader, whereas Zerubbabel was a popular but unofficial leader at the same time. However, we take the view that Sheshbazzar and Zerubbabel were the same person, just as Daniel's name, meaning, *my God is Judge*, had been changed to Belteshazzar, meaning, *whom Bel favors*. His three companions experienced the same tactic; Hananiah, *whom Jehovah hath favored,* was named Shadrach, *inspired by the sun god*. Mishael, *who is comparable to God,* was given the name of Meshach, meaning, *who is like Venus*. Azariah, *whom the Lord helps,* was renamed Abednego, *servant of the shining fire*. It was a Babylonish scheme to cause these men to lose their identity. However, even though Babylon changed their names, they never succeeded in changing their nature. God was still in all their thoughts. Zerubbabel's name means, *born in Babylon*, while Sheshbazzar means, *worshipper of fire*. His first name correctly identified the place of his birth, but his second name incorrectly described the object of his worship. He worshipped not fire, but rather the God of the everlasting burnings.

Numbers and Weights

God records the number and weight of the treasure. "And this is the number of them: thirty chargers of gold, a thousand chargers of silver, nine and twenty knives, Thirty basons of gold, silver basons of a second sort four hundred and ten, and other vessels a thousand. All the vessels of gold and of silver were five thousand and four hundred. All these did Sheshbazzar bring up with them of the captivity that were brought up from Babylon unto Jerusalem." (Ezra 1:9-11). If you add the vessels in verse ten they amount to 2,499, yet in verse eleven it states that 5,400 were taken to Jerusalem. There is no discrepancy, since more than likely the larger and most prominent vessels were numbered in verse ten, whereas in verse eleven all the vessels were counted, even those not enumerated. This is the view of ancient interpreters.

A Careful Look at Cyrus

Before leaving the gates of Babylon, let us for a moment consider this great man Cyrus. The Lord spoke of him as, " the man that executeth My counsel" (Isa. 46:11); "a righteous man" (Isa. 41:2); "My shepherd" (Isa. 44:28); and, "His anointed" (Isa. 45:1). God employed him in the fulfilling of His purposes in the releasing of His people and the rebuilding of His holy dwelling place in Jerusalem.

In executing the counsel of God, Cyrus thought that he was pursuing his own interests, but in reality, he was only fulfilling the divine plan of God for His people, Israel. How remarkably God works on heathen hearts to fulfill His own unique designs. God's ways are the same today. Governments are motivated and move seemingly according to their own interests, little realizing that behind all their schemes and plans lies the providence of God, moving them like puppets to fulfill His own sovereign design and will.

Let us remember that the great Controller of kings, dictators, presidents and prime ministers, is not only our God, but also our Father. He is on the throne, and we are in His hand. Need we fear? "He ruleth by His power for ever; His eyes behold the nations" (Psa. 66:7). Daniel confessed, "And all the inhabitants of the earth are reputed as nothing: and He doeth according to His will in the army of heaven, and among the inhabitants of the earth: and none can stay His hand, or say unto Him, What doest Thou?" (Dan. 4:35). What a great God we have, yet how feeble is our appreciation of Him!

Why should we fear, O Lord our God,
When nations in Thy hand are moved.
All to fulfill Thy plan divine,
We wait on Thee, thus faith is proved.

Cyrus, a righteous man! This is God's appraisal of him. How can a heathen be a righteous man? The answer is simple. History informs us that he was a habitually upright man, a man conscientious about inflicting wrong. Because of his upright character, his countrymen held him in very high esteem. His private life was irreproachable. In speaking thus of Cyrus, we are reminded of the testimony of God regarding a Roman. "There was a certain man in Caesarea called Cornelius, a centurion of the band called the Italian band, A devout man, and one that feared God with all his house, which gave much alms to the people, and prayed to God alway" (Acts 10:1,2).

God said he was His shepherd. A shepherd protects and provides for his flock. Certainly Cyrus fulfilled this description in his manifested care for the welfare of God's people, encouraging them to return to their land while at the same time making contributions at his own expense to further God's design for His remnant people. It is interesting to note that only two persons are termed, "My Shepherd," in the Holy Scriptures. The other One we know very well. "Awake, O sword, against My Shepherd, and against the Man that is My fellow, saith the LORD of hosts: smite the Shepherd, and the sheep shall be scattered: and I will turn Mine hand upon the little ones" (Zech.13:7). The sword of Cyrus was in the sheath, sleeping. The victory was won and the sheep of Israel were called upon to gather together to return to the land. What a contrast when we consider our blessed Lord as God's Shepherd. The sword had been removed from the sheath, ready to be plunged into His bosom, and the sheep of Israel were soon to be scattered.

The next description we find of Cyrus is that he was called, "God's anointed." Kings were anointed with oil to their kingly position, but Cyrus was more than a merely anointed king – he was the Lord's anointed. What a distinguished position! God in His providence had appointed this mighty man, who ruled over the Lord's captive people, to restore His people to their own land and to restore the worship of Jehovah in Jerusalem. Thus, as the Lord's anointed, the purposes of God were accomplished.

This mighty monarch's name is discovered twenty-three times in Holy Scripture, but whether his name is written in heaven I know not. I would like to think that such a benevolent man toward the people of God would find Israel's God to be his God, but we must wait the day when the saints all meet on the heavenly shore to discover if he ever found shelter beneath the wings of Jehovah or not.

CHAPTER THREE

Zerubbabel

The Great Gathering Together

THE SECOND CHAPTER of Ezra may prove uninteresting to the casual reader because of all the names recorded. However, to the careful reader of Holy Scripture (which all of us should be), there are nuggets of gold along the trail of names that contain vital and precious truths. As we walk among the multitude of returnees, let us grasp the scattered golden nuggets and learn their valuable truths.

Who would have thought among these thousands of people, that their family names would be indelibly recorded in the page of holy scripture? Through the following ages, their names have been viewed by the readers of God's word. How carefully God observes His people, even those that appear insignificant. Regarding us, the Lord said that even the hairs of our head are numbered, and Job exclaimed, "Thou numberest my steps" (Job 14:16). We are closely observed and certainly not obscure to the eye of our God.

The returning remnant's names were written in God's book. The Lord said regarding us, "Rejoice, because your names are written in heaven" (Lk. 10:20).

Names and Numbers

God is a God of order, thus we see a divine order in the list of names. The leaders are mentioned first, eleven including Zerubbabel. However, in Nehemiah 7:7, there are twelve names. Some of the names are spelled differently but a marginal reading in most Bibles clears the apparent discrepancy. Nahamani is the only name missing in the list in Ezra 2:2. The name means, "he comforted me," or, "repenting." The meaning of that name certainly reminds us of the condition and experience of the nation at that time. They had repented of their sins, never again to return to idolatry, and they were experiencing the comforting hand of God through the attitude and decree of Cyrus for them to return to their native land. We may also note that the names Nehemiah and Mordecai, mentioned in chapter two, are not the same persons as mentioned in the Book of Nehemiah and Esther.

The number "twelve" in scripture is interesting and can be found at least 168 times. God mentions twelve wells of water to a thirsty multitude at Elim (Ex.15: 27); twelve cakes set on the table of shewbread for the eye of God to feast upon (Lev. 24:5); twelve stones to be placed in Jordan and twelve stones to be taken out of Jordan as a memorial (Josh. 4:8,9); twelve apostles chosen of our Lord to further the gospel (Lk. 6:13); the heavenly Jerusalem with twelve gates of pearl, and the city, twelve thousand furlongs square (Rev. 21:21,16) containing the tree of life bearing twelve manner of fruits (Rev.22:2). In the mention of twelve names we have a representation of the twelve tribes of Israel, thus the whole nation of Israel is represented.

Priests and Levites

There is a distinct order to Ezra chapter two. The list is according to the families, then all the cities situated in the neighborhood of Jerusalem. The number of priests that returned was 4,289, while the Levites numbered only seventy-four. One may wonder why so few Levites responded to the call to return to Jerusalem. Perhaps the answer could be found in Ezekiel 44:9-16, where, because of their disobedience to God, they were placed in a lower function, not acceptable to them. Evidently the prophet's message was obeyed, for in Ezra chapter two we see them being separated from the priests in the arrangement. Perhaps, through sulking resentment, they balked at the thought of doing just a menial service; thus their aloofness from an expedition of rebuilding the temple. Another thought is, they had no inheritance in the land, for the Lord was their inheritance, so why return when no material gain was in prospect? Following their mention, we notice, "The singers: the children of Asaph, an hundred twenty and eight." (Ezra 2:41). They too were Levites, but a separate class from the seventy-four previously mentioned. Next on the list were the children of the porters, one hundred and thirty-nine, followed by the Nethinims and the children of Solomon's servants, three hundred and ninety and two. Thus in Ezra chapter two we have various ranks and duties of those who returned. The priests (vs.36-39), the Levites who assisted the priests (vs. 40), the Levitical singers (vs.41), the Levitical gate-keepers or porters (vs.42), the Nethinims, who performed the more servile and laborious duties (vs. 43-54), and the children of Solomon's servants, who were slaves and did the lowest work of all (vs. 55-60).

It has been supposed that the Nethinims were the descendants of the Gibeonites, who were made hewers of wood and drawers of water. Solomon's servants were war captives made slaves and assigned to the work of building the first temple. Now we see their children, still slaves, ready to be employed in the construction of the second temple.

As it was then, so it is today in an assembly of God; there are various spheres of service. The truth of First Corinthians chapter twelve comes before us. "Now there are diversities of gifts, but the same Spirit. And there are differences of administrations, but the same Lord. And there are diversities of operations, but it is the same God which worketh all in all. But the manifestation of the Spirit is given to every man to profit withal" (vs. 4-7).

Following this scripture, various gifts are mentioned, and then we read, "But all these worketh that one and the selfsame Spirit, dividing to every man severally as He will" (vs. 11). There is a good exhortation for us all in Romans chapter twelve, verses six to eight. "Having then gifts differing according to the grace that is given to us, whether prophecy, let us prophesy according to the proportion of faith; Or ministry, let us wait on our ministering: or he that teacheth, on teaching; Or he that exhorteth, on exhortation: he that giveth, let him do it with simplicity; he that ruleth, with diligence; he that sheweth mercy, with cheerfulness."

The Urim and Thummin

All seemed to be in order, except for one thing. Just as the children of Solomon's servants, and the Nethinims "could not shew their father's house, and their seed, whether they were of Israel" (vs.59), some children of the priests "sought their register among those that were reckoned by genealogy, but they were not found: therefore were they, as polluted, put from the priesthood" (vs. 62).

Thus we see a definite attitude in maintaining purity regarding the priesthood. We could apply this by saying that there are people today who claim to be Christians but have never experienced the new birth. It is only those who are born again who can show their father's house (show their register). One could hardly accept into a gathered out assembly of God's people a person who lacked the credentials of the new birth. These uncertified priests were not allowed to eat of the holy things until a priest rose up with the Urim and Thummim. One may ask just what were the Urim and the Thummim? Whatever they were (perhaps two different stones) they were incorporated into the breastplate of the high priest (Ex. 28:30; Lev.8:8), and were used to discern the mind of God on various occasions (Num. 27:21; 1 Sam. 28:6).

Since the claim of these people of being priests could not be verified, Zerubbabel set them aside until a time would arise when the high priest would be endowed with God's power to be able to accurately discern through the Urim (lights) and Thummim (perfections) the true status of those held in question. As far as we know, that day never came. Unlike in a former day, Israel lacked the Urim and

Thummim, the ark and the shekinah presence of Jehovah.

Numerical Values

Hebrew words, unlike our language, contain numerical values. It is very interesting to observe the numerical value of the words employed in Ezra 2:63. "And the Tirshatha (the governor, Zerubbabel) said unto them, that they should not eat of the most holy things, till there stood up a ***priest* (75) *with Urim* (287) *and with Thummim* (526)**." Add those six words with their numerical values and you arrive at **888**, which is the numerical value of the name ***JESUS!*** It is also interesting to notice the initial letters of Urim and Thummim. **Urim** is **Aleph**, made to represent the head of an ox, indicating sacrifice. **Thummim** is **Tav**, a letter shaped like a cross. These letters, being the first and last letters in the Hebrew alphabet, equal the word **"WHOM"** employed in Zechariah 12:10 – "And I will pour upon the house of David, and upon the inhabitants of Jerusalem, the spirit of grace and of supplications: and they shall look upon Me **WHOM** they have pierced, and they shall mourn for Him, as one mourneth for his only son, and shall be in bitterness for Him, as one that is in bitterness for his firstborn." At that future time, the Nation of Israel will fully realize the sacrifice made by their Messiah on the cross. The numerical value of the word "WHOM," is 232, which equals, "JEHOVAH." It is amazing the truths that the Holy Spirit has woven into the text of Holy Writ in the Hebrew language.

It is also worthy of note that the word **URIM** means **LIGHTS**, indicating the deity of our blessed Lord Who was the light of the world. The word **THUMMIM** means **PERFECTIONS**, pointing to the fact of our Lord's impeccable humanity. Thus we see Jehovah, Jesus our Lord, His essential deity, His sinless humanity, combined eternally for His future activity with His earthly people when He shall officiate as a priest upon His throne. Thus the prophecy of Zechariah to the returning remnant - "Then take silver and gold, and make crowns, and set them upon the head of Joshua the son of Josedech, the high priest; And speak unto him, saying, Thus speaketh the LORD of hosts, saying, Behold the man whose name is The BRANCH; and He shall grow up out of His place, and He shall build the temple of the LORD: Even He shall build the temple of the LORD; and He shall bear the glory, and shall sit and rule upon His throne; and ***He shall be a priest upon His throne:*** and the counsel of peace shall be between them both" (Zech. 6: 11-13). What a glorious portion awaits His earthly people in a soon-coming day!

Zerubbabel and the Journey

However, for the present time, let us now go back to Zerubbabel and his company, making their way through the desert to Jerusalem. It might be said of these people that they were a purposeful people. Their purpose of heart was to rebuild the altar and temple and initiate sacrifices unto their God in the place that He had chosen to place His name. They valued the place and they longed to be able to sacrifice unto their God once again. What a pure purpose of heart! We rejoice when we see this attitude amongst the saints today, a deep and devoted appreciation for the assembly of God, and a longing to be with God's gathered out people.

The very fact that there were so few willing to make the sacrifice involved in returning is a discredit to those who remained comfortably in Babylon. They were not occupied with the testimony of Jehovah, much less making sacrifices for the LORD. They had found their Babylonish surroundings quite comfortable and satisfying. Why leave the comforts, the prosperity, and the pleasures of Babylon, to become returned exiles, to suffer hardship, and reproach, in a far off land? Does this not strike a similarity in our day? How sad to see some that have lost their attraction to the assembly, thus they are found in places of worldly company and entertainment that can never fill the soul that has tasted of His love. Many of God's people are immersed in a world system; they find themselves quite comfortable indulging in its pleasures. The path of separation and reproach, connected with a scriptural testimony, has no appeal to them. They are saved, but it seems that their acceptance of Christ as their Saviour amounts only as an escape hatch from going to hell in their minds. They have never laid themselves upon the altar for God. They have never bid a total farewell to the world's pleasures. Consequently, they have become like those who go down to the pit, and any resemblance of Christ in their lives is very dim. The injunction of the Holy Spirit through the apostle Paul remains. "I beseech you therefore, brethren, by the mercies of God, that ye present your bodies a living sacrifice, holy, acceptable unto God, which is your reasonable service. And be not conformed to this world: but be ye transformed by the renewing of your mind, that ye may prove what is that good, and acceptable, and perfect, will of God" (Rom. 12:1,2). May the Lord keep us a people with a pure purpose of heart.

Not only were they purposeful, they were a praising people. I often wonder what psalms were employed by the singers as they trudged along the desert from Babylon to the City of God? One hundred and twenty-eight trained voices, filling the atmosphere with notes of praise and gladness to the returning pilgrims. How beautiful!

We are not told exactly which route the caravan took through the wild and rugged country. If the route was the usual one, by Palmyra, the eight hundred miles would have taken several months, for when Ezra came from Babylon to Jerusalem, seventy-eight years later, it is recorded that the journey took four months (Ezra 7:8,9). However, if the easier, but longer way by Aleppo were taken, the journeying time would have even been longer. Perhaps the fifteen songs of degrees (Psa. 120 to 134) were sung along the way. Would not the words of Psalm 121 encourage them through the hot desert? "I will lift up mine eyes unto the hills, from whence cometh my help. My help cometh from the LORD, which made heaven and earth. He will not suffer thy foot to be moved: He that keepeth thee will not slumber. Behold, He that keepeth Israel shall neither slumber nor sleep. The LORD is thy keeper: the LORD is thy shade upon thy right hand. The sun shall not smite thee by day, nor the moon by night. The LORD shall preserve thee from all evil: He shall preserve thy soul. The LORD shall preserve thy going out and thy coming in from this time forth, and even for evermore."

Would not Psalm 122 fill their hearts with confidence and hope? "I was glad when they said unto me, Let us go into the house of the LORD. Our feet shall stand within thy gates, O Jerusalem. Jerusalem is builded as a city that is compact together: Whither the tribes go up, the tribes of the LORD, unto the testimony of Israel, to give thanks unto the name of the LORD. For there are set thrones of judgment, the thrones of the house of David. Pray for the peace of Jerusalem: they shall prosper that love thee. Peace be within thy walls, and prosperity within thy palaces. For my brethren and companions' sakes, I will now say, Peace be within thee. Because of the house of the LORD our God I will seek thy good." The singing of Psalm 126 would express the fact that they were overjoyed at the thought of such sudden permission to return to their God-given land. "When the LORD turned again the captivity of Zion, we were like them that dream. Then was our mouth filled with laughter, and our tongue with singing: then said they among the heathen, The LORD hath done great things for them. The LORD hath done great things for us; whereof we are glad" (vs. 1-3). They also would realize the importance of God's presence through the words of Psalm 127. "Except the LORD build the house, they labour in vain that build it: except the LORD keep the city, the watchman waketh but in vain" (vs. 1). Also appreciated would be the importance and sweetness of unity among themselves. "Behold, how good and how pleasant it is for brethren to dwell together in unity! It is like the precious ointment upon the head, that ran down upon the beard, even Aaron's beard: that went down to the skirts of his garments; As the dew of Hermon, and as the dew that descended upon the mountains of Zion: for there the LORD commanded the blessing, even life for evermore" (Psa. 133). The remnant were a praising people.

Not only was this company a people of purpose and praise, it could be said of them that they were materially poor. They only had one slave to every six persons. For every fifty-eight persons, there was only one horse. For every one hundred seventy and three persons, there was only one mule. For every ninety-eight souls, there was only one camel, and for every seven persons, only one ass. What a contrast to Job who possessed seven thousand sheep, three thousand camels, five hundred yoke of oxen, and five hundred she asses! When the people were numbered in Sinai, there were 603,550 able men to go to war. How different in Zerubbabel's day, when the whole congregation numbered a mere 42,360, plus servants and maids (Ezra 2:64,65).

However, little is much if God is in it. No doubt there would be some among them who were people of means. How wonderful to see their attitude when they arrived at their longed-for destination. "And some of the chief of the fathers, when they came to the house of the LORD which is at Jerusalem, offered freely for the house of God to set it up in his place: They gave after their ability unto the treasure of the work threescore and one thousand drams of gold, and five thousand pound of silver, and one hundred priests' garments. So the priests, and the Levites, and some of the people, and the singers, and the porters, and the Nethinims, dwelt in their cities, and all Israel in their cities" (Ezra 2:68–70).

It must have been quite an emotional experience for these dear souls to return to the land of their fathers, to stand on the very ground on which their fathers had worked and raised their families, the very ground where their fathers had brought their offerings to Jehovah. Yes, and the very land in which some of their fathers had disobeyed their God, following after the idols of the heathen. Perhaps the thoughts of many hearts were revealed as they would commune with one another over their return to the city of God.

Godly Giving

No doubt their emotions would be touched as they gazed on that pile of rubble that had once been the monument of the greatest kingdom seen, when Solomon, in all his wisdom and glory, commanded the respect and admiration of all the surrounding nations. They would view the burned gates, the foundations of former dwellings, the uncultivated barren land, lying in total waste, waiting for the day of revival, when once again, it would bring forth nourishment to the sower. I picture tears on that occasion as well as joy. But I see something else in these people, I see love, a love for the place where Jehovah had been pleased to place His name, thus we read, "They offered freely…they gave after their ability." They were a passionate and providing people. When I read these words, I am reminded of two New Testament churches, Antioch and Corinth. Notice Acts chapter eleven. "And in these days came prophets from Jerusalem unto Antioch. And there stood up one of them named Agabus, and signified by the Spirit that there should be great dearth throughout all the world: which came to pass in the days of Claudius Caesar. Then the disciples, every man ***according to his ability,*** determined to send relief unto the brethren which dwelt in Judaea: Which also they did, and sent it to the elders by the hands of Barnabas and Saul" (Acts 11:27-30). Antioch, some two hundred and forty miles north of Jerusalem was the first Gentile assembly, planted not by apostles, but rather by the persecuted saints that had fled Jerusalem. Prophets had traveled from Jerusalem to Antioch to help them in a spiritual way, and now the Jerusalem saints needed help in a temporal way, due to a great dearth. The assembly at Antioch responded immediately. This is the first record in the human race, of a people of a foreign nation and culture, taking a collection to help those of another nation.

True Christianity manifests a love and deep concern for others. Let me ask you, are you concerned for the welfare of others, even saints that you have never met? Would you spend money needlessly on yourself, or perhaps your family, and never consider saints in distant places that may need temporal assistance? Or are you aware of the needs of other saints perhaps even near you? Consider the family that has been brought into severe trials. Are you aware? More than that, are you aware of their needs? More than that, are you willing to help them with your substance? Remember, God does not look necessarily on how much you give. What He considers is not how much you give, but rather how much you retain for yourself after you have given. It is nothing for a man with $100,000 in his bank account to give $1,000. He still has $99,000 for himself. But a widow with a bank account of only $500, if she gave the Lord $200, that would be a sacrifice, would it not? What would you think of a person living in a mansion, owning a luxury car and possessing a bulging savings account, putting $100 into the offering, and the widow in the same assembly, living in a low-income apartment, owning no car, and living from hand to mouth, placing $10 into the offering? Did the rich man give ten times as much to God as the poor widow? If you answer yes, think again! She deposited far more in her heavenly account than he. Consider the observation and words of our Lord. "And He saw also a certain poor widow casting in thither two mites. And He said, Of a truth I say unto you, that this poor widow hath cast in more than they all: For all these have of their abundance cast in unto the offerings of God: but she of her penury hath cast in all the living that she had" (Lk. 21:2-4). They gave after their ability. Do we?

They offered "freely." Their giving was spontaneous! It is interesting the kind of giver God appreciates. He makes His mind known to the Corinthians. "Every man according as he purposeth in his heart, so let him give; not grudgingly, or of necessity: for God loveth a cheerful giver" (2 Cor. 9:7). The word "cheerful," means "prompt" and it means "hilarious." It carries the thought of seeing a situation and acting on the spur of the moment, giving one's substance with exceeding great joy. The giver "laughs" as he parts with his material substance. How contrary to the ways of the earth dweller, who has all his aspirations, hopes, and gains centered on earth and its material things.

Paul, in his exhortation to the Corinthians relative to giving, supplies us with some vital truths and promises. Notice his exhortations. "But this I say, He which soweth sparingly shall reap also sparingly; and he which soweth bountifully shall reap also bountifully" (2 Cor. 9:6). Thus he sets before them nature's law. Any farmer will tell you that the more seed he sows the larger the harvest-crop he receives. A corn of wheat lying in a sack in the barn will yield him nothing. But let him sow that seed into the earth and it will yield him a multitude of grain. If you sow of your substance on earth, you will reap a great harvest at the Bema of Christ. Many wing their way to heaven and leave all their substance behind – in a bank account for their children to enjoy. However, their treasure chest in the glory is empty.

Paul now exposes us to the proper attitude in giving –, "so let him give; not grudgingly, or of necessity: for God loveth a cheerful giver" (vs 7). Not grudgingly, as if you were paying your taxes, or of necessity, as if you were being pressured into giving. Oh no, that will never do. One must give willingly. How much? The answer lies in this same verse, "As he purposeth in his heart." Some give 10% of their income, others more. I knew of a man that gave 95%, but the 5% he kept for himself amounted to a higher income than many. In 1 Corinthians 16:2 Paul says, "Upon the first day of the week let every one of you lay by him in store, as God hath prospered him, that there be no gatherings when I come." Thus the giving is habitual. Do also note that it is individual, it is singular, "every one of you." That means that the wife, as well as the husband, purposes in her heart what she will personally give from her own hand. It is not the husband's responsibility to put the wife's contribution into the offering for her. He does not sing for her. He does not eat the bread and drink from the cup for her. She is an individual priest as much as he and it is her own personal responsibility to put into the offering what the Lord has laid upon her own heart.

Having dealt with the attitude of the giver, Paul moves on to convince the Corinthians that God is able to supply the cheerful giver with more to give. "And God is able to make all grace abound toward you; that ye, always having all sufficiency in all things, may abound to every good work:

(As it is written, He hath dispersed abroad; he hath given to the poor: his righteousness remaineth for ever. Now He that ministereth seed to the sower both minister bread for your food, and multiply your seed sown, (or, "for sowing") and increase the fruits of your righteousness;) Being enriched in every thing to all bountifulness, which causeth through us thanksgiving to God" (2 Cor. 9:8-11).

Thus Paul reveals that the source of their giving was God Himself and that He guaranteed them a multiplication of substance to be employed in future giving. He then reveals the visible results of their giving. "For the administration of this service not only supplieth the want of the saints, but is abundant also by many thanksgivings unto God; Whiles by the experiment of this ministration they glorify God for your professed subjection unto the gospel of Christ, and for your liberal distribution unto them, and unto all men; And by their prayer for you, which long after you for the exceeding grace of God in you" (2 Cor. 9:12-14).

Consequently the giver honors God and insures for himself a blessing. "Honour the LORD with thy substance, and with the firstfruits of all thine increase: So shall thy barns be filled with plenty, and thy presses shall burst out with new wine" (Prov. 3:9,10). He manifests his appreciation of God. "What shall I render unto the LORD for all His benefits toward me?" (Ps. 116:12). He proves the sincerity of his love to the Lord. "Therefore, as ye abound in every thing, in faith, and utterance, and knowledge, and in all diligence, and in your love to us, see that ye abound in this grace also. I speak not by commandment, but by occasion of the forwardness of others, and to prove the sincerity of your love.

For ye know the grace of our Lord Jesus Christ, that, though He was rich, yet for your sakes He became poor, that ye through His poverty might be rich" (2 Cor. 8:7-9).

Our giving, in supplying the wants of the saints, causes them to thank God for His grace to them. They also, upon receiving from the giver, pray for him, and long after them with love. What tremendous effects cheerful giving produces!

Sad to say, not everyone is a cheerful giver. I have a good friend who many years ago gave up his professional business, and went forth as an evangelist, taking nothing of the nations. Along life's pathway, the Lord enabled him to purchase a new Buick LeSabre automobile. A self-centered brother, upon seeing the evangelist driving such a nice vehicle, sarcastically said to him, "That's a pretty big and expensive car you have there." The preacher, being of Irish descent, quickly replied, "Oh don't feel bad, there was none of your money helped pay for it!" I wonder how big the complaining brother's bank account was in heaven – if he had any?

A Remarkable Incident

Many years ago, in Indiana, Pennsylvania, the late David L. Roy, a godly minister of the word, was conducting meetings. He received word from Cleveland, Ohio, that his wife was dying. He told me that he didn't even have three cents in his possession to buy a postage stamp. In faith he acted, asking the brother with whom he was staying, to please take him to the bus terminal, as he had to return home immediately. The brother took him to the station and waited on a side bench while Mr. Roy got in line for his ticket –

without one penny in his possession. As the line moved him closer to the ticket agent he earnestly prayed that God would supply his need. Finally, he arrived as the next customer, and the ticket agent asked him where he was going. Mr. Roy said, "I need a one-way ticket to Cleveland, Ohio. While the agent was preparing the ticket, Mr. Roy lifted his heart to God and cried, "Lord, what do I do now?" Just as the agent presented the ticket, the brother who had conveyed him to the station rushed up to the ticket window and earnestly blurted out, "Brother Roy, keep your wallet in your pocket, I am paying for your ticket!" The spontaneous giver never did discover that the Lord's servant had no money. Mr. Roy took the ticket, thanked the man, got on the bus, and praised God all the way home for meeting his dire need. God loveth a spontaneous, cheerful giver! Upon seeing the ruins of God's dwelling place, the people "offered freely…they gave after their ability."

I've found a Friend; O such a Friend!
He bled, He died to save me;
And not alone the gift of life,
But His own self He gave me.
Naught that I have, mine own I'll call
I'll hold it for the Giver:
My heart, my strength, my life, my all,
Are His, and His for ever.

Not only were these people purposeful, praising, poor, passionate, and providing people, but they were also protected. The journey was infested with Bedouin Arabs, who often assaulted and robbed travelers. However, these faithful souls were guided, preserved and protected by the Lord God of Israel, in Whom they had placed their hope, confidence, and trust. Are we not reminded of the Lord's promises that we possess? How precious, how comforting, how assuring they are. "Lo, I am with you alway, even unto the end of the world. Amen" (Matt. 28:20). "Let your conversation (life-style) be without covetousness; and be content with such things as ye have: for He hath said, I will never leave thee, nor forsake thee" (Heb. 13:5). Certainly we ought to be able to sing with confidence Fanny Crosby's famous hymn.

> ***"All the way my Saviour leads me;***
> ***What have I to ask beside?***
> ***Can I doubt His tender mercy***
> ***Who through life has been my guide?***
> ***Heavenly peace, divinest comfort,***
> ***Here by faith in Him to dwell;***
> ***For I know, what'er befall me,***
> ***Jesus doeth all things well."***

Consider the fact that when they came to the rubble and ruins of what had once been the house of God, in their hearts the house of God still stood. It does not say when they came to the complete ruins, but rather, when they came to the house of God. As far as God was concerned, His dwelling place still remained there, even though they had vacated the land for seventy years.

"So the priests, and the Levites, and some of the people, and the singers, and the porters, and the Nethinims, dwelt in their cities, and all Israel in their cities" (Ezra 2:70).

The Restoration of Spiritual Worship

The third chapter of the Book of Ezra could be well

titled, *The Restoration of spiritual worship.* It commences with a gathering together. "And when the seventh month was come, and the children of Israel were in the cities, the people gathered themselves together as one man to Jerusalem" (vs.1).

The seventh month would bring us in time to the Feast of Tabernacles. Of the seven feasts of Jehovah, the Feast of Tabernacles was the seventh and last for the year. What prophetic lessons we discover in them. Consider them in this way as viewed in Leviticus chapter twenty-three.

The first four feasts were held in the spring of the year, and relate to the church age. The last three feasts occurred in the fall, during the seventh month, and relate to Israel. Looking at the last three feasts we notice:

(1) The Feast of Trumpets, reminding us of that day yet to come, when Israel will be awakened, thus repenting of their sin;

(2) the great day of atonement, when cleansing and restoration will be the portion of God's earthly people;

(3) finally, the feast of tabernacles, prefiguring the day when Israel's God will usher in the millennial reign of Christ, and Israel under His rule will be the head of the nations and not the tail.

What an era that will be when our blessed Lord will have dominion from sea to sea, ruling from the river to the ends of the earth, God making His enemies the footstool of His feet. How fitting then for this weak and feeble remnant to commence God's testimony in the land during the feast that speaks of such a glorious future blessing for the nation.

It is worthy of notice that "the people gathered themselves together as one man." That word 'together' reappears in verses nine, eleven, and chapter four and verse three. There was togetherness, a divine unity manifested on that occasion. Such manifestations were rare in Israel, but these people seemingly were in their first love, thus the oneness of heart. Turning to our dispensation we see the same unity on the day of Pentecost, when the Holy Spirit descended, empowering the believers on the birthday of the Church which is His body. Sad to say, the unity of the Church did not last long. Today we find departure, sects and various systems involving believers. However, in many local assemblies this unity of oneness can still be seen. Paul's ministry was presented to accomplish that end, as we notice in I Corinthians 1:10. "Now I beseech you, brethren, by the name of our Lord Jesus Christ, that ye all speak the same thing, and that there be no divisions among you; but that ye be perfectly joined together in the same mind and in the same judgment." To the Ephesians he writes, " Endeavouring to keep the unity of the Spirit in the bond of peace" (4:3). To Rome he writes, " Be of the same mind one toward another" (12:16). Notice his exhortation to the Philippians, "Only let your conversation be as it becometh the gospel of Christ: that whether I come and see you, or else be absent, I may hear of your affairs, that ye stand fast in one spirit, with one mind striving together for the faith of the gospel" (1:27).

The Remnant's Priorities

How encouraging to see the priorities of this remnant. Their country laid desolate, the ground had ceased to produce fruit, many dwellings were in severe need of repair and other homes lay in ashes. There would be the need of much cleansing, cultivation, renovation and construction. However, all of this was set aside until they had rebuilt the altar of the Lord, restored worship to Jehovah, and kept the feast of tabernacles. Let me ask you, when private interests urgently call for your attention, but at the same time a work has to be done for God, which avenue do you choose? True, we have secular responsibilities, but do we let those responsibilities occupy the priority in our life? When it comes time to meet with the Lord's people in an assembly gathering, are we hindered in attending as a result of "more important" things to do? It is to our shame if this is the case. These people had their priorities right, the building of the altar and the restoration of worship to Jehovah took preeminence in their lives. Their guarantee of future crops and a fine home in which to live were secondary.

Jeshua the High Priest

At this tremendous self-imposed gathering we see certain men coming into view. "Then stood up Jeshua the son of Jozadak, and his brethren the priests, and Zerubbabel the son of Shealtiel, and his brethren, and builded the altar of the God of Israel, to offer burnt offerings thereon, as it is written in the law of Moses the man of God" (Ezra 3:2). Thus Zerubbabel of the royal line, and Jeshua of the priestly line, foreshadow Christ, Who will be the Priestly King sitting on His throne. "Behold the man whose name is The BRANCH; and He shall grow up out of His place, and He shall build the temple of the LORD: Even He shall build the temple of the LORD; and He shall bear the glory, and shall sit and rule upon His throne; and He shall be a priest upon His throne: and the counsel of peace shall be between them both" (Zech 6:12,13). Although Jeshua is not called the high priest in the Book of Ezra, yet we find him positioned as such by the prophets Haggai and Zechariah (Hag. 1:1,14; Zech. 3:1,8; 6:11).

The testimony was to be both priestly and royal, reminding us of what Peter writes, "Ye also, as lively stones, are built up a spiritual house, an holy priesthood, to offer up spiritual sacrifices, acceptable to God by Jesus Christ. ...But ye are a chosen generation, a royal priesthood, an holy nation, a peculiar people; that ye should shew forth the praises of Him Who hath called you out of darkness into His marvellous light" (1 Pet. 2:5,9). As a holy priesthood, we enter the sanctuary to worship. As a royal priesthood, we enter the street to witness. Do remember the order Peter sets forth, teaching us that worship to God is more important than witnessing to sinners, for if I am not a diligent worshipper, my witnessing will have no power.

Through the direction of Jeshua and Zerubbabal, the work proceeded in the building of the altar. It is enlightening to observe the statement, "as it is written in the law of Moses the man of God." Zerubbabel and Jeshua were men of the Book. Moses had written that they were to come to the place which the Lord their God had chosen, to the place of His habitation, to offer their sacrifices. The command was, "thou shalt come." Thus the work of providing an altar for sacrifice commenced. These godly men fully realized the importance of giving Jehovah His place. To insure divine protection it must be secured on the ground of the efficacy of the sacrifices offered upon God's altar, at God's prescribed place. Though very feeble, yet the remnant manifested a wonderful attitude of total dependence upon God.

What pleasure it must have brought to the heart of God to see the labors of His returned people, building a God-appointed altar, positioning God first in all their endeavors, as the result of a dedicated heart.

One is reminded of incidents of first love depicted in the early days of the church. Peter, in love to his Lord exclaimed, "We have left all and followed Thee" (Lk.18:28). Mary, of Bethany poured her treasure (a year's wages for a working man) on her blessed Lord. Christ said, "She hath wrought a good work on Me...She hath done what she could" (Mk. 14:6,8). The Thessalonians, upon hearing the gospel, "turned to God from idols to serve the living and true God" (1 Thess. 1:9). The Ephesians, "many of them also which used curious arts" upon experiencing salvation, immediately "brought their books together, and burned them before all men: and they counted the price of them, and found it fifty thousand pieces of silver" (Acts 19:19). Paul the apostle laid himself on the altar of God as a sacrifice, saying, "But what things were gain to me, those I counted loss for Christ. Yea doubtless, and I count all things but loss for the excellency of the knowledge of Christ Jesus my Lord: for whom I have suffered the loss of all things, and do count them but dung, that I may win Christ" (Phil.3:7,8). Let us individually weigh ourselves in the balances of the divine sanctuary and ask ourselves, "am I found wanting?" What pleasure the devotion of a redeemed soul brings to the heart of God!

The God of Israel

It is instructive to observe the description of God and of Moses. God is called, "The God of Israel." Such an expression is associated with His testimony. David expressed this as he met Goliath and the testimony of God was at stake. "Then said David to the Philistine, Thou comest to me with a sword, and with a spear, and with a shield: but I come to thee in the name of the LORD of hosts, the God of the armies of Israel, whom thou hast defied" (1 Sam.17:45). In the LORD of hosts we are made aware of His power, and authority. In the God of the armies of Israel, we see His Testimony. Hannah, in her prayer addresses God as the "LORD of hosts," referring to His power to give her a child. Eli, who was the high priest and directly connected with the testimony, speaks of God as "the God of Israel." Regarding the testimony, a man of God appears on the scene at Shiloh and rebukes Eli, speaking for "the LORD God of Israel" (1 Sam. 1:11,17: 2:30).

The expression, "Moses the man of God," is found six times in the Scriptures: (1) In association with him blessing the children of Israel before his death (Deut. 33:1); (2) referred to by Caleb, when rehearsing the spying out of the land (Josh. 14:6); (3) as listed in the genealogy of the sons of Kohath (1Chr. 23:14); (4) mentioned in relation to the great passover during Hezekiah's reign (2 Chr. 30:16); (5) regarding the reinstituting of worship in the land (Ezra 3:2); (6) described as the man of God in the title of Psalm 90, he wrote depicting the eternity and greatness of God.

The Altar Set

"And they set the altar upon his bases; for fear was upon them because of the people of those countries: and they offered burnt offerings thereon unto the LORD, even burnt offerings morning and evening. They kept also the feast of tabernacles, as it is written, and offered the daily burnt offerings by number, according to the custom, as the duty of every day required" (Ezra 3:3,4). The revised version reads, "They set the altar in its place." This proves interesting for it projects a vital truth. Do we give Christ (the altar) His proper place, in the assembly, in our home, in our business? To give Christ His place in the assembly, do we bow to His commandments, and seek to obey His shepherds? In the home, is He honored through the daily reading of His Word to our children? Have we eliminated the influence of a godless world in our dwellings? In our business, are we honest in our dealings, upright in our motives, as we either work for an employer, or engage in our own business? The altar was set in its rightful place!

Burnt offerings were immediately offered to Jehovah, thus assuring the weak remnant of the power, presence, and protection of the Lord of hosts, the God of Israel. May we say that, if we are to expect the presence of God with us, His mighty power and His unlimited protection, there must be a divine link between Him and us. That link is Christ, the burnt offering, providing us our standing before God in all the acceptance of Him, Who "hath given Himself for us an offering and a sacrifice to God for a sweetsmelling savour" (Eph. 5:2). May God enable us to appreciate the work of our blessed Lord to a fuller degree. There were neither modern notions nor unscriptural innovations as to the method of keeping the feast of tabernacles. Human reasoning could have suggested a multitude of changes, but that would never do. It was kept *AS IT IS WRITTEN!*

Today we are being bombarded with new innovations.

So-called "better methods" are being practiced for the reaching of the lost. It was not too late for the remnant in Zerubbabel's day to follow the divine pattern, and neither is it too late for us to continue to follow the New Testament pattern for all of our activities for the Lord. "Religious movies," puppet shows, play acting, refreshment stands, welcome centers, and a host of other activities too numerous to mention, are foreign to the divine pattern, thus unnecessary in winning souls. True, we seek to win the confidence of souls with friendliness, help them perhaps even in a temporal way, but let us remember, the divine pattern is, "it pleased God by the foolishness of preaching to save them that believe" (1 Cor.1:21).

God says, "He that winneth souls is wise" (Prov.11:30). What does this mean? Notice J.N. Darby's translation. "The wise winneth souls." In other words, one is not wise because he wins souls, but rather he wins souls because he is wise. A wise man understands that, apart from the demonstration and power of the Holy Spirit, his presentation of spiritual truths will amount to nothing. It is the preaching of the gospel in the power of the Spirit that God honors and uses in the salvation of sinners. Follow the life of Paul through the Book of the Acts and notice the manner of his activities in winning souls for Christ. The wise man, the true soul winner, considers the divine pattern and follows it. *IT IS WRITTEN* for our learning, thus the wise man takes heed. A quotation from H. A. Ironside would be fitting here. *"The moment expediency usurps the place of subjection to the revealed will of the Lord, the whole principle of faith is given up, and a walk by sight takes its place. For we cannot walk by faith except as we yield unhesitating obedience to the word of God, which leaves no place for human will or human arrangements."*

Salvation – A Dramatic Change!

In fifty years of preaching the gospel I have often observed total strangers attending a series of gospel meetings for the first time and being immediately arrested by the Holy Spirit, convicted of their sins and trusting Christ as their Saviour. Recently when I was conducting a series of gospel meetings, a twenty-two year old woman, living an addicted and sinful life, entered the hall and listened intently. It was her first exposure to the gospel. She returned the following night. At the close of the meeting, as people were leaving, she stood near the exit door with tear-filled eyes, literally trembling. She was thanked for attending the meeting and given a gospel tract, nothing else was said to her. Returning to her dwelling, she phoned us one hour later to tell us that she was saved. Immediately she came to our dwelling to tell us and others how it happened. The first night that she heard the gospel she was convicted that her sins were against God. The second night she realized that her sins were taking her to hell. Returning to her dwelling, she read the gospel tract, recalled to her mind the words preached in the meeting and saw plainly that Christ had died for her sins, and that through trusting Him as her Saviour, she would be saved. She was illuminated to the fact that His blood could cleanse her of all her sins. Obediently, she trusted the Lord Jesus Christ and was given the full assurance of possessing salvation! Immediately her sinful life was terminated and one week after her salvation, she was seen in a local mall handing out gospel tracts, spreading the good news to others. "Therefore if any man be in Christ, he is a new creature: old things are passed away; behold, all things are become new" (2 Cor. 5:17). Her case is only one of many that I have observed in my gospel labors for God. Let us forever keep in mind, that the imparting of salvation to a sinner is totally the work of the Holy Spirit of God. We are but the heralds, but God is the Healer. "Salvation is of the Lord" (Jonah 2:9).

Even though the foundation of the temple of the LORD had not yet been laid, with the authority of God's word filling their hearts, they immediately commenced to offer burnt offerings unto the LORD. Not only this, "They gave money also unto the masons, and to the carpenters; and meat, and drink, and oil, unto them of Zidon, and to them of Tyre, to bring cedar trees from Lebanon to the sea of Joppa, according to the grant that they had of Cyrus king of Persia" (Ezra 3:7). *Meat* reminds us of the fragrant life of Christ, *drink*, of the joy of the Lord, and *oil* of the power of the Spirit. These three items were given in exchange for materials for the construction of the temple. The Sidonians and Tyrians were situated in mountainous terrain, not suitable to agriculture and would welcome the provisions given in exchange for timber. Perhaps the same method of transportation for the cedar trees was used as in Solomon's day. The trees were rafted on the sea from Lebanon to Joppa, which was located thirty-five miles northwest of Jerusalem, then transported by oxen or camels to the construction site. Ezra records, "Now in the second year of their coming unto the house of God at Jerusalem, in the second month, began Zerubbabel the son of Shealtiel, and Jeshua the son of Jozadak, and the remnant of their brethren the priests and the Levites, and all they that were come out of the captivity unto Jerusalem; and appointed the Levites, from twenty years old and upward, to set forward the work of the house of the LORD" (3:8). Up to that period of time, they had cleared the land, prepared the soil, and had harvested the crops to pay for the timber they had received. They had been diligent in laboring to tend the olive gardens, and trim the vines for a good surplus of produce. There seemingly was no hoarding of their crops like the rich farmer in Luke 12, but rather a cheerful giving of what they had produced to finance the building of the house of the Lord.

Offering Freely

Not only was there the ministry of one's substance seen in Babylon, prior to the departure of the remnant, but as soon as the work of God commenced in the land, as we have previously noticed – "some of the chief of the fathers, when they came to the house of the LORD which is at Jerusalem, **offered freely** for the house of God to set it up in his place…They gave after their ability…They gave money also to the masons, and to the carpenters" (Ezra 2:68,69; 3:7). One old disciple remarked, "When God saved our souls, He also converted our pocketbooks."

Scripture lays down for us examples of giving. God is a great Giver. John 3:16 proves that. Christ is a great Giver. "The Son of God, Who loved me, and gave Himself for me" (Gal. 2:20). "Christ also loved the church, and gave Himself for it" (Eph. 5:25). David was a great giver, donating 171 tons of gold and 427 tons of silver to the house of his God. Israel at one time in their history, gave so much for the construction of the tabernacle that they were restrained from bringing any more. Jacob promised to give a tenth; Zacchaeus fifty percent; the poor widow with the two mites gave one hundred percent. Mary Magdalene, Joanna, and Susanna ministered unto Him of their substance.

Giving to the Lord honors God, and insures blessing (Prov.3:9,10); it conveys my real appreciation of the Lord "What shall I render unto the LORD for all His benefits toward me?" (Psa. 116:12); proves the sincerity of my love (2 Cor.8:8); encourages the hearts of others; and lays up for the giver treasure in heaven. Shepherds are told to "support the weak" (Acts 20:35). Assemblies are told to support widows that are widows indeed (1 Tim. 5:3). We are told to give to him that needeth (Eph.4:28). We are enjoined upon to support financially "they which preach the gospel" (1 Cor. 9:14). Such giving is considered by the Lord to be a priestly-offered sacrifice (Phil.4:18; Heb. 13:16). Assemblies are encouraged to finance the cost of a full-time laborer's expense in coming to them or even in leaving them to go elsewhere.

While Paul and Barnabas abode at Antioch, the assembly determined that they should go to Jerusalem regarding a problem. We then read, "And being brought on their way by the church" (Acts 15:3). Paul, in purposing to journey to the saints in Rome, writes, "Whensoever I take my journey into Spain, I will come to you: for I trust to see you in my journey, and to be brought on my way thitherward by you, if first I be somewhat filled with your company" (Rom. 15:24). John writes to Gaius regarding brethren purposing coming, "whom if thou bring forward on their journey after a godly sort, thou shalt do well" (3 Jn. 1:6).

The first Gentile assembly was planted in Antioch through the efforts of common believers. The Jerusalem Assembly sent teachers to help them spiritually. When a great dearth came upon the land, the Antioch Assembly responded to the temporal needs of the Jerusalem saints; thus we read, "Then the disciples, every man according to his ability, determined to send relief unto the brethren which dwelt in Judaea" (Acts 11:29). True to divine principles, the returned remnant "gave after their ability."

Building the Temple

In the commencement of the temple construction we observe two important needs: The need of devotion to the LORD, as seen in the sacrifices offered, followed by the need of skilled workers. When any scriptural assembly has been planted, two great things have been observed: (1) An intense devotion to, and a deep appreciation of the Lord Jesus Christ, wherein great sacrifices are made; (2) God raising up men of skill in divine things, skill in presenting the gospel, and men with shepherd hearts. Without these vital features, a true collective testimony of God will hardly commence, and will never survive. It is saddening, and soul searching to see in some areas once-healthy assemblies deteriorating almost to the point of extinction, simply because of the lack of wise and devoted shepherds.

At this point in the remnant's history, Jeshua the high priest comes into prominent view. A quick survey of this great man reveals him in association with the building of the altar (Ezra 3:2); appointing workmen (3:9); defending the testimony (4:3); affected by the word (5:2); honored by a son (8:33; and finally, disappointed by his sons (10:18).

The setting forward of the work of the house of the Lord simply means that the Levites were to have the oversight regarding the work. When the builders laid the foundation of the temple, the priests in their new white vestments blew their silver trumpets, the sons of Asaph sounded their cymbals to praise the Lord. What a beautiful scene that must have been, to see a multitude gathered together as one man, singing, and bursting forth with loud shouts of joy in their holy praise, as the foundation was laid.

Would it surprise you to know that in the scriptures praise to God is never a spectator sport? It never conveys the thought of entertaining an audience. The basic purpose of praise is to publicly exalt the Person of God and His marvelous works. We seek to praise the name of God with a song, and to magnify Him with thanksgiving. The psalmist exclaimed, "Praise ye the LORD. I will praise the LORD with my whole heart, in the assembly of the upright, and in the congregation" (Psa. 111:1). It is a type of worship that saints join in, not a program that people watch.

Weeping Old Saints

However, it was not only a day of audible excitement, but it was also a day of weeping, for the older saints, when they reflected upon the glory of the former days when Solomon's temple stood. Many of us today could well weep as we think of the glory of the former days, when there was more of the fear of God about us, and a greater display of the marching of God with us. However, let us who remember the former days not allow our memory of the past to bring us to the place of despair and inactivity. Youth brings with it enthusiasm; old age brings sobriety and memories of the past. Sobriety is a valuable asset, but let us who are older beware of unduly reminiscing to the point of becoming critical and faultfinding. Constantly criticizing the young is a good way of driving them away. Let us be careful to diligently guide our younger brethren, and at the same time encourage them in their endeavors for God. Let us who are older not chill the fervency of those who are young by a continuous critical spirit. We need each other! How valuable and refreshing to see a godly older saint seeking to guide the young in the paths of holy scripture, yet at the same time, manifesting a cheery spirit and a true love for others. To be an effective counselor, one must genuinely love the ones he seeks to counsel. He will faithfully correct them, but he will also be there to help them, materially, or spiritually, when the occasion calls for it. The young men shouted for joy, and the ancient men wept. What a scene!

CHAPTER FOUR

The Adversaries

WHENEVER A WORK for God is going to be accomplished, the devil is sure to commence his work in seeking to destroy that work from being fulfilled. No sooner had the foundation of the temple been laid, than the adversaries began to work. The devil wastes no time in seeking to hinder the work of God, neither has it ever been recorded that he takes vacations. He was very quick to mar the work of God manifested in Eden. He was very much alert in his effort to destroy Job. When the Father announced our Lord as His beloved Son in Whom He was well pleased, immediately the devil came on the scene to try the Lord (Matt.3:17; 4:1). When the sower went forth to sow the word of God, as the seed fell, immediately the devil came to steal away the seed (Mk. 4:15). The devil is diligent, tireless, powerful, cunning, wise, effective, and ruthless. Apart from the Holy Spirit within us, we are no match for him.

How quickly the scene of praise and joy changes! "Now when the adversaries of Judah and Benjamin heard that the children of the captivity builded the temple unto the LORD God of Israel; Then they came to Zerubbabel, and to the chief of the fathers, and said unto them, Let us build with you: for we seek your God, as ye do; and we do sacrifice unto Him since the days of Esar-haddon king of Assur, which brought us up hither" (Ezra 4:1,2).

The Adversarys' Background

Who were these people? A careful look at 2 Kings 17:24 provides the answer. "And the king of Assyria brought men from Babylon, and from Cuthah, and from Ava, and from Hamath, and from Sepharvaim, and placed them in the cities of Samaria instead of the children of Israel: and they possessed Samaria, and dwelt in the cities thereof." When the king of Assyria took the ten tribes of the Northern Kingdom away captive, in 722 B.C., he forcibly replaced the population of Samaria with these foreigners. Because they lacked the fear of the LORD, the LORD sent lions among them which slew some of them. An appeal was made to the king of Assyria for help, since the people knew not the manner of the God of the land. The king sent a Jewish priest to dwell among them to teach them the manner of the true God, and how they should fear the LORD. "Howbeit every nation made gods of their own, and put them in the houses of the high places which the Samaritans had made, every nation in their cities wherein they dwelt…So they feared the LORD, and made unto themselves of the lowest of them priests of the high places, which sacrificed for them in the houses of the high places. They feared the LORD, and served their own gods, after the manner of the nations whom they carried away from thence" (2 Ki. 17:29,32,33).

Thus we see the true character of these people. They worshipped their own gods and simply included the name of Israel's God (Yahweh) in their long list, to appease the god of the land in which they were now living. These people never experienced Egyptian bondage, a Passover lamb sacrificed for their redemption, the shedding and application of the blood. Yet now, they assume the same position and place as the people of God who had returned to their land. How subtle are their words to Zerubbabel and to the chief of the fathers, seeking to convince them that they, too, were as they were, and that they wanted to help them in their work for God. In reality, it was a devilish plot to ruin the work of God.

False Professors Today

Are there people today of the same character as these foreigners? Absolutely! There are multitudes today who make a profession of Christianity, but have never experienced redemption by His blood. They have never experienced the forgiveness of their sins. They have never been "born again." The Lord speaks of such in Luke 6:46-49. "And why call ye Me, Lord, Lord, and do not the things which I say? Whosoever cometh to Me, and heareth My sayings, and doeth them, I will shew you to whom he is like: He is like a man which built an house, and digged deep, and laid the foundation on a rock: and when the flood arose, the stream beat vehemently upon that house, and could not shake it: for it was founded upon a rock. But he that heareth, and doeth not, is like a man that without a foundation built an house upon the earth; against which the stream did beat vehemently, and immediately it fell; and the ruin of that house was great." These false professors profess to fear the Lord, but they serve their own gods. Christendom is full of such people. They love the world with all its amusements and ways. The divine appraisal is simply this, "If any man love the world, the love of the Father is not in him" (1 Jn. 2:15).

It is interesting to notice the impression such people seek to convey that they are Christians. The expression, "Lord, Lord," is only found in connection with such. Our Lord brings this to light in the following passages. "Not every one that saith unto me, Lord, Lord, shall enter into the kingdom of heaven; but he that doeth the will of my Father which is in heaven. Many will say to Me in that day, Lord, Lord, have we not prophesied in Thy name? and in Thy name have cast out devils? and in Thy name done many wonderful works? And then will I profess unto them, I never knew you: depart from Me, ye that work iniquity" (Matt. 7:21-23). In Matthew 25:1 we notice ten *virgins* with lamps. The lamp conveys the thought of maintaining a Christian profession. However, five virgins were foolish, they had no oil in their vessel, indicating a lack of the indwelling of the Holy Spirit. Romans 8:9 is clear on this point, "Now if any man have not the Spirit of Christ, he is none of His." The ten virgins were waiting for the coming of the bridegroom and when He came, only those who possessed oil in their vessels entered in with Him to the marriage feast. Then we read, "Afterward came also the other virgins, saying, Lord, Lord, open to us. But He answered and said, Verily I say unto you, I know you not" (Matt. 25:11,12). Some professors had even done miraculous works, supposedly for the Lord. yet they were not genuine believers.

In Luke's Gospel we find the Lord exposing the false professor. "Strive to enter in at the strait gate: for many, I say unto you, will seek to enter in, and shall not be able. When once the Master of the house is risen up, and hath shut to the door, and ye begin to stand without, and to knock at the door, saying, Lord, Lord, open unto us; and He shall answer and say unto you, I know you not whence ye are: Then shall ye begin to say, We have eaten and drunk in Thy presence, and Thou hast taught in our streets. But He shall say, I tell you, I know you not whence ye are; depart from Me, all ye workers of iniquity" (Lk. 13:24-27). Talk is cheap, and the Lord rebukes false professors with these stern words. "And why call ye Me, Lord, Lord, and do not the things which I say?" (Lk. 6:46).

When unregenerate people infiltrate the assemblies of God, they can cause serious problems. The love of the world remains in them. The lusts of the flesh still control them. The things of God hold no attraction to them. Christ is not the motivating factor in their lives. They have never been willing to forsake all as disciples, taking up their cross to follow Him. They lack the power to do so, simply because they have never been born again, they have never been indwelt with the Spirit of God. They can talk about the Bible, they can utter prayers that are scriptural, they can even feebly witness to others, but the solemn fact remains, they are still on the broad way that leads to destruction, while at the same time, defiling the local assembly into which they have been received. After the apostles passed off the scene there was a marked departure in the testimonies of God. Christians' children were taken into the assemblies without experiencing the new birth. Baptismal-regeneration was recognized, and a clergy-laity program was introduced. Thus the assemblies of the Lord's people became defiled with false professors, who, in time, introduced unscriptural practices into the churches so that we have today an unholy mixture and powerless churches.

Godly Discernment

Zerubbabel and Jeshua were not only men of devotion and determination, but they were also men of discernment. They recognized the truth of Solomon's words, "Faithful are the wounds of a friend; but the kisses of an enemy are deceitful" (Prov. 27:6). The words of the people of the land were convincing, but not convincing enough for Zerubbabel, Jesuah and the rest of the chief of the fathers of Israel. How subtle Satan is in his approaches to hinder and destroy the work of God. Godly discernment, how valuable it is! The apostle Paul was a man of keen discernment. Regarding Satan he exclaimed, "we are not ignorant of his devices" (2 Cor. 2:11). Paul in writing to Timothy is very concerned about the activities of the wicked one. He mentions imitators, "Having a form of godliness, but denying the power thereof: from such turn away" (2 Tim. 3:5). He brings to Timothy's attention that through imitation, they resist the truth. "Now as Jannes and Jambres withstood Moses, so do these also resist the truth: men of corrupt minds, reprobate concerning the faith" (2 Tim. 3:8). He warns that conditions will wax worse. "But evil men and seducers shall wax worse and worse, deceiving, and being deceived" (2 Tim. 3:13). In writing to the Corinthians, Paul warns, "But I fear, lest by any means, as the serpent beguiled Eve through his subtilty, so your minds should be corrupted from the simplicity that is in Christ" (2 Cor. 11:3). He warns the teachers of that assembly – "According to the grace of God which is given unto me, as a wise masterbuilder, I have laid the foundation, and another buildeth thereon. But let every man take heed how he buildeth thereupon" (1 Cor. 3:10). He manifests a fearful concern for the welfare of the Ephesian Assembly, warning the elders, saying, "I have not shunned to declare unto you all the counsel of God. Take heed therefore unto yourselves, and to all the flock, over the which the Holy Ghost hath made you overseers, to feed the church of God, which He hath purchased with His own blood. For I know this, that after my departing shall grievous wolves enter in among you, not sparing the flock. Also of your own selves shall men arise, speaking perverse things, to draw away disciples after them. Therefore watch, and remember, that by the space of three years I ceased not to warn every one night and day with tears. And now, brethren, I commend you to God, and to the word of His grace, which is able to build you up, and to give you an inheritance among all them which are sanctified" (Acts 20: 27-32).

A Bombarded Church

Thus today, the church is being bombarded with Hollywood-style evangelism, religious books that water down the truth of God and cast away precious divine principles. Many have been led astray from the pilgrim path of separation through the deceptive devices of the devil. What is the solution? The solution is simply this, read diligently and meditate constantly upon the holy scriptures. In other words, *know your Bible!* We are living in a day of rush and constant activity. Christians are not spending time in solitude with God and His word as in days gone by. Thus, they are more vulnerable to the subtle attacks of the wicked one.

Psalm 119 gives us an insight to the psalmist's appreciation of God's word. "Wherewithal shall a young man cleanse his way? by taking heed thereto according to Thy word" (Ps.119:9). "Thy word have I hid in mine heart, that I might not sin against Thee" (vs.11). "Thy testimonies also are my delight and my counsellors" (vs. 24). "Behold, I have longed after Thy precepts: quicken me in Thy righteousness" (vs. 40). "I will never forget Thy precepts: for with them Thou hast quickened me" (vs. 93). "O how love I Thy law! it is my meditation all the day" (vs. 97). "Thy word is a lamp unto my feet, and a light unto my path" (vs. 105). "The entrance of Thy words giveth light; it giveth understanding unto the simple" (vs. 130). It was with the word of God that our Lord rebuked Satan (Lk. 4:1-12).

Then we read about Satan, that he departed from Him for a season. His attack utterly failed. As for us, we would do well to heed the exhoration of James. "Submit yourselves therefore to God. Resist the devil, and he will flee from you" (Jas. 4:7). Through the obedient reading of the holy scriptures we intelligently submit ourselves to God, thus obtaining the power to resist the devil. Brother, sister, how much attention and time do you give to your Bible? Zerubbabel and Jeshua, men well versed in the law of God, gave their reply to the adversaries. "Ye have nothing to do with us to build an house unto our God; but we ourselves together will build unto the LORD God of Israel, as king Cyrus the king of Persia hath commanded us" (Ezra 4:3).

The Natural Man

These adversaries are what the New Testament scriptures would define as, "the natural man" (1 Cor. 2:14). They receive not (reject) the things of the Spirit of God. They put on a front, but when a discerning saint gives them the place that the truth puts them in - they deeply resent it. A scripturally conducted assembly of God will be severely criticized by the religious world as being narrow minded, or accused of thinking themselves better than everybody else, simply because they do not open their doors to the public to come and worship with them. Ah no, such would never do. In the first place, regarding a local testimony, there is a distinct within and a distinct without (1 Cor. 5:12,13). If an unsaved person enters, he is given the seat of the unbeliever. He is not received into the fellowship of that assembly, simply because he has never been born again. He is still dead in trespasses and sins. He is in need of divine life. He is still unrighteous, having never been washed in the blood of the Lamb. He abides in spiritual darkness. Concerning such, God says, "Be ye not unequally yoked together with unbelievers: for what fellowship hath righteousness with unrighteousness? and what communion hath light with darkness?" (2 Cor. 6:14). He comes into the building, not to participate, but to be an observer. Many "religious buildings" display this sign on their bulletin board, "Come, worship with us." Such is a total denial of the teachings of Holy Scripture!

The Unlearned

Then we have another class of person who is saved, but totally ignorant of divine principles. Perhaps he has never been baptized. Perhaps he is still addicted to tobacco and drink. Perhaps he has never severed himself, as a pilgrim and a stranger, from the world. Perhaps he is not doctrinally clear on certain truths. He is unlearned. Thus, upon entering the building, he is given the place of the unlearned, to sit as an observer. He occupies what the scripture terms, "the room of the unlearned" (1 Cor.14:16).

Receiving into an Assembly

Every local church is autonomous, and answerable only to the Lord Himself. A scriptural church has no headquarters or branches. Paul compares it to a human body composed of various parts, all functioning together. Just as our human body employs all the various parts (eyes, nose, ears, hands, legs, organs, head) for its survival and activity, so in like manner the local church has members, all functioning together for its effective testimony. A careful study of 1 Corinthians chapter 12 supports this. To receive one into the fellowship of the church is a very serious procedure. Paul warned the Ephesian Church, "Lay hands suddenly on no man, neither be partaker of other men's sins: keep thyself pure" (1 Tim. 5:22). This warning was in relation to the placing of elders within the local church, bringing them into the elderhood. The laying on of hands was no mysterious act, it simply means giving one's approval of the person. How much more then should this warning be heeded in receiving total strangers into the local church? Receiving a defiled person into the assembly automatically defiles the whole assembly. If you were aware that a certain vial of substance caused cancer, would you drink it, would you receive it into your body? Absolutely not! How much more then receiving a stranger into the assembly fellowship?

Just look for a moment at Saul upon his conversion to God. "And when Saul was come to Jerusalem, he assayed to join himself to the disciples: but they were all afraid of him, and believed not that he was a disciple. But Barnabas took him, and brought him to the apostles, and declared unto them how he had seen the Lord in the way, and that He had spoken to him, and how he had preached boldly at Damascus in the name of Jesus. And he was with them coming in and going out at Jerusalem" (Acts 9: 26-28).

They were not about to lay the hands of approval upon Saul and consequently receive him into their fellowship of the assembly at Jerusalem. However, when Barnabas came, whom they knew, and gave them a good report of Saul, not until then was he received into the assembly. Since a person's WAYS speak volumes more than his WORDS, how do we determine if a person is really saved? The answer is simple – we observe them. What is their attitude to the Bible? Do they love it, read it daily and obey its precepts? Holy Scripture says, "We know that we have passed from death unto life, because we love the brethren. He that loveth not his brother abideth in death" (1 Jn. 3:14). Do they love the brethren? Have they manifested a love to the Father by separating themselves from the harmonious arrangement, or constitution and adornment of this present evil world?

Remember, "Love not the world, neither the things that are in the world. If any man love the world, the love of the Father is not in him" (1 Jn. 2:15). Divine life in a saved sinner manifests itself, and this is the only way a believer can assuredly believe that the person is truly saved. I greatly rejoice when I hear of souls professing salvation, but it annoys me when I hear believers say concerning them, quote, "They GOT saved." How do they really know? A careful reading of the sower in Luke chapter eight would discount such a careless statement. Notice the four types of soil on which the seed was sown. Notice the ground with underlying rock. "They on the rock are they, which, when they hear, receive the word with joy; and these have no root, which for a while believe, and in time of temptation fall away" (Lk.8:13). They hear the word and receive it with joy. They profess and there is a lot of happiness. I can just see the saints rejoicing and reporting to others, "They GOT saved." Did they? Why no, they really weren't saved at all, they just professed and you have ended up telling others something that really never took place. Yes, you may say, but they seemed so real. True, for the activity of the flesh can be very deceiving. When sinners profess, let us rejoice in their profession. Then let us watch them for a few months and rejoice when we see them walking in God's path for the true believer. Let us be careful of our vocabulary. "The preacher sought to find out acceptable words…even words of truth" (Eccl.12:10), even so should we.

When professors have proved themselves by a godly life, seeing the truth of separation from the world's adornment, separation from religious christendom, and seeing the truth of gathering solely to the name of our Lord Jesus Christ, then and only then are they suited to be received into the fellowship of the assembly in their locality. When saints are thus convinced of divine life in that person, then they are glad to witness the baptism of that person, and their reception into all the activities and responsibilities of that assembly where they desire fellowship.

When visitors from other scriptural assemblies come to a local assembly, they should bring a letter of commendation from their assembly to the assembly they are visiting, thus giving confidence to that assembly concerning their person (2 Cor.3:1). Upon being received they are privileged to function in their priestly capacity while visiting. No one is ever received just to the Lord's supper, they are received into the assembly itself, to function with the believers there until they depart to return home.

The Answer to the Adversaries

Let us now return to Jerusalem and listen again to the words of those noble men. "But Zerubbabel, and Jeshua, and the rest of the chief of the fathers of Israel, said unto them, Ye have nothing to do with us to build an house unto our God; but we ourselves together will build unto the LORD God of Israel, as king Cyrus the king of Persia hath commanded us" (Ezra 4:3).

True to form, the devil now springs into open opposition. If he cannot beguile them, he will batter them. If he cannot fool them, he will frustrate them. He is relentless in his activity to destroy any testimony for God. Living for God produces problems. Stating the past experiences of his life for Christ, the apostle Paul exclaims, "Persecutions, afflictions, which came unto me at Antioch, at Iconium, at Lystra; what persecutions I endured: but out of them all the Lord delivered me." Then he faithfully tells Timothy and the Ephesian saints, "Yea, and all that will live godly in Christ Jesus shall suffer persecution." (2 Tim. 3:11,12). Christ speaks of the narrow way (Matt.7:14). The word narrow conveys the thought of, "trouble, affliction, to suffer tribulation, to press as grapes (pressure), to be in distress" and is translated that way in other portions of Holy Scripture. Becoming a Christian is not an escape from earthly trouble, it is an escape from eternal torment. It is not an escape from temporary problems, it is an escape from eternal perdition. Having become a Christian, the person takes the narrow way of life. Is it worth it, persecutions, trouble, afflictions and distress - for Christ? Absolutely! For it is the way that leads to life, eternal life in all its fullness, becoming like Christ, and being with Christ in that glorious home above. The end of the way is what makes the journey on the narrow way worthwhile!

Adversary Activity

"Then the people of the land weakened the hands of the people of Judah, and troubled them in building, And hired counsellors against them, to frustrate their purpose, all the days of Cyrus king of Persia, even until the reign of Darius king of Persia. And in the reign of Ahasuerus, in the beginning of his reign, wrote they unto him an accusation against the inhabitants of Judah and Jerusalem" (Ezra 4:4-6).

The hands that were strengthened in Babylon, prior to their return (Ezra 1:6) are now weakened by the people of the land surrounding Jerusalem. The once enthusiastic builders now became disheartened, their hands became slack. Through the enemy's tactics and words, they were troubled, meaning disturbed and terrified. In Persian times it was common to bribe the Persian governors, and this tactic was employed to frustrate the purpose of the remnant. Such a tactic shattered them, defeated their purpose, and caused the work to cease. The adversaries wrote Ahasuerus an accusation. The word "accusation" is extremely interesting and reveals the source of the activity against the builders. The word is "sitnah" and it is found only here in all the

Bible. Sitnah (accusation) means, "to attack, to be an adversary, opposition," cognate with the noun, "Satan." Thus we readily see the source of all the trouble – Satan! As a result of the adversaries' letter to the king, the king gave commandment to cause the work to cease in letter form. "Now when the copy of king Artaxerxes' letter was read before Rehum, and Shimshai the scribe, and their companions, they went up in haste to Jerusalem unto the Jews, and made them to cease by force and power" (Ezra 4:23).

In the beginning of the church's testimony on earth, Satan raised up many accusations against the Christians, and presented them to the Roman Empire, which in turn, brought the church into times of great tribulation. Christians spoke of communion with their Lord as eating His flesh and drinking His blood (Jn.6:54), thus they were accused of being cannibals. They held love feasts, times of joyfully eating together, consequently they were accused of holding "orgies of lust." Christ came, causing divisions in families, (Lk. 12:51), so Christians were accused of splitting families. The saints refused to worship Caesar as god, and the accusation was leveled at them that they were atheists. The saints gave Christ first place in their life, thus they were accused of being politically disloyal. Christians spoke of hell fire and the end of the universe melting with fervent heat, so they were labeled "incendiaries." Satan did his work well and the beloved children of God suffered tribulation, just as Paul had warned them, " that we must through much tribulation enter into the kingdom of God" (Acts 14:22). Thus the returned remnant, with weakened hands, troubled minds, and their purpose frustrated "ceased the work of the house of God which is at Jerusalem. So it ceased unto the second year of the reign of Darius king of Persia" (Ezra 4:24). Not until sixteen years later did the work on the temple resume, being in the second year of Darius.

The Ceasing of the Work

From 536 to 520 B.C. the work of rebuilding God's house hibernated. During this lull, the interests of the people drifted from the temple to their own possessions. Their own dwellings became the priority in their lives. With threats of military intervention from the adversaries, it was far less dangerous to turn one's energy to domestic improvement, rather than building a testimony for God. As long as the remnant ceased to produce something for God, they had peace from the enemy. Things have not changed, even to our day. Do nothing for God and you will experience little, if any, trouble from the devil. The people of the land will live peaceably with you, and you will not suffer reproach, or experience tribulation from the ungodly - all will be "smooth sailing." However, stir yourself up to accomplish something for God and see the drastic change. Satan will trouble you in manifold ways. How serene and peaceful was the countryside as long as the remnant gave all their attention to their own homes while the temple of God lay undeveloped. However, two great men suddenly appeared on the scene, which drastically changed the atmosphere.

CHAPTER FIVE

The Awakening Call

Haggai & Zechariah

FOR SIXTEEN YEARS the love of many had waxed colder and colder. Temporal things became paramount in their lives and the things of God had taken last place. One is reminded of the lament of the beloved apostle Paul, "For all seek their own, not the things which are Jesus Christ's" (Phil. 2:21). It is interesting to note that they were truly occupying a right *position.* They were at the place where the Lord had chosen to place His name. However, their spiritual *condition* was not in keeping with their position – their work for God had ceased. This sad parallel can be seen even in our day. There are Christians who scripturally gather to the name of our Lord Jesus Christ. They occupy the right position. They can pray intelligently, having learned Biblical truths in the days of their first love. They can declare the gospel in a doctrinally correct fashion. However, even though their prayers and their worship may be scripturally proper, there is something lacking. There is an evident emptiness to it. They seem to be going through a ritual. The listener cannot find fault as to the correctness of the expressions employed, but for some reason, their prayer doesn't seem to grip the heart. Stock expressions are used time and time again, until they become "threadbare." There is nothing warm and fresh from the heart. Their brain is employed in grasping stored phrases, to be mechanically uttered by their lips. What does God get out of such acting? Very little, if anything. The same is evidenced in the preaching of the gospel, the doctrines are correct, but spiritual warmth and grip is missing. Paul related to the Corinthians, "And I was with you in weakness, and in fear, and in much trembling. And my speech and my preaching was not with enticing words of man's wisdom, but in demonstration of the Spirit and of power: That your faith should not stand in the wisdom of men, but in the power of God." (1 Cor. 2:3-5). Unlike the apostle, confidently they rise, the fear and trembling are missing. Man's wisdom is manifested with intellectual words, but alas, the sinner's conscience is untouched. Some even employ sheets of notes, reading half of what they proclaim. Since their message is without Holy Spirit power, instead of piercing the hearer's heart, it hardens his heart. They are in the right position, but with a wrong condition.

There is another way of looking at *position* and *condition*. Many take a scriptural position, professedly gathering without the camp (Heb.13: 13), breaking bread every Lord's Day, employing, as the scripture teaches, one loaf and one cup. The sisters veil their heads according to the teaching of 1 Corinthians 11:6. They remain silent in the church, according to 1 Corinthians 14:34, and 1 Timothy 2:11,12. There are no hired clergy, the government of the local assembly being elders (1 Tim. 3:1-10). Yet, alas, the condition of some does not correspond to their professed position. The world has entered their hearts. The sports, the theater, the various amusements, and the covetous business principles of the world have overtaken their hearts. The love of money, the love of worldly entertainment, and even the love of worldly recognition, have captured their souls, turning their once-fervent heart into a virtual igloo. One is reminded of the rebuke of the Lord given to the once-fervent assembly in Ephesus. "I know thy works, and thy labour, and thy patience, and how thou canst not bear them which are evil: and thou hast tried them which say they are apostles, and are not, and hast found them liars: And hast borne, and hast patience, and for My name's sake hast laboured, and hast not fainted. Nevertheless I have somewhat against thee, because thou hast left thy first love" (Rev. 2: 2-4). Paul warns the Corinthians of the danger of living for self. "For the love of Christ constraineth us; because we thus judge, that if One died for all, then were all dead: And that He died for all, that they which live should not henceforth live unto themselves, but unto Him which died for them, and rose again" (2 Cor. 5:14,15).

Ezra chapter five brings us to that point in the remnant's history. They had lavished upon themselves earthly goods. Their houses had been remodeled to excess. There is nothing wrong in providing for ourselves comfortable dwellings, but are we excessive? Is it essential to have the square feet in our dwellings twice as much as necessary? Are the furnishings ornate? Is the dwelling luxurious, or does it manifest only what we essentially need? Our homes certainly should be neat, tidy, and respectable, for our testimony's sake. What a disgrace to see a Christian dwelling dilapidated and shoddy. But to pour our income into furnishings and properties and then meagerly give a trickle of our income to the house of God and the work of the Lord, betrays the same condition that prevailed in the remnant's day. It is sad to see saints loading themselves with expensive nonessentials, while at the same time just giving a small amount of their income for the furtherance of the things of God.

The injunction remains, dear brethren, "Lay not up for yourselves treasures upon earth, where moth and rust doth corrupt, and where thieves break through and steal: But lay up for yourselves treasures in heaven, where neither moth nor rust doth corrupt, and where thieves do not break through nor steal: For where your treasure is, there will your heart be also" (Matt. 6:19-21).

An Old Amishman

Boarding a train in Chicago I met an old Amishman who said something that greatly impressed me. I believed him to be a saved man, and here is what he said, "Brother Surgenor, the more that one possesses down here, the less excited he is about going to heaven." He was absolutely right, for the more we live for God down here, this world will hold no attraction to our hearts, and our desire to see our Lord face to face will become more intense.

Looking at the Amishman it was very evident that he possessed little of this world's goods. As the train pulled out of the station for Cleveland the two of us discussed the Holy Scriptures for hours. He delighted in the law of his God, and the glow of heaven seemed to radiate on his face. It was a wonderful experience for me. He might not have been in the exactly proper position scripturally, but his condition of soul was to be coveted.

Paul, who possessed nothing of this world's goods, exclaimed, "For I am in a strait betwixt two, having a desire to depart, and to be with Christ; which is far better" (Phil. 1:23). Are you "excited" about going to heaven?

Haggai and Zechariah

"Then the prophets, Haggai the prophet, and Zechariah the son of Iddo, prophesied unto the Jews that were in Judah and Jerusalem in the name of the God of Israel, even unto them. Then rose up Zerubbabel the son of Shealtiel, and Jeshua the son of Jozadak, and began to build the house of God which is at Jerusalem: and with them were the prophets of God helping them" (Ezra 5:1,2).

The instruments were the prophets; the action was, they prophesied; their audience was the Jews; the location being Jerusalem; their authority, in the name of the God of Israel; and the result was, they rose up and began to build the house of God.

I have termed Haggai, "the piercing prophet." He was tremendously outspoken. There were no "smooth utterances." He was bold and exceedingly blunt, challenging and charging the people of God. His name means, "festive." His prophecies are four, each one being dated in his book. All four were delivered within four months, in 520

B.C. You have perhaps noticed in your reading of the scriptures, that prophets were always raised up in times of declension and departure. If the remnant had been pleasing to God, the prophecies of Haggai would never have been needed.

We hear much today of the need of Christ-exalting ministry, and such ministry is encouraging to the redeemed soul. However, God is a God of balance, and we are living in days of serious departure, and the character of Haggai-like ministry is sorely needed. It may not be appreciated by carnal saints, yet it is needed. Not all preachers have the fortitude of Haggai, but I thank God for those who do. Paul told the Ephesian elders, "Wherefore I take you to record this day, that I am pure from the blood of all men. For I have not shunned to declare unto you all the counsel of God" (Acts 20:26,27). Paul was not interested in popularity, money, or compliments. His sole purpose was to glorify God, edify the body of Christ, and be faithful to His word. He exhorted Timothy, "Preach the word; be instant in season, out of season; reprove, rebuke, exhort with all longsuffering and doctrine" (2 Tim. 4:2). Paul is God's model for the minister of the word today. May such be followers, imitators of him, as even he was of Christ (1 Cor. 11:1).

Haggai's Message

The blunt prophet's message commences with a question. It has been rightfully said, that a question provokes an answer, and in order to give an answer, one's brain has to spring into a thinking process. Haggai wanted them to engage their minds as he commenced to address them. The mind and the heart are used interchangeably in scripture and mean almost the same thing. Haggai desired his words to sink into their hearts, for out of the heart are the issues of life (Prov. 4:23).

The first thing we notice is that the Lord spoke to the prophet, before the prophet spoke to Zerubbabel, the governor, and Joshua, the high priest. Zerubbabel, being the political man, and Haggai, the priestly man. "Thus speaketh the LORD of hosts, saying, This people say, The time is not come, the time that the LORD'S house should be built." (Hag. 1:2).

It is imperative, if a man is a spokesman for God, that he first be in communion with God. It is true today that we do not have the gift of receiving divine revelations, or foretelling the future, apart from what has been written in the holy scriptures. However, the church does possess the gift of forthtelling the revealed mind of God as contained in the scriptures. To engage in this ministry, the speaker must know his Bible, and know his God in an intimate way. To receive a word from the Lord is a tremendous thing. To declare that word to others is a serious thing – faithfulness is required. Paul speaks of this in Romans 12:6-8. "Let us prophesy according to the proportion of faith…He that teacheth, on teaching…Or he that exhorteth, on exhortation." The thought being that the one possessed with a certain gift, give himself wholly to it. This carries the thought of earnestness and diligence. Haggai certainly did fit that criteria.

Excuses

As previously noticed, the people were saying, "The time is not come, the time that the Lord's house should be built." Thus we see that these self-centered people were making excuses for themselves. One wonders if these people were applying Jeremiah's prophecy of the exile of seventy years (Jer. 25:11,12) to the Temple. The seventy years of exile had passed, but only sixty-eight years had passed since the destruction of Solomon's Temple, so perhaps they were excusing their indifference to the house of God reasoning that perhaps it was the time to rebuild, not now, but two years later in the future. They had been back in the land sixteen years and in the second year of their return the foundation had been laid (Ezra 3:8-10). By now more than likely the weeds had overtaken the premises and the area was returning to nature, parched and ruined.

It should be understood, that people of that day determined how highly another nation thought of their god by how magnificent a temple they built for him. Looking upon the LORD'S temple, with only a foundation laid and lying there for fourteen years, what could the heathen have thought other than that the Jews must have held their God in low esteem? What a grief to Jehovah! What a disgrace to His testimony! The prophet speaks in no uncertain terms. "Is it time for you, O ye, to dwell in your cieled houses, and this house lie waste?" (Hag. 1:4). Their cieled houses were a mark of luxury. Not only were the walls paneled with the finest of wood, but also the ceilings. Such construction was common in the dwellings of kings.

Solomon is an example. "Then he made a porch for the throne where he might judge, even the porch of judgment: and it was covered with cedar from one side of the floor to the other" (1 Ki. 7:7). They were living like kings, while God's house lay poverty stricken! We deplore such a condition, but can we truthfully sing James Small's hymn?

> ***"I've found a Friend; O such a Friend!***
> ***He bled, He died to save me;***
> ***And not alone the gift of life,***
> ***But His own self He gave me.***
> ***Naught that I have, mine own I'll call,***
> ***I'll hold it for the Giver:***
> ***My heart, my strength, my life, my all,***
> ***Are His, and His for ever."***

Haggai, having assured them that it was the Lord Who was speaking through him, and exposing their sinful thoughts relative to the building of God's house, and challenging the people with a searching question, he goes on to enjoin them to consider their ways. "Thus saith the LORD of hosts; Consider your ways" (Hag. 1:7). He speaks of God as, "the LORD of hosts." The expression is first used in 1 Samuel 1:3. David employed it as he went out to meet Goliath (1 Sam. 17:45). Holy seraphim acknowledged the preincarnate Christ as such. "And one cried unto another, and said, Holy, holy, holy, is the LORD of hosts: the whole earth is full of His glory" (Isa. 6:3). The expression denotes His power, authority, and holiness.

Considering one's ways can be a very humbling experience. Are we not humbled and perhaps ashamed when we look back over our own steps since conversion's day? How often we have acted unwisely. How foolishly we have wasted precious time with trivial things! How many times we have passed up opportunities to witness for Him to the ungodly! How little we have accomplished for God! The moments spent with God in prayer and meditation over His word have been so limited. In contrast, the times spent for our own comfort, pleasure, and monetary wealth have been so abundant. It is healthy to consider our ways, for then we will be aware of our true state and hopefully seek to correct our ways. David came to this station in his life and cried out, "Search me, O God, and know my heart: try me, and know my thoughts: And see if there be any wicked way in me, and lead me in the way everlasting" (Ps. 139:23,24). As we diligently and prayerfully read the holy scriptures, they search us out, and as we bow to their precepts, they correct us and lead us in the way everlasting.

God's Displeasure

The prophet proceeds. After challenging them with a question, and calling upon them to consider their ways, he then proceeds to present evidence of God's displeasure to them.

"Ye have sown much, and bring in little; ye eat, but ye have not enough; ye drink, but ye are not filled with drink; ye clothe you, but there is none warm; and he that earneth wages earneth wages to put it into a bag with holes" (Hag. 1:6). In neglecting their duty to God, none of their efforts had prospered. When a person cheats God, in reality he really cheats himself. They had diligently worked their fields and planted their crops only to experience a failure in their harvest. They had sown much, but instead of reaping much, they brought in little. They had worked their fields thoroughly, only to have their crops fail. The LORD of hosts had brought them to poverty. Their reward for all their toil was an empty stomach.

In Moses' day, God threatened His people with plagues

for disobedience. We list only one. "And when I have broken the staff of your bread, ten women shall bake your bread in one oven, and they shall deliver you your bread again by weight: and ye shall eat, and not be satisfied" (Lev. 26:26). Two hundred and sixty years prior to Haggai's day, the prophet Hosea uttered similar words as a result of the people's disobedience. "For they shall eat, and not have enough: they shall commit whoredom, and shall not increase: because they have left off to take heed to thc LORD" (Hos. 4:10).

Sowing to the Flesh

In our day we have a similar warning. "Be not deceived; God is not mocked: for whatsoever a man soweth, that shall he also reap. For he that soweth to his flesh shall of the flesh reap corruption; but he that soweth to the Spirit shall of the Spirit reap life everlasting. And let us not be weary in well doing: for in due season we shall reap, if we faint not. As we have therefore opportunity, let us do good unto all men, especially unto them who are of the household of faith" (Gal. 6:7-10). The word "mocked" is only found here in the New Testament and bears the thought of "turning up the nose." When one sows to the flesh, he turns up his nose at God. A serious act indeed! We sow to the flesh with wrong company, fraternizing with the world. We sow to the flesh reading wrong literature. Most Christians are careful to avoid pornography, but some consider fiction acceptable. Let me explain something before going further. If you have a comprehensive dictionary, a complete book of synonyms, or Thayer's Lexion, you will discover what the word fiction actually means. Paul warns the saints, "Neither give heed to fables" (1 Tim. 1:4). Thayer's Lexion describes the word "fable" as, "a fiction, an invention, a falsehood." Take this word to a book of synonyms and you will discover the following description – " fiction, fabrication, fantasy, invention, falsehood, lie, misrepresentation, untruth." To term a book, "Christian fiction," is a gross misnomer. Who ever heard of a Christian lie, a Christian falsehood, a Christian untruth? The idea is absurd. Such books classified as such are misnamed and to be avoided. The Lord was Truth incarnate, and spoke nothing but the truth. His parables were certainly not fables, but actual events that had taken place. Let us regulate our reading to writings that are true. Our time is too limited and valuable to waste it reading fantasies, which in reality are lies.

We sow to the flesh by listening to wrong music. The world has its songs. To term some Rap and Rock musicals as "Christian," is a flagrant denial of sacredness. We can even sow to the flesh with activity, engaging in the sports of the world, traveling wearisome miles to see the sights of the world, joining the clubs, lodges, and a host of other things that this dark world has to offer. We can sow to the flesh by spending an excess of money on ourselves, on our pleasures, and on our comfort.

Sowing thus to the flesh reaps corruption. Things of this life fade with age. They lose their luster and their value as time marches on, until nothing is left at the end. We are living in a decaying society. Those who sow to the flesh not only discover at the end the vanity of it all, they also lose an eternal reward that could have been theirs, if only they had sown to the Spirit. May God give us spiritual discernment and the wisdom to sow to the Spirit and thus reap life everlasting in all its fullness.

A Bag with Holes

The prophet continues. "Ye clothe you, but there is none warm." Insufficiency of clothing had overtaken them, and he that earned wages only earned it to put it into a bag with holes, meaning that their income had been reduced to be able only to meet the bare necessities of life. Israel was God's earthly people, we, of this dispensation of grace, are His heavenly people. When the LORD punished Israel, He removed material blessings. When He punishes us, He withdraws spiritual blessings. Their seeming prosperity had been turned into poverty, simply because their priorities were not right. God had been given second place in their lives, consequently He withdrew blessing. The exhortation of our Lord comes to mind. "But seek ye first the kingdom of God, and His righteousness; and all these things (the necessities and blessings of life) shall be added unto you" (Matt 6:33).

The Exhortation

Haggai now exhorts them to act. "Go up to the mountain, and bring wood, and build the house; and I will take pleasure in it, and I will be glorified, saith the LORD" (Hag. 1:8). God made the material accessible, but it took human effort to obtain it. "Go" – There seems to be urgency in that word. It was to be an urgent effort and a united effort. The work would be uphill – "Go up to the mountain." Can you not picture them? Their food was scarce, their clothing scant, their means were short, nevertheless God said, "GO!" I can see them gathering what tools were available, ropes, chains, saws, and making their way out of the city and up to the mountain, dragging their equipment with them, perhaps on beasts of burden. When they dwelt comfortably in their ceiled houses they had "looked for much, and, lo, it came to little." Whatever they had brought home, God had blown upon it. The heavens had been affected and instead of providing dew, there was drought. Instead of the ground producing fruit, there was famine. The preaching of Haggai had produced obedience to the word of God, "and the people did fear before the LORD" (Hag. 1:12).

Words of Assurance

It was the first day of the sixth month when God had first spoken to them through Haggai (1:1) On the twenty-fourth day of that same month we read, "Then spake Haggai the LORD'S messenger in the LORD'S message unto the people, saying, I am with you, saith the LORD. And the LORD stirred up the spirit of Zerubbabel the son of Shealtiel, governor of Judah, and the spirit of Joshua the son of Josedech, the high priest, and the spirit of all the remnant of the people; and they came and did work in the house of the LORD of hosts, their God, In the four and twentieth day of the sixth month, in the second year of Darius the king" (Hag. 1:13-15). Haggai is described as "the LORD'S messenger in the LORD'S message." The people were convinced that Haggai was a spokesman for God, and that his cutting message, and his comforting message, were directly from the throne of God to them. "I am with you saith the LORD." What assurance, what comfort, from God Himself as they launched forward for Him in the work of building His house. When we come to the climax of Matthew's Gospel we find a similar expression as the disciples are about to set forward in labor for their risen Lord. He gives them a definite work to do and assures them, "Lo, I am with you alway, even unto the end of the world. Amen" (Matt. 28:20).

Commencement of the Work

No time had been wasted; in three weeks, there had been enough wood cut and brought to the temple site to commence the work in the house of the LORD of hosts, their God. Out of the thirty-eight verses in Haggai's book, we find that expression, "the LORD of hosts" fourteen times. It is found no less than two hundred and thirty-six times in the Bible and is solely an Old Testament expression. It is touching to notice the expression, "the LORD of hosts, their God." This particular expression is found only twice in the scriptures, Haggai 1:14, and Zechariah 12:5. When God first addressed these people, He spoke of the remnant as, "This people," not, "My people." It was not because He had disowned them, but rather because He was wearied with them for their sluggishness and slothfulness regarding His work. But now the pleasure of the Lord was upon them once again, due to their revival, and God was spoken of as, "their God." A relationship had been re-established. God had taken pleasure in their efforts and was glorified (Hag. 1:8).

It took effort to climb uphill to secure the wood, but far better to climb a mountain and drag the wood downhill, than walk down into a valley and haul the timber uphill. I have found that when we desire to do something for God, it seems hard to get started, but once we get into the work, the Lord makes the burden light. The Lord had the wood waiting for them, not in a valley, but in the mountain.

Various Works for God

"They came and did the work" (Hag. 1:14). What a gathering that must have been. The dying embers had been fanned through Haggai's word to a fervently burning flame. How refreshing to see the saints gathering and doing a work for God, the work of prayer. One is reminded of Epaphras, of whom it was said, "always labouring fervently for you in prayers" (Col. 4:12). When Peter was in prison, we read, "prayer was made without ceasing of the church unto God for him" (Acts 12.5). How vital to the testimony is collective prayer.

There is something very interesting that I have noticed through the years. The gatherings of the Lord's people always have a set time, and at most gatherings the saints are there in good time, except for one type of meeting. The meeting that I am referring to is very important, but seemingly not considered so by many. Hardly any seem to be at this meeting on time, and usually the percentage of attendance is low. You ask, "What meeting are you referring to?" The answer is, the prayer meeting preceding the gospel meeting on Lord's Day evenings. Brethren that are always at work on time, at the doctor's office on time, at the airline gate on time, never seem to get to this prayer meeting on time. What is the problem? The problem is the importance of supplicating God prior to the presentation of the gospel by the assembly is lacking. Haggai said, "They came and did the work."

The True Shepherd

We also have the work of visitation by the elders. One widow recently told me that she has not had a visit from an elder since her husband died ten years ago. What a shame. The word "overseers," found in Acts 20:28, as a description of the elders, is also used in Luke 19:44, and 1 Peter 2:12 and is translated there, "visitation." A true elder is a shepherd who visits the flock when the assembly is not corporately gathered together. Their responsibility is to counsel the young, comfort the sorrowing, encourage the discouraged, and restore the wandering. It is a full-time occupation demanding time. They visit, visit, visit. A true shepherd will be able to sit down with a young couple contemplating marriage and give them godly counsel. He will feel a responsibility to support the weak with his substance (Acts 20:35). He will read the scriptures and pray with the saint confined to a hospital room. He will seek to guide the lambs in the assembly with rich and wholesome food from the Book. He will encourage any developing gift seen in a young saint.

In the Books of Isaiah and Ezekiel we have a graphic description of a true shepherd. Notice: "He shall feed His flock like a shepherd (*satisfaction*): He shall gather the lambs with His arm (*security*), and carry them in His bosom (*support*), and shall gently lead those that are with young" (*sympathy*) (Isa. 40:11).

"I will feed my flock (*a minister of food*), and I will cause them to lie down (*a promoter of peace)*, saith the Lord GOD. I will seek that which was lost (*a restorer of the fallen*), and bring again that which was driven away (*a recoverer of the stolen*), and will bind up that which was broken (*a skillful surgeon)*, and will strengthen that which was sick (*a wise physician*): but I will destroy the fat and the strong; I will feed them with judgment" (*a protector of the flock) (*Ezek. 34:15,16).

In the New Testament consider the shepherds this way.

(1) Their Producing – Acts 20:28
(2) Their Pointing out – Acts 14:23
(3) Their Pedigree – 1 Tim. 3:1–7
(4) Their Purpose – 1 Tim. 3:5; 5:17
(5) Their Placing – 1 Tim. 5:22–25
(6) Their Protection – 1 Tim. 5:19
(7) Their Punishment – 1 Tim. 5:20

Five shepherds are graphically presented to us in the Old Testament Scriptures and all of them point to Christ Who is the Good Shepherd, the Great Shepherd, and the Chief Shepherd.

(1) Abel – The death of the shepherd.
(Christ the Righteous Shepherd)
(2) Jacob – His care for the sheep.
(Christ the Resourceful Shepherd)
(3) Joseph – He fed the flock.
(Christ the Rejected Shepherd)
(4) Moses – He watered and protected.
(Christ the Returning Shepherd)
(5) David – Jeopardized his life for sheep
(Christ the Royal Shepherd)

What a valuable asset to a scriptural flock are shepherds. The flock can rise no higher spiritually than the overseers. They are to be ensamples, models to the flock and watchmen, for their protection. In many places, assemblies are in sore need of true shepherds. In these perilous times, may the Lord raise up in our midst shepherds, so that every assembly will be able to exclaim like Haggai, "They came and did the work."

Haggai's Prophecies

The prophecies of Haggai were five, the first and second being on the sixth month, the first day (1:1-15). In the first utterance, words were proclaimed to arouse and stir up the people to give the LORD His rightful place, by commencing again the work of His house, as we have noticed. The second word came assuring the people that the Lord was with them in their endeavor.

The third prophecy was delivered almost two months later, being the seventh month and the twenty-first day (2:1-9). It was a message to strengthen and support the workers, exhorting them to be strong, and giving them the promise of His abiding spirit, and also pointing them on to a future day of glory.

The fourth utterance of the prophet was given on the twenty-fourth day of the ninth month, two months after the second prophecy (2:10-19). It was a searching word, reminding them of their past disobedience, yet assuring them that the LORD would bless them from that day onward, thus supporting, confirming, and endorsing their work.

The fifth message took place on the ninth month and the twenty-fourth day (2:20-23). It was delivered solely to Zerubbabel. What a word of encouragement as the prophet points the governor on to the day of Messiah's reign when all the nations of the earth shall bow before Him, Who is King of kings, and LORD of Lords.

Haggai's third message commences with a question. "Who is left among you that saw this house in her first glory? and how do ye see it now? is it not in your eyes in comparison of it as nothing?" (2:3). As noticed in the Book of Ezra, when the foundation had been laid fourteen years prior to Haggai's prophecies, the ancient men, who had seen the splendor and glory of Solomon's temple, wept with a loud voice, while others, who had never beheld the glory of the first house, shouted for joy. Haggai rightly analyzes the thoughts of the ancient men, they considered the present work "as nothing."

Coming to our day, we who are older can relate to this condition. Looking back many years, and then observing conditions today, older saints see dramatic changes. Gospel efforts continued for weeks on end. It was normal to see brethren engaged in tent meetings for nine, or even more weeks. Today what do we see? In comparison we see similar labors lasting only three or four weeks. The interest is small, few strangers attend and the saints seem to be easily tired after three or four weeks, thus we are prone to say, "Ah, this is as nothing." How often do you hear of one or two hundred sinners coming nightly to hear the gospel proclaimed? Many years ago it was heard of – today, hardly ever. I heard of a man who pitched a tent and preached all summer, into the fall of the year. As the weather turned cold, he moved his gospel effort into a little building alongside a corn field and continued. People came, carrying their kitchen chairs, as he didn't have enough seating available for all. He went on nightly for over fifty-four weeks, and many were saved. Saints of a bygone day were absolutely devoted to the LORD.

Comparison With Former Days

In 1970, I pitched a tent in a new area in the hills of West Virginia. I went into the area a total stranger to all.

People came and the tent being small could only hold perhaps one hundred and seventy people. It was packed nightly. We preached under that canvas for twelve weeks, then because of the coming winter, moved into a building and continued for twenty-five more weeks. The result was a testimony formed for the glory of God. After thirty-seven weeks of labor, I went home to visit my wife for a few days, before returning to minister spiritual food to those who had professed salvation during my labors. At the time of this writing, it is now thirty-three years later and my tent was pitched only ten miles from the first site. How long did I stay? Not very long, only six weeks. During that time, we traveled about 1,500 miles up and down the valleys, visiting folks with an invitation and a nice wall plaque for their homes. The result was, hardly a soul came to hear the gospel. Three professed faith in Christ, but the numbers never rose above fifty, and the sixth week they dropped into the thirties. Could I not say, in comparison of the former days, it was as nothing?

Christian Priorities

Older brethren have often remarked to me the order in the Christian's priorities. The order was this; (1) The house of God first; (2) The family second; (3) Their employment third. However, the order has sadly changed. The order today seems to be; (1) Their employment; (2) Their family; (3) The house of God. The zeal for the things of God today, in comparison to former days – is as nothing.

However, the prophet is not a pessimist; he interjects with these encouraging words, "Yet now be strong, O Zerubbabel, saith the LORD; and be strong, O Joshua, son of

Josedech, the high priest; and be strong, all ye people of the land, saith the LORD, and work: for I am with you, saith the LORD of hosts: According to the word that I covenanted with you when ye came out of Egypt, so My spirit remaineth among you: fear ye not" (2:4,5). "Be strong," is a primitive root; "to fasten upon;" hence, "to seize, courageous, to conquer, be established, play the man, be urgent, behave self valiantly." What good advice for older saints that may have a tendency to look morosely to the past. The constant cry that things are not what they used to be will never prompt us to do much for today. No, brethren, in spite of conditions, let us look up and be strong, and do what we can for God in spite of prevailing conditions. True, we are living in the day of small things, but let us remember, little is much if God is in it. The greatest strength we can possess is to have the LORD with us as our strength. Samuel Barnard grasped this truth and composed these words, often sung by believers.

"Jehovah is our strength,
And He shall be our song;
We shall o'ercome at length,
Although our foes be strong:
In vain then Satan doth oppose,
For God is stronger than our foes.

The Lord our refuge is,
And ever will remain;
Since He hath made us His
He will our cause maintain:
In vain our enemies oppose,
For God is stronger than His foes."

The Warrior

Paul rejoiced in the fact that, "If God be for us, who can be against us?" (Rom. 8:31). Paul exhorts us, "Finally, my brethren, be strong in the Lord, and in the power of His might. Put on the whole armour of God, that ye may be able to stand against the wiles of the devil. For we wrestle not against flesh and blood, but against principalities, against powers, against the rulers of the darkness of this world, against spiritual wickedness in high places. Wherefore take unto you the whole armour of God, that ye may be able to withstand in the evil day, and having done all, to stand. Stand therefore, having your loins girt about with truth, and having on the breastplate of righteousness; And your feet shod with the preparation of the gospel of peace; Above all, taking the shield of faith, wherewith ye shall be able to quench all the fiery darts of the wicked. And take the helmet of salvation, and the sword of the Spirit, which is the word of God: Praying always with all prayer and supplication in the Spirit, and watching thereunto with all perseverance and supplication for all saints" (Eph. 6:10-18).

Thus, we gird our loins about with truth, that is, we characterize ourselves with sincerity and truthfulness. We wear the breastplate of righteousness, we manifest uprightness in our life. Our feet are shod with the preparation of the gospel of peace, our footing is secure, we slip not. Holding the shield of faith, we express our utter dependence on God and our confidence in God. Putting on the helmet of salvation, we have the full assurance in our minds of eventual deliverance. Finally, in our hand we hold the sword of the Spirit, having a word from God to our fellowmen to suit the occasion. Thus strengthened – we work the work of the Lord!

The Future

From that encouraging declaration, Haggai projects God's people into the future, saying, "For thus saith the LORD of hosts; Yet once, it is a little while, and I will shake the heavens, and the earth, and the sea, and the dry land; And I will shake all nations, and the desire of all nations shall come: and I will fill this house with glory, saith the LORD of hosts. The silver is mine, and the gold is mine, saith the LORD of hosts. The glory of this latter house shall be greater than of the former, saith the LORD of hosts: and in this place will I give peace, saith the LORD of hosts" (Hag. 2:6-9).

Some have thought that this utterance was to be fulfilled in Haggai's day. However, no heavens and earth were ever shaken in the prophet's time. The Persian Empire at that time covered two million square miles and there is no record of serious disruptions within. The prophet's words contain a Messianic prophecy. In God's reckoning the fulfillment of this is but "a little while." God's way of reckoning time is vastly different than ours. A thousand years in His sight is but a moment. Haggai brings his hearers to apocalyptic times. As stated, the shaking of all nations certainly does not refer to the various uprisings seen at a later date in the Persian and Greek Empires. The prophet goes further than that, to the time when God in His omnipotence will make the kingdoms of this world to tremble, replacing them by the righteous and kingly rule of Messiah. It is the manifestation of the Son of man in power and in glory that is in view. This will be an event that will be unparalleled in human history. The poetic words of James Montgomery come to mind.

> ***"Kings shall fall down before Him,***
> ***And gold and incense bring;***
> ***All nations shall adore Him,***
> ***His praise all people sing:***
> ***For He shall have dominion***
> ***O'er river, sea, and shore,***
> ***Far as the eagle's pinion***
> ***Or dove's light wing can soar."***

Thus the prophet encourages God's people, assuring them of His presence with them, His covenant for them, the abiding of His spirit among them, and the promised return of their King to set up His earthly kingdom. Projecting the future to Israel had desired effects. The Lord works with us the same way. Constantly in scripture we are exhorted to look ahead. We are exhorted to "look for the Saviour, the Lord Jesus Christ: Who shall change our vile body, that it may be fashioned like unto His glorious body, according to the working whereby He is able even to subdue all things unto Himself" (Phil. 3:20,21). What a comfort to older saints who are experiencing the deterioration of aging bodies "Beloved, now are we the sons of God, and it doth not yet appear what we shall be: but we know that, when He shall appear, we shall be like Him; for we shall see Him as He is. And every man that hath this hope in Him purifieth himself, even as He is pure" (1 Jn. 3:2,3). Thus looking for His coming has a purifying effect on our lives. "And that, knowing the time, that now it is high time to awake out of sleep:

for now is our salvation nearer than when we believed. The night is far spent, the day is at hand: let us therefore cast off the works of darkness, and let us put on the armour of light. Let us walk honestly, as in the day; not in rioting and drunkenness, not in chambering and wantonness, not in strife and envying. But put ye on the Lord Jesus Christ, and make not provision for the flesh, to fulfil the lusts thereof" (Rom. 13:11-14). Looking to the future has the effect of making us awake and aware. It prompts us to a spiritual walk, not making provision for the flesh.

The All-Sufficiency of God

Haggai also assures the remnant workers of His all-sufficiency – the One able to meet their every need. "The silver is Mine, and the gold is Mine, saith the LORD of hosts" (2:8). Whatever was needed for the construction of His house, He would abundantly, and graciously supply. Brethren, Zerubbabel's God is our God, " I am the LORD, I change not" (Mal. 3:6). Are you afraid to give your time and substance abundantly to God?

Notice the assurance the Philippian Assembly received after giving abundantly of their substance for the furtherance of the work of God. They had given of their substance to Paul on more than one occasion. Were they the poorer for it? Absolutely not. What words of assurance Paul writes to that unselfish assembly. "But I have all, and abound: I am full, having received of Epaphroditus the things which were sent from you, an odour of a sweet smell, a sacrifice acceptable, wellpleasing to God. But my God shall supply all your need according to His riches in glory by Christ Jesus" (Phil. 4:18,19).

The same thought is projected to the Corinthian Church. To those who gave they are assured, "But this I say, He which soweth sparingly shall reap also sparingly; and he which soweth bountifully shall reap also bountifully. Every man according as he purposeth in his heart, so let him give; not grudgingly, or of necessity: for God loveth a cheerful giver. And God is able to make all grace abound toward you; that ye, always having all sufficiency in all things, may abound to every good work: (As it is written, 'He hath dispersed abroad; he hath given to the poor: his righteousness remaineth for ever.' Now He that ministereth seed to the sower both minister bread for your food, and multiply your seed sown, and increase the fruits of your righteousness)" (2 Cor. 9 :6-10).

Haggai's Fourth Prophecy

Approaching Haggai's fourth prophecy we hear these solemn words. "Thus saith the LORD of hosts; Ask now the priests concerning the law, saying, If one bear holy flesh in the skirt of his garment, and with his skirt do touch bread, or pottage, or wine, or oil, or any meat, shall it be holy? And the priests answered and said, No. Then said Haggai, If one that is unclean by a dead body touch any of these, shall it be unclean? And the priests answered and said, It shall be unclean. Then answered Haggai, and said, So is this people, and so is this nation before me, saith the LORD; and so is every work of their hands; and that which they offer there is unclean. And now, I pray you, consider from this day and upward, from before a stone was laid upon a stone in the temple of the LORD: Since those days were, when one came to an heap of twenty measures, there were but ten: when one came to the pressfat for to draw out fifty vessels out of the press, there were but twenty. I smote you with blasting and with mildew and with hail in all the labours of your hands; yet ye turned not to Me, saith the LORD. Consider now from this day and upward, from the four and twentieth day of the ninth month, even from the day that the foundation of the LORD'S temple was laid, consider it. Is the seed yet in the barn? yea, as yet the vine, and the fig tree, and the pomegranate, and the olive tree, hath not brought forth: from this day will I bless you" (2:11-19).

A Call to Consider

Two months after his last utterance, Haggai now brings before the remnant a divine principle. The time of the year was when an early rain could be expected to nourish the young crops. In the past they had experienced drought and severe disappointment. Their harvests had been a complete failure, the reason being that they had given attention to their own possessions to the total neglect of the house of God. True, they had been offering their sacrifices upon the altar for the past sixteen years, but in front of their eyes stood the foundation of the temple, possibly grown over with brush and weeds, a disgrace to the testimony.

The question now arises, since they had been awakened and revived and the work of the temple had once again commenced, would the LORD change the desperate conditions that prevailed? They had been brought low, would their God now lift them up? Haggai answers these inquiries in his fourth prophecy. He turns the people to the priests, who knew God's law and were commissioned by God to interpret it as we see in Deuteronomy 17:8,9. "If there arise a matter too hard for thee in judgment, between blood and blood, between plea and plea, and between stroke and stroke, being matters of controversy within thy gates: then shalt thou arise, and get thee up into the place which the LORD thy God shall choose; And thou shalt come unto the priests the Levites, and unto the judge that shall be in those days, and enquire; and they shall shew thee the sentence of judgment."

In this prophecy, Haggai is indirectly describing the remnant as they appeared before the LORD in their disobedience – they had been unclean. Being in this state of uncleanness, their offerings upon the existing altar were unclean. In their disobedience, they forwarded the results of that disobedience to their offerings on the altar, which rendered their sacrifices unprofitable to God. It has been well stated, "A healthy person cannot communicate his health to a dying person, but a dying person can communicate his disease to a healthy one." Thus, the law firmly taught that ceremonial cleanness was not transferrable from one person to another, but ceremonial uncleanness was. This is proclaimed in Leviticus 22:5,6. "Whosoever toucheth any creeping thing, whereby he may be made unclean, or a man of whom he may take uncleanness, whatsoever uncleanness he hath; The soul which hath touched any such shall be unclean until even, and shall not eat of the holy things, unless he wash his flesh with water." Also Numbers 19:11. "He that toucheth the dead body of any man shall be unclean seven days." Since the people in their disobedience were unclean, consequently their offerings were unacceptable, they too were unclean.

To parallel this with today, we would say a Christian

not living according to the will of God may fool himself into thinking that his worship is acceptable, but in reality, he is only, as they say, "going through the motions." The psalmist said, "If I regard iniquity in my heart, the Lord will not hear me" (Ps. 66:18). Samuel informed Saul, "Hath the LORD as great delight in burnt offerings and sacrifices, as in obeying the voice of the LORD? Behold, to obey is better than sacrifice, and to hearken than the fat of rams" (1 Sam. 15:22). Let us be soberly aware of this: If my life is not consistent with the teachings of God's word, if I am not walking according to the commandments of the Lord, my worship amounts to nothing. A man can pray intelligently, emotionally and tactfully, but if his walk is not consistent with his profession, in God's ears his words are only" as sounding brass, or a tinkling cymbal" (1 Cor. 13:1). He may charm the ears of the hearers, but God receives nothing. It is a godly walk that gives weight to a person's prayers. Should not this truth alone give us an incentive to live holy lives?

The LORD proceeds to inform His people only of what they were all aware – they had experienced desperate crop failures. Expecting twenty measures, they received only ten. The pressfat yielded only twenty measures when they fully expected fifty. In spite of the blasting (from excessive drought), mildew (from excessive moisture) and hail (from excessiveness turbulence), designed to humble them and bring them to repentance, they had refused to return. In view of this cheerless history, God said to them, "CONSIDER." They had been reminded of the past, now they are called upon to consider from that very day onward. The harvest was yet to come. Would it be a good harvest? God assures them that even though the seed is not yet in the barn and the fruit bearing trees and vines have not yet brought forth their fruit, yet from that day He would bless them. Thus with the assurance of His spirit with them, and His blessing of a fruitful harvest in view, they put their back to the work of God.

Haggai's Fifth and Last Prophecy

The fifth and final prophecy was delivered the same day, but to only one individual – Zerubbabel. "Speak to Zerubbabel, governor of Judah, saying, I will shake the heavens and the earth; And I will overthrow the throne of kingdoms, and I will destroy the strength of the kingdoms of the heathen; and I will overthrow the chariots, and those that ride in them; and the horses and their riders shall come down, every one by the sword of his brother. In that day, saith the LORD of hosts, will I take thee, O Zerubbabel, my servant, the son of Shealtiel, saith the LORD, and will make thee as a signet: for I have chosen thee, saith the LORD of hosts" (2:21-23).

Before our eyes arises the battle of Armageddon. God will overthrow, not the thrones of kingdoms, but "the ***throne*** of kingdoms," indicating that the kingdoms of this world have been fused into that one world system controlled by Satan and under the dictatorship of Antichrist. The chariots, instruments of war, shall be eliminated to usher in peace. "The horses and their riders shall come down, every one by the sword of his brother." The LORD will even employ civil strife to accomplish His divine purposes in ushering in a millennium of peace.

The name Zerubbabel does not refer to the present governor, but rather to the office he filled as ruler in Judah, and the One who would eventually appear to rightfully fulfill that office in all its completeness. The implication is that through Zerubbabel the Messiah was to come. You will notice that in the genealogy of Christ Zerubbabel's name appears (Matt.1:12, Lk.3:27). This man is honored in being chosen to portray a picture, a shadow, of Christ. The Person referred to was to be as a signet. To an Oriental a signet was a valuable item, denoting honor and authority. It was a ring employed by the owner for the signing of important documents. Zerubbabel's ministry would be invested with honor and authority, but at the same time, Haggai is prefiguring the value, authority, and honor of Christ in His coming kingdom. Zerubbabel, being in Messiah's line of succession, was honored to be the one to point to the Messiah, "I have chosen thee." What confidence the governor would have in the days of work that lay before him, knowing that the LORD Himself would represent him, and give him the authority in all his labors for Jehovah. As the signet was the sign of delegated authority, so our blessed Lord, in that day of His exaltation, will manifest His undisputed authority, which He confessed possessing after His glorious resurrection from among the dead. "All power is given unto Me in heaven and in earth" (Matt. 28:18). "For the Father judgeth no man, but hath committed all judgment unto the Son" (Jn. 5:22). What a day awaits us, when we shall reign with Him!

Zechariah – Prophet, Priest, Young Man.

Haggai climaxed his prophecies "in the seventh month, in the one and twentieth day of the month" (2:1). "In the eighth month, in the second year of Darius, came the word of the LORD unto Zechariah, the son of Berechiah, the son of Iddo the prophet" (Zech. 1:1). The omission of the day implies it was on the first day, or on the feast of the new moon. Zechariah was not only a prophet, but he was of priestly descent. Attention is drawn to this fact in Nehemiah 12:10-16. It seems that Biblical names draw attention to the character of the person so named. The father of Zechariah was named Berechiah, which means, ***Jehovah will bless.*** The prophet's grandfather was Iddo, meaning, ***the appointed time.*** Zechariah's name means, ***Jehovah remembers.***

It is very interesting to notice that these names give us a panoramic outline of the prophecies of this great man. He brings before the children of God that Jehovah has remembered them. The days of captivity are over, and according to His promise Jehovah has brought them back to their land. He also projects them into the future to such an extent that his prophecy is the same in the Old Testament as the Book of the Revelation is to the New Testament. The books of Zechariah and Revelation have both been termed the *Apocalypse*, meaning, the *unveiling*.

This mighty prophet has more utterances concerning our blessed Lord, His accomplished work and His manifested glory, than all of the other minor prophets combined, and in those prophecies we observe with wonder the blessing that God has in store for His beloved earthly people. Zechariah is diligent to point out in his prophecies that there is an appointed time for the realization of Jehovah's blessings upon the nation. That appointed time has not yet arrived. Thus we see that ***Jehovah remembers, Jehovah will bless,*** and that at ***the appointed time***.

Four Sections of Zechariah's Book

Zechariah's book is presented to us in four distinct sections. The prophet commences in the eighth month of 520 B.C., with a call to repentance, followed by the second section consisting of eight visions, in the eleventh month of the same year. The third section (chapters 7,8), the message was delivered in the ninth month of 518 B.C. and considered the subject of fasting, and the future day of blessing that Jehovah had for His people. No date is given for the fourth section, commencing at chapter nine and continuing to the end of the book. This final section considers the overthrow of world-power and the glorious establishment of Messiah's kingdom.

Haggai was much older than Zechariah, who was called, "this young man" (Zech. 2:4). Yet the younger priestly man is given more profound visions than his older companion Haggai. Notice, godly men do not envy, nor do they hold any resentment toward younger men that may be used by the Lord to a greater degree than they. In a local assembly of believers, for an older believer to "put down" a younger man simply because the younger man is more gifted, is an evil worthy of rebuke. We who are older should heartily welcome and encourage any spark of gift that we see in younger men. After all, the future of any testimony for God depends on them. Let us be careful to have a right spirit.

Unflattering Utterances

The commencement of Zechariah's utterances is certainly not very flattering! "The LORD hath been sore displeased with your fathers" (Zech.1:2). Their fathers had been brought almost to the place of abhorrence. Because of this terrible condition, the Lord of hosts pleads with them to turn unto Him, that He might turn unto them. The LORD is seeking fellowship. How gracious of the LORD to ever consider them. James brings the same picture to our attention, saying, "Submit yourselves therefore to God. Resist the devil, and he will flee from you. Draw nigh to God, and He will draw nigh to you. Cleanse your hands, ye sinners; and purify your hearts, ye double minded. Be afflicted, and mourn, and weep: let your laughter be turned to mourning, and your joy to heaviness. Humble yourselves in the sight of the Lord, and He shall lift you up" (Jas.4:7-10). Zechariah reminds them of the warnings that their fathers had received from the former prophets and the fact that their fathers simply turned a deaf ear to the pleadings of their God.

The prophet continues, "Your fathers, where are they? and the prophets, do they live for ever?" setting before them the common fate that befell their forefathers. The passing also of the prophets would warn them that there is brevity associated with the opportunity to repent, and to bow to the claims of their God. This was the time of their opportunity, but it was a quickly-passing occasion!

****** *THE EIGHT NIGHT VISIONS* ******

As mentioned, the second section of Zechariah's book contains eight visions: **(1)** The red-horse rider among the myrtle trees (1:7-17); **(2)** the four horns and the four carpenters (1:18-21); **(3)** a man with a measuring line in his hand (Ch.2); **(4)** the cleansing of Joshua the high priest (Ch. 3); **(5)** the golden lampstand and the two olive trees (Ch. 4); **(6)** a flying roll (5:1-4); **(7)** the woman in the ephah (5:5-11); **(8)** the four chariots (Ch.6).

One wonders with what depth these prophesies were perceived in the year they were given. There is an old statement regarding the Old and the New Testaments:

The New is in the Old concealed.
The Old is in the New revealed.

The New Testament writings unfold with divine clarity the writings of Zechariah. However, it is not the purpose of this book to go into these prophecies with an in-depth study, but only to skim the surface to support a few practical exhortations.

THE FIRST VISION

In Zechariah's first vision he sees in the night, "a man riding upon a red horse, and he stood among the myrtle trees that were in the bottom; and behind him were there red horses, speckled, and white." Thus we have a group of myrtle trees growing in a low place, and amongst them angelic horsemen. There is also an interpreter standing in the myrtle grove, who answers Zechariah's questions. Let us be clear the prophet is not dreaming, he is fully conscious as this vision comes before his eyes. Nebuchadnezzar's invasion of Jerusalem had involved three attacks, namely in the first, eighth, and seventeenth year of his reign, the last being about 590 B.C. The 70 years of indignation commenced at this point and now, exactly 70 years later, he began to see these eight visions. When you read of the *cap-*

tivity, it is referring to the condition of the people during those 70 years. The word *desolations* refers to the land during that same period.

The Myrtle Tree

The myrtle tree occupies a prominent place in Holy Scripture. It was a beautiful shrub to behold. The shiny dark green leaves when bruised gave forth a fragrant odor. Its white flowers were sweet to the smell. Brides adorned themselves with its flowers. The feast of tabernacles also employed this lovely shrub, along with olive, pine, and palm branches, using them in the construction of their booths (Neh.8:15). The myrtle tree was a symbol of Israel in a joyful and happy state. Isaiah even spoke of it in relation to the day when, instead of the briar, there would come up the myrtle tree, being to the Lord for a name and an everlasting sign that would not be cut off (Isa.55:13).

However, in Zechariah's vision there is no joy, there is no exaltation. Haggai, four months prior to Zechariah's vision, had prophesied, "For thus saith the LORD of hosts; Yet once, it is a little while, and I will shake the heavens, and the earth, and the sea, and the dry land; And I will shake all nations, and the desire of all nations shall come: and I will fill this house with glory, saith the LORD of hosts. The silver is mine, and the gold is mine, saith the LORD of hosts. The glory of this latter house shall be greater than of the former, saith the LORD of hosts: and in this place will I give peace, saith the LORD of hosts" (Hag.2:6-9). As previously explained, Haggai was projecting them on to the far distant future of the battle of Armageddon. When Zechariah commenced his prophesies, there had been no shaking, Haggai's prophecy was not being fulfilled as they had anticipated. The people were perplexed. Thus, in response to their frustration and bewilderment, Zechariah receives his first vision.

The prophet sees the myrtle trees in a low place. This describes the low condition of the nation at that time. They were in a state of humiliation. The Gentile powers still held authority over them. It is well to also consider the word, *bottom*, where the myrtle trees are positioned. It has also been translated *valley*, and some writers say that it represents Babylon where the nation had been held in captivity for seventy years. However, we reject such interpretation. A better rendering would be, *in the deep.* It is rendered thus in Psalm 88:6, "Thou hast laid Me in the lowest pit, in darkness, in the deeps. Thy wrath lieth hard upon Me, and thou hast afflicted Me with all thy waves. Selah." How fitting a picture of Israel over whom the waves of Gentile oppression had been rolling for so many years. The times of the Gentiles had commenced with their being carried away. The Gentile power, represented by the sea, the Satan-like power of the world had strongly exercised its dominion, especially since their captivity seventy years prior to this vision. How wonderful to see, that in all of their disobedience, departure, and discipline from God, the Lord was concerned over them. His power on their behalf had been withdrawn, but His presence remained. The prophet Isaiah projects this promise to God's people, "When thou passest through the waters, I will be with thee; and through the rivers, they shall not overflow thee" (Isa. 43:2). "In all their affliction He was afflicted, and the angel of His presence saved them: in His love and in His pity He redeemed them; and He bare them, and carried them all the days of old" (Isa. 63:9). How gratifying to know, that even in our day, when God's beloved people err and stray from His commandments, He is near. His power may be withdrawn, and His communion with us may be broken, yet the promise remains, "I will never leave thee, nor forsake thee" (Heb. 13:5).

Angels and Horses

Among the myrtle trees we discover angels and varied colored horses. The prophet inquired, "O my lord, what are these?…And the man that stood among the myrtle trees answered and said, These are they whom the LORD hath sent to walk to and fro through the earth" (Zech. 1:10). Having completed their mission, they report that "all the earth sitteth still, and is at rest." The meaning of the report is simple. Judah's blessing, according to Haggai's prophecy, would require first an overthrow of the nations, to Israel's favor. God had made known, through His prophet Haggai, that He would shake the heavens and the earth; and would overthrow the throne of kingdoms, and, destroy the strength of the kingdoms of the heathen. The nation realized that such an event would never occur when God was punishing them for their sins, by removing them from the land for seventy years, but now that time had expired and yet no overthrow of the nations had taken place, Israel was still under Gentile rule. The Babylonian Empire who had taken them captive no longer existed, but now the Persian Empire ruled so effectively that there was a rest upon the earth. Persia had full sway, and Israel was under their rule. Of course this caused much perplexity among the remnant, their cry, even many years later being, "Behold, we are servants this day, and for the land that Thou gavest unto our fathers to eat the fruit thereof and the good thereof, behold, we are servants in it" (Neh. 9:36). The nations were at rest, enjoying peace and prosperity, but the little remnant were still under the Gentile yoke, their land still lying in waste, the burned and crumbled walls still surrounding them as a testimony to their disobedience. There they were, a remnant surrounded by an ocean of enemies, with no sight of their God overthrowing the kingdoms of the world to their exaltation and blessing.

The question now arises in the vision, "Then the angel of the LORD answered and said, O LORD of hosts, how long wilt thou not have mercy on Jerusalem and on the cities of Judah, against which thou hast had indignation these threescore and ten years?" (Zech. 1:12). Over 2060 years have passed since the vision, and the cry remains, "O LORD of hosts, how long." Even though Israel is now an established state, she is still partially under Gentile power, and her people are still scattered throughout the world.

The Lord Speaks

The prophet now receives "good words and comfortable words," which were sweet, precious and soothing to the perplexed heart. The LORD of hosts announces His jealousy for Jerusalem. The correct rendering is, "I have given a token of My jealously and am now eased," the reference being to some great act of God in the past, on behalf of His people. This act was the bringing back of His people out of captivity.

The LORD goes on to say, "And I am very sore displeased with the heathen (nations) that are at ease: for I was but a little displeased, and they helped forward the affliction (evil)" (Zech. 1:15).

God had used the Gentiles as His instrument to punish His people, but the Gentiles had gone beyond the intentions of God in their severity. In their cruelty and rage, their extremes resulted in wickedness and evil. "Therefore thus saith the LORD; I am returned to Jerusalem with mercies: My house shall be built in it, saith the LORD of hosts, and a line shall be stretched forth upon Jerusalem. Cry yet, saying, Thus saith the LORD of hosts; My cities through prosperity shall yet be spread abroad; and the LORD shall yet comfort Zion, and shall yet choose Jerusalem" (Zech. 1:16,17). "I am returned to Jerusalem with mercies." Consider the tense, it is in the *past*. However, the *past historical perfect,* in this case, indicates a *prophetic perfect,* indicating that with absolute certainty an event still future is considered as having already taken place.

What words of hope and comfort! Even though the full realization of these promises could only be in the future, they were announced for the present comfort of the discouraged little remnant. When the Lord appears the second time, He will physically return to the beloved city with mercies. The prophet proclaims the Lord's message. "And it shall come to pass ***in that day***, that I will seek to destroy all the nations that come against Jerusalem. And I will pour upon the house of David, and upon the inhabitants of Jerusalem, the spirit of grace and of supplications: and they shall look upon Me Whom they have pierced, and they shall mourn for Him, as one mourneth for his only son, and shall be in bitterness for Him, as one that is in bitterness for his firstborn" (Zech. 12:9,10).

The Words of Isaiah

The prophet Isaiah also has much to say regarding ***that day.***

"***And in that day*** there shall be a root of Jesse, which shall stand for an ensign of the people; to it shall the Gentiles seek: and His rest shall be glorious" (Isa. 11:10).

"And it shall come to pass ***in that day***, that the Lord shall set His hand again the second time to recover the remnant of His people, which shall be left, from Assyria, and from Egypt, and from Pathros, and from Cush, and from Elam, and from Shinar, and from Hamath, and from the islands of the sea" (Isa. 11:11).

"And it shall come to pass ***in that day,*** that the LORD shall punish the host of the high ones that are on high, and the kings of the earth upon the earth" (Isa. 24:21).

"And it shall be said ***in that day,*** Lo, this is our God; we have waited for Him, and He will save us: this is the LORD; we have waited for Him, we will be glad and rejoice in His salvation" (Isa. 25:9).

"And it shall come to pass ***in that day,*** that the great trumpet shall be blown, and they shall come which were ready to perish in the land of Assyria, and the outcasts in the land of Egypt, and shall worship the LORD in the holy mount at Jerusalem" (Isa. 27:13).

"***In that day*** shall the LORD of hosts be for a crown of glory, and for a diadem of beauty, unto the residue of His people" (Isa. 28:5).

THE SECOND VISION

Zechariah continues. "Then lifted I up mine eyes, and saw, and behold four horns. And I said unto the angel that talked with me, What be these? And he answered me, These are the horns which have scattered (winnowed) Judah, Israel, and Jerusalem" (Zech. 1:18,19).

The prophet lifts up his eyes. His head had evidently been bowed in meditation over the awesomeness of the first vision. The question now arises, what are the four horns? The horns are not horns for blowing announcements, but rather animal horns that depict the power and energy of that animal, such as a ram. Thus the horns in our vision typify the strength and power of four distinct empires. These horns have been responsible for scattering and viciously abusing God's earthly people.

As noted, the word *scattered* means *winnowed.* Israel had been treated like grain beaten out on the threshing floor to separate it from the chaff. The word *scattered* is in the perfect tense, and could be interpreted as a complete action in the past. However, according to Hebrew scholars, "the Hebrew verbal system describes the *kind* of action, and *not* the past, present, or future tense. The perfect presents *finished* or *completed* action either in past, present, or future depending upon the *context.*" Considering the scope of all the other night visions, we feel comfortable placing this vision as a *present* perfect. Thus we see four great kingdoms represented by four horns, namely the Babylonian, Persian, Grecian, and Roman Empires. At the time of the vision the Babylonian Empire had passed away, and the present ruling Empire was the Persian. Two more Empires were to come, the Grecian and Roman Empires. In the activities of these four great Gentile powers we see Israel scattered, abused, afflicted and plowed upon.

There are fifteen Psalms grouped together and titled, *A Song of degrees* (or Ascents). As the children of Israel approached the former temple, in all its glory, these Psalms were sung. They commence with Psalm 120 and end with Psalm 134. Psalm 129 is especially interesting in view of our previous statements. "A Song of degrees. Many a time have they afflicted me from my youth, may Israel now say: Many a time have they afflicted me from my youth: yet they have not prevailed against me. The plowers plowed upon my back: they made long their furrows. The LORD is righteous: He hath cut asunder the cords of the wicked. Let them all be confounded and turned back that hate Zion. Let them be as the grass upon the housetops, which withereth afore it groweth up: Wherewith the mower filleth not his hand; nor he that bindeth sheaves his bosom. Neither do they which go by say, The blessing of the LORD be upon you: we bless you in the name of the LORD."

The full realization of Israel upon their enemies has not yet come to fruition. The plowers are still plowing upon her back and making long their furrows. At the time of this writing, the Palestinian murderer Arafat is continually conniving to exterminate God's earthly people. However, the day is coming when He Who has the right to reign will come. The apostle John beholds that day and writes, "And I saw heaven opened, and behold a white horse; and He that sat upon him was called Faithful and True, and in righteousness He doth judge and make war. His eyes were as a flame of fire, and on His head were many crowns; and He had a name written, that no man knew, but He himself. And He was clothed with a vesture dipped in blood: and His name is called The Word of God. And the armies which were in heaven followed Him upon white horses, clothed in fine linen, white and clean. And out of His mouth goeth a sharp sword, that with it He should smite the nations: and He shall rule them with a rod of iron: and He treadeth the winepress of the fierceness and wrath of Almighty God. And He hath on His vesture and on His thigh a name written, KING OF KINGS, AND LORD OF LORDS" (Rev. 19:11-16). Israel has much to endure yet before that glorious day arrives.

Four Carpenters

Zechariah beholds four *carpenters*, or, *smiths*. The word denotes *craftsmen that worked* to construct. However, these craftsmen are employed in destroying. "And the LORD shewed me four carpenters. Then said I, What come these to do? And He spake, saying, These are the horns which have scattered Judah, so that no man did lift up his head: but these are come to fray them, to cast out the horns of the Gentiles, which lifted up their horn over the land of Judah to scatter it" (Zech. 1:20-21). Fray means, *to discomfit, to make tremble*. The destroying craftsmen are employed in casting out. The first time that expression, cast out, is employed in scripture is in Genesis 21:10. "Wherefore she said unto Abraham, Cast out this bondwoman and her son: for the son of this bondwoman shall not be heir with my son, even with Isaac." Thus Hagar lost her position in the house of Abraham. The second occasion is found in Exodus 34:24, and is a promise given to Israel upon entering the land. "For I will cast out the nations before thee, and enlarge thy borders: neither shall any man desire thy land, when thou shalt go up to appear before the LORD thy God thrice in the year." The four carpenters represent four kingdoms, one following the other.

The Babylonian Empire 605–539 B.C. Ruled 66 years.
The Persian Empire 539–336 B.C. Ruled 203 years
The Grecian Empire 336–300 B.C. Ruled 36 years.
The Roman Empire 300 B.C.–476 A.D. Ruled 776 years.
The first carpenter, Persia, cast out Babylon.
The second carpenter, Greece, cast out Persia.
The third carpenter, Rome, cast out Greece.

The Roman Empire began its hibernation in 476 A.D., but will be revived again after the rapture of the church. Governed by Satan himself, and represented by antichrist, she will display tremendous influence and power to the four corners of the earth. Israel will enter a bloodbath unparalleled in human history, until He comes, Whose right it is to reign. The fourth carpenter will cast out the Roman Empire, and our Lord's kingdom will be established as Zechariah foretells. "And I will cut off the chariot from Ephraim, and the horse from Jerusalem, and the battle bow shall be cut off: and He shall speak peace unto the heathen: and His dominion shall be from sea even to sea, and from the river even to the ends of the earth" (Zech. 9:10).

When the prophet refers to the river, he is speaking of the Euphrates, one of the four rivers that flowed out from the garden of Eden, the very cradle of the human race. Then, and not until then, shall all the promises of future blessing for the nation of Israel be fully realized and enjoyed. A careful reading of Revelation, chapters five to nineteen, will enlighten you further on this intriguing subject of the final overthrow of the Roman Empire and the divine establishment of the kingdom of our Lord, and of His Christ (Rev.11:15).

THE THIRD VISION

Once more the prophet lifts up his eyes and beholds a man with a measuring line in his hand. This man is on his way to Jerusalem to measure its breadth and length. The second vision brought before us the total destruction, the casting out of Israel's enemies, and the setting up of our Lord's glorious kingdom. Now, in this third night vision we behold the wonderful restoration of Israel as a nation, and the establishment of Jerusalem as the center of the earth. What a tremendous city Jerusalem will be in the millennial reign of Christ, far larger, and by far more illustrious, than what meets our eye today. The angel runs to tell young Zechariah that Jerusalem " shall be inhabited as towns without walls for the multitude of men and cattle therein." There will be no invading armies, consequently no need of walls. As in ancient villages, this mighty city will contain pasture for the herds of cattle owned by the inhabitants. The great city of New York cannot even boast of such an accommodation in our day. Not only this, "the LORD, will be unto her a wall of fire round about, and will be the glory in the midst of her" (Zech 2:5). Isaiah exclaims, "And the LORD will create upon every dwelling place of mount Zion, and upon her assemblies, a cloud and smoke by day, and the shining of a flaming fire by night: for upon all the glory shall be a defence" (Isa. 4:5). Every eye shall behold Him, Whose right it is to reign, when His glory, visible to all, will be exposed in the land. He will be a wall of fire encompassing them. The protectiveness of God will be fully seen, the Lord Himself being the wall of defence for the city. Just as fire drives away wolves from a flock of sheep, so Jehovah will repel any thinking to do His people harm. He will also be "the glory in the midst of her."

As the times of the Gentiles dawned and God's earthly people came under Gentile dominion, the Shekinah Presence departed from Jerusalem as Ezekiel relates. "Then did the cherubims lift up their wings, and the wheels beside them; and the glory of the God of Israel was over them above. And the glory of the LORD went up from the midst of the city, and stood upon the mountain which is on the east side of the city" (Ezek. 11:22,23). In the millennial reign of our Lord the Shekinah Presence will once more be a reality. Ezekiel is projected by the Spirit into the future and exclaims, "And, behold, the glory of the God of Israel came from the way of the east: and His voice was like a noise of many waters: and the earth shined with His glory…And the glory of the LORD came into the house by the way of the gate whose prospect is toward the east. So the Spirit took me up, and brought me into the inner court; and, behold, the glory of the LORD filled the house" (Ezek. 43:2,4,5). Isaiah bears record of the same. "The wilderness and the solitary place shall be glad for them; and the desert shall rejoice, and blossom as the rose. It shall blossom abundantly, and rejoice even with joy and singing: the glory of Lebanon shall be given unto it, the excellency of Carmel and Sharon, they shall see the glory of the LORD, and the excellency of our God" (Isa. 35:1,2).

Those in Babylon

Having prophesied of the coming glory, Zechariah focuses on those who remained in Babylon. Rather than suffer hardship, danger and toil, they had chosen to remain in their comfortable surroundings in the land where they had been taken captive. They had melted into the Babylonish system and felt at home. The testimony of the Lord in Jerusalem had never captivated their soul. Of course they were in sympathy with it, but not willing to suffer for it. To return would mean giving up all their prospects, investments, pleasures and comforts of Babylon.

Through Zechariah, the LORD speaks. "Ho, ho, come forth, and flee from the land of the north, saith the LORD: for I have spread you abroad as the four winds of the heaven, saith the LORD. Deliver thyself, O Zion, that dwellest with the daughter of Babylon. For thus saith the LORD of hosts; After the glory hath He sent Me unto the nations which spoiled you: for he that toucheth you toucheth the apple of His eye. For, behold, I will shake Mine hand upon them, and they shall be a spoil to their servants: and ye shall know that the LORD of hosts hath sent Me" (Zech. 2:6-9).

Astonishment and Wondering

To solemnly arrest the attention, the prophet cries, "Ho, ho." He is about to admonish and warn those who chose to remain in Babylon. Even though Babylon lay only slightly north and almost directly east of Jerusalem, it is spoken of as the land of the north, because armies and merchants from that land came around what is called the *fertile crescent* and entered Israel's land from the north. Jeremiah speaks of Nebuchadnezzar as from the north. "And the word of the LORD came unto me the second time, saying, What seest thou? And I said, I see a seething pot; and the face thereof is toward the north. Then the LORD said unto me, Out of the north an evil shall break forth upon all the inhabitants of the land...Set up the standard toward Zion: retire, stay not: for I will bring evil from the north, and a great destruction. The lion is come up from his thicket, and the destroyer of the Gentiles is on his way; he is gone forth from his place to make thy land desolate; and thy cities shall be laid waste, without an inhabitant" (Jer.1:13,14; 4:6,7).

Assyrian Captivity

Assyria also is spoken of as from the north. Two centuries prior to this prophecy, the ten tribes had been carried away by the Assyrians. Many of God's people were placed in Hamath in northern Syria, others taken to Mesopotamia (northeast of Hamath), and also into Media. Later, Nebuchadnezzar had deported Judah to Babylon, some later to be scattered throughout the 127 provinces of the Persian empire from India to Ethiopia. God truly had scattered them "as the four winds of heaven." Now these scattered ones are called upon to "deliver themselves," that is, to flee, as the judgment upon Babylon was nearing. They were about to lose their complacent way of life, their comfortable homes and vineyards were about to be lost, their prosperity would soon be converted into poverty –Jerusalem was beckoning. History records two great rebellions in Babylon and the two captures of that city, one by Darius, then one by his generals. God warned them to leave and return to Jerusalem that they might escape the impending evil and also experience the goodness of their God extended to those in the land of promise.

Christendom

Perhaps you will allow me to apply this ancient narrative to our day. Christendom could well be likened to Babylon in our day – a place of confusion. Paul warned Timothy, "Now the Spirit speaketh expressly, that in the latter times some shall depart from the faith, giving heed to seducing spirits, and doctrines of devils; Speaking lies in hypocrisy; having their conscience seared with a hot iron; Forbidding to marry, and commanding to abstain from meats, which God hath created to be received with thanksgiving of them which believe and know the truth" (1 Tim.4:1-3). The fullness of this departure commenced in 606 A.D. three years after the death of Gregory (bishop of Rome). Emperor Phocas conferred the title of *Universal Bishop* upon Boniface, thus the papacy was born. Later, her priests were forbidden to marry and her people were commanded to abstain from eating certain meats on designated days. Prior to her birth, departure from the scriptural pattern laid down for churches was well on its way. Not long after the death of the apostle John corruption set in - a deviation from the pattern laid down for the churches in the New Testament writings. A hierarchical government soon developed, and there was an approved episcopal office beyond the limits of the local company. There was an unscriptural recognition of clergy and laity. The baptism of infants and the false doctrine of baptismal regeneration were introduced. Prayers for the dead were initiated in 310 A.D. The worship of Mary was introduced in 431 A.D., and the sad doctrine of purgatory in 593 A.D. By the year 600, people were praying to

Mary and other dead saints. "Peter the Hermit" introduced the rosary in 1090, and the Church of Rome accepted the vile doctrine of transubstantiation.

Denominations

It is appalling to see the rapid departure of professed Christianity. In reality, the whole system had become a spiri tual Babylon. There are all sorts of so called "Christian denominations" today, but God's people are exhorted to leave such and to come out of it all, and gather alone to the peerless Name and Person of our Lord Jesus Christ. The promise of His words to the local assembly of believers still remains, "For where two or three are gathered together in My name, there am I in the midst of them" (Matt. 18:20).

Separation

Paul exhorted the Corinthian believers, "Wherefore come out from among them, and be ye separate, saith the Lord, and touch not the unclean thing; and I will receive you" (2 Cor. 6:17). We find a similar exhortation to the Jewish believers, but applicable to all true saints today. "Wherefore Jesus also, that He might sanctify the people with His own blood, suffered without the gate. Let us go forth therefore unto Him without the camp, bearing His reproach" (Heb. 13:12,13). There is a reproach connected with leaving a religious and unscriptural system that approves a clergy and a laity, one-man salaried ministers, and a host of other deviations from the plain blueprint of Holy Scripture.

Dublin, Ireland

In Dublin, Ireland (1827), there were a number of prominent Christian men who met together to diligently search the truth of the Word of God regarding the scriptural function of a local church. They saw the truth of gathering to the Name and Person of Christ alone, owning no other name. They discovered the unscripturalness of a local assembly having only one pastor, and the unscripturalness of that pastor receiving a salary for his labors. Some of these men were high in the ecclesiastical system of the day, but through their diligent searching, with humble spirit they bowed to the truth of God and left the system they had discovered to be unscriptural.

The cost was tremendous. From every quarter they were reproached, but as they ministered, God worked mightily and hundreds were added to the Lord, and eventually scriptural assembles were planted throughout the world. The silence of women in the church, their long hair, their wearing of a veil (or hat), the plurality of elders as the only form of government, the Lord's supper carried out every first day of the week, using one cup and one loaf of bread, the absence of instrumental music, the priesthood of all believers, the acknowledgment of the Holy Scriptures as the only guide and authority for the local assembly, the eternal security of the believer, the passing of the miraculous sign gifts, and the fervent proclamation of the gospel every Lord's day are things tenaciously held by such scriptural gatherings. They are not a cult or a denomination. They take no other name than that which the scriptures give, such as, believers, saints, Christians, children of God, sons of God, and disciples. Figuratively speaking, the call came to arise and leave Babylon and return to God's appointed dwelling place – Jerusalem.

God's Affection

God assures the remnant of His tender affection toward them. "For thus saith the LORD of hosts; After the glory hath He sent me unto the nations which spoiled you: for he that toucheth you toucheth the apple of His eye" (Zech. 2:8). How tender is the pupil of the eye. Touching it affects the whole body. The enemies who touched, or abused, Israel may as well have touched God Himself. He is very sensitive toward His people. C.H. Spurgeon once said, "Lay your hand upon a child's head, and you touch a mother's heart." The same relationship could be said of the Lord of hosts and Israel. Moses expresses the same. "He found him in a desert land, and in the waste howling wilderness; He led him about, He instructed him, He kept him as the apple of His eye" (Deut. 32:10). David prayed for that same relationship with his God, saying, "Keep me as the apple of the eye, hide me under the shadow of Thy wings" (Ps.17:8). The same is true in our day. Saul of Tarsus was persecuting the saints, but on the day of his conversion the Lord apprehended him with these searching words, "Saul, Saul, why persecutest thou Me? And he said, Who art thou, Lord? And the Lord said, I am Jesus whom thou persecutest: it is hard for thee to kick against the pricks" (Acts 9:4,5).

He who persecutes His own,
Is persecuting Christ.
For they are members of His body,
Of His flesh, and of His bones.

One cannot help but notice the occurrence of that expression, t*he Lord of hosts*, so frequently seen in the writings of Zechariah. It is in every chapter except chapter eleven, and is found fifty-two times. The expression conveys to us His authority and power. He is the Lord of armies. Daniel relates, "And all the inhabitants of the earth are reputed as nothing: and He doeth according to His will in the army of heaven, and among the inhabitants of the earth: and none can stay His hand, or say unto Him, What doest Thou?" (Dan. 4:35). What a solemn warning to those who had abused God's people. Their punishment was coming.

The Manifestation of God

The vindication of the LORD, His coming to the nations to shake His hand upon them, putting them down, and exalting His people Israel, is spoken of as, "after the glory." It seems that we are being directed to a day yet to come, when Messiah will display the glory of God by His appearing as King of kings and Lord of lords and with rapid movements setting up His earthly kingdom.

In other words, it is the Second Advent of Christ in power and glory to smite the nations with the rod of His anger and to bring salvation to His people. "For, behold, I will shake (brandish) Mine hand upon them, and they shall be a spoil (prey, booty) to their servants: and ye shall know that the LORD of hosts hath sent Me" (Zech. 2:9). The almighty hand of God will be manifested in no uncertain terms. The nations have touched the apple of His eye. His sensitive feelings toward His people will react with a shaking of the nations. The day of His manifestation is graphically described in the second Psalm. "Why do the heathen rage (throng together), and the people imagine (meditate) a vain thing? The kings of the earth set themselves, and the rulers take counsel together, against the LORD, and against His Anointed, saying, Let us break Their bands (which fasten yoke to the neck) asunder, and cast away Their cords (reins, that which keeps an animal under control) from us. He that sitteth in the heavens shall laugh: the Lord shall have them in derision (ridicule, scorn). Then shall He speak unto them in His wrath, and vex them in His sore displeasure. Yet have I set My King upon My holy hill of Zion. I will declare the decree: the LORD hath said unto Me, Thou art My Son; this day have I begotten Thee. Ask of Me, and I shall give Thee the heathen for Thine inheritance, and the uttermost parts of the earth for Thy possession. Thou shalt break them with a rod of iron; Thou shalt dash them in pieces like a potter's vessel. Be wise now therefore, O ye kings: be instructed, ye judges of the earth. Serve the LORD with fear, and rejoice with trembling. Kiss the Son (a sign of homage, loyalty), lest He be angry, and ye perish from the way, when His wrath is kindled but a little. Blessed are all they that put their trust in Him."

Matthew mentions the same event.

"Immediately after the tribulation of those days shall the sun be darkened, and the moon shall not give her light, and the stars shall fall from heaven, and the powers of the heavens shall be shaken: And then shall appear the sign of the Son of man in heaven: and then shall all the tribes of the earth mourn, and they shall see the Son of man coming in the clouds of heaven with power and great glory. And He shall send His angels with a great sound of a trumpet, and they shall gather together His elect from the four winds, from one end of heaven to the other" (Matt. 24:29-31).

Paul Speaks

Paul relates this tremendous event to the Thessalonian believers.

"And to you who are troubled rest with us, when the Lord Jesus shall be revealed from heaven with His mighty angels, In flaming fire taking vengeance on them that know not God, and that obey not the gospel of our Lord Jesus Christ: Who shall be punished with everlasting destruction from the presence of the Lord, and from the glory of His power; When He shall come to be glorified in His saints, and to be admired in all them that believe (because our testimony among you was believed) in that day" (2 Thess. 1:7-10).

John Speaks

Finally, John bears witness to the coming of Christ to shake the nations.

"And I saw heaven opened, and behold a white horse; and He that sat upon him was called Faithful and True, and in righteousness He doth judge and make war. His eyes were as a flame of fire, and on His head were many crowns; and He had a name written, that no man knew, but He himself. And He was clothed with a vesture dipped in blood: and His name is called The Word of God. And the armies which were in heaven followed Him upon white horses, clothed in fine linen, white and clean. And out of His mouth goeth a sharp sword, that with it He should smite the nations: and He shall rule them with a rod of iron: and He treadeth the winepress of the fierceness and wrath of Almighty God. And He hath on His vesture and on His thigh a name written, KING OF KINGS, AND LORD OF LORDS" (Rev.19:11-16).

The Millennial Reign

The coming of the Lord to redeem the nation will usher in His millennial reign on earth. The prophet proceeds – "Sing and rejoice, O daughter of Zion: for, lo, I come, and I will dwell in the midst of thee, saith the LORD. And many nations shall be joined to the LORD in that day, and shall be My people: and I will dwell in the midst of thee, and thou shalt know that the LORD of hosts hath sent Me unto thee. And the LORD shall inherit Judah His portion in the holy land, and shall choose Jerusalem again. Be silent, O all flesh, before the LORD: for He is raised up out of His holy habitation" (Zech.2:10-13).

What a glorious day that will be when in the midst of Jerusalem their Lord will visibly be present. They will sing and rejoice. How different today for that nation. Still under Gentile domination, they are still scattered throughout the earth, and those who have returned to the land, (which was declared a State in 1948), are in a state of unrest and terrorism from the Arab world. The ultimate goal of the Arab nations is to completely destroy the nation of Israel from the face of the earth, but, unknown to them, Israel's God has far different plans for His people. Seven years after the rapture of the Church, Israel shall behold their Messiah, residing in the beloved city – and they shall sing aloud.

Israel's Blindness

Ask any unconverted Jew today about the events just described, and you will find him totally oblivious to the facts. Israel still abides in a state of unbelief. The veil is still upon the nation's heart, but the day is coming when God will remove the veil and they shall acknowledge the truth of Isaiah's prophecy. Their confession in that day will be, "Surely He hath borne our griefs, and carried our sorrows: yet we did esteem Him stricken, smitten of God, and afflicted. But He was wounded for our transgressions, He was bruised for our iniquities: the chastisement of our peace was upon Him; and with His stripes we are healed. All we like sheep have gone astray; we have turned every one to his own way; and the LORD hath laid on Him the iniquity of us all. He was oppressed, and He was afflicted, yet He opened not His mouth: He is brought as a lamb to the slaughter, and as a sheep before her shearers is dumb, so He openeth not His mouth. He was taken from prison and from judgment: and who shall declare His generation? for He was cut off out of the land of the living: for the transgression of my people was He stricken" (Isa. 53:4-8).

In the Midst

It is interesting to notice that expression, "in the midst," relative to our Lord in the New Testament.

(1) HIS PERCEPTION – **IN THE TEMPLE**

"And it came to pass, that after three days they found Him in the temple, sitting ***in the midst*** of the doctors, both hearing them, and asking them questions" (Lk. 2:46).

(2) HIS PROVISION – **AMONG THE TRIBES**

"Ye men of Israel, hear these words; Jesus of Nazareth, a Man approved of God among you by miracles and wonders and signs, which God did by Him ***in the midst*** of you, as ye yourselves also know" (Acts 2:22).

(3) HIS PASSION – **ON THE TREE**

"Where they crucified Him, and two other with Him, on either side one, and Jesus ***in the midst***" (Jn. 19:18).

(4) HIS PRESENCE – **IN THE TESTIMONY**

"For where two or three are gathered together in My name, there am I ***in the midst*** of them" (Matt. 18:20).

(5) HIS POWER & PREEMINENCE –**ON THE THRONE**

"And I beheld, and, lo, ***in the midst*** of the throne and of the four beasts, and in the midst of the elders, stood a Lamb as it had been slain, having seven horns and seven eyes, which are the seven Spirits of God sent forth into all the earth" (Rev. 5:6).

(6) HIS PERCEPTION, PROVISION, PASSION, PRESENCE, POWER, PEACE, AND PREEMINENCE – **AMONG THE TROUBLED**

"Then the same day at evening, being the first day of the week, when the doors were shut where the disciples were assembled for fear of the Jews, came Jesus and stood ***in the midst,*** and saith unto them, Peace be unto you" (Jn. 20:19).

In the coming day of Israel's glory, He again shall be in their midst, but what a difference! In His first appearance He came unto them, as the prophet declared, "Rejoice greatly, O daughter of Zion; shout, O daughter of Jerusalem: behold, thy King cometh unto thee: He is just, and having salvation; lowly, and riding upon an ass, and upon a colt the foal of an ass" (Zech. 9:9). However, He was taken, and by wicked hands was crucified and slain (Acts 2:23).

At His next appearing to the nation of Israel, they will gladly receive Him and He will " cut off the chariot from Ephraim, and the horse from Jerusalem, and the battle bow shall be cut off: and He shall speak peace unto the heathen: and His dominion shall be from sea even to sea, and from the river even to the ends of the earth" (Zech. 9:10).

THE FOURTH VISION

We now find the prophet confronted with a problem, but also a promise. "And He (the Lord of hosts) shewed me Joshua the high priest standing before the angel of the LORD, and Satan standing at his right hand to resist him. And the LORD said unto Satan, The LORD rebuke thee, O Satan; even the LORD that hath chosen Jerusalem rebuke thee: is not this a brand plucked out of the fire? Now Joshua was clothed with filthy garments, and stood before the angel. And he answered and spake unto those that stood before him, saying, Take away the filthy garments from him. And unto him He said, Behold, I have caused thine iniquity to pass from thee, and I will clothe thee with change of raiment. And I said, Let them set a fair mitre upon his head. So they set a fair mitre upon his head, and clothed him with garments. And the angel of the LORD stood by. And the angel of the LORD protested unto Joshua, saying, Thus saith the LORD of hosts; If thou wilt walk in My ways, and if thou wilt keep My charge, then thou shalt also judge My house, and shalt also keep My courts, and I will give thee places to walk among these that stand by. Hear now, O Joshua the high priest, thou, and thy fellows that sit before thee: for they are men wondered at: for, behold, I will bring forth My servant the BRANCH. For behold the stone that I have laid before Joshua; upon one stone shall be seven eyes: behold, I will engrave the graving thereof, saith the LORD of hosts, and I will remove the iniquity of that land in one day. In that day, saith the LORD of hosts, shall ye call every man his neighbour under the vine and under the fig tree" (Zech. 3).

Joshua the High Priest

Joshua, named Jeshua by Ezra, now comes to our attention. We enter a courtroom scene. Having returned with the remnant of 49,697 from Babylon to Jerusalem, he had officiated as high priest for sixteen years. As representing the nation, he is seen to be clothed in filthy garments (excrement-soiled garments). Joshua is being accused, the prosecutor being Satan. The nation of Israel is on trial. The charge is that, since God is holy, He was obligated to reject Jeshua and His people, the reason being that Joshua had allowed the people to cease building the temple, and furthermore, the nation was contaminated with sin. The charge was serious, but alas, true.

The Defense Attorney

The Lord comes to the front as "Israel's defense Attorney." The Great Advocate for His people rebukes Satan and speaks, "Take away the filthy garments from him. And unto him (Joshua) He said, Behold, I have caused thine iniquity to pass from thee, and I will clothe thee with change of raiment. And I said, Let them set a fair mitre upon his head. So they set a fair mitre upon his head, and clothed him with garments. And the angel of the LORD stood by" (Zech. 3:4,5). God is justified in His action because of His sovereign choice; He willed it so. Another reason for His justification of Joshua and the nation was that they had suffered for their sin, and were as brands plucked from the burning, thus God had cleansed them. The case is closed. Satan, the prosecuting attorney, stands speechless.

Has the role of Satan changed from Joshua's day? Absolutely not. As the age begins to close and the millennial reign of Christ is about to be unfolded, he is still seen as "the accuser of our brethren" (Rev. 12:10).

Our Advocate

We have not reached heaven yet, brethren, and "if we say that we have no sin, we deceive ourselves, and the truth is not in us" (1 Jn.1:8). We still possess a nature prone to sin. However, John continues his revelation and exposes to us a wonderful fact, namely, "My little children, these things write I unto you, that ye sin not. And if any man sin, we have an advocate with the Father, Jesus Christ the righteous" (1 Jn. 2:1).

What is an advocate? He is one who pleads another's cause before a judge, a counsel for defense, a legal assistant. That is exactly what our Lord is for us, beloved brethren. How wonderful that "the blood of Jesus Christ His Son cleanseth us from all sin," whether they be past, present or future (1 Jn.1:7). Charles L. Bancroft grasped the truth of this, as conveyed in his hymn.

"Before the throne of God above
I have a strong, a perfect plea,
A great High Priest, whose name is love,
Who ever lives and pleads for me.

When Satan tempts me to despair,
Telling of evil yet within,
Upward I look, and see Him there
Who made an end of all my sin.

Because the sinless Saviour died,
My sinful soul is counted free;
For God, the Just, is satisfied
To look on Him and pardon me."

The filthy, excrement-soiled garments can be compared to Isaiah's blunt statement, which in reality was Jehovah's divine appraisal of the nation. "But we are all as an unclean thing, and all our righteousnesses are as filthy rags; and we all do fade as a leaf; and our iniquities, like the wind, have taken us away" (Isa. 64:6). However, God removed the filthy garments, and caused their iniquity to pass from them, clothing them with "a change of raiment," or, "rich apparel." God bestowed the gift of righteousness upon them, even though unworthy. How gracious is our God!

A Pure Mitre

An eminent promise is now exposed. "And I said, Let them set a fair mitre (a clean turban) upon his head. So they set a fair mitre upon his head, and clothed him with garments. And the angel of the LORD stood by" (Zech.3:5). What a change in the high priest, what a change in the nation he represented. A pure mitre is placed upon the head of Joshua. The garments would be the holy garments of the priest worn for glory and for beauty, made of gold, blue, purple, scarlet, and pure white fine linen, the coat also made of fine linen (Ex. 28:4,5). This conveys to us the fact that

Joshua would be retained in his office as high priest. To the mitre would be attached a plate of pure gold. Moses writes, "And thou shalt make a plate of pure gold, and grave upon it, like the engravings of a signet, HOLINESS TO THE LORD. And thou shalt put it on a blue lace, that it may be upon the mitre; upon the forefront of the mitre it shall be. And it shall be upon Aaron's forehead, that Aaron may bear the iniquity of the holy things, which the children of Israel shall hallow in all their holy gifts; and it shall be always upon his forehead, that they may be accepted before the LORD" (Ex. 28:36-38).

Joshua a Picture

Joshua is now equipped and fitted for his high priestly duties, the nation also being assured of their acceptance before Jehovah and the removal of their guilt. Would not Joshua present to us a picture of the believer in this dispensation? How vile we were, our garments totally stained with sin, yet God in His sovereign grace plucked us as brands from the burning, and cleansed us through the blood of His dear Son, thus projecting us into a holy and a royal priesthood. Peter perhaps had this ancient incident in mind, for he writes of the laying aside of a garment prior to being brought into a priesthood - notice. "Wherefore laying aside all malice, and all guile, and hypocrisies, and envies, and all evil speakings" (1 Pet. 2:1). The verb, "laying aside" is in the aorist participle, indicating something done in the past at a distinct point of time, and could read, "Having laid aside." The thought is the removal of a garment to put on another. He then takes us to the priesthood in verses five and nine. "Ye also, as lively stones, are built up a spiritual house, an holy priesthood, to offer up spiritual sacrifices, acceptable to God by Jesus Christ" (vs.5). "But ye are a chosen generation, a royal priesthood, an holy nation, a peculiar people; that ye should shew forth the praises of Him who hath called you out of darkness into His marvellous light" (vs. 9). As holy priests we enter the sanctuary to worship the Father. As royal priests, we enter the street to witness to the world. It is most interesting that in 1 Peter 2, he also mentions a stone, and Zechariah does the same in the portion of his book that we are presently considering.

Angelic Announcement

The angel of the LORD now speaks as the representative of the LORD of hosts. "And the angel of the LORD protested (testified) unto Joshua, saying, Thus saith the LORD of hosts; If thou wilt walk in My ways, and if thou wilt keep My charge, then thou shalt also judge My house, and shalt also keep My courts, and I will give thee places to walk among these that stand by. Hear now, O Joshua the high priest, thou, and thy fellows that sit before thee: for they are men wondered at: for, behold, I will bring forth My servant the BRANCH" (Zech. 3:6-8).

What a profound utterance – we would do well to consider it. Joshua is given a conditional promise. The word "protested" signifies that God is called to witness. The statement made is very important and quite solemn indeed. "If thou wilt walk in My ways." Thus Joshua is exhorted to loyalty and faithfulness in his personal walk for God. The following exhortation, "keep My charge," involves his faithful function as a priest for the nation and to God. Moses was faithful in all God's house as a servant (Heb. 3:5). So the LORD expected from Joshua faithfulness in his personal and official life. The reward for his faithfulness would be that the LORD would entrust to him the high honor of judging God's house (His people) and keeping (to hedge about) His courts.

The House of God – Behavior

In our dispensation we have the house of God, the local assembly, and proper behavior is expected (1 Tim.3:15). In that house we have men raised up by the Spirit to fulfill the work of overseers. Their qualifications are listed in 1 Timothy chapter three, qualifications that far exceed the requirements of the world to a political office - even the presidency. Maintaining proper behavior in the house of God calls for men that are walking in God's ways, guarding His charge. When a local assembly of believers lacks men of this caliber, it is headed for ruin. How valuable are such men amongst us today. Men that meet the qualifications of an elder are to be honored, prayed for, and obeyed.

Boldness to Enter

Following the charge and the present work for Joshua to accomplish, the LORD goes further, saying, "I will give thee places to walk among those that stand by." Some have suggested that those standing by were angels, and now the prophecy is projected into the world to come, when in the eternal day he would be moved to a much higher service in heaven, where he would literally walk in the presence of the angels. However, we feel that this statement simply means that Joshua was promised entrance into the immediate presence of God, as were angels, while ministering as priest for the nation. We as priests today can claim the same, as the writer to the Hebrews says. "Having therefore, brethren, boldness to enter into the holiest by the blood of Jesus, By a new and living way, which He hath consecrated for us, through the veil, that is to say, His flesh; And having an High Priest over the house of God; Let us draw near with a true heart in full assurance of faith, having our hearts sprinkled from an evil conscience, and our bodies washed with pure water" (Heb. 10:19-22).

The Branch – The Stone

Joshua is now called to attention. "Hear now, O Joshua the high priest, thou, and thy fellows that sit before thee: for they are men wondered at: for, behold, I will bring forth My Servant the BRANCH. For behold the Stone that I have laid before Joshua; upon one Stone shall be seven eyes: behold, I will engrave the graving thereof, saith the LORD of hosts, and I will remove the iniquity of that land in one day. In that day, saith the LORD of hosts, shall ye call every man his neighbour under the vine and under the fig tree" (Zech. 3:8-10).

The "men wondered at," simply means that they were "men of portent," or, "men of sign." In other words, through their cleansing and deliverance from deserved punishment, they had been made acceptable as priests before their God. In reality, they were but a sign, a picture, of a future day when men would be taken from the dunghill of sin and placed among His people, having been made holy and royal priests to their God. This has become a reality following the death, burial, and resurrection of Christ, as the First Epistle of Peter reveals.

The Messiah as the BRANCH is now introduced. The word is, a "SPROUT," or "SHOOT." After the fall of Jerusalem to Nebuchadnezzar, the royal house of David sank into obscurity – thus the royal tree (the Davidic family) was cut down. From that seemingly hopeless condition there sprang out of that dead trunk a shoot, or sprout. Laid in a manger (a feeding trough), then raised in a humble dwelling in a despised city called Nazareth, came the Branch. His name was Jesus. How insignificant He was at first, but as time moved on, what a glorious Tree He became, a Tree stately and fruitful. An even greater day awaits our Lord, when He as King will have dominion from sea to sea. Isaiah portrays Him thus - "And there shall come forth a rod out of the stem of Jesse, and a Branch shall grow out of his roots" (Isa. 11:1). "For He shall grow up before Him as a tender plant, and as a root out of a dry ground: He hath no form nor comeliness; and when we shall see Him, there is no beauty that we should desire Him" (Isa. 53: 2).

It is profitable to note the fourfold reference to Messiah as the BRANCH, and their correspondence to the four gospels, where we have our Lord portrayed as a King in Matthew, a Servant in Mark, a Man in Luke, and the Son of God in John. Let us begin with the King and turn to Jeremiah.

"Behold, the days come, saith the LORD, that I will raise unto David a righteous **Branch**, and a **King** shall reign and prosper, and shall execute judgment and justice in the earth. In His days Judah shall be saved, and Israel shall dwell safely: and this is His name whereby He shall be called, THE LORD OUR RIGHTEOUSNESS" (Jer. 23:5,6). "In those days, and at that time, will I cause the Branch of righteousness to grow up unto David; and He shall execute judgment and righteousness in the land. In those days shall Judah be saved, and Jerusalem shall dwell safely: and this is the name wherewith she shall be called, The LORD our righteousness" (Jer. 33:15,16).

Satan Bound

There are certain words that seem to stand out in this profound prophecy, namely - "reign and prosper, judgment, justice, saved, and dwell safely." He shall ascend the throne and have good success. He will execute formal decrees, all of which will be morally correct. How unlike the courts of men today! John's vision relates, "And I saw an angel come down from heaven, having the key of the bottomless pit and a great chain in his hand. And he laid hold on the dragon, that old serpent, which is the Devil, and Satan, and bound him a thousand years, And cast him into the bottomless pit, and shut him up, and set a seal upon him, that he should deceive the nations no more, till the thousand years should be fulfilled: and after that he must be loosed a little season" (Rev.20:1-3). Israel will then experience true peace under Messiah's reign.

How different from today, where we see that little nation bombarded from every side by the Arab nations with their agenda of seeking to totally eliminate Israel from the face of the earth. Israel will dwell in peace and safety as their King executes righteous judgment and justice.

The Servant

The Gospel of Mark portrays our Lord as Jehovah's Servant. Notice Zechariah's prophecy. "Hear now, O Joshua the high priest, thou, and thy fellows that sit before thee: for they are men wondered at: for, behold, I will bring forth my **Servant** the **BRANCH**" (Zech.3:8). As the Servant, Paul writes of Him. "Let this mind be in you, which was also in Christ Jesus: Who, being in the form of God, thought it not robbery to be equal with God: But made Himself of no reputation, and took upon Him the form of a **servant**, and was made in the likeness of men: And being found in fashion as a man, He humbled Himself, and became obedient unto death, even the death of the cross" (Phil. 2:5-8).

The Man

The Gospel of Luke reveals Him to be the perfect **Man**. His impeccable humanity comes before our gaze. Thus we read, "And speak unto him, saying, Thus speaketh the LORD of hosts, saying, Behold the **Man** whose name is The **BRANCH**; and He shall grow up out of His place, and He shall build the temple of the LORD: Even He shall build the temple of the LORD; and He shall bear the glory, and shall sit and rule upon His throne; and He shall be a priest upon His throne: and the counsel of peace shall be between them both" (Zech. 6:12,13). Thus in a coming day, that Person of Whom Pilate said, "Behold the Man " (Jn. 19:5), shall build the Millennial temple and shall rule in priestly character, sitting upon His throne.

The Son of God

Finally, John, in his gospel of maturity, conveys to us the uniqueness of our blessed Lord as the **Son of God. "In** the beginning was the Word, and the Word was with God, and the Word was God" (Jn.1:1). Thus we immediately see at the commencement of this unique gospel, His eternal pre-existence as Jehovah, His equality and essential unity with God, and His essential deity and personal distinctness.

Isaiah's Testimony

In speaking of the BRANCH, Isaiah recognizes Him in this capacity. "In that day shall the **Branch** of the LORD (**Jehovah**) be beautiful and glorious, and the fruit of the earth shall be excellent and comely for them that are escaped of Israel" (Isa. 4:2). The day will come when Israel will confess to their shame, "For He shall grow up before Him as a tender plant, and as a root out of a dry ground: He hath no form nor comeliness; and when we shall see Him, there is no beauty that we should desire Him. He is despised and rejected of men; a Man of sorrows, and acquainted with grief: and we hid as it were our faces from Him; He was despised, and we esteemed Him not" (Isa. 53:2,3).

Israel's Salvation

In that great day of our Lord's reign, Israel will appreciate the beauty of the Lord and the splendor of His Person. The fruit of the earth shall be excellent. "The wilderness and the solitary place shall be glad for them; and the desert shall rejoice, and blossom as the rose. It shall blossom abundantly, and rejoice even with joy and singing: the glory of Lebanon shall be given unto it, the excellency of Carmel and Sharon, they shall see the glory of the LORD, and the excellency of our God. Strengthen ye the weak hands, and confirm the feeble knees. Say to them that are of a fearful heart, Be strong, fear not: behold, your God will come with vengeance, even God with a recompense; He will come and save you" (Isa. 35:1-4). Isaiah continues with his words of coming prosperity and peace (Isa 51:3). "For the LORD shall comfort Zion: He will comfort all her waste places; and He will make her wilderness like Eden, and her desert like the garden of the LORD; joy and gladness shall be found therein, thanksgiving, and the voice of melody…Break forth into joy, sing together, ye waste places of Jerusalem: for the LORD hath comforted His people, He hath redeemed Jerusalem…The LORD hath made bare His holy arm in the eyes of all the nations; and all the ends of the earth shall see the salvation of our God" (Isa. 51:3; 52:9,10).

Ezekiel

Then Ezekiel adds, "And they shall say, This land that was desolate is become like the garden of Eden; and the waste and desolate and ruined cities are become fenced, and are inhabited" (Ezek. 36:35). It will truly be a glorious day for the nation when "the plowman shall overtake the reaper, and the treader of grapes him that soweth seed; and the mountains shall drop sweet wine, and all the hills shall melt" (Amos 9:13).

The Stone

Having considered Messiah as the Branch, Zechariah now climbs to the mountain top of his prophecy and reveals that coming One as a stone. Could not this be termed a prophetic summary of the predictions of the former prophets? The words of Isaiah come immediately to mind. "Therefore thus saith the Lord GOD, Behold, I lay in Zion for a foundation a stone, a tried stone, a precious corner stone, a sure foundation: He that believeth shall not make haste" (Isa. 28:16). Calvary is in view. Complementing this we have the words of the psalmist, "The stone which the builders refused is become the head stone of the corner" (Ps. 118:22), the rejection and ultimate exaltation of our Lord being in view. Daniel views Him as the Stone. "Thou sawest till that a stone was cut out without hands, which smote the image upon his feet that were of iron and clay, and brake them to pieces. Then was the iron, the clay, the brass, the silver, and the gold, broken to pieces together, and became like the chaff of the summer threshingfloors; and the wind carried them away, that no place was found for them: and the stone that smote the image became a great mountain, and filled the whole earth" (Dan. 2: 34,35), thus projecting us on to the day when Messiah will put down all His enemies under His feet, and bring to an end "the times of the Gentiles."

Commanding the prophet's undivided attention, the Lord speaks. "For behold the stone that I have laid (set) before Joshua; upon one stone shall be seven eyes: behold, I will engrave the graving thereof, saith the LORD of hosts, and I will remove the iniquity of that land in one day. In that day, saith the LORD of hosts, shall ye call every man his neighbour under the vine and under the fig tree" (Zech. 3:9,10).

Seven Eyes – The Engraving

As we have seen, Joshua and his fellow priests prefigure the nation, fully redeemed, restored, and formed into a priestly nation. Prophetically set before Joshua is a stone, a stone that would smite the kingdoms of the earth prior to the establishment of the millennial reign. Upon this stone are seven eyes, bringing before us the fact that the Messiah, the Stone, will manifest divine intelligence and wisdom. Upon this Stone God's hand engraves "the graving thereof." Immediately my mind turns to Calvary, where, through the determinate council and foreknowledge of God, He was engraved, wounded for our transgressions. Five precious engravings, His hands, His feet, His side. What an eternal witness to the heavenly host, whether they be men or angels, of His obedience to the Father (Thy will be done), and of His undisputed and eternal love to us! Rising from the tomb, a Victor over death, hell, and the grave, our blessed Redeemer chose to retain the wounds of the Cross inflicted upon His lovely body. The wounds inflicted in Pilate's judgment hall were gone. No longer were there shreds of flesh , mingled with blood, hanging from His body. No longer were the wounds on His blessed brow, inflicted by cruel thorns. No longer was the flesh torn from His cheeks. No, beloved brethren, all the wounds inflicted before the cross were gone, but oh, the cruel wounds of Calvary itself remain.

The Spirit of Grace and of Supplication

In the day of His glorious manifestation, He "will remove the iniquity of that land in one day," that day being the day of judgment for Israel's foes, and the day of blessing for the nation. Zechariah relates to this in chapter 12:9,10. "And it shall come to pass in that day, that I will seek to destroy all the nations that come against Jerusalem. And I will pour upon the house of David, and upon the inhabitants of Jerusalem, the spirit of grace and of supplications: and they shall look upon Me Whom they have pierced, and they shall mourn for Him, as one mourneth for his only son, and shall be in bitterness for Him, as one that is in bitterness for his firstborn." Thus Zechariah's fourth vision closes.

> ***As I view the wounds of Jesus,***
> ***Inflicted on the accursed tree***
> ***I bow in humble, holy wonder,***
> ***To think He bore it all for me.***

THE FIFTH VISION

The prophet now experiences his fifth vision. He beholds a candlestick (lampstand) all of gold, above it is a bowl. Seven pipes for each of the seven lamps on the stand carry by gravity the oil from the bowl to the lamps. Beside this lampstand stand two olive trees, one on the right side and the other on the left side. What does this strange vision convey? Considering other portions of scripture, such as Exodus 25:31; Revelation 1:20, the candlestick represents Christ in union with His people, and also the local testimony of the Lord relative to a company of believers gathered unto His name.

The Lampstand

The lampstand set before the gaze of Zechariah was different from that of the Tabernacle. Over this lampstand is a bowl, constantly and abundantly supplying the lamps with oil. As most know, oil is an emblem of the Holy Spirit. Thus we see that the lampstand, which symbolizes Israel's calling to be a witness to the nations surrounding her, of God's salvation through Christ in the millennial reign, shall in the full power of the Holy Spirit of God accomplish this vocation. Thus we see her high calling in relation to the

Gentile nations. Israel will be in full fellowship with Jehovah, a position in which she failed miserably in Old Testament times.

Israel's Testimony

In this vision, no mortal priest appears to trim the wicks, supply the oil, and attend the lights morning and evening (Ex. 27:20,21). Through Messiah's manifestation to the nation, her testimony will be brilliant, spontaneous, pure, and without the need of human constraint. The Holy Spirit will be the motivation, abundantly working in the heart of the nation. Israel's coming glory, her coming power and authority over all nations, will not be realized by the art of crafty politicians, nor the experience of commanders. No, brethren, Israel will be fitted and enabled by one Person alone – the Holy Spirit of God. The oil flowed freely to the seven lamps in abundant supply.

Pentecost

In consideration of this coming glorious event, are we not reminded of the day of Pentecost, after the return of our Lord to heaven? What tremendous power in witnessing we see, when the Spirit of God descended upon the believers, and indwelt them. As a result of the Spirit's power indwelling the believers, the message went forth with such power that we read, "Then they that gladly received His word were baptized: and the same day there were added unto them about three thousand souls. And they continued stedfastly in the apostles' doctrine and fellowship, and in breaking of bread, and in prayers. And fear came upon every soul: and many wonders and signs were done by the apostles" (Acts

2: 41-43).

Diminished Power

It is sad, but true, the power among us has diminished, and as the Church nears the time of its homecall, we see weakness. What ominous signs are portrayed in the churches mentioned in Revelation chapters two and three.

Ephesus, "thou hast left thy first love."

Pergamos, "But I have a few things against thee, because thou hast there them that hold the doctrine of Balaam…So hast thou also them that hold the doctrine of the Nicolaitanes, which thing I hate." The loss of pilgrim character and an introduction of clergy and laity.

Thyatira, "Notwithstanding I have a few things against thee, because thou sufferest that woman Jezebel, which calleth herself a prophetess, to teach and to seduce My servants to commit fornication, and to eat things sacrificed unto idols." Thus we see an oversight failing to maintain godly order and the Word of the Lord set aside.

Sardis, "Thou hast a name that thou livest, and art dead." A galvanized corpse!

Laodicea, "I know thy works, that thou art neither cold nor hot…thou art wretched, and miserable, and poor, and blind, and naked." Need we say more? Yes, perhaps one more testimony, which should characterize every godly testimony gathered unto His name.

Philadelphia, "I know thy works: behold, I have set before thee an open door, and no man can shut it: for thou hast a little strength, and hast kept My word, and hast not denied My name."

The Olive Trees

Alongside the pure golden lampstand, Zechariah beholds two olive trees, termed, "sons of oil," or, "anointed ones." They are symbols of Zerubbabel the prince, and Joshua the high priest, both having been anointed into their particular office with anointing oil. These two men are mentioned at the end of the vision as "the two anointed ones, that stand by the Lord of the whole earth" (Zech. 4:14). That is, in religious and civil duties, Joshua and Zerubbabel are responsible to perform their sacred duties before the One supreme. They are called upon to direct the nation, in the power of the Spirit and under the authority of God, so that she might be an effective witness to the nations. The trees also symbolize Christ, Who in His millennial reign shall occupy both kingly and priestly functions, as He sits upon His throne as Zechariah relates, in His eighth nightly vision (6:13), as we shall notice later.

"Then he answered and spake unto me, saying, This is the word of the LORD unto Zerubbabel, saying, Not by might, nor by power, but by My spirit, saith the LORD of hosts. Who art thou, O great mountain? before Zerubbabel thou shalt become a plain: and he shall bring forth the headstone thereof with shoutings, crying, Grace, grace unto it. Moreover the word of the LORD came unto me, saying, The hands of Zerubbabel have laid the foundation of this house; his hands shall also finish it; and thou shalt know that the LORD of hosts hath sent me unto you. For who hath despised the day of small things? for they shall rejoice, and shall see the plummet in the hand of Zerubbabel with those seven; they are the eyes of the LORD, which run to and fro through the whole earth" (Zech. 4:6-10).

Thus we see that nothing can stay the work of God, if God be in it. It is not by might (human forcefulness), or by power (human capacity and ability) that the work of God is accomplished – it is only by the Holy Spirit. Paul relates to this when writing the Corinthians. "And I, brethren, when I came to you, came not with excellency of speech or of wisdom, declaring unto you the testimony of God. For I determined not to know any thing among you, save Jesus Christ, and Him crucified. And I was with you in weakness, and in fear, and in much trembling. And my speech and my preaching was not with enticing words of man's wisdom, but in demonstration of the Spirit and of power: That your faith should not stand in the wisdom of men, but in the power of God" (1 Cor. 2:1-5). Paul recognized the fact that intellectual power only amounted to the mind imparting to the mind mere words. He was aware that soulish (psychic) power would only influence the emotions. It was spiritual power that he coveted, for such power in the preaching of the gospel convinces, then convicts, and finally converts the sinner.

The Great Mountain

Zerubbabel is informed that the great mountain (a tremendously great obstacle, or difficulty) would become a plain, disappearing through the operation of the Holy Spirit. As long as they were obedient to the Lord, no outside forces of the enemy could hinder the work. The promise was, "he shall bring forth the headstone thereof with shoutings, crying, Grace, grace unto it" (Zech. 4:7). Zerubbabel would crown the work of rebuilding the temple by laying the headstone. He had laid the foundation about sixteen years prior to these visions, and now he is assured that he would see the last stone (the headstone) fitted into its place. Certainly this word from the LORD would encourage the workers in the midst of their enemies. On that occasion, the bringing forth of the head stone, there would be shoutings of joy from the builders, crying, "How perfectly graceful it is!"

Ephesians

I cannot help but think of the truths projected by the Spirit in the Epistle to the Ephesians. In that epistle, the Church is likened to a temple under construction. "Now therefore ye are no more strangers and foreigners, but fellowcitizens with the saints, and of the household of God; And are built upon the foundation of the apostles and prophets, Jesus Christ Himself being the chief corner Stone; In Whom all the building fitly framed together groweth unto an holy temple in the Lord: In Whom ye also are builded together for an habitation of God through the Spirit" (Eph. 2:19-22). But as we move on in that profound epistle, we see the Church viewed as the Bride of Christ, and we can almost hear the shoutings of joy in that coming day, so graphically displayed in the following verses. "That He might present it to Himself a glorious church, not having spot, or wrinkle, or any such thing; but that it should be holy and without blemish" (Eph. 5:27). Soon the Temple shall be completed, the Bride will be forever united with her Bridegroom, and the joy of that glorious occasion can never be fully apprehended in our sojourn here, but it will be a day when we may well shout, "What hath grace wrought!"

Another aspect of the same event can be seen in another way. As for completing our work for God here, we may claim the same. If God has given us a work to do, as long as we are obedient to His precepts, He will allow us the time and give us the strength to accomplish that particular work. As the apostle Paul neared the end of his journey, he could exclaim, with confidence, "I have fought a good fight, I have finished my course, I have kept the faith" (2 Tim. 4:7). I do trust that all of us will be able to say the same.

Ancient Men Despising

Then the question arises. "For who hath despised the day of small things? for they shall rejoice, and shall see the plummet in the hand of Zerubbabel with those seven; they are the eyes of the LORD, which run to and fro through the whole earth" (Zech. 4:10). As the work of the temple progressed, there were ancient men that seemingly despised the effort. What they were viewing was not as elaborate or as great as the former temple. They considered the day a day of small things. Of course, such critics could never contribute to the work. In reality, they could only discourage those who had put their mind to the work.

As it was then, so it is now. We have a class of brethren that are constantly living in the past, crying, "Oh, things are not what they used to be." Now, brethren, that may be true. We do not see as many coming to the Lord through our efforts as we once did. We do not see the power of God with us as in former days, and this should concern us and drive us to our knees in prayer. However, does standing off at a distance and criticizing what little is being done for God help the work? Assuredly not – it hinders it! The eyes of God were resting with divine satisfaction upon that noble work by Zerubbabel and his co-workers. Who did these people think they were by despising that work? Perhaps God has given you a task to accomplish and it is not an elaborate work at all, it is just some simple, small task. How do you look upon it, with delight, or with despising? It is not for us to draw an appraisal on the allotted work; who are we to judge? If God has called you to a particular service, small it may be, but rejoice that you have been chosen and do that work faithfully for Him. The eyes of the Lord are running to and fro upon the face of the earth, beholding every little thing we may be seeking to do for Him. His all-seeing eye misses nothing. The plummet was in Zerubbabel's hand to make sure that the walls were in perfect alignment, and that the completion of the temple would be with absolute perfection. We too, at the rapture will be presented perfect. "Beloved, now are we the sons of God, and it doth not yet appear what we shall be: but we know that, when He shall appear, we shall be like Him; for we shall see Him as He is" (1 Jn. 3:2).

The first five night-visions of the prophet, which we have considered, were relative to the future glory of Israel, and the overthrow of all their enemies. Such utterances proved to be an encouragement to the builders of the temple. Three night-visions remain, and are of a completely different character, being visions of God's judgment. We shall consider them but not as extensively as the first five visions.

THE SIXTH VISION

"Then I turned, and lifted up mine eyes, and looked, and behold a flying roll. And he said unto me, What seest thou? And I answered, I see a flying roll; the length thereof is twenty cubits, and the breadth thereof ten cubits. Then said he unto me, This is the curse that goeth forth over the face of the whole earth: for every one that stealeth shall be cut off as on this side according to it; and every one that sweareth shall be cut off as on that side according to it. I will bring it forth, saith the LORD of hosts, and it shall enter into the house of the thief, and into the house of him that sweareth falsely by My name: and it shall remain in the midst of his house, and shall consume it with the timber thereof and the stones thereof" (Zech. 5:1-4).

The Flying Roll

The prophet now beholds a most unusual flying roll, measuring twenty cubits by ten cubits, with writings on both sides. Its measurements correspond to the tabernacle, and also to the porch gracing Solomon's temple. God will weigh out their transgressions in the light of the sanctuary. The tabernacle reminds us of an holy God dwelling in the midst of His people as they journeyed through the wilderness. The same measurements of the roll seem to indicate that the holy requirements of God have not diminished now that they are in the land, and that, if His presence in their midst is to be realized, then sin must be judged.

One side of the roll contained cursings for those who violated their fellow men by stealing, the other side contained curses written regarding those accused of swearing (perjury), a violation against God Himself. Men had been guilty of breaking God's law; consequently the flying roll, displaying God's law and its curses, became the means of God's curse to be laid upon the guilty. The holiness of God demands the absolute punishment for sin. Nothing escapes His eye. "Neither is there any creature that is not manifest in His sight: but all things are naked and opened unto the eyes of Him with Whom we have to do" (Heb. 4:13). We are reminded of the words of Moses to Israel. "But if ye will not do so, behold, ye have sinned against the LORD: and be sure your sin will find you out" (Num. 32:23). Men find a sense of security in their own house, but even if they seek refuge there, the flying roll (God's judgments) shall enter there.

Not only this, but the roll shall "remain in the midst of his house, and shall consume it with the timber thereof and the stones thereof." Thus we see an absolute cleansing, nothing left unturned. The roll is flying, indicating the swiftness with which God will overcome the wicked in His judgments. There is none that can stay His almighty hand. What was true in Zechariah's day will be true in that coming day, when Israel shall recognize their Messiah at His manifestation as King of kings, and LORD of lords.

The Holiness of God

As for our day, we would do well to recognize the holiness of God, confessing, "Thou art of purer eyes than to behold evil, and canst not look on iniquity" (Hab.1:13). Certainly, "God is greatly to be feared in the assembly of the saints, and to be had in reverence of all them that are about Him" (Ps. 89:7). "Thy testimonies are very sure: holiness becometh Thine house, O LORD, for ever" (Ps. 93:5).

Thus proper behavior is expected. The key verse to the First Epistle to Timothy is found in chapter three and verse fifteen - "But if I tarry long, that thou mayest know how thou oughtest to behave thyself in the house of God, which is the church of the living God, the pillar and ground of the truth" (1 Tim. 3:15). Thus that epistle contains at least thirty exhortations relative to behavior in the house of God. In the early days of the church, how sudden were the judgments of God. Ananias and his wife Sapphira lied to the Holy Spirit, consequently, the same day, were slain by God (Acts 5:1-10). Some of the Corinthian believers were not discerning in the emblems, the body and blood of the Lord, thus God struck them with weakness, sickness, and some with death (1 Cor. 11:27-30).

In the last days of the history of the church on earth, we see less of the presence of God, thus a lower degree of His immediate and severe judgment for sin.

THE SEVENTH VISION

"Then the angel that talked with me went forth, and said unto me, Lift up now thine eyes, and see what is this that goeth forth. And I said, What is it? And he said, This is an ephah that goeth forth. He said moreover, This is their resemblance through all the earth. And, behold, there was lifted up a talent of lead: and this is a woman that sitteth in the midst of the ephah. And he said, This is wickedness. And he cast it into the midst of the ephah; and he cast the weight of lead upon the mouth thereof. Then lifted I up mine eyes, and looked, and, behold, there came out two women, and the wind was in their wings; for they had wings like the wings of a stork: and they lifted up the ephah between the earth and the heaven. Then said I to the angel that talked with me, Whither do these bear the ephah? And he said unto me, To build it an house in the land of Shinar: and it shall be established, and set there upon her own base" (Zech. 5:5-11).

The Ephah

In the former vision, Zechariah sees Jehovah judging the transgressors of His law and removing them. In this vision we see the removal of wickedness itself. Upon seeing the vision, the prophet inquires as to its meaning and the angel answers. He sees an ephah, something similar to our bushel, and considered the largest measurement in use at that time. The bushel is a symbol of commerce. God's people had been shepherds, living simple lives. However, due to their captivity living in Babylon, they had become accustomed to the Babylonian way of life and had developed into self-centered, greedy, materialistically-minded people. That characteristic continues even to this day. Their unlawful business dealings, buying and selling in the land, had spread even to the point of affecting judicial judgments in their courts of law. A Roman historian writes concerning the city of Babylon, "Nothing could be more corrupt than its morals, nothing more fitted to excite and allure to immoderate pleasures. The rites of hospitality were polluted by the grossest and most shameless lusts. Money dissolved every tie, whether of kindred, respect or esteem. Drunkenness and the grossest immoralities were practiced in public."

Others believe that the ephah has no reference to "great commercial enterprise" but rather indicating that the ephah is a symbol of measurement, "telling us that God shall weigh and measure Judah's sin…with unerring accuracy; also that the woman is a symbol of a religious character – idolatry. Some link this woman with Jezebel, who corrupted the assembly at Thyatira. Since Babylon is the mother of all idolatry, some interpreters go on to say that this woman will be "transported rapidly to the mother source of idols – the land of Shinar – that it might be set there in its congenial haunt: why should it pollute the land of Jehovah?" (William Kelly). This we agree with, but also can see the ephah as a symbol of materialism and unscrupulous commerce.

Israel, submerged in such an atmosphere for seventy years, had taken on its characteristics. Many had acquired an inordinate lust for gain at the cost of all moral principles. The words of Amos, spoken three hundred years prior to this, come to life. "Hear this, O ye that swallow up the needy, even to make the poor of the land to fail, Saying, When will the new moon be gone, that we may sell corn? and the sabbath, that we may set forth wheat, making the ephah small, and the shekel great, and falsifying the balances by deceit? That we may buy the poor for silver, and the needy for a pair of shoes; yea, and sell the refuse of the wheat?" (Amos 8:4-6). As far as the returned exiles were concerned, Jehovah demanded that the land be cleansed.

Idolatry and Materialism

Looking at the whole situation, are we not reminded of our own day? Moral principles have been trashed for the sake of material gain. The dollar has become the god of many corporations. Deception prevails, corporation accounts are altered to avoid taxes, advertising is deceptive, and the public is deceived as manufacturers and merchants move dishonestly to make a dollar. Not only this, do we not see in our day the rise of idolatry in the religious systems that surround us? Rome, with its worship of images and relics; Islam, with its worship of the moon god, Allah; Humanism, with its worship of self; Christendom, with its worship of crafty men. The list could go on and on. Even the majority of Jews in Israel today are atheistic. As the end time draws near, idolatry and materialism increase.

The Woman Inside the Ephah

The prophet beholds the ephah's round lid of lead being lifted, revealing a woman sitting inside. She is wickedness personified. At first the woman seems quite content with her surroundings, it is her dwelling place. She is enjoying her luxury and holdings. She is settled in her environment, satisfied and content with the commercial wickedness that supports her. However, when the lid is raised, she immediately realizes that the time has come for God's judgment on such activities and she seeks to escape, in order to continue in her wicked activities. Wickedness is not willing to accept restriction, but seeks to roam at its own selfwill. However, the angel casts her into the midst of the ephah and flings the heavy lid upon the mouth of the ephah, confining the woman. This indicates that wickedness is to be secured so firmly as to prevent her escape.

Two Women

The main point of the vision is not the punishment, or the restraint of wickedness, but rather its complete removal from the land. Thus two women appear on the scene, with stork-like wings and wind in their wings. The explanation is simple, the interpretations are many. Some believe that the two women represent instruments of God's justice. Others look upon them as wicked instruments taking the woman away to free her from the coming judgment of God. Some go so far as to suggest that these two women represent civil government that has broken the cords of restraint, denying God, thus resulting in a corrupt and anti-God society composed of both Jew and Gentile. This interpretation seems fanciful, to say the least.

Wings

There are four things to consider concerning the two women. First, their wings; second, the wind in their wings; third, the altitude of their flight; fourth, the destination of their flight. Consider now their wings. They were like the wings of a stork. Some have sought to link this with Leviticus 11:19, showing that the stork is an unclean bird. However, this does not seem to be the thought. The stork was a migrating bird, plentiful in that area, and noted for its strong wings. The wings like a stork indicated the ability of these two women to lift the heavy, lead-lidded ephah containing the woman. The mission would be a total success.

Wind

The second observation is that the wind was in their wings. The wind would propel the powerful wings to greater speed. Commercial jet pilots take advantage of what is called, "the jet stream." This stream of air travels at high speed, flowing from the north to the east. Flying toward the east, a pilot, by entering the jet stream, can accelerate his ground speed one to two hundred miles per hour. The women had wind in their wings; the carrying away of wickedness would be exceedingly swift.

Altitude

The third consideration is the altitude of their flight. It was between the earth and the heaven. When storks fly from one nearby place to another, their flight is at low altitude. However, when they migrate to distant destinations, they fly at a much higher altitude. Commercial airlines follow the same principle. Flying from Cleveland, Ohio to Detroit, Michigan, a distance of one hundred and fifty miles, you will discover that the plane flies at a much lower altitude than a jet taking off from Cleveland, to Seattle, Washington, a distance of over two thousand miles.

Destination

The winged women were taking wickedness on a long journey from Israel, all the way back to the land of Shinar. This land is mentioned seven times in the Bible, the first is Genesis 10:10, the last here, in Zechariah 5:11. Shinar has always been associated with rebellion against God. Here paganism had its foundation and man's first attempt to establish a world empire in opposition to God. The wickedness that permeated the Jewish race had its origin in Babylon, and was now being divinely forced to leave the land of promise, and return to Shinar, whence it originated, there to be settled, then eventually crushed by the Almighty. We find the woman comfortably dwelling in Shinar, in her own house. Thus the wickedness carried away from the region of the children of God will have its permanent rest in the bounds of the domineering power that is opposed to Almighty God. The whole operation was for this ultimate purpose. The revised version of 1899 reads, "Then said I to the angel that talked with me, Whither do these bear the ephah? And he said unto me, To build her an house in the land of Shinar: and when it is prepared she shall be set therein her own place" (Zech. 5 10,11).

Earth's Coming Judgment

In the light of this, John, the apocalyptic writer, foretells of a coming day when Messiah shall establish His kingdom on earth, after snatching away His bride, the Church. At that great event divine judgments will fall upon earth's Christless society. Earth will experience the wrath of the Lamb. John projects us to that scene, writing, "And I beheld when He had opened the sixth seal, and, lo, there was a great earthquake; and the sun became black as sackcloth of hair, and the moon became as blood; And the stars of heaven fell unto the earth, even as a fig tree casteth her untimely figs, when she is shaken of a mighty wind. And the heaven departed as a scroll when it is rolled together; and every mountain and island were moved out of their places. And the kings of the earth, and the great men, and the rich men, and the chief captains, and the mighty men, and every bondman, and every free man, hid themselves in the dens and in the rocks of the mountains; And said to the mountains and rocks, Fall on us, and hide us from the face of Him that sitteth on the throne, and from the wrath of the Lamb: For the great day of His wrath is come; and who shall be able to stand?" (Rev. 6:12-17).

Babylon the Mother of Harlots

Corrupt, idolatrous Christendom will feel the weight of God's judgments in that awesome day. "And there came one of the seven angels which had the seven vials, and talked with me, saying unto me, Come hither; I will shew unto thee the judgment of the great whore that sitteth upon many waters...And upon her forehead was a name written, MYSTERY, BABYLON THE GREAT, THE MOTHER OF HARLOTS AND ABOMINATIONS OF THE EARTH. ... And the ten horns which thou sawest upon the beast, these shall hate the whore, and shall make her desolate and naked, and shall eat her flesh, and burn her with fire. For God hath put in their hearts to fulfil His will" (Rev.17:1-5).

The World's Commerce

The evil world's commerce will also experience the severe judgments of God. Due to God's judgments on Babylon, we read, "And the merchants of the earth shall weep and mourn over her; for no man buyeth their merchandise any more: The merchandise of gold, and silver, and precious stones, and of pearls, and fine linen, and purple, and silk, and scarlet, and all thyine wood, and all manner vessels of ivory, and all manner vessels of most precious wood, and of brass, and iron, and marble, And cinnamon, and odours, and ointments, and frankincense, and wine, and oil, and fine flour, and wheat, and beasts, and sheep, and horses, and chariots, and slaves, and souls of men. And the fruits that thy soul lusted after are departed from thee, and all things which were dainty and goodly are departed from thee, and thou shalt find them no more at all. The merchants of these things, which were made rich by her, shall stand afar off for the fear of her torment, weeping and wailing, And saying, Alas, alas, that great city, that was clothed in fine linen, and purple, and scarlet, and decked with gold, and precious stones, and pearls! For in one hour so great riches is come to nought. And every shipmaster, and all the company in ships, and sailors, and as many as trade by sea, stood afar off, And cried when they saw the smoke of her burning, saying, What city is like unto this great city! And they cast dust on their heads, and cried, weeping and wailing, saying, Alas, alas, that great city, wherein were made rich all that had ships in the sea by reason of her costliness! for in one hour is she made desolate" (Rev. 18:11-19).

Thus the vision of the removal of the Ephah was not only relevant to Zechariah's day, but points us on to a far greater day to come, when God's unwavering righteousness and holiness, accompanied by divine judgments, shall be meted out to a wicked world.

THE EIGHTH VISION

In the last of the eight night visions we see the two mountains, and four chariots, linked with red, black, white, and grisled and bay horses. "And I turned, and lifted up mine eyes, and looked, and, behold, there came four chariots out from between two mountains; and the mountains were mountains of brass. In the first chariot were red horses; and in the second chariot black horses; And in the third chariot white horses; and in the fourth chariot grisled and bay horses. Then I answered and said unto the angel that talked with me, What are these, my lord? And the angel answered and said unto me, These are the four spirits of the heavens, which go forth from standing before the Lord of all the earth. The black horses which are therein go forth into the north country; and the white go forth after them; and the grisled go forth toward the south country. And the bay went forth, and sought to go that they might walk to and fro through the earth: and he said, Get you hence, walk to and fro through the earth. So they walked to and fro through the earth. Then cried he upon me, and spake unto me, saying, Behold, these that go toward the north country have quieted my spirit in the north country" (Zech. 6:1-8).

The scene is most interesting and the interpretations by expositors are quite varied. Some consider the mountains totally symbolic, while others feel that they refer to actual mountains, namely, Zion and Olivet. It is between these two mountains that the Valley of Jehoshaphat lies, (known today as the Valley of Kidron) where the final conflict of God with the nations shall take place, prior to the millennial reign of Christ. The word "Jehoshaphat" means, "Jehovah shall judge." The reason for considering these mountains to be literal mountains is because in the Hebrew language the definite article "the" is present before the word "mountains," indicating that these two mountains were well known.

They are termed as mountains of brass (bronze). The scripture speaks of the brazen altar, associated with the tabernacle in the wilderness. It also speaks of the serpent of brass, lifted up in the wilderness. John, in the Revelation of Jesus Christ, beholds the exalted Lord, in the midst of the seven churches of Asia, "His feet like unto fine brass, as if they burned in a furnace. He is judging the churches. Brass thus identifies itself with righteous judgment of God manifesting itself to deal with sin. This judgment will emanate from the holy city, Jerusalem, in the region of these two mountains. None will be able to stand before the inflexible power and judgment of Almighty!

Four Chariots

Please notice the agents employed for this tremendous event. Zechariah beholds four chariots with horses harnessed to them. What can this mean? A sensible consideration reveals that the agents are certainly not mortal human beings, but rather angels. The question is asked by the prophet to the angel, "What are these, my lord?" The reply comes, "These (chariots) are the four spirits (winds) of the heavens, which go forth from standing before the Lord of all the earth" (Zech. 6:5). Angels in heaven are usually described as standing before the Lord. Gabriel stood before the Lord (Lk.1:19). Micaiah saw angels standing beside the Lord, as He sat upon a throne (1 Ki. 22:19). Daniel viewed many thousands of these heavenly beings standing before their Lord (Dan. 7:10). Thus we conclude the chariots to symbolize holy angels invested with divine power. The horses convey to us the judgments meted out upon earth. Thus we see in the vision, holy angels pouring out the judgments of God upon those who dwell on earth.

Colors

Some see no significance in the varied color of the horses. But let us ask ourselves, why does the Spirit emphasize the varied colors? There must be a reason. The answer is provided in Revelation chapter six. Zechariah sees red horses, black horses, white horses, and finally grisled and bay horses (grisled strong horses). John views a white horse first, indicating Antichrist riding in victory; second, a red horse, speaking of bloodshed; followed by a black horse, indicating famine; and finally a pale horse – with a rider called, "Death."

There is an earnestness, clothed with rapidity, conveyed in the chariots hitched with horses in Zechariah's vision. The judgment will be swift and the victory will be sure. Then Messiah will take the priestly throne to rule with a rod of iron. The direction of the horse-drawn chariots is exceedingly interesting. The first horse (red) is not the first one to move. "The black horses which are therein go forth into the north country; and the white go forth after them; and the grisled go forth toward the south country" (Zech. 6:6).

It was from the north where most of Israel's enemies came to invade Israel -the Assyrians, Babylonians, Persians, and Romans. In that direction race the black horse-drawn chariots (famine and death), and the white horse-drawn chariots (dominion and victory). The age-old enemy of Israel dwelling toward the south is Egypt, which would include the Arab world. Toward that kingdom race the grisled horse-drawn chariots. The revised version says, "dappled and strong," perhaps an indication of inflicting pestilence and plague. How varied are God's ways in dealing with His enemies, through invisible forces – the angels. It was to the north that man first rebelled against God and erected his first empire in opposition to God. It was from the north that the Gentile yoke was still felt by Israel. Seemingly her sins were the greater, thus judgment begins there. There are no angelic movements to the west or the east, for the Mediterranean Sea lay to the west, and the vast Arabian Desert to the east. However, it seems that, when the northern and southern kingdoms have come under the judgments of God, the red horse-drawn chariot (war and bloodshed) commence to move worldwide. In the first of the eight night visions we see divine agencies moving throughout the earth on a scouting mission, surveying Israel's enemies (Zech 1:7-10). The last vision shows us angels, in accordance with the information gleaned in the first mission, now moving to execute judgement. The ledger was full, and now the lashing out of God's wrath was inevitable. "Then cried he upon me, and spake unto me, saying, Behold, these that go toward the north country have quieted My spirit in the north country" (Zech. 6:8). Such news revealed that the judgments executed in the north country had satisfied the justice of God, thus the anger of God was pacified. What a word of encouragement for God's people. They had been gravely abused by the northern nations, but God had His people in remembrance and He would vindicate them in His own time and in His own way.

The Crown of Gold and Silver

As these visions drew to a close, certain brethren came from Babylon bringing with them an offering of gold and silver for the temple that was still in construction. Josiah, being a hospitable man, took the visitors into his own home. It certainly was an act of kindness to lodge these strangers, named Heldai, Tobijah, and Jedaiah. The gold and silver were to be woven into a crown (Zech. 6:11, R.V.) and placed upon the head of Joshua the high priest. In the K.J.V. the word crown is in the plural, but what is meant is that it was a single "splendid royal crown," made from a number of gold and silver strands woven into one. While being crowned, he was to hear these words from Zechariah. "Thus speaketh the LORD of hosts, saying, Behold the man whose name is The BRANCH; and He shall grow up out of His place, and He shall build the temple of the LORD: Even He shall build the temple of the LORD; and He shall bear the glory, and shall sit and rule upon His throne; and He shall be a priest upon His throne: and the counsel of peace shall be between them both" (Zech. 6:12,13).

A Typical Act

The crown was not be continually worn by Joshua, for the placing of the crown upon his head was but a brief typical act. The words uttered at this crowning were Messianic. Notice the first utterance, "Behold the Man." The words were spoken to Joshua, but they cannot possibly be made to apply to him. The Man is Christ. The first occurrence of those words is when God spoke of Adam (Gen. 3:22). The last mention of that phrase is found in John 19:5, as Pilate brings the mocked and abused Lord forth before the gaze of Israel's chief priests, his words ring out, "Behold the Man!" What a contrast! In Genesis, the first Adam had sinned and was about to be excommunicated from the garden, having ruined mankind. In the Gospel of John, the last Adam, Who never could sin, had left the garden to be crucified and slain, in order to redeem us.

Zechariah's Messianic prophecy points to that glorious day, when the Messiah shall come in glory and power to establish His kingdom, occupying His throne as a Priest. Presently He is building a spiritual temple composed of living stones (Matt.16:18; Eph. 2:21;1 Pet. 2:5), but at His glorious manifestation another literal temple will be built. As the King of Kings, and LORD of Lords, He will rightfully possess His inheritance. The Nation of Israel will recognize Him, and, like the Jewish brethren coming from Babylon with their gifts of gold and silver for Jehovah's house, God's earthly people will return to the beloved city Jerusalem with their offerings and sacrifices for Him.

"And the counsel of peace shall be between them both" (6:13), meaning that the two offices of Priest and King will be combined in the Messiah, and functioning in these two offices, He will secure salvation, resulting in peace for His own people Israel during His reign. What a tremendous day of glory that will be!

A Memorial Crown

Following this tremendous Messianic utterance, the prophet goes on to say, "And the crowns shall be to Helem, and to Tobijah, and to Jedaiah, and to Hen the son of Zephaniah, for a memorial in the temple of the LORD (Zech. 6:14).

You will notice that verse ten names three visitors, yet in verse fourteen a fourth name is added to the list, namely the word *Hen*. The word *Hen* is not a proper name but means *grace*. The Revised Version margin reads, "And the crowns shall be to Helem, and to Tobijah, and to Jedaiah, and for the kindness of the son of Zephaniah, for a memorial in the temple of the LORD." That person was Josiah, the man who had graciously opened his home for the visiting brethren from Babylon. He had showed them kindness, and God looked upon his hospitality with pleasure, thus the crown was to be laid up and displayed in the temple as a memorial of these worthy men. Let us bring this noble incident into New Testament teaching. Many of the Hebrew saints experienced persecution, even to the spoiling of their goods. Some lost their employment and thus wandered from place to place seeking employment. How were they to be treated when they came upon fellow-believers? The answer is found in Hebrews 13:1,2. "Let brotherly love continue. Be not forgetful to entertain strangers." The word *entertain* is *hospitality.* For those who showed such kindness, God gave them this assurance – "For God is not unrighteous to forget your work and labour of love, which ye have shewed toward His name, in that ye have ministered to the saints, and do minister" (Heb. 6:10).

Let me ask you, what is your attitude to "strangers," who are brethren visiting? I remember being with an older servant who taught me many lessons in the Lord's work as an evangelist. On one occasion we visited an assembly for the Lord's Day. Arriving on Saturday, not one opened their home to take us in. We rented a motel room and on Lord's Day morning had our breakfast there. After the breaking of bread, we sought to help the saints in their Bible reading. After the reading, the saints shook our hand and inquired if we were going to be with them for the gospel meeting that evening, to which we replied, "Yes." "Fine," they said, and leaving the building, they all drove away, leaving my older companion and me standing on the sidewalk. The snow was coming down quite heavy, and about four inches lay on the ground. I said to my older brother, "What do we do now?" He grinned and said, "We sit in the car until the gospel meeting." The gospel meeting was at 7:30 P.M. and it was only a few minutes past 1 P.M. I remember saying, "No way!" I drove to a phone booth and called a brother connected with another assembly about one hour's drive away and asked if we could come for a little visit to get warm. "You get right over here," he exclaimed, so away we went. Upon arriving at this brother's house we found a quick meal all ready for us. What a relief! What a wonderful time we had that afternoon.

Traveling back to the other assembly building for the gospel meeting, we fulfilled our promise to be there, and preached the gospel. After the meeting, one suggested that it would be nice for us to come for a series of meetings. I pictured myself paying out a motel bill and eating alone in a restaurant daily during my stay there. Needless to say, I never returned. My older companion said, "I brought you here to teach you something," and I certainly did learn something that day! I learned the preciousness of hospitality. May the Lord preserve us from being so self-centered that we cannot open our homes to saints visiting our locality.

I remember preaching in another place and the young woman who attended for two nights professed. Immediately she saw the sin of living with a man, not being married to him. The night she professed, what was she to do, where would she sleep? There was no hesitation on the part of a brother and his wife. They immediately took her in and gave her a bedroom until she could get settled on her own. What is this, brethren? It is love! It is true Christianity in action! It is a sacrifice that God is not unrighteous to forget. The memorial in the temple was a display to all who entered of the kindness and grace of Josiah, the son of Zephaniah. Remember, God is not unrighteous to forget your hospitality, either.

"And they that are far off shall come and build in the temple of the LORD, and ye shall know that the LORD of hosts hath sent me unto you. And this shall come to pass, if ye will diligently obey the voice of the LORD your God" (Zech. 6:15).

The Crown - A Pledge

The prophet closes the first section of his prophecies with words of hope and promise. The depositing of the crown in the temple also would serve as a pledge of great things yet to come. Jews scattered worldwide shall return to their land and share in the great work of building the millennial temple in Jerusalem. Those who diligently obey His voice will have the high honor of contributing to this work.

His Manifestation in Glory

Israel is presently surrounded by 22 Arab monarchies and dictatorships, filled with rage and violence against them. Their agenda is to wipe Israel off the face of this world. However, what the enemies of God do not realize is that the God of His people Israel is still on the throne. He is waiting, and when His appointed time comes, the heaven will be opened and with great military power the LORD shall come and in righteousness He will judge and make war. John writes, " His eyes were as a flame of fire, and on His head were many crowns; and He had a name written, that no man knew, but He Himself. And He was clothed with a vesture dipped in blood: and His name is called The Word of God. And the armies which were in heaven followed Him upon white horses, clothed in fine linen, white and clean. And out of His mouth goeth a sharp sword, that with it He should smite the nations: and He shall rule them with a rod of iron: and He treadeth the winepress of the fierceness and wrath of Almighty God. And He hath on His vesture and on His thigh a name written, KING OF KINGS, AND LORD OF LORDS" (Rev.19:11-16). The heaven will depart as a scroll when it is rolled together; and every mountain and island will be moved out of their places. And the kings of the earth, and the great men, and the rich men, and the chief captains, and the mighty men, and every bondman, and every free man, will hide themselves in the dens and in the rocks of the mountains; and will cry to the mountains and rocks, "Fall on us, and hide us from the face of Him that sitteth on the throne, and from the wrath of the Lamb: For the great day of His wrath is come; and who shall be able to stand?" (Rev. 6:14-17). What a day of reckoning for a wicked world, what a day of glory for Israel, His purchased people.

CHAPTER SIX

The Temple Completed

WITH ALL THE PROPHECIES we have considered, the effect of them was positive upon the people of God. "Then rose up Zerubbabel the son of Shealtiel, and Jeshua the son of Jozadak, and began to build the house of God which is at Jerusalem: and with them were the prophets of God helping them" (Ezra 5:2). You can be sure that, any time God's people rise up to work for God, Satan rises up to thwart that work. "At the same time came to them Tatnai, governor on this side the river, and Shethar-boznai, and their companions, and said thus unto them, Who hath commanded you to build this house, and to make up this wall? Then said we ("they," the enemies, cp. vs.10) unto them after this manner, What are the names of the men that make this building?" The purpose was to bring them to the Persian court. (Ezra 5:3,4). Tatnai was the Persian governor of the province, his jurisdiction covering Syria, Palestine, and Judah. Shethar-boznai was seemingly a government servant to the governor. Gathering other Persian officials, they approached the laboring Jews and presented their challenge. The unsettled state in the Persian Empire at that time may have helped to arouse their suspicions, but whatever the cause was, one can readily see the workings of Satan behind their challenge. When the remnant were employed fervently building their own houses for their own comfort, there was never any disturbance from the enemy. However, as soon as the trowel, the hammer, and other tools were taken up and used for the construction of God's house, the inquiries begin. Is there a lesson in this? –Yes! Consider a brother totally engrossed with his home, his yard, and his belongings. Is Satan bothering him? Absolutely not! However, what takes place if that person sets his priorities right? The results are very evident. When he begins to show attention to the house of God, and seeks to live for God, Satan becomes aroused, he becomes very concerned, and consequently the restored brother finds opposition and difficulties in the way. This corresponds to what Paul wrote Timothy, "Yea, and all that will live godly in Christ Jesus shall suffer persecution" (2 Tim. 3:12). It was true in Zerubbabel's day, it was true in Timothy's day, and it is still true in our day! The devil's activities remain unchanged.

Enemies

In all fairness, we must admit that the enemies in Ezra chapter five were not as adamant and abusive as the enemies of chapter four. Those men were termed "adversaries," and rightly so, for they "weakened the hands of the people of Judah, and troubled (terrified) them in building: (4:4). Consequently the work ceased. Tatnai, the governor, and Shethar-bozani, his secretary, with their companions, were of a less brutal nature. Their attack was much weaker. They were only fulfilling their duty to the empire they served, in making their inquiry as to the vigorous movements of the Jews. Unreasonableness and maliciousness do not seem to be evident. Their inquiry is twofold: First – the authority of the builders, "Who hath commanded you to build this house, and to make up this wall?" Second – the names of the builders, "What are the names of the men that make this building?" Comparing Ezra 5:4, with 5:10, those asking the names were not the builders, but the enemies. The fourth verse should read, "Then said they," not, "Then said we." As stated, verse 10 upholds this interpretation.

The Eye of God

Suddenly the chronicler interjects, "But the eye of their God was upon the elders of the Jews, that they could not cause them to cease, till the matter came to Darius: and then they returned answer by letter concerning this matter" (Ezra 5:5). You will notice it was not *the hand of God*, nor the *outstretched arm of God,* but simply *the eye of God.* There would be no miracles taking place, nor a wondrous manifestation of His almighty power. Knowing that the eye of their God rested on them would certainly give them the assurance of His presence with them, and His intense interest in their activities for Him. My dear brother, my dear sister, the eye of God is upon you wherever you are and in whatever you may be engaged. Certainly the knowledge of this should tend to govern our movements and activities. "For the eyes of the LORD run to and fro throughout the whole earth, to shew Himself strong in the behalf of them whose heart is perfect toward Him" (2 Chr. 16:9). "For the ways of man are before the eyes of the LORD, and He pondereth all his goings" (Prov. 5:21). "The eyes of the

LORD are in every place, beholding the evil and the good" (Prov. 15:3). "For the eyes of the Lord are over the righteous, and His ears are open unto their prayers" (1 Pet. 3:12).

The very fact that the eye of their God was upon the elders of the Jews betrays the seriousness of the situation. As far as the builders were concerned, the will of God was being carried out, His authority was being acknowledged, and on a daily basis, they were seeking His grace. They had put their trust in God, honoring Him by their loyal obedience to His word, spoken to them through the prophets, Haggai and Zechariah. Tatnai, the governor, and his associates were totally ignorant of Israel's God, of His purposes and plans, thus their officious inquiry. Having absolute authority over the region where Israel abode, the Gentile governor sought to cause the Jews to cease their construction of God's house. At this particular point, Israel, seemingly, was close to their God, thus not even the high Persian official's inquiry and warnings could stop them from their work. Tatnai sought to have them cease until the matter could come before Darius and a reply be given. There was no modern mail system as we experience today; a reply would involve a long period of time. To cease the work for months, waiting for confirmation, would definitely have a cooling effect. The governor's request went unheeded. We are reminded of the words of Peter to the authorities when he was told not to preach the name of Jesus in Jerusalem. "We ought to obey God rather than men" (Acts 5:29).

However, Tatnai was a wise man. Considering the zeal of the Jewish workers and their determination to continue in their labors, he perceived that it would be prudent for him not to act until he had received direct orders from the king. Zerubbabel had informed him that Cyrus, the former king of Babylon, had issued a decree to build the house of God, sixteen years ago, in B.C. 536 (Ezra 5:13).

Word Sent

Immediately the governor sent word to King Darius with this request. "Now therefore, if it seem good to the king, let there be search made in the king's treasure house, which is there at Babylon, whether it be so, that a decree was made of Cyrus the king to build this house of God at Jerusalem, and let the king send his pleasure to us concerning this matter" (Ezra 5:17). Prior to this request, the governor made known to the king what he had observed and the remarks to him from the Jewish elders. He observed the great stones being employed in the structure of the house of God, and the timber. There would be tremendous effort in placing great stones. They are termed, *stones of rolling,* meaning they were so large that they had to be transported by rolling them on the ground. The Persian governor also noticed the earnestness and zeal of the workers, exclaiming, "this work goeth fast on, and prospereth in their hands" (5:8). The opposers were greatly impressed.

Let me ask, as you seek to labor and live for God, are the ungodly who observe you impressed? Are those impressions spiritual and deep? Are you halfhearted or zealous in the work of your Lord? What is the quality of the material you are putting into the house of God? The large stones indicate durability. Is your work of that nature? Are you strengthening the assembly in which you have been divinely placed? Will your labors stand the test at the judgment seat of Christ? What kind of impression are you leaving on this godless world? The workers in B.C. 520, Zerubbabel's day, made great impressions!

The Answer Given

The next thing to observe is the answer of the elders to Tatnai, when he asked their names. They returned him answer, saying, "We are the servants of the God of heaven and earth" (Ezra 5:11). I believe that this is the only place in the entire Scripture where you will find God described in these exact words. It indicates His universal and absolute dominion. What a bold confession of their true status. They were not merely servants, but servants of the God of heaven and earth. Do we possess the holy boldness to convey to a sinful world to Whom we belong and where we stand? Are we ashamed to confess His name, not only in words, but also in our ways? If we openly confess Christ, is our walk consistent with our talk? The builders openly confessed their spiritual status. Thus we have their confession of what they were. Next they relate what they were doing, "we build the house that was builded these many years ago, which a great king of Israel builded and set up" (vs.11).

What They Had Been

Then they relate what they had been. "But after that our fathers had provoked the God of heaven unto wrath, He gave them into the hand of Nebuchadnezzar the king of Babylon, the Chaldean, who destroyed this house, and carried the people away into Babylon" (Ezra 5:12). What an open confession! The pride is gone, their humbleness is manifest. They openly acknowledged the fact that sin had ruined them as a nation and a righteous God had punished them. Is not their attitude a lesson for us today? I remember an old quaint Irish Gospel preacher advising me thus, "When you preach the gospel and tell sinners how vile they are in God's sight, never forget to include yourself, lest you convey the thought to their hearts that you consider yourself better than they." How right he was! I look at the scum of society and silently say to myself, "There but by the grace of God, go I." Let us never forget what we were, and let us ever rejoice in what we now are – all through His wondrous grace!

The Orphan Boy

Let me further illustrate. Many years ago in an orphanage, a severe problem arose. A lad nearing sixteen was giving the facility of the orphanage quite a problem due to his misbehavior. He was brought into the office, a defiant youngster. The head of the orphanage looked compassionately upon him, and not saying a word took from his desk drawer a large photo of a bedraggled little boy in a terrible condition. He was scantily clothed in rags, bruised and dirty. The administrator set the photo on the desk for the youth to see. Not a word was said – the boy began to weep. From that moment he was a changed youngster, and the trouble he was causing ceased. Who was the little fellow in the photo? It was himself, an abandoned, abused little child, when the orphanage took him in to care tenderly for him. He was reminded of what he was, and what he now was, and the reminder filled him with gratitude to those who had befriended him. Brethren, let us ever remember what we were, and what we now are, by the grace of God – it will produce a greater degree of gratitude and love in our hearts for the Lord Who died to save us. Let me also say, when love burns fervently in our hearts to Christ, absolute obedience to His word is always the fruit.

What They Had Been Told

Next Zerubbabel and Jeshua related to the enemies what they had been told. "But in the first year of Cyrus the king of Babylon the same king Cyrus made a decree to build this house of God" (Ezra 5:13). That was in B.C.536, and the year was now B.C. 520. Sixteen years had rolled their course and nothing had been done. The adversaries had done their work well, but, through the prophesying of Haggai and Zechariah, there was a rising up from self-centeredness and complacency to get busy for God.

Secular history tells us that Darius had the utmost regard and respect for Cyrus and the founder of the Persian Empire, and was always prepared to act upon what Cyrus had decreed. One of the great rules of the Persian empire was that the laws of the Medes and Persians never changed. This is emphasized three times in the book of Daniel (Dan.6:8,12,15). The setting could not have been more appropriate for the Jews than at this time. In this we observe that the ways of God are not always similar when we seek to do something for God. There are occasions where bitter opposition is encountered, while at other times things seem to go very favorably. This may seem very strange to us, but when we reach our heavenly abode, all will be made clear. Let us not question the mysterious ways of God, but seek in a humble way to just go on for Him, whether the sun shines or the sky is dark with ominous clouds.

What They Had Done

The last point they made in their reply was what they had done. "And the vessels also of gold and silver of the house of God, which Nebuchadnezzar took out of the temple that was in Jerusalem, and brought them into the temple of Babylon, those did Cyrus the king take out of the temple of Babylon, and they were delivered unto one, whose name was Sheshbazzar, whom he had made governor; And said unto him, Take these vessels, go, carry them into the temple that is in Jerusalem, and let the house of God be builded in his place" (Ezra 5:14-15).

The Vessels

As pointed out previously, Sheshbazzar was another name for Zerubbabel. Having considered the vessels in chapter two, we won't elaborate except to say that Zerubbabel was faithful in his handling of divine things. Ezra chapter ones gives the number of the vessels, being "five thousand and four hundred." Consider the fact that these vessels were vital in restoring scriptural worship in the temple. There were no modern implements employed in the restored functioning and worship of the LORD. The vessels were the same as formerly used.

From this we learn that "improved" tactics, and modernized methods are not the solutions for godly and effective worship today. Let us beware of so-called "changes for the better." A scriptural assembly has sacred "vessels," the same vessels committed to, and employed in the assemblies mentioned in the Holy Scriptures. Times change, but God's way of functioning, whether it be witnessing or worshipping, have not changed. "Thus saith the LORD, Stand ye in the ways, and see, and ask for the old paths, where is the good way, and walk therein, and ye shall find rest for your souls." Those in Jeremiah's day said, "We will not walk therein" (Jer. 6:16). However, in Zerubbabel's day, the people of God had learned their lesson – they were willing to obey and walk in God's ways. Zerubbabel dealt faithfully with the things of God.

A Reply of Prudence and Piety

Considering the prudence of their reply, there was also piety connected with it. They made it plain that their project was not a matter of human adventure, but rather one of divine charge and approval. They made it known that the temple that they were building was not an invention of their own thinking, but that, in reality, they were restoring the temple that Solomon had erected on that very spot nearly five hundred years ago. They realized that the destruction of the former temple was the result of their sad departure from God's ways, and that God's judgment upon them was just. They freely acknowledged that they forsook God, consequently God forsook them. Also made known was the fact that they were certainly not opposing royal authority, but were acting in accordance with the former king's decree, and that the king had actually helped them financially to commence the work. Perhaps the enemies feared that this great and sturdy edifice would be a military fort. However, Zerubbabel made it very clear that the purpose of their labor was to restore worship to their nation. One is reminded of Solomon's words on this occasion. "A soft answer turneth away wrath: but grievous words stir up anger" (Prov. 15:1).

As chapter five draws to a close, we read, "Then came

the same Sheshbazzar, and laid the foundation of the house of God which is in Jerusalem: and since that time even until now hath it been in building, and yet it is not finished. Now therefore, if it seem good to the king, let there be search made in the king's treasure house, which is there at Babylon, whether it be so, that a decree was made of Cyrus the king to build this house of God at Jerusalem, and let the king send his pleasure to us concerning this matter" (Ezra 5:16,17). It is hard to distinguish whether verse 16 was said of the builders, or was the writing of the enemies. We are inclined to believe the latter. Having heard the humble, honest, and honorable reply, Tatnai the governor mentions how long the building had been going on, and requests that search be made in the king's treasure (record or library) house as to whether the claims of the builders were true or not.

What If?

Even though there is no mention, one wonders if there might have been an air of suspense in the hearts of the builders as the search was being made. Having received the letter from Tatnai and those associated with him, the Persian officials would initiate a search. *What if* the letter were not found in the Persian archives? *What if* those in charge of the records were careless in their search, or were ignorant as to the whereabouts of that particular writing. Or, *what if* some unscrupulous person, who hated Jews, upon finding the precious record, would destroy it? What would the final outcome be if no record were found? Have you ever noticed the various *what ifs* in your own life? It is like trying to cross a difficult bridge even before coming to it. People plagued with doubts and fears never seem to accomplish much for God. Take, for example, one seeking to witness for their Lord. They approach a person, but then the thought strikes them, "*What if* the person gets angry? Or, *what if* they hit me? Consequently, they remain silent, they have become ineffective because of *what ifs*. No, I do not believe that these Jews were worried. They had the assurance that the eye of God was upon them and that the work they were seeking to do was ordained by Him. They had nothing to fear. Everything was in the hand of their God, and He would, in His own time and in His own way, accomplish His purposes.

David's Confession

Brethren, absolute confidence in our God is a wonderful thing to possess. How fitting are the words of David, their former king. "The LORD is my light and my salvation; whom shall I fear? the LORD is the strength of my life; of whom shall I be afraid? When the wicked, even mine enemies and my foes, came upon me to eat up my flesh, they stumbled and fell. Though an host should encamp against me, my heart shall not fear: though war should rise against me, in this will I be confident. One thing have I desired of the LORD, that will I seek after; that I may dwell in the house of the LORD all the days of my life, to behold the beauty of the LORD, and to enquire in His temple. For in the time of trouble He shall hide me in His pavilion: in the secret of His tabernacle shall He hide me; He shall set me up upon a rock. And now shall mine head be lifted up above mine enemies round about me: therefore will I offer in His tabernacle sacrifices of joy; I will sing, yea, I will sing praises unto the LORD" (Ps. 27:1-6).

Darius' Thorough Search

In urging for a search to be made, no doubt the enemies felt that no such record could be produced, that there was no foundation to the reply that they had received from Zerubbabel. Upon receiving the letter, King Darius commanded that a search be made among the archives in Babylon. Alas, no record was found! However, this did not deter the king. He did not look upon the whole matter lightly. He continued his search, going to his summer residence in Achmetha (Ecbatana), where the document was found. It can be said of Darius that he was very thorough in his search, dealing very honorably with his Jewish subjects. Here we have a picture of the truth of Proverbs 21:1. "The king's heart is in the hand of the LORD, as the rivers of water: He turneth it whithersoever He will."

Another thing we learn from this incident is the fact that, whenever any thorough and sincere investigation of true Christianity takes place, it will contribute to its progress. It is when people with prejudiced minds, and people who are not thorough in their queries regarding the absolute truth of God investigate, that their conclusions are harmful to the cause of God. True, the investigation of Christendom could rightly produce some very negative conclusions; however, an absolutely honest and unprejudiced mind could never find fault with divine Christianity, for it in itself is pure.

What a blessing written history can be as it was in this case. The document was found and its contents made known. Never did the enemies that sent the inquiry expect such an outcome. They were totally defeated in their cause. Would you not like to have seen their faces when they received the report?

Measurements

The record not only gave permission to rebuild the temple, but it also provided information concerning the measurements of that temple. Comparing these measurements with those of Solomon's temple in 1 Kings 6:2, we discover, much to our surprise, that the temple in the mind of Cyrus was to be twice as high and three times as wide as Solomon's great temple. However, this seemingly never materialized, for the question arose; "Who hath despised the day of small things" (Zech. 4:10); "Who is left among you that saw this house in her first glory? and how do ye see it now? is it not in your eyes in comparison of it as nothing?" (Hag. 2:3). Then the record in Ezra 3:12 further confirms my statement. "But many of the priests and Levites and chief of the fathers, who were ancient men, that had seen the first house, when the foundation of this house was laid before their eyes, wept with a loud voice; and many shouted aloud for joy."

However, though not as great as the former temple, it was to be the greatest edifice of that day, simply because it was a God-ordained work. Even though it would lack the ark that was in the first temple, the tables of the covenant, the cherubim that covered it, fire from heaven, the Shekinah glory, and the Urim and Thummim, yet it was the place where the Lord had placed His name. It has been 2,000 years since the Church was born. What glory, what power, what godliness was manifested then in comparison to our present day. Can we all not admit that we are living in the day of small things? Yet, as weak as some local testimonies have become, are they not still precious in God's eyes? In weakness the name of Christ is still upheld. One is reminded of the commendation of our Lord to the church in Philadelphia. "I know thy works: behold, I have set before thee an open door, and no man can shut it: for thou hast a little strength, and hast kept My word, and hast not denied My name" (Rev. 3:8). Our Lord is kept alive in the world by the assemblies' obedience to the word and their loyalty to Christ.

A Strongly Laid Foundation

What tremendous results this revived document produced. Cyrus had decreed that "the foundations thereof be strongly laid." The word *strongly* comes from a root word meaning a *burden*, or, *to bear*. It seems to imply the thought of much toil in accomplishing the work. Regarding the foundation of the Corinthian church, Paul wrote, "According to the grace of God which is given unto me, as a wise masterbuilder, I have laid the foundation" (1 Cor. 3:10). Laying that foundation was teaching fundamental truth concerning the Person and work of the Lord Jesus Christ. It was no easy task. It involved sleepless nights, many tears, physical weariness, and largeness of heart. Paul, the layer of many strong foundations, could say, "But by the grace of God I am what I am: and His grace which was bestowed upon me was not in vain; but I laboured more abundantly than they all: yet not I, but the grace of God which was with me" (1 Cor. 15:10). The psalmist lamented, "If the foundations be destroyed, what can the righteous do?" (Ps. 11:3). The need today is for men in the assemblies of God who can labor to the point of exhaustion for God. To maintain truths in a local testimony takes spiritual sweat and toil on the part of those who shepherd the sheep; men who can "earnestly contend for the faith which was once (for all) delivered unto the saints" (Jude 1:3); men that will "labour in the word and doctrine" (1 Tim. 5:17). A strongly laid foundation is essential to a healthy testimony. Cyrus called for a strongly laid foundation that the house might continue for a long time.

The Gold and Silver Vessels

The decree also mentioned the golden and silver vessels. These are mentioned in Ezra chapter one, but something is added in 6:5, they were to be restored and "brought again unto the temple…every one to its place, and thou shalt put them in the house of God" (RV). Paul exhorted Timothy, "Study to shew thyself approved unto God, a workman that needeth not to be ashamed, rightly dividing the word of truth" (2 Tim. 2:15). Let us properly place truths lost by Christendom, but restored to the gathered out companies of God's people, owning no name but the Lord's. Let us never be guilty of misapplying Scripture to further our own views, but let us with an honest and sincere heart keep the vessels, the truths of God, in their proper place.

Darius' Command

Next, King Darius issues a command. "Now therefore, Tatnai, governor beyond the river, Shethar-boznai, and your companions the Apharsachites, which are beyond the river, be ye far from thence: Let the work of this house of God alone; let the governor of the Jews and the elders of the Jews build this house of God in his place" (Ezra 6: 6,7). A New Testament parallel to this would be Acts 9:31. "Then had the churches rest throughout all Judaea and Galilee and Samaria, and were edified; and walking in the fear of the Lord, and in the comfort of the Holy Ghost, were multiplied." That rest was obtained by the Lord arresting Saul of

Tarsus and saving him at noonday on the road to Damascus (Acts 9). The very person the devil was using to destroy the churches was to be the very person deity was going to use to develop the churches. In the remnant's case, it was a Gentile king who provided rest for them as they sought to build and establish the house of God. How varied are the instruments God takes up to fulfill His purposes. Nothing can stay His hand. King Nebuchadnezzar lifted his eyes unto heaven and confessed, "All the inhabitants of the earth are reputed as nothing: and He doeth according to His will in the army of heaven, and among the inhabitants of the earth: and none can stay His hand, or say unto him, What doest Thou?" (Dan. 4:35). The words of the Lord Jesus fit here. "With men it is impossible, but not with God: for with God all things are possible" (Mk. 10:27).

The Tribute Money

Not only were these official men ordered to let the work of the house of God alone, and not even to be on the premises, but they were also commanded to make provision for the furtherance of the work. The tribute money from Tatnai's district, instead of being sent to Darius, was to be given to the Jews for the work on the house of God. Also, young bullocks, and rams, and lambs, for the burnt offerings to the God of heaven, along with wheat, salt, wine and oil, to accompany the meal offerings, were all to be provided on a daily basis, accompanied with the warning, "WITHOUT FAIL!" (Ezra 6:9).

One may think it strange that Darius should be so concerned regarding even the offerings of the Jewish priests. However, the next verse explains the reason for his interest and concern. "That they may offer sacrifices of sweet savours unto the God of heaven, and pray for the life of the king, and of his sons" (Ezra 6:10). Darius recognized the fact that the God of the Jews was a powerful God, and he looks to God's people to pray for his life and his sons. Here we find a Gentile king with a consciousness of God and a love for his family. It is good to see the fear of God in men, especially kings, or any that occupy the place of authority. We are told to pray for them. "I exhort therefore, that, first of all, supplications, prayers, intercessions, and giving of thanks, be made for all men; For kings, and for all that are in authority; that we may lead a quiet and peaceable life in all godliness and honesty" (1 Tim. 2:1,2).

West Virginia's Brook High

How often in our dealing with sinners we have heard them say, "Pray for me." I remember many years ago preaching in the West Virginia hills, in a little village named Purgitsville. In that village was the most unique grocery store I have ever seen. The owner, Brook High, was related to that famous statesman, Will Rodgers. The store was heated with a little coal stove. There was no cash register, Brook simply kept the money in rolls, inside his pockets. There was no alarm system except Brook's handgun, a 45-caliber automatic kept four inches under the counter. One light bulb hung from the ceiling, dimly illuminating the place, and a little radio played as it sat on the counter. Nothing was sold that needed refrigeration, for he had no such "modern inventions," as he called them. Fellows gathered daily in the store, just to chat and pass the time away. My gospel tent was pitched across the little road from his store.

He owned the lot, and when I tried to pay him for the use of it he said, in no uncertain terms, "Preacher, that lot is God's property and you are preaching God's word. Put your tent up there and put that money back in your pocket!"

As my gospel meetings continued, daily, I would walk into his quaint store and immediately upon entering, without fail, he would turn the radio off, and tell the men to "hush up, the preacher's going to pray." Then looking at me he would say, "Preacher, don't pray for my business, just pray for our souls."

Nightly Brook would sit on a bench outside the tent and listen. Two years later, word reached me that he was dying. I drove 320 miles to visit him on his deathbed, and sought to point that dear man to Christ. The evening came, and I left in tears, only to hear a week later that dear Brook had gone into eternity to meet his God. As far as I know, this dear man that requested prayer, never made a profession of faith in Christ. Darius said, "Pray for me and my sons."

Darius' Threat

Following the king's request for prayer from the Jews, comes a threat of punishment to his own officers. "Also I have made a decree, that whosoever shall alter this word, let timber be pulled down from his house, and being set up, let him be hanged thereon; and let his house be made a dunghill for this. And the God that hath caused His name to dwell there destroy all kings and people, that shall put to their hand to alter and to destroy this house of God which is at Jerusalem. I Darius have made a decree; let it be done with speed" (Ezra 6:11,12). The king with a generous disposition could also manifest a savage and vicious spirit.

According to Herodotus, this king had impaled three thousand men at Babylon, after recapturing the city. The modern view of humanitarianism was totally unknown by ancient dictatorial world-rulers. This attitude can still be seen in parts of the Arab world today, they are hospitable, but intolerant and cruel to those who violate their civil and religious laws. The United States discovered this in a pronounced way, especially since their war with Iraq in 2003.

Urgency

Tatnai knew better than not to follow orders immediately, thus we read, "Then Tatnai, governor on this side the river, Shethar-boznai, and their companions, according to that which Darius the king had sent, so they did speedily" (Ezra 6:13). David was well aware of a servant's responsibility to a king – "And David said unto Ahimelech, …the king's business required haste" (1 Sam. 21:8). Bring this to our day, does not our Lord's business require haste? The word haste means, *urgent.* When it comes to winning souls for Christ, are we urgent? When it comes to attending assembly meetings, are we urgent? When it comes to searching the Holy Scriptures, are we urgent? We are living in a day of ease and complacency, a "ho hum" sort of attitude. May God preserve us from a sleepy condition. May the Lord help us to be "God's minute men, "stedfast, unmoveable, always abounding in the work of the Lord" (1 Cor. 15:58). When the king commanded, the servants acted – immediately!

The builders had three things helping them. (1) God was for them, His eye was upon them, strengthening them daily for their task. (2) The government was for them, supplying them with the necessary items to complete the work. (3) The word of God was prospering (advancing) them through the preaching of the prophets, Haggai and Zechariah.

The House Finished

"And this house was finished on the third day of the month Adar, which was in the sixth year of the reign of Darius the king" (Ezra 6:15). The foundation had been laid about twenty years prior to the completion. Time had been spent on self and no progress had been made, but once the revival took place, through the preaching of the two prophets, the work was finished in four years, five months, and ten days, the date being between February and March according to our calender. The last seven verses of Ezra chapter five record the joyous results of that historic event.

The House Dedicated

"And the children of Israel, the priests, and the Levites, and the rest of the children of the captivity, kept the dedication of this house of God with joy" (Ezra 6:16). The word *dedication* simply means that they were giving the building over to the use of God. It is found in different forms at least twenty-eight times in the Old Testament, but never once in the New Testament. In Solomon's dedication of his temple, 22,000 oxen, and 120,000 sheep were sacrificed. On the occasion we are considering we read, "And they offered at the dedication of this house of God an hundred bullocks, two hundred rams, four hundred lambs; and for a sin offering for all Israel, twelve he goats, according to the number of the tribes of Israel" (Ezra 6:17 R.V.). It was the day of small things, but please notice with me – there was joy!

The Day of Small Things – Rejoice!

As the dispensation of grace draws to a close, we must confess that we are living in the day of small things, yet, brethren, it is possible to rejoice. To be pessimistic can ruin our effectiveness. Later in Israel's history, Nehemiah and Ezra told the people to mourn not, nor weep, and not to be grieved, for the joy of the Lord was their strength (Neh. 8:9,10). Paul, in writing to the Thessalonian believers, exhorted them saying, "Rejoice evermore" (1 Thess. 5:16). To the Philippians he exhorts the same. "Rejoice in the Lord alway: and again I say, Rejoice" (Phil. 4:4).

You may say, "Oh, but the days are so dark, the times are so distressing, things are just not like they used to be." This is true, and it causes much concern to the spiritual soul, but let me ask you, are you rejoicing? When David sinned and was convicted of his sin, he cried, "I am troubled; I am bowed down greatly; I go mourning all the day long" (Ps. 38:6), and rightfully so.

However, I am not talking about personal sin in the believer's life, I am talking about deteriorating conditions surrounding the spiritual soul. Are you in a constant state of mourning because of outside conditions, or are you rejoicing? Are you strong and doing exploits for God? How can you be if you are not rejoicing? You may ask the question, "What is there to rejoice over?" Now that is a good and a healthy question, my friend. Let me give you the answer. Recently my dear wife underwent a serious operation. She is seventy-two and the recovery was painfully slow. At the same time I received word that a small assembly of believers held a gospel series nightly and that five sinners had professed faith in Christ. Needless to say, I rejoiced.

How often severe trials come into the believers' lives. What are they to do? – Rejoice! "What!" you say, "Rejoice?" Yes! They are to rejoice. Isn't that what God tells us? "Rejoicing in hope; patient in tribulation; continuing instant in prayer" (Rom. 12:12). Consider Peter and the other apostles, beaten by the council and put to shame. What did they do? We are told that "they departed from the presence of the council, rejoicing that they were counted worthy to suffer shame for His name" (Acts 5:41). With bleeding backs and bruised bodies – they rejoiced! Look down into that dingy mud-hole of the inner prison in Philippi, and what do you see? You see two men with scourged backs, their feet made tight in the cruel stocks, they are torn and weary, they have suffered official abuse all day and now it is midnight. "Oh my, poor fellows," you may say. Yes, poor in this world's goods, but exceedingly rich in spiritual blessings, and what are they doing? Read the divine record. "And at midnight Paul and Silas prayed, and sang praises unto God: and the prisoners heard them" (Acts 16:25) – they rejoiced! Brother, sister, in spite of all your trials take advice from Johnson Oatman's hymn.

When upon life's billows you are tempest tossed,
When you are discouraged, thinking all is lost,
Count your many blessings name them one by one,
And it will surprise you what the Lord hath done.

Are you ever burdened with a load of care?
Does the cross seem heavy you are called to bear?
Count your many blessings, every doubt will fly,
And you will be singing as the days go by.

Count your blessings, name them one by one,
Count your blessings, see what God hath done.
Count your blessings, name them one by one;
Count your many blessings, see what God hath done.

Consider the Lord

Look at the blessed Saviour. The cruel cross is looming before Him, His own disciples have forsaken Him, the ungodly are shouting for His crucifixion, His soul is exceeding heavy, even unto death. He has endured the agony of Gethsemane, the lash of the Roman government, the mockery and the shame, and now they are leading Him away. Consider the divine record over this dark occasion. "Who for the **joy** that was set before Him endured the cross, despising the shame, and is set down at the right hand of the throne of God" (Heb. 12:2). Joy? Yes, joy! What was there to rejoice about? First of all, He was accomplishing the Father's will; second, He was about to purchase His bride, the Church. In the midst of all that darkness – He rejoiced!

What a divine example for us! Dare we grumble and feel discouraged after considering such witnesses? You have a great High Priest Who is able to enter into every pang of your heart – rejoice! You have an Advocate with the Father, Who pleads your cause – rejoice. You have been blessed with all spiritual blessings in the heavenlies in Christ – rejoice! Christ said, "Blessed are ye, when men shall hate you, and when they shall separate you from their company, and shall reproach you, and cast out your name as evil, for the Son of man's sake. Rejoice ye in that day, and leap for joy: for, behold, your reward is great in heaven: for in the like manner did their fathers unto the prophets" (Lk.

6:22,23). Finally, we "rejoice in hope of the glory of God" (Rom. 5:2). The day is coming when we shall behold the splendor, the glory of God, and we also shall be manifested in glory. In our glorified state, we shall be glorified with Christ. Look up, the coming of the Lord draweth nigh, and as you continue to look up your soul will be filled with holy anticipation, and you will REJOICE! The house was finished. The house was dedicated, and there was JOY!

The Offerings

The chronicler moves on in his report and brings us to the functioning of the dedication. They "offered at the dedication of this house of God an hundred bullocks, two hundred rams, four hundred lambs; and for a sin offering for all Israel, twelve he goats, according to the number of the tribes of Israel. And they set the priests in their divisions, and the Levites in their courses, for the service of God, which is at Jerusalem; as it is written in the book of Moses" (Ezra 6:17,18).

Notice the awareness of sin. Even though it was a time of rejoicing, the sin of the nation could not be overlooked. There could be no remission of sins apart from the shedding of blood, thus twelve he goats were offered. Even though this solemn occasion only involved a small remnant of that nation, yet the offerings were on the behalf of all Israel. In other words, the remnant were judging the sin in which the whole nation has participated. The sin offerings were not individual, but national. The nation had been punished as a result of its collective sin, thus it was necessary to have a collective expiation of sin. Of course all of these sacrifices pointed to the final and greatest sacrifice of all, the atoning sacrifice of Christ. The writer to the Hebrews informs us that "without shedding of blood is no remission" (9:22), that it was "not possible that the blood of bulls and of goats should take away sins" (10:4), thus the necessity of a human sacrifice that could satisfy the throne of God in absolutely removing all sin. The answer could only be found in Christ. Thus, "once in the end of the world hath He appeared to put away sin by the sacrifice of Himself" (9:26). The writer defines the quality of the sacrifice of Christ, speaking of it in the plural as, "better sacrifices than these" (9:23). The word *sacrifices* exposes the fact that the Saviour's sacrifice was the fulfillment of all the Levitical offerings. He was the burnt offering, the sin offering, the trespass offering, the peace offering, and the meal offering. Every sacrifice of old only pointed to the great sacrifice offered at Calvary. Christ encompassed all!

Divisions and Courses

Not only did they offer, they offered orderly and scripturally, " as it is written in the book of Moses." The priests were set in their divisions, and the Levites functioned according to their courses. The book of Moses is mentioned, but in vain will you find the divisions of priests and the courses of the Levites mentioned. What then is the solution to this report? The solution is simple. The divisions and courses had been instituted by David as First Chronicles 23:6-23; and 24:1-19 show. David arranged this order, based on the ordinances of the law respecting the offices of the two orders, written in the Book of Numbers 3:6-10, and 7:6-26. So that, even though the courses themselves were not established until David, yet they were according to the writing of the book of Moses. It is statements of this nature that cause skeptics to fault the Bible, claiming that it makes mistakes. However, their conclusions only betray their total ignorance of the divine record, and the satanic blindness of their degenerate hearts. Thus, "the natural man receiveth not (rejects) the things of the Spirit of God: for they (the holy scriptures) are foolishness unto him: neither can he know thcm, because they are spiritually discerned" (1 Cor. 2:14). The holy scriptures cannot be understood apart from the new birth.

Diversity of Operations

The priests had their responsibilities, and the Levites had their own work to accomplish, thus we see diversity in the service of God. We also see obedience to the blueprints of God, all was done "as it is written." Considering a local assembly, we see a multiplicity of gifts for its function in divine things. This seems to be the leading theme of First Corinthians chapter twelve. Not all have the same work, but all are necessary to accomplish that which projects a scriptural testimony for God. All functioning must be in accordance with what is written, thus we see the importance of the Holy Scriptures for the proper functioning of an assembly. Man is not left to his own human understanding, nor his innovations. The assembly of God is not an organization, but rather an organism, the various members functioning through the power and guidance of the Holy Spirit of God. "What saith the Lord," is paramount – an absolute must! Paul likens the local testimony to a human body, composed of various parts, all functioning for the good of that body. He points out that every member is needed.

"The eye cannot say unto the hand, I have no need of thee: nor again the head to the feet, I have no need of you. Nay, much more those members of the body, which seem to be more feeble, are necessary" (1 Cor. 12:21,22). The thought of one man doing it all and receiving a salary is never envisioned in New Testament teaching.

In conclusion of this theme, we close with the apostle's writing. "Now there are diversities (distribution) of gifts, but the same **Spirit**. And there are differences of administrations (ministry), but the same **Lord**. And there are diversities of operations (energy working), but it is the same **God** which worketh all in all" (1 Cor.12:4-6). Thus we see the trinity of the Godhead functioning. The Spirit administering, or distributing, the particular gift. The Lord regulating the various forms of service, His lordship being acknowledged. Finally, God empowering to accomplish the assignment, through the gift given. The priests and the Levites were set for the service of God.

The Passover

The religious New Year arrived, which brought them to the month of Abib. Fourteen days later, according to the law of Moses, the passover was kept. There are only eight mentions of the passover in holy scripture; the first one at its institution (Ex.12); the second, when Israel entered into the land and encamped at Gilgal (Josh. 5:10); the third, in the wilderness of Sinai, "the second year after they were come out of the land of Egypt" (Num. 9:1); the fourth, during the reign of Hezekiah (2 Chr. 30:15); the fifth, during the reign of Josiah (2 Chr. 35:1); the sixth, the following month after the dedication of the temple in Zerubbabel's day (Ezra 6:19); the seventh, when the Lord was twelve years of age (Lk. 2:24); the eighth, in all four gospels prior to the crucifixion of our Lord; and the ninth, the Lord Himself – "For even Christ our passover is sacrificed for us" (1 Cor. 5:7). Scripture speaks of the passover in five different ways in Exodus 12. It was a **memorial**, for their memory (vs.14); a **feast**, for fellowship (vs.14); an **ordinance**, being an appointed law (vs. 24); a **service**, to accomplish a ministry (vs. 26); and a **sacrifice**, being a form of worship (vs.27).

Purity

It is instructive to observe how the passover was kept. It was no haphazard function. Because it was a most solemn feast, those responsible for its carrying out must be pure. Thus we read, "For the priests and the Levites were purified together, all of them were pure, and killed the passover for all the children of the captivity, and for their brethren the priests, and for themselves" (Ezra 6:20). They were purified, uncontaminated, morally innocent or holy. God requires holiness to handle holy things.

Those who rule in a local assembly MUST be blameless, that is, no serious charge laid to their account. When a believer is excommunicated because of sin, even though repentance takes place and that person is received back into the fellowship, yet there remains a serious blot on that individual; they are not blameless, although forgiven. The degree of one's reverence to God and their understanding of His holiness are measured by the degree in which they abhor sin. The two coincide. In 1 Timothy 3, we discover the qualifications of an elder and are impressed with God's standard for such, the list revealing ten things he should be, and six things he should not be. The priests and Levites were purified together.

Sanctification

The next thing noted is that "the children of Israel, which were come again out of captivity, and all such as had separated themselves unto them from the filthiness of the heathen of the land, to seek the LORD God of Israel, did eat, And kept the feast of unleavened bread seven days with joy: for the LORD had made them joyful" (Ezra 6:21,22).

The Holy Spirit now directs us from the purifying of the priests and Levites to the sanctification of those Jews who had married heathen women. Sad to say, we find a recurrence of this almost eighty years later in Ezra's day. "And Ezra the priest stood up, and said unto them, Ye have transgressed, and have taken strange wives, to increase the trespass of Israel. Now therefore make confession unto the LORD God of your fathers, and do His pleasure: and separate yourselves from the people of the land, and from the strange wives" (Ezra 10:10,11).

The land was unclean, filthy, filled with abominations (Ezra 9:11), yet in spite of this, there had been those who, from fleshly lusts had, as it were, "jumped the fence," and gone out to take to themselves heathen women for their wives. They may have been Israelites who had lived in Palestine through the captivity, perhaps members of the ten tribes who had been scattered throughout the northern kingdom. The Canaanite and Babylonian ways of living were grossly immoral. At any rate, they had become immersed in heathen associations, and there must be a cleansing before they could participate in the holy ordinances of the LORD.

Are there not lessons in this for today? Paul exhorts those of the Corinthian Church, "Let us cleanse ourselves from all filthiness of the flesh and spirit, perfecting holiness in the fear of God" (2 Cor. 7:1). James exhorts the believers, "Pure religion and undefiled before God and the Father is this, To visit the fatherless and widows in their affliction, and to keep himself unspotted from the world" (Jas. 1:27).

The Feast of Unleavened Bread

As the scene closes we read they "kept the feast of unleavened bread seven days with joy: for the LORD had made them joyful, and turned the heart of the king of Assyria unto them, to strengthen their hands in the work of the house of God, the God of Israel" (Ezra 6:22). In the seven feasts of the LORD you will notice that the one-day feasts portray what God *has done for us*, while the period feasts convey *what God is doing in us.* The passover pictures the death of Christ for us – salvation. That is what God has done *for us.* The seven-day feast of unleavened bread conveys the thought of a complete period of time, our whole Christian experience, characterized by the removal of all uncleanness (leaven) in our lives. This is what God is doing *in us* presently. In view of the sacrifice of Christ, Paul exhorts the Corinthians "Purge out therefore the old leaven, that ye may be a new lump, as ye are unleavened. For even Christ our passover is sacrificed for us: Therefore let us keep the feast, not with old leaven, neither with the leaven of malice and wickedness; but with the unleavened bread of sincerity and truth" (1 Cor. 5: 7,8). "Let us keep the feast" refers to our whole life for God here. The leaven on that occasion was the assembly's toleration of evil.

The World

As noticed, James speaks of the defiling character of this world, warning us to keep ourselves unspotted from it. Indulge in the world's amusements and it will spot your garment. Visit the musicals, the theater, the sports arena, the seemingly innocent games of pool, bowling, and golf, and you will, in God's eyes be wearing spotted garments. The injunction still remains, "Love not the world, neither the things that are in the world. If any man love the world, the love of the Father is not in him. For all that is in the world, the lust of the flesh, and the lust of the eyes, and the pride of life, is not of the Father, but is of the world" (1 Jn. 2:15,16). John closes his epistle with these pungent words. "Little children, keep yourselves from idols. Amen" (1 Jn. 5:21).

Reasons For Rejoicing

The cause of rejoicing was manifold. First of all, the LORD Himself made them joyful. What a wonderful God we have! Perhaps it costs us the satisfying of our flesh to present our bodies a living sacrifice unto Him, not conforming ourselves to this world (Rom.12:1,2), but the reward is tremendous, God fills our heart with joy. Do you want to experience a joy this world had never experienced? Separate yourself from the world's false ways, keep yourselves clean, and God will fill you with joy. Even though to cease from sin will cause suffering in the flesh (1 Pet. 4:1), do remember, the Lord's yoke is easy and His burden is light

(Matt. 11:30).

Another reason for rejoicing was the fact that God had turned the heart of the king to their favor. Those of us who live in a land of freedom, How much do we rejoice in the fact that the government is favorable toward us, and that there are no severe repercussions for spreading the gospel, and gathering collectively together to worship the Lord? Let us who live in such lands ever be thankful and rejoice.

The third occasion of their rejoicing was the fact that their hands were strengthened to complete the work which they had commenced. Paul could rejoice as he penned these memorable words to his son in the faith, Timothy: "I have fought a good fight, I have finished my course, I have kept the faith" (2 Tim. 4:7). May the Lord give us the daily grace to finish our course well. I have seen dear saints on their deathbed lamenting the fact that they had wasted most of their God-given time on the frivolous things of this world. Time that could not be recalled, thus tears, instead of joy, ended their journey here. Not so with Paul, and certainly not so with our divine example, the Lord Jesus Himself. "I have glorified Thee on the earth: I have finished the work which Thou gavest Me to do" (Jn.17:4).

"Consecrate me now to Thy service, Lord,
By the power of grace divine;
Let my soul look up with a steadfast hope,
And my will be lost in Thine"

CHAPTER SEVEN

Zechariah and The Men of Bethel

FOLLOWING THE EIGHT NIGHT VISIONS of Zechariah, he proceeds in his prophetic utterances to instruct and encourage the people of God. This commences at chapter seven of his book, two years after the eight night visions, and two years before the completion of the temple. The pronouncements continue to the end of the book. We introduce some of these declarations seeing that they were uttered as the temple work progressed, thus bringing encouragement to the laborers of God.

Ministry is manifold. Not only do we need to be corrected, yea, even at times rebuked, but we also need to be encouraged. The spiritual minister of the word is not lopsided, with all "Christ-exalting ministry," or with all rebuking ministry, there must be a balance. Just as a wise nursing home employs a nutritionist to arrange well-balanced meals for the residents to maintain good health, so a wise minister of the word balances his ministry for the well-being of the saints. God's eye was upon the builders and He was strengthening them spiritually, and perhaps even physically, as they labored in love for Him.

The Delegation From Bethel

As the seventh chapter of Zechariah opens, we find a most interesting, and unusual situation. Verse one -"And it came to pass in the fourth year of king Darius, that the word of the LORD came unto Zechariah in the fourth day of the ninth month, even in Chisleu;" Verse two - "When they had sent unto the house of God Sherezer and Regem-melech, and their men, to pray before the LORD;" Verse three - "And to speak unto the priests which were in the house of the LORD of hosts, and to the prophets, saying, Should I weep in the fifth month, separating myself, as I have done these so many years? Mr. J.N. Darby's rendering of verse two is more accurate, it reads, "when Bethel (i.e. those of Bethel) had sent Sherezer and Regem-melech, and his men, to supplicate Jehovah." *Bethel* literally means *House of God,* but verse two is referring to the city of Bethel, not to the house of God, as one would be led to believe through the King James Version. It is enlightening to observe that the expression, "house of God" ("house of El") in verse two is never used for *the* temple or for *a* temple. The expressions "house of *the Lord*" and "house of *Elohim*" alone are used.

The city of Bethel lay about twelve miles to the north of Jerusalem. It was there Jeroboam had set up the golden calf, which positioned this city as the idolatrous-religious capital of the ten northern tribes, which ultimately were carried into captivity by Assyria (1 Ki. 12:28–13:1). There were those who, coming up out of Babylon, settled in Bethel (Ezra 2:28; Neh. 11:31). The delegation being sent to Jerusalem reveals that, even though Bethel had been the religious capital of Israel before the Assyrian captivity, the inhabitants of this city recognized Jerusalem as God's gathering center and the priests in Jerusalem as ordained of God.

Two Self-Imposed Fasts

When taken into Babylonian captivity the Jews initiated two special fasts, neither of them required by God. The first fast was in memory of the destruction of Jerusalem and the temple, when for four days in the fifth month (August) the fires blazed, consuming the city to ashes (2 Ki. 25:8,9). The second self-imposed fast was commemorative of Gedaliah's murder in the seventh month (2 Ki. 25:25). These fasts had been observed for seventy years throughout the captivity and involved the wearing of sackcloth, rending of one's garments, abstaining from food, and weeping.

More than likely at the beginning of this self-imposed ritual, there was genuine remorse, tears, and grief, as they thought upon their beloved city and the beautiful temple brought to absolute ruin. The murder of Gedaliah, a man who sought their good, had also filled them with great grief, resulting in sincere mourning on the appointed fast day. It was a season of sincere humbling of self and remorsefulness for their sin. The rite was designed to express their total dependence upon their God, Who had punished them for their sin.

However, as time went on, the fast days merely became a legalistic ritual, a mechanical formalism. Seeing that the temple was nearing completion, and that the divine order of worship was being established, the people of Bethel wondered if the fast, in which they had no heart, meant anything at all. They directed their inquiry to the priests and prophets (Haggai and Zechariah), was it necessary to continue these fasts? While the temple lay in ruins, the fast had a meaning, but now another temple was nearly complete, would their fasting be meaningless? During the seventy years in Babylon they had observed the fast, commemorating a past national tragedy, but why continue to mourn when present abundance and success were being experienced? Thus the question is asked, "Should I weep in the fifth month (August) separating myself, as I have done these so many years?" The inhabitants of Bethel are speaking as one man, thus the first person ("I") is used in the inquiry. The whole city was concerned.

A Stinging Answer

Seeing that this commemorative observance had degenerated into a heartless form, the answer from the LORD of hosts through the prophet Zechariah was quite stinging and severe. "Speak unto all the people of the land, and to the priests, saying, When ye fasted and mourned in the fifth and seventh month, even those seventy years, did ye at all fast unto Me, even to Me? And when ye did eat, and when ye did drink, did not ye eat for yourselves, and drink for yourselves?" (Zech. 7:5,6). What an exposure of their hypocritical hearts! The rebuke was merited. Not only did the rebuke involve the city of Bethel, it encompassed all the people of the land, and even the priests! What a deplorable condition!

Perhaps if you had observed these people on their fast days you would have been greatly impressed with their supposedly humble and contrite spirit. However, "man looketh on the outward appearance, but the LORD looketh on the heart" (1 Sam. 16:7). "I the LORD search the heart, I try the reins, even to give every man according to his ways, and according to the fruit of his doings" (Jer. 17:10). The fruit of their doings in this case, was the public rebuke of God. Even though all looked proper outwardly, yet inwardly they were performing their "little act," with absolutely no heart at all. They were eating and drinking for themselves, not Jehovah. They were tired of it, but had continued, keeping up a front. When they asked the question, "should I weep, separating myself," they were as much as saying, "O that I might cease from these practices!"

Christendom and Christianity

To parallel this, we mention Christendom with their man-made ordinances and rituals. Their manifold observances are a dishonor to the Lord and only satisfy the self-interests of the people. The chanting of prayers, the burning of incense, the counting of beads, the acts of penance, and many more humanly contrived religious inventions, are nothing less than an abomination to God.

Let us who are saved also consider. Is there not a danger, in our functioning as priests today, of deteriorating into a similar frame of mind as those of the captivity? Oh, how earnest we were when first saved! The things of God were so appealing to our souls. In love we were so willing to make sacrifices for God. We willingly presented our body a living sacrifice and ceased to be conformed to this world (Rom.12:1). Our worship was from fervent hearts and we delighted to be with the Lord's people collectively, at the prayer meeting, the Bible study, the breaking of bread, and the gospel meeting.

Let us ask ourselves, are all these activities now a burden? Have the fires of a devoted heart ceased to burn fervently? Are we present at the assembly gatherings because we feel it our duty? Do we pray because we feel that we are expected to do so? Are we glad when the hour is over, so that we can get away, and return home, or engage in other activities? These are all very heart-searching questions, but is it not good to examine ourselves? Are we sincerely enjoying all the privileges, responsibilities, and activities of assembly fellowship, or are we simply "going through the motions?"

Comparison of Men

When you consider the men from Bethel (ch. 7) with the three men from Babylon (ch.6), there is a vast difference, not only in their names and position, but also in their attitude. The three men from Babylon, Heldai (Helem), Tobijah, and Jedaiah, with humbleness and gratitude, brought gifts for the temple. Their names are meaningful as they relate to Jehovah. The two men from Bethel, Sherezer, Regem-melech, came with nothing to offer except their frustration. Unlike the men from Babylon, their names were foreign, being associated with the idol-worship of their conquerors. More than likely their names were derived because of their occupation, perhaps having held office in the court of their oppressors, either in Babylon or Assyria. In like manner, Daniel and his companions had their names changed by the king of Babylon, seeing they were to serve in his court. So we observe, it was the rank and file of God's people that brought silver and gold for the temple, while the dignitaries of the Bethel delegation brought nothing but statements and grumbling. It is usually the poorer of the Lord's people that possess the greatest awareness of the needs of others, and are willing to part with what little they possess.

Peter, Paul, Barnabas, and Christ

Keep in mind, the apostle Peter was poor. He confessed, "Silver and gold have I none" (Acts 3:6). The apostle Paul was poor. "As poor, yet making many rich; as having nothing, and yet possessing all things" (2 Cor. 6:10). Barnabas made himself materialistically poor. "Having land, sold it, and brought the money, and laid it at the apostles' feet" (Acts 4:37). Then we have the greatest example of all, our blessed Lord, of Whom it was said, "For ye know the grace of our Lord Jesus Christ, that, though He was rich, yet for your sakes He became poor, that ye through His poverty might be rich" (2 Cor. 8:9).

James' Warning

James warns us regarding our attitude toward the poor. He relates to his readers, that when a rich man came into their assembly they bestowed great favors upon him and made a great ado, but when a poor man entered no respect was given to him. His pen writes, "Are ye not then partial in yourselves, and are become judges of evil thoughts? Hearken, my beloved brethren, Hath not God chosen the poor of this world rich in faith, and heirs of the kingdom which He hath promised to them that love Him? But ye have despised the poor. Do not rich men oppress you, and draw you before the judgment seats?" (Jas. 2:4-6).

A Sobering Reminder

Following the divine reply to the Bethel delegation, the prophet reminds the people of the disobedience of their fathers and the cause of the captivity. God had sent His messengers to them but they had refused to hearken, and pulled away their shoulder, and stopped their ears. They had made their hearts as an adamant stone, therefore great wrath came from the LORD. Destroying the temple and the city, He scattered them with a whirlwind among all the nations whom they knew not. Thus the land was desolate after them, that no man passed through nor returned: for they laid the pleasant land desolate (Zech. 7:11-14). What a sad history, what terrible results. However, the judgment was now past, they were back in the land, and the temple services were about to be initiated once again – there was joy.

A Glorious Future

Again the word of the LORD of hosts came to Zechariah (8:1). He projects the people from the desolation of the past to the prosperity of the future. He reveals God's jealousy for the city and the fact that in a coming day He would dwell in the midst of Jerusalem, and that the city would be called, "a city of truth." The inhabitants of that city would not only be old men and old women, but the streets would be full of boys and girls playing. There would be no fear in the streets, peace and tranquility would be the norm of the day. The devastation of war would be a thing of the past. With God all things are possible and even though this future blessing may have seemed marvelous (too hard) in the remnant's eyes, God will bring it to pass.

"Thus saith the LORD of hosts; Behold, I will save My

people from the east country, and from the west country; And I will bring them, and they shall dwell in the midst of Jerusalem: and they shall be My people, and I will be their God, in truth and in righteousness. Thus saith the LORD of hosts; Let your hands be strong, ye that hear in these days these words by the mouth of the prophets, which were in the day that the foundation of the house of the LORD of hosts was laid, that the temple might be built" (Zech. 8:7-9).

The expression from the east country and from the west country simply means the whole earth. You will find the same language in Psalm 113:3; Malachi 1:11. "From the rising of the sun (the east) unto the going down of the same (the west)." Compare also Psalm 50:1 for a similar expression.

Israel had never been scattered to the four corners of the earth until the destruction of the temple in A.D. 70 by the Roman Army under the siege of Titus. This worldwide dispersion of the Jewish people still remains today, but after the rapture of the Church, Israel shall return to the land as their Messiah initiates His glorious millennial reign. "And it shall come to pass in that day, that the Lord shall set His hand again the second time to recover the remnant of His people… and shall assemble the outcasts of Israel, and gather together the dispersed of Judah from the four corners of the earth" (Isa. 11:11,12). God promises them, "Fear not: for I am with thee: I will bring thy seed from the east, and gather thee from the west; I will say to the north, Give up; and to the south, Keep not back: bring My sons from far, and My daughters from the ends of the earth" (Isa 43:5,6).

Having said this, the prophet from verse 9 to 17, reveals the ways of God, relative to the conduct of men. There are seven statements contained in seven verses that are worthy of notice.

(1) Proclamation - Zech. 8:9

"Thus saith the LORD of hosts; Let your hands be strong, (in other words, *be of good courage*) ye that hear in these days these words by the mouth of the prophets (Haggai and Zechariah), which were in the day that the foundation of the house of the LORD of hosts was laid, that the temple might be built." In other words, be of good courage to continue in obedience to My word. In verse ten, God reminds them of the former days of disobedience and the sobering results. In verses eleven to thirteen we find that since there had been a turning to Him in dependence, He promises better days. In verse fourteen God brought grievous days, but in verse fifteen, God brought good days.

For the minister of the word, it is very encouraging to see positive results on the part of his listeners as a result of his ministry. Nothing is so disheartening than to faithfully minister the word of God, only to have it go unheeded. As the older Haggai and the younger Zechariah beheld the progress of the work resulting from their continual and faithful ministry, it must have filled their souls with joy. Remember the beloved apostle John, how faithfully he ministered the truth. What encouraged him the most? It was when he saw his ministry having the desired effect in the hearts of his children. His interesting words come to mind. "I have no greater joy than to hear that my children walk in truth" (3 Jn. 1:4).

(2) Punishment - Vs. 10

"For before these (those) days there was no hire for man, nor any hire for beast; neither was there any peace to him that went out or came in because of the affliction: for I set all men every one against his neighbour."

What a contrast is presented to their present circumstances. He takes them back to thc days before the temple work had resumed, those days had been characterized by their disobedience to His word. Previous to B.C. 520 there had been severe times economically. They had been excusing themselves saying that the time had not yet come to build the temple. Their interests were totally on their own possessions, not on the things of God. They would certainly have been reminded of the words of Haggai, spoken at the time of their awakening to divine responsibilities. "Is it time for you, O ye, to dwell in your cieled houses, and this house lie waste?" (Hag. 1:4).

Employment had been scarce, there was no work for animals, thus they remained idle, and it had become unsafe to even travel. The word *peace* (shalom) meaning, *quietness, tranquility, safety, security.* Internal strife had become normal behavior. There was no unity, and brethren were suspicious of one another. What a deplorable condition! Let us be aware of the fact that this condition was brought upon them due to one thing – their disobedience to the word of the Lord. At that time they certainly couldn't exclaim like the psalmist, "Behold, how good and how pleasant it is for brethren to dwell together in unity!" (Ps. 133:1). The prophet was reminding them of past conditions due to past failures to impress them with a truth that never changes – "them that honour Me I will honour, and they that despise Me shall be lightly esteemed" (1 Sam. 2:30).

(3) Promise - Vs. 11

"But now I will not be unto the residue of this people as in the former days, saith the LORD of hosts."

They are now reminded of the changed attitude of God toward them. God is a God of restoration. Not only this, He is a God of longsuffering. The longsuffering of God waited in the days of Noah, but there was no repentance on the part of the world, thus the judgment of Almighty fell. How different concerning the wicked believer in the Corinthian Assembly. Put away for grossly immoral sin, God allowed him to be delivered unto Satan, that is, outside the protective wall of the assembly and into the sphere where Satan reigns. What distresses came upon him we are not told, but the God of restoration began to work in his soul, finally bringing him to sorrow and tears. Upon his restoration, the attitude of God changed and the Lord, through the writing of Paul, exhorted the assembly to receive him back into the fellowship of the assembly and to confirm their love to him (1 Cor. 5 with 2 Cor. 2). As the temple neared completion, we see a changed people from a former day, consequently their God acting differently toward them. This teaches us how beneficial it is for us to keep right with God.

(4) Prosperity – Vs. 12

"For the seed shall be prosperous; the vine shall give her fruit, and the ground shall give her increase, and the heavens shall give their dew; and I will cause the remnant of this people to possess all these things."

The opening of the verse could read, "At the time of sowing seed, there shall be peace." This reading supports the fact that the vine, being the choicest of all plants, requires peaceful times in order to yield its fruit. Luther translates it, "the seed shall be prosperous." Under divine blessing the crops would yield their produce abundantly, thus the remnant would inherit an abundant harvest. God said that they would *inherit* it, indicating that they were not necessarily worthy, but their filled barns would be an evident token of the grace of God toward them.

(5) Protection – Vs. 13

"And it shall come to pass, that as ye were a curse among the heathen, O house of Judah, and house of Israel; so will I save you, and ye shall be a blessing: fear not, but let your hands be strong."

Because of their disobedience, they had been a curse before the nations. The word *curse* comes from the root *qalal*, meaning, to *be made, or held contemptible.* God had inflicted such punishment upon them that consequently they were held in contempt by the surrounding nations. Their former glory had departed, and instead of being admired and feared, they were scorned and held in utter contempt by the nations. What shame! What disgrace!

There are people today who were once held in admiration, but because of exposed sin in their life have been lowered in the eyes of the populace to a place of contempt and scorn. The result of Israel's restoration to God, pictured in the remnant, was that the contempt of the heathen would fade, and that they would prove to be a blessing to those who had formerly scorned them. With the protection of God upon them, they are exhorted to make their hands strong.

(6) Provoking – Vs.14

"For thus saith the LORD of hosts; As I thought to punish you, when your fathers provoked Me to wrath, saith the LORD of hosts, and I repented not."

What a grim reminder, what a warning to disobedience! They had provoked their God to wrath, consequently, He punished them, meaning, *to spoil* (literally, by breaking to pieces); figuratively, *to make good for nothing*. Calamities had befallen them from the hand of God. Loved ones were slain, the temple destroyed, and they themselves carried into captivity.

Very often, even in our day, calamities which befall God's people can be traced to the hand of God as a result of disobedience. However, we should be very slow in attributing all calamities to disobedience, for on some occasions God allows severe trials in our life to prove us, or to make us better men and women for God, as was the case with Job, Daniel, and the apostle Paul, who were godly men.

(7) Pleasant Days – Vs. 15

"So again have I thought in these days to do well unto Jerusalem and to the house of Judah: fear ye not."

Consider the word, *do well;* (yatab) a primitive root; to *be made well*, they had been spiritually sick. Literally the word means, *sound, beautiful;* figuratively it means, *happy, successful, right:– be accepted.* It also carries the thought, *to make cheerful, be comely, be content.* What pleasant and delightful words of encouragement to the struggling remnant as they neared the completion of a temple to Jehovah. Once sick, but now spiritually sound; once unattractive to God, but now beautiful in His eyes; once a heavyhearted people, now happy; once unsuccessful in accomplishing anything for God, but now successful; once wrong, but now right. Accepted and rejoicing before their God, they possessed a contentment that only God could give.

In closing this section, let us bear in mind that the previous seven verses that we have examined basically point on to that future day when the reign of Christ in His millennial kingdom shall be realized. What we have observed in Zerubbabel's day was only a little shadow of greater things to come.

Exhortation to Bethel

Given glimpses of Israel's illustrious future, both at hand and in the distant future, the prophet now exhorts the delegation from Bethel to proper conduct. A similar exhortation had just been given in chapter 7:9,10. God is a holy God and as such, He demands holiness in His people. Thus we read, "These are the things that ye shall do; Speak ye every man the truth to his neighbour; execute the judgment of truth and peace in your gates: And let none of you imagine evil in your hearts against his neighbour; and love no false oath: for all these are things that I hate, saith the LORD" (Zech. 8:16,17). Four things God expected, the first two are positive, the last two are negative. Notice the word is not, "these things shall ye hear," but rather, "these things shall ye do." James reminds us, "But be ye doers of the word, and not hearers only, deceiving your own selves" (Jas.

1:22).

First, they were to be truthful. A similar injunction was written to the saints at Ephesus. "Wherefore putting away lying, speak every man truth with his neighbour: for we are members one of another" (Eph. 4:25). The psalmist exclaimed, "Behold, Thou desirest truth in the inward parts" (Ps. 51:6). Let us ever be aware that our God is a God "that cannot lie" (Titus 1:2), and that He expects the same of His children.

Second, they were to execute the judgment of truth and peace in their gates. The gate was the area inside the city wall near the entrance where public court was held. Their judicial judgments in their courts should be in such a way that they would effect peace. Honesty should prevail, that justice be satisfied. In the local assembly today we have a court, where elders judge various cases that come to their attention. Paul warns the Corinthian assembly that only in the mouth of two or three witnesses shall every word be established (2 Cor. 13:1). Saints are not to judge motives, but elders are certainly enjoined of God to judge sin in the camp. "Do not ye judge them that are within?" (1 Cor. 5:12).

A Saddening Story

Let us be emphatic, sin cannot be judged and righteously dealt with apart from more than one witness. There was a most distressing case that came to my attention years ago. A godly elder in an assembly (we will call him Mr. G.), was hated by one of its woman members. The woman was probably not saved. One day, in tears she came to the overseers of that assembly and laid an accusation at their feet concerning Mr. G. She confessed that he had an affair with her many months ago. The elders were shocked, for this elder was one of the most godly men in that assembly. He was brought in for questioning and vehemently denied the charges. The man's wife was driven to distress, and their two mature daughters were brought to tears. The man maintained his innocence. The accusing woman was approached again and questioned. She sounded so convincing, and was broken down in tears as she spoke to the elders. The case was judged, and in spite of the godly man's absolute denial, he was put away from the assembly as a wicked person.

Soon afterward, the accusing woman left the assembly. The whole assembly was distressed, to think that this man had committed such an ungodly deed. As the days passed by, the accused brother never missed an assembly meeting. Meekly he sat back during the breaking of bread in silence. His voice was not allowed to be heard at the prayer meetings or the Bible readings, yet he came faithfully to every gathering. He was godly, and had committed his cause unto the Lord, Who judgeth all things righteously.

As time went on, his own wife and daughters began to lose confidence in his claim of innocence. The family life was affected, and the happiness in that godly home began to evaporate. However, after two years or so, something happened. One day a sister in that assembly was shopping in a super market. She overheard two women talking in the next aisle and one of them was the woman who had accused Mr. G. She was laughing as she related to her ungodly friend how that she had really "fixed" Mr. G. She related how she had conjured up her story so that he would be disgraced, but assured her friend that she never was involved with him in any way. Hurriedly, the sister informed the elders of her experience in the store. What the rest of the details were I am not prepared to say, but the falsely accused brother was exonerated and brought back into the fellowship with apologies. However, the episode had made its mark on him and his family, and he never seemed quite the same. The brethren had severely wounded him, simply because they had not followed God's pattern in the scriptures regarding judging a case. They had acted on the testimony of one witness, and a false one at that. What shame! Do remember, God emphatically says, "In the mouth of TWO or THREE witnesses!"

Third, they were not to devise evil in their hearts against one another. The word *heart* really refers to the *intellect* or *mind*, and the thought is that their mind was not to be engaged in contaminating thoughts against others. The law forbid them to even have a thought of revenge or injury against the wronging party.

Proper Conduct

Peter records, by the Spirit, the conduct of the true believer. "Wherefore laying aside all malice, and all guile, and hypocrisies, and envies, and all evil speakings" (1 Pet. 2:1). The word *laying aside,* is in the aorist participle, indicating something accomplished in the past, and should read, *having laid aside*. Peter is assuming that malice, guile, hypocrisies, envies, and all evil speakings, like a garment, have been discarded for a better garment. He is not necessarily exhorting them to cease this ungodly behavior, but he is relating to his readers what he assumes has already taken place upon their conversion to Christ. Another thought on this third law: The Septuagint renders it, "Let none of you remember in your hearts the malice of your brother."

Dark Brown Stains

About forty-five years ago I went to a dentist to whom I had often witnessed for Christ. He examined my teeth and noticed some very dark brown stains on the backside. Looking at the stains, he remarked how pronounced they were. I asked him, "Why?" He stammered and with an apologetic voice said, "Perhaps too many cigarettes?" Of course, I immediately told him that being a Christian, I certainly didn't smoke. He then suggested that the stains must have come from drinking very strong coffee. I told him that I hardly ever drank coffee, but that I enjoyed tea. Surprised he exclaimed, "You must drink it very strong." I informed him that I only drank from eight to twelve cups a day and used two two-cup bags per cup, steeping them for at least ten minutes. He gasped, and calling his assistant said, "Come here and look at a case of extreme vegetation stains!"

The reason for the story is this. Have you ever considered what malice and envy are? Malice is the harboring of evil thoughts, the building up of grudges. Envy is jealously, being tormented by another's good. These things are like tea bags. Put them into your mind and just like a tea bag, the longer they "steep," the darker and more bitter the mind becomes. A tea bag at first releases caffeine, but if left in for a longer period, it begins to release tannic acid, so much so that the brew even stains the cup. There are minds that brew malice and envy until their whole mind is stained. Brethren, this should not be among us as the people of God. Eliminate immediately any malicious or envious thoughts that may inadvertently fall into your mind. Keep thyself pure. Peter speaks of a "pure mind" (2 Pet. 3:1).

Fourth, they were not to love a false oath. They were not to tolerate perjury. To lie under oath is a most grievous sin. It can obstruct justice and free the guilty, or it can condemn the falsely accused. God states through Moses. "If a false witness rise up against any man to testify against him that which is wrong; Then both the men, between whom the controversy is, shall stand before the LORD, before the priests and the judges, which shall be in those days; And the judges shall make diligent inquisition: and, behold, if the witness be a false witness, and hath testified falsely against his brother; Then shall ye do unto him, as he had thought to have done unto his brother: so shalt thou put the evil away from among you" (Deut. 19:16-19). If this law were upheld in our courts today, there certainly would be far less lying under oath.

To apply this in another sphere, permit me to say that, even though telling the truth to an employer might cost the Christian his employment, he is obligated to tell the truth, no matter what the consequences might be. "Lie not one to another, seeing that ye have put off the old man with his deeds" (Col. 3:9).

Israel's Future Restoration

Zechariah, having encouraged the men from Bethel with seven expressions, and four laws relative to proper conduct (8:9-17), now concludes the chapter with utterances regarding the full and future restoration of Israel, and its unparalleled joy during the millennial reign of Christ (verses 18–

23). Israel's fasts would be turned into feasts, and nations that presently despise the Jew, shall in that day beg to be associated with them. Dignitaries will be sent to Jerusalem to pray before the LORD. He will be recognized by all as "the LORD of hosts", meaning, "LORD of armies." He shall rule with a rod of iron, and His dominion shall be from sea to sea. "Thus saith the LORD of hosts; In those days (the millennial reign) it shall come to pass, that ten men shall take hold out of all languages of the nations, even shall take hold of the skirt of him that is a Jew, saying, We will go with you: for we have heard that God is with you" (Zech. 8:23). Ten men taking hold of the skirt of a Jew. What does this unusual verse mean? Ten indicates a large indefinite number. Taking hold of the skirt of one's garment is often seen in little children when a stranger draws near. In their parent they recognize protection and care. They are totally dependent upon them. As Gentiles make their way to the holy city, Jerusalem, they will desire to be associated with the Jew, realizing them to be a benefit to them, bringing them protection, well being, and care. In taking hold of the Jew's skirt, they are manifesting a desire to share the nation's privileges, being united in fellowship with it. Who could ever bring about such a change in a wicked world's attitude to God's earthly people? – only God Himself! With God all things are possible!

Need We Be Anxious?

Brethren, consider for a moment, this Almighty God is our Father in heaven! Need we be overanxious regarding conditions? Never! True, we should be concerned about many things, but needless worry and fretting should not be part of the Christian's agenda. "Be careful (anxious, troubled with cares) for nothing; but in every thing by prayer and supplication with thanksgiving let your requests be made known unto God" (Phil. 4:6). This is an excellent exhortation, for it will save us from many physical ailments. Have you ever considered the cause of high blood pressure, ulcers, digestive disorders? You can often trace it to anxiety!

If you want good medical advice, let us go to a good Christian doctor and see what he says. Notice! "Take no thought (over anxiousness) for your life, what ye shall eat; neither for the body, what ye shall put on. ...Consider the ravens: for they neither sow nor reap; which neither have storehouse nor barn; and God feedeth them: how much more are ye better than the fowls? And which of you with taking thought can add to his stature (life-span) one cubit? ...If then God so clothe the grass, which is to day in the field, and to morrow is cast into the oven; how much more will He clothe you, O ye of little faith? And seek not ye what ye shall eat, or what ye shall drink, neither be ye of doubtful mind. For all these things do the nations of the world seek after: and your Father knoweth that ye have need of these things. But rather seek ye the kingdom of God; and all these things shall be added unto you" (Luke 12:22-31). The good doctor writing is Luke the physician, and He is simply quoting the words of the greatest Physician Who ever lived, the Lord Jesus Christ.

It is amazing how we can trust God for our eternal destiny, yet in so many circumstances, we cannot seemingly trust Him for our little sojourn here. Some time ago, I was shocked while talking to a young Christian father who managed his own business. His wife was also employed at another establishment, both having good incomes. What stunned me was when he told me that he had a large life insurance policy, so that in case he passed away, his family would be provided with the necessary things of life. A chill ran up my back and I thought, "But where is the Lord?" Seemingly, he had excluded the greatest Provider out of his plans. He had turned from total dependence on the Lord, to an arm of flesh.

The salient question arises, is the God that provided for us eternal life, able to provide for us in this life? I am fully persuaded that He is! His promise is unmistakably plain, "Let your conversation (manner of life) be without covetousness; and be content with such things as ye have: for He hath said, I will never leave thee, nor forsake thee" (Heb. 13:5). Isn't that little word NEVER a big word? What a weighty promise – *NEVER!* "We trust in the living God, who is the Saviour of all men, **specially** of those that believe" (1 Tim. 4:10).

In the time of trial Abraham failed and went down into Egypt, because of a famine in the land. Had he stayed where he was, he would have been able to prove God like Elijah at the brook Cherith (1 Ki. 17:5). Who would have ever thought that unclean birds like ravens would have enough sense to search for meat and then when finding it, not eat it for themselves, but fly away with it to feed God's trusting prophet? The man of the world cannot visualize such a strange thing, it is unreal, unnatural, and extreme. How God loves to prove Himself.

Those that place their implicit trust in Him have the blessed opportunity of allowing God to work on their behalf. On the occasion in Genesis chapter twelve, Abraham missed it, but in I Kings fifteen, Elijah gained it. Not only did Abraham miss the privilege of proving God, he got himself and his wife into serious trouble, which could have been avoided, if he had only placed unwavering trust in his God.

The business man with the working wife seemingly could not lay hold on God's promises for survival. Consider men with excellent employment, who at the call of God, laid their secular work aside, and their employer's pay checks, and went forth into the harvest field, taking nothing of the Gentiles. Consider them, I say again, consider them! Have you ever seen one of them begging on Skid Row, destitute with no roof over their head and no food for their stomach? Have you ever seen their families crying in desperation for a crumb? Why no, they are living as well as when they were employed. They have had the unspeakable joy of proving God, and in so honoring God, God's heart has been constantly moving on their behalf. Brethren, if the riches of Christ are unsearchable, as the Bible says, do you not think that He can give us help in time of need? I close this little discourse with this promise. "When thou passest through the waters, I will be with thee; and through the rivers, they shall not overflow thee: when thou walkest through the fire, thou shalt not be burned; neither shall the flame kindle upon thee. For I am the LORD thy God, the Holy One of Israel, thy Saviour…Since thou wast precious in My sight, thou hast been honourable, and I have loved thee…Fear not: for I am with thee" (Isa. 43:2-5).

CHAPTER EIGHT

Zechariah's Two Great Burdens

ONLY THREE TIMES do we read in the whole Bible these words, "The burden of the word of the Lord." They are found in, Zechariah 9:1; 12:1; and Malachi 1:1. This expression forms two main divisions in Zechariah's prophecies. Chapter nine begins the second great division and continues on to the end of the book. This section of six chapters involves two great burdens, which project the reader into the future. They are not as relevant to the little remnant as are the first eight chapters of Zechariah's prophecies. However, they were spoken in the remnant's day for the purpose of projecting their minds to a far greater day of Messiah's glory, thus beaming strength and hope into their hearts.

Our Interest in Prophecy

Some Christians may say, "Why be interested in prophecy, it has nothing to do with our present times?" What an attitude! Let me say, even though I will not be here on earth when prophetic actions on earth will materialize, yet I am intensely interested in them. Why? Simply because I am in love with the central Person involved in future events – my blessed Lord, Who in that great day will be revealed as King of kings, and LORD of lords! Why should I not be interested in all that is to take place for His honor and His unsurpassed glory? How wonderful, how satisfying, how joyous to behold, that in a coming day, the despised and rejected One will receive all **glory and dominion,** for ever and ever (Rev. 1:6).

Doxologies

Let us not stop there; in Revelation 4:11 the doxology increases. "Thou art worthy, O Lord, to receive **glory and honour and power:** for Thou hast created all things, and for Thy pleasure they are and were created." Let us go further. In Revelation 5:13, we read, "And every creature which is in heaven, and on the earth, and under the earth, and such as are in the sea, and all that are in them, heard I saying, **Blessing, and honour, and glory, and power,** be unto Him that sitteth upon the throne, and unto the Lamb for ever and ever." Let us go even further to Revelation 7:11:12. "And all the angels stood round about the throne, and about the elders and the four beasts, and fell before the throne on their faces, and worshipped God, Saying, Amen: **Blessing, and glory, and wisdom, and thanksgiving, and honour, and power, and might**, be unto our God for ever and ever. Amen."

The Kingdom

See how the doxology, the heavenly praise, increases as time goes on? That is one reason why I am interested in prophecy, for it conveys to me, even in a greater measure than the gospels, the essential attributes of Almighty that are resident in our blessed Lord, Who is God manifest in the flesh. I am interested in what He told His disciples to pray, namely, "Thy kingdom come. Thy will be done, as in heaven, so in earth" (Lk.11:2). I am not only interested in His kingdom, I am *intensely* interested! Why? Simply because I am going to be positioned in that coming kingdom. "Verily, verily, I say unto thee, Except a man be born again, he cannot see the kingdom of God" (Jn.3:3). Since I have been born again, I have been placed into that kingdom. I will grant you that presently it is in its invisible form, if I may put it that way; however the day is coming when that kingdom shall be visible and that is what most of prophecy is about.

Consider the grand announcement in Revelation 11:15. "And the seventh angel sounded; and there were great voices in heaven, saying, The kingdoms of this world are become the kingdoms of our Lord, and of His Christ; and He shall reign for ever and ever" Consider the fact that Paul encouraged Timothy with these sublime words. "If we suffer, we shall also reign with Him: if we deny Him, He also will deny us" (2 Tim 2:12). Since we are going to reign with Him in His visible kingdom, let us proceed with Zechariah's prophecies and glean a few grand and glorious glimpses of the future; not only glimpses of yet future events, but also observations of events that were future in the remnant's day but are history today.

The First Burden – Alexander

Zechariah's first burden reveals the conquests of the young and proud world conqueror, Alexander the Great (Zech. 9:1-8). The announcements are a burden, meaning that they are heavy, and permeated with woe and judgment.

The word "burden," comes from the root *nasa*, meaning "to lift up." Zechariah's name had been previously mentioned in his book, twice in chapter one, and twice in chapter seven. However, in the last section of his prophecies, from chapter nine to the end of the book, his name never occurs. The final messages are not merely utterances, but burdens.

The Overthrow of Tyrus (Tyre)

For centuries the nation of Israel had suffered from the active antagonism of their neighbors, but in the burdens it is made clear that their time of God's judgment had come. Alexander was a tool in the hand of God, to bring judgment upon various cities for their idolatry. God, at times, uses strange forces to accomplish His end. Syria, Phoenicia, and Philistia are first mentioned in the prophecy, but let us just consider the city of Tyrus. Her history goes back further than 2700 B.C. It was a double city, one section on an island, one-half mile from the shore, the other part on the mainland. The city on the mainland was protected by a wall 150 foot high, containing 40,000 inhabitants. However, it was destroyed 240 years before Alexander by Nebuchadnezzar. The island city submitted to the Persians about 525 B.C., becoming a vassal state during the existence of the Persian Empire.

"And Tyrus (Tyre) did build herself a strong hold, and heaped up silver as the dust, and fine gold as the mire of the streets. Behold, the Lord will cast her out, and He will smite her power in the sea; and she shall be devoured with fire" (Zech. 9:3,4).

The prophet's description of the military movements

and victories of the Macedonian Empire in chapter nine are so amazingly accurate that they offer one of the strongest proofs of the divine inspiration and absolute reliability of Holy Scripture. At the age of 22, Alexander, upon defeating the Persian army, conquered Asia Minor, sweeping on to subdue Syria and Phoenicia, the city of Tyrus being crushed with great difficulty. In fact, of all of his conquests, Tyrus was the most difficult to defeat. One by one all of the Syrian cities surrendered without resistance. As the Macedonian conqueror approached Sidon, the city immediately surrendered. Not so with Tyrus! This strong and exceedingly proud city considered herself absolutely impregnable. Alexander was refused entry. Enraged, the mighty youth of war made his plan of attack. Zechariah describes Tyrus as a stronghold, that had heaped up silver as the dust, and gold as the mire in the streets. The streets, not being paved, would in the dry season produce dust, which the wind would occasionally blow away. In the wet weather, the dusty streets would be turned to mire. The city had treasured up silver and gold as plentiful as the dust and mire of her streets; she was exceedingly rich. The city also boasted of its wisdom, but as the dust of the street, her riches, strength, pride and wisdom were soon to be swept away by the onslaughts of Alexander. She was destined to be cast out, her power smitten, and devoured by fire. God had said it, and God would bring it to pass – using Alexander as His instrument.

The island city was twenty miles in circumference, and had massive walls 150 feet high surrounding it. Their weapons of war to defend the city came behind no fortress of that day. The question arose, how could a land army attack an island fortress? Previously in history, the city had withstood a five-year siege from the Assyrians, and later a fifteen-year siege from the Chaldeans. Alexander stripped the old mainland city of its stones and built a causeway out from the mainland to the island. There were vicious attacks on his project, but Alexander continued, and after seven months of conflict, captured the city. He slew all 10,000 of its guards in hand-to-hand sword combat, sold the remainder of the populace of 30,000 into slavery and burned the city with fire, just as Zechariah had prophesied. At this point, notice the prediction of Ezekiel regarding this fortress city. "And I will make thee like the top of a rock: thou shalt be a place to spread nets upon; thou shalt be built no more: for I the LORD have spoken it, saith the Lord GOD" (Ezek. 26:14). To this day, fishermen can be seen drying their nets, out from the mainland, on the very stones of Alexander's causeway.

Jerusalem Spared

Another historical fact worthy of notice is, in Alexander's conquest of many cities, he passed by Jerusalem a number of times without harming the city. It is recorded that he had tender feelings toward the Jewish people, thus the prophecy of Zechariah was fulfilled, "And I will encamp about Mine house (God's Temple, thus including the people) because of the army, because of him that passeth by, and because of him that returneth: and no oppressor shall pass through them any more: for now have I seen with Mine eyes" (Zech 9:8). God had observed them, He had entered into every trial and affliction that was theirs. He had seen their affliction in Egypt, He had seen their affliction after returning to the land, and in a coming day, as the nation enters the great tribulation, prior to the return of their King to establish His millennial kingdom, His eye in pity and deliverance will be upon them. "For the eyes of the LORD run to and fro throughout the whole earth, to shew Himself strong in the behalf of them whose heart is perfect toward Him" (2 Chr. 16:9). David recognized this fact and said, "The eyes of the LORD are upon the righteous, and His ears are open unto their cry" (Ps. 34:15). Let us take courage, brethren, our God does not change, and just as His eyes were upon His ancient people, so His eyes are also upon us today.

Two Dreams

History records the reason for Alexander's tender feeling toward God's people. After conquering Gaza, Alexander purposed invading Jerusalem. Israel's high priest ordered the people of Jerusalem to offer sacrifices to God and pray for their safety.

God spoke in a dream to the high priest telling him to go outside the city to welcome Alexander when he arrived. As the great warrior approached the city, the priest, with other priests, went forth from the city's gates to greet Alexander. When he saw Israel's high priest arrayed in purple and scarlet with the mitre on his head, having a golden plate with the name of God upon it, and accompanied with many priests in white linen robes, he adored the name of Jehovah and saluted the high priest. What is most remarkable is that prior to this, Alexander had seen the priest in his priestly garments in a dream at Dios in Macedonia!

The Coming of the King

Having considered the greatest king of that day, the prophet now projects us over three hundred years to the greatest King of all, our blessed Lord. What a striking contrast to Alexander. Notice His introduction. "Rejoice greatly, O daughter of Zion; shout, O daughter of Jerusalem: behold, thy King cometh unto thee: He is just, and having salvation; lowly, and riding upon an ass, and upon a colt the foal of an ass" (Zech 9:9).

The prophet calls for the remnant to rejoice over the coming King. Matthew and John relate this prophecy to Christ's triumphal entry into Jerusalem on the Lord's Day of the week in which He was crucified (Matt.21:5; Jn. 12:15).

The first thing noticed in the prophet's Messianic statement is **the consideration of the King:** "Behold thy King cometh unto thee." He comes as their King, but also as their Helper. The more strict rendering is, "your King comes for you," that is, He comes for your good. This indicates a deliverance with His coming. However, that deliverance never came, for as John pens, "He came unto His own, and His own received Him not" (Jn. 1:11).

Second, **the character of the King:** "He is just." He was righteous in character and practice. His royalty excelled all others. Peter recognized this quality in Jesus of Nazareth and laid the charge to Israel. "But ye denied the Holy One and the Just, and desired a murderer to be granted unto you" (Acts 3:14). In like manner Stephen testifies. "Which of the prophets have not your fathers persecuted? and they have slain them which shewed before of the coming of the Just One; of Whom ye have been now the betrayers and murderers" (Acts 7:52). Paul relates Ananias' words to him at his conversion. "And he said, The God of our fathers hath chosen thee, that thou shouldest know His will, and see that Just One, and shouldest hear the voice of His mouth" (Acts 22:14). Later Peter speaks again of Christ as the Just One. "For Christ also hath once suffered for sins, the Just for the unjust, that He might bring us to God, being put to death in the flesh, but quickened by the Spirit" (1 Pet. 3:18). Thus it was made known that the coming King would be purely righteous, a quality rarely seen in a king.

Third, we see **the charity of the King:** "Having salvation." Brought as a babe less than two months old, into the temple in Jerusalem, Simeon, upon embracing the Lord to his own breast, exclaimed, "Lord, now lettest Thou Thy servant depart in peace, according to Thy word: For mine eyes have seen Thy salvation" (Lk. 2:29,30). This is the only occasion on which the expression, "Thy salvation," is employed in the New Testament. Salvation is not merely a gift, it is a Person to be received. Our Lord brought something no other could bring. He brought salvation within our grasp, He brought it within our means, the Lord being nigh unto all that call upon Him, and salvation provided at no expense to us whatsoever. It is a great salvation, and there is no escape if we neglect it (Heb. 2:3). It is a great salvation, because of the One Who brought it. It is great because of the cost to procure it – the death of our Lord. It is great because it is unto all and upon all that call upon Him.

Fourth, we notice t**he condescension of the King:** "lowly." What a striking contrast to the proud young conqueror, Alexander! The Lord was humble, "meek and lowly in heart" (Matt. 11:29). The Spirit through Paul testifies. "And being found in fashion as a man, He humbled Himself, and became obedient unto death, even the death of the cross" (Phil. 2:8). However, the word *lowly* has a deeper meaning than just humble. It also carries the thought of one bowed down and afflicted. It also embraces the meaning of being poor and needy. Notice Matthew's report of the King. "The foxes have holes, and the birds of the air have nests; but the Son of man hath not where to lay His head" (Matt. 8:20). The word also carries the thought of being afflicted, and truly our holy Lord was afflicted by wicked men. What a comprehensive word *lowly* is, and the Lord fulfilled every meaning of it in His sojourn here.

Fifth, **the credentials of the King:** "and riding upon an ass, and upon a colt the foal of an ass." While Alexander rode the finest horse available, the greatest of all kings rode on a lowly beast – an ass. There was a time in Israel's history when nobility rode on asses, but this completely changed during David's reign when horses were introduced. From that day on, people of rank, and those of nobility rode horses, leaving the ass as a burden bearer, totally unsuitable for kings and their families to ride. There was no dignity to riding an ass, as Jeremiah reveals. "Then shall there enter into the gates of this city kings and princes sitting upon the throne of David, riding in chariots and on horses, they, and their princes, the men of Judah, and the inhabitants of Jerusalem: and this city shall remain for ever" (Jer. 17:25). When the time had come for Messiah's triumphal entry into Jerusalem, His credentials were that He would be riding on an ass, accompanied with a colt. One can readily see why the men who went into the city and found the ass and colt, said to those who questioned them, "The Lord hath need of them" (Matt.21:1-7). "All this was done that it might be fulfilled which was spoken by the prophet, saying, Tell ye the daughter of Sion, Behold, thy King cometh unto thee, meek, and sitting upon an ass, and a colt the foal of an ass" (Matt. 21:4,5).

Omission

It is very striking to notice that, when this incident is mentioned in the gospels, the second part of Zechariah 9:9 is quoted, but the first part of the verse is entirely omitted. "Rejoice greatly, O daughter of Zion; shout, O daughter of Jerusalem." The reason is that Israel could not be called upon to rejoice while rejecting her King.

Messiah's Future Reign

After announcing the entry of the King into the beloved city of God, the prophet projects us to the future, revealing an event that will not take place until after the rapture of the Church. "And I will cut off the chariot from Ephraim, and the horse from Jerusalem, and the battle bow shall be cut off: and He shall speak peace unto the heathen: and His dominion shall be from sea even to sea, and from the river even to the ends of the earth" (Zech. 9:10).

Various world leaders through the ages have sought for world peace. Their efforts are vain as long as the King of kings is despised and rejected of men. When Christ comes to reign, He will cut off the chariot from Ephraim and the horse from Jerusalem, and the battle bow. All weapons of war will be abolished, and the world will experience a peace unparalleled in its history. "But I will have mercy upon the house of Judah, and will save them by the LORD their God, and will not save them by bow, nor by sword, nor by battle, by horses, nor by horsemen" (Hos.1:7). Satan will be bound and confined 1,000 years in hell, thus depriving him of influencing the minds of men. All the kings of the earth will bow in submission to the King of kings, the Man with the pierced hands, feet, and side. Oh the wonder of it all, the despised and rejected Jesus of Nazareth, ruling as sovereign Lord over all creation.

Even the brute creation will be changed, "And righteousness shall be the girdle of His loins, and faithfulness the girdle of His reins. The wolf also shall dwell with the lamb, and the leopard shall lie down with the kid; and the calf and the young lion and the fatling together; and a little child shall lead them. And the cow and the bear shall feed; their young ones shall lie down together: and the lion shall eat straw like the ox. And the sucking child shall play on the hole of the asp, and the weaned child shall put his hand on the cockatrice' den. They shall not hurt nor destroy in all My holy mountain: for the earth shall be full of the knowledge of the LORD, as the waters cover the sea" (Isa. 11:5-9).

His dominion shall be from sea to sea and from the river (Euphrates) to the ends of the earth, indicating that it will be worldwide. "He will speak peace unto His people, and to His saints" (Ps. 85:8). What a day of glory that will be for His earthly people as we, His heavenly people, orbit the earth in the heavenly Jerusalem.

The prophet continues encouraging the nation in view of their blessed future, their conflict with godless paganism, the Lord defending them, and saving them as the flock of His people. The ninth chapter closes with Israel's appreciation and realization of their kingdom blessing expressed.

"For how great is His goodness, and how great is His beauty."

The Corner Stone

Entering the tenth chapter, we find another description of the Lord from the prophet. "Out of him (Judah) came forth the Corner, (Corner Stone) out of him the Nail, out of him the Battle bow, out of him every oppressor together" (Vs. 4). Having considered Christ as the Stone on pages 153–155, we will simply add this. Just as a corner stone supports a building on a sloping incline, so to Israel, the Messiah will be their sole support, uniting them, ruling them, and prospering them. Zechariah no doubt had the prophecy of Isaiah in mind during these Messianic utterances and his allusion to the stone. " Behold, I lay in Zion for a foundation a stone, a tried stone, a precious corner stone, a sure foundation: he that believeth shall not make haste" (Isa. 28:16).

The Nail

He is also the Nail. The thought is of a tent peg driven into the pole inside the tent to hang precious things for display. Isaiah records, "And I will fasten Him as a nail in a sure place; and He shall be for a glorious throne to His Father's house. And they shall hang upon Him all the glory of His Father's house" (Isa. 22:23,24). The weight, the responsibility of government shall be upon His shoulder, and unlike most leaders, He will not fail. His rule will be righteous with utmost authority.

The Battle Bow

As the Battle-bow, He will put down all political and military oppressors. His kingdom will be characterized by peace. "Thine arrows are sharp in the heart of the king's enemies; whereby the people fall under Thee" (Ps. 45:5). Again the words spoken by Isaiah come to our attention. "Wherefore art Thou red in thine apparel, and Thy garments like him that treadeth in the winefat? I have trodden the winepress alone; and of the people there was none with Me: for I will tread them in Mine anger, and trample them in My fury; and their blood shall be sprinkled upon My garments, and I will stain all My raiment. For the day of vengeance is in Mine heart, and the year of My redeemed is come" (Isa.63:2-4). This Messianic revelation corresponds exactly with Revelation 19:11-18, where our Lord is seen coming out of heaven as KING OF KINGS, AND LORD OF LORDS, to execute judgment upon His enemies.

Every Oppressor

In doing so, He will drive every oppressor out of Judah. The *oppressors* here are tyrants. The word is *nagas,* a primitive root meaning, "to drive a workman, harass, tyrannize, distress, oppress, a taskmaster." That is the meaning of the word *oppressor*. From him (Judah) they shall depart. There are more than one, for they shall go out *together.* We are not convinced that the word *oppressor* refers to Christ as some writers claim. Chapter nine and verse eight seem to support this interpretation, "no oppressor shall pass through them anymore." Isaiah's words come again to mind. "…I will also make thy officers peace, and thine exactors righteousness. Violence shall no more be heard in thy land, wasting nor destruction within thy borders; but thou shalt call thy walls Salvation, and thy gates Praise" (Isa. 60:17,18).

The Lord will rid the land of such. What a great Shepherd He will be to His gathered flock, the restored nation of Israel. "Behold, I will gather them out of all countries, whither I have driven them in Mine anger, and in My fury, and in great wrath; and I will bring them again unto this place, and I will cause them to dwell safely" (Jer. 32:37). How tender are His promises to His people. "Behold, the Lord GOD will come with strong hand, and His arm shall rule for Him: behold, His reward is with Him, and His work before Him. He shall feed His flock like a shepherd: He shall gather the lambs with His arm, and carry them in His bosom, and shall gently lead those that are with young" (Isa. 40:10,11). Thus He will **satisfy** His people; He will give them **security**; He will **support** them; and "gently lead those that are with young" – His lovely **sympathy**.

The Second Burden – Jerusalem

The prophet now commences his second and last burden in chapters twelve to fourteen. This burden is concerned primarily with the coming of Messiah in power to establish His kingdom. In this last section we find that phrase, "in that day" sixteen times. The expression relates to the day of the LORD, when divine judgments will be poured out and the sufferings of the tribulation will fall upon man until the Son of Man returns in power.

A Cup of Trembling

Prior to the Lord's coming God will make Jerusalem "a cup of trembling and a burdensome stone for all people…All that burden themselves with it shall be cut in pieces, though all the people of the earth be gathered together against it" (Zech.12:2,3).

"A cup of trembling," is an interesting phrase. J.N. Darby translates it, "a cup of bewilderment." The ASV translates it," a cup of reeling," and both convey the true meaning. The thought is a goblet of wine that causes intoxication. When the nations gather together for their final war against Jerusalem, in a united effort to wipe Israel off the face of the earth, they will be intoxicated with pleasure in doing so. However, like a drunken man unable to accomplish his desires, they shall find themselves helpless to conquer the city, Not only will the city be a cup of reeling, it will also be to them a burdensome stone, a heavy stone, hard to lift. Those who try to lift the stone will seriously injure themselves. They shall be "sore wounded," simply meaning that they shall tear themselves, their injury will be grievous.

"In that day, saith the LORD, I will smite every horse with astonishment, and his rider with madness: and I will open Mine eyes upon the house of Judah, and will smite every horse of the people with blindness" (Zech. 12:4).

God will fight for Israel! The cavalry of the enemy will be thrown into total disarray. The horses, going blind, will be terrified, the riders will be unable to control their steeds, and will become insane – there will be total panic. The inspired words of the psalmist come to mind. "Why do the heathen rage (throng together), and the people imagine (meditate) a vain thing? The kings of the earth set themselves, and the rulers take counsel together, against the LORD, and against His Anointed, saying, Let us break Their bands asunder, and cast away Their cords from us. He that sitteth in the heavens shall laugh: the Lord shall have them in derision. Then shall He speak unto them in His wrath, and vex them in His sore displeasure. Yet have I set My King upon my holy hill of Zion. I will declare the decree: the LORD hath said unto Me, Thou art My Son; this day have I begotten Thee" (Ps. 2;1-7).

Nations Destroyed

Zechariah continues. "And it shall come to pass in that day, that I will seek to destroy all the nations that come against Jerusalem. And I will pour upon the house of David, and upon the inhabitants of Jerusalem, the Spirit of grace and of supplications: and they shall look upon Me Whom they have pierced, and they shall mourn for Him, as one mourneth for his only son, and shall be in bitterness for Him, as one that is in bitterness for his firstborn" (Zech. 12:9,10).

"God will seek to destroy all the nations." The thought is certainly not that God will hopefully accomplish His purpose, but rather that He will give all His attention to destroying His people's enemies. He will allow nothing to distract Him from accomplishing His purpose. Not only this, He will pour out the Spirit of grace and supplication on His people. Those of His own who have survived the great tribulation shall experience a great spiritual visitation from on high. Christ poured out His soul unto death (Isa. 53:12). God will pour out His Spirit unto once dead Israel. This will enable them to recognize their Messiah, and will fit them for the multitude of blessings that will be graciously bestowed upon them during their Messiah's millennial reign.

The Great Look

" They shall look upon Me Whom they have pierced."

Let us be very clear on the word, "pierced." It is not in a figurative sense, as some writers suggest. Neither does it mean to profane the name of God, or to wound by insulting. The word is *dakar*, meaning *to thrust through.* The thought of looking ***upon*** Him means, *looking* ***unto*** *Him,* which gives the thought of looking to Him in confidence and faith, as a child looks to its parent to meet its need.

Whom

"Me Whom they pierced." There is a wealth of thought in the word *Whom*. It is composed of the first and last letter of the Hebrew alphabet, *aleph* (shaped like the head of an ox), and *tav* (shaped like a cross). He is the Alpha and Omega, the beginning and the end (Rev. 1:11; 22:13), alpha being the first letter and omega being the last letter of the Greek alphabet. The ox would remind us of the sacrifice of our Lord and the cross tells us where that sacrifice took place. These also are the initial letters of *Urim* (lights) and *Thummim* (perfections), which are explained on page 35. Lights speak of His deity ("God is light," 1 Jn. 1:5)), and perfections of His impeccable humanity ("In Him is no sin," 1 Jn. 3:5).

As this book is being composed, Israel is being bombarded on every side by its Arab neighbors. The Arabs have broken every peace treaty made, since the nation became a sovereign state in 1948. Their agenda is to completely wipe out the nation of Israel. Israel today is basically atheistic. Only a small remnant acknowledge God and the writings of Moses.

What a transformation in the nation —"in that day!"

The prophet reveals that, "they shall mourn for Him, as one mourneth for his only son, and shall be in bitterness for Him, as one that is in bitterness for his firstborn."

At this point, the account of this event by the Lord Himself is worthy of our attention. Matthew records – "Immediately after the tribulation of those days shall the sun be darkened, and the moon shall not give her light, and the stars shall fall from heaven, and the powers of the heavens shall be shaken: And then shall appear the sign of the Son of man in heaven: and then shall all the tribes of the earth mourn, and they shall see the Son of man coming in the clouds of heaven with power and great glory. And He shall send His angels with a great sound of a trumpet, and they shall gather together His elect from the four winds, from one end of heaven to the other" (Matt. 24: 29-31).

The National Mourning

Never in the history of the nation has there been a day like this! The Jewish people will make their way from the four corners of the earth to which they have been scattered, back to Israel, recognizing their Messiah to be none other than Jesus. The mourning will take place. A whole nation in mourning! What a sight that will be! They will wail and strike their breasts in deep grief. Their confession will be, "Surely He hath borne our griefs, and carried our sorrows: yet we did esteem Him stricken, smitten of God, and afflicted. But He was wounded for our transgressions, He was bruised for our iniquities: the chastisement of our peace was upon Him; and with His stripes we are healed. All we like sheep have gone astray; we have turned every one to his own way; and the LORD hath laid on Him the iniquity of us all" (Isa. 53: 4-6). Paul writes of their national status in these words, "And so all Israel shall be saved: as it is written, There shall come out of Sion the Deliverer, and shall turn away ungodliness from Jacob" (Rom. 11:26).

Josiah

The prophet continues to inform us of the place and the nature of Israel's mourning. "In that day shall there be a great mourning in Jerusalem, as the mourning of Hadadrimmon in the valley of Megiddon" (Zech. 12:11). The question arises, what is meant by, "the mourning of Hadadrimmon in the valley of Megiddon?" Hadadrimmon was a city near Jezreel, where Josiah, the last good king of the nation was slain by Pharaoh-Necho in 609 B.C. (2 Chr. 35:22). So tremendous was the loss to Judah, that we read, "And all Judah and Jerusalem mourned for Josiah. And Jeremiah lamented for Josiah: and all the singing men and the singing women spake of Josiah in their lamentations to this day, and made them an ordinance in Israel: and, behold, they are written in the lamentations" (2 Chr. 35:24,25).

Families

Zechariah continues in His utterance to mention mourning families, namely; the house of David; the house of Nathan; the house of Levi; and the house of Shemei. Thus we see the royal, prophetic, and priestly families all in mourning. Every individual will search his own heart, the wives apart from their husbands, and the husbands apart from their wives. Every individual will face his own sin, with a private outpouring of tears.

False Professions

Today we see professions made with no contrition, no mourning over one's sin, no true repentance, and no tears. What is the result? Virgins with no oil in their vessel (Matt. 25:3)! False professors, with no foundation (Lk.6:49). Of such the Lord says, "And why call ye Me, Lord, Lord, and do not the things which I say?" (Lk. 6:46). David, when convicted of his sin, cried, "For Thine arrows stick fast in me, and Thy hand presseth me sore. There is no soundness in my flesh because of Thine anger; neither is there any rest in my bones because of my sin. For mine iniquities are gone over mine head: as an heavy burden they are too heavy for me. My wounds stink and are corrupt because of my foolishness. I am troubled; I am bowed down greatly; I go mourning all the day long. For my loins are filled with a loathsome disease: and there is no soundness in my flesh. I am feeble and sore broken: I have roared by reason of the disquietness of my heart" (Ps. 38:2-8).

"Only Believe" ? ?

It is very distressing to see so-called "soul-winners" telling souls to "only believe." Christ said, "I tell you, Nay: but, except ye repent, ye shall all likewise perish" (Lk. 13:3). What is needed in gospel preaching is the preaching of sin and its terrible consequences, for unless there is a solemn awakening to the stark facts, there can be no true repentance wrought in the soul, and apart from true repentance, there can be no salvation. David L. Roy, a godly servant of the Lord, made tremendous impressions on our heart. He advised me, "When preaching the gospel, give them a big rope of law at the beginning, and a wee thread of grace at the end." Good advice! The late William Warke, with whom I labored for twelve years, lamented, "We are living in the day of tearless professions." Israel will weep, lament, mourn, and smite their breasts over their sin – then God will save them. Again I say, what a glorious day that will be!

A Fountain

Zechariah moves on from families to a fountain. "In that day there shall be a fountain opened to the house of David and to the inhabitants of Jerusalem for sin and for uncleanness" (Zech. 13:1). The force of the word *opened* is, *shall remain open.*

One writer states, "There is the washing of water by the word. There is no such thing in scripture as a fountain of blood, spite of our own poet Cowper. To be cleansed by blood is not enough. We need to be bathed in water and to wash our feet also day by day…it is the water not the blood. Here the Spirit uses the word as the moral power of the death of Christ doubtless; but still it is the word" (The Minor Prophets by William Kelly). Another writer states, "The day of atonement brings them to the cross. The next step is the laver, to which the fountain answers. Observe well, it is not, as poets have sung, 'a fountain filled with blood,' but of living *water* – the word of God applied in the Spirit's power to their consciences" (Notes on the Minor Prophets, by H.A, Ironside).

However, in scripture there ARE fountains of blood. The woman who gave birth to a child, on the day of her purifying the priest was to offer her sacrifice "before the

LORD, and make an atonement for her; and she shall be cleansed from the issue (fountain) of her blood. This is the law for her that hath born a male or a female" (Lev. 12:7). We also have these words in Leviticus 20:18, "the fountain of her blood." In both instances we have uncleanness associated with the fountain of blood. How different is the fountain in Zechariah 13:1. It is opened for sin and uncleanness. Being washed in the blood is certainly a scriptural expression. John, by the Spirit exclaims, "Jesus Christ, who is the faithful witness, and the first begotten of the dead, and the Prince of the kings of the earth. Unto Him that loved (loveth) us, and ***washed*** us from our sins in His own blood" (Rev.1:5).

That blessed fountain was opened at Calvary as William Cowper beautifully wrote.

"There is a fountain filled with blood
Drawn from Immanuel's veins,
And sinners plunged beneath that flood
Lose all their guilty stains."

A Closed Fountain

That fountain is opened to every individual on earth today, and its cleansing is available to all, including every Jew on an individual basis. However, as far as the nation of Israel is concerned, that fountain, nationally speaking, was closed to the nation upon their rejection of the Messiah. The final message of the nation was sent to God at the murder of Stephen, "We will not have this Man to reign over us" (Lk.19:14; Acts 7:54-60). Thus the nation has been set aside until that day comes, when it will experience atonement. Presently the state of the nation is described by Paul. "And not as Moses, which put a vail over his face, that the children of Israel could not stedfastly look to the end of that which is abolished: But their minds were blinded: for until this day remaineth the same vail untaken away in the reading of the old testament; which vail is done away in Christ. But even unto this day, when Moses is read, the vail is upon their heart. Nevertheless when it (the godly remnant of Israel) shall turn to the Lord, the vail shall be taken away" (2 Cor. 3:13-16). Their turning to the Lord will be "in that day," which we have been considering. We have a similar thought in Romans 11:25-27. "Blindness in part is happened to Israel, until the fulness of the Gentiles be come in. And so all Israel shall be saved: as it is written, There shall come out of Sion the Deliverer, and shall turn away ungodliness from Jacob: For this is My covenant unto them, when I shall take away their sins." Then God will open the Fountain for that nation.

The Shepherd and the Opened Fountain

Opening the Fountain at Calvary involved an announcement. "Awake, O sword, against My Shepherd, and against the Man that is my Fellow, saith the LORD of hosts: smite the Shepherd, and the sheep shall be scattered: and I will turn Mine hand upon the little ones" (Zech. 13:7).

In the New Testament, the Lord is described as a Shepherd in different aspects. In the Gospel of John, chapter ten He is portrayed as the good Shepherd. "I am the good Shepherd: the good Shepherd giveth His life for the sheep…I am the good Shepherd, and know My sheep, and am known of Mine" (Vs.11-14). The word *good* carries the thought of: better; honest; excellent; genuine, approved; beautiful by reason of purity of heart and life, and hence praise worthy; affecting the mind agreeably, comforting and confirming."

In Hebrews chapter thirteen, we find this description; "Now the God of peace, that brought again from the dead our Lord Jesus, that great Shepherd of the sheep, through the blood of the everlasting covenant, Make you perfect in every good work to do His will, working in you that which is wellpleasing in His sight, through Jesus Christ; to Whom be glory for ever and ever. Amen" (Vs. 20,21). The word *great* indicates a person of rank, a person eminent for ability, virtue, authority, and power, One esteemed highly for his importance and excellence.

Peter addresses elders regarding the Lord; "And when the chief Shepherd shall appear, ye shall receive a crown of glory that fadeth not away" (1 Pet. 5:4). The word chief indicates Christ as the Head of the Church, which is His body.

In the Good Shepherd, we see the excellence and approval of His atoning sacrifice in the eyes of God. He is beautiful to us, thus praiseworthy.

In the Great Shepherd, we discover One raised from amongst the dead, now seated at the right hand of the Majesty on high, engaged in priestly activity for us. As such, we appreciate His ability, authority, and power, thus we esteem Him highly for His excellence.

In the Chief Shepherd, elders recognize the Head, controlling all the members. They have been exhorted to "feed the flock of God," and in doing so, "not as being lords over God's heritage, but being ensamples to the flock." Having acted according to the will of their Head, He will, as the Chief Shepherd, reward them with a crown of glory, that shall never fade away.

Zechariah points us to God's Shepherd Who endured the cross (Zech. 13:7). There is absolutely no doubt as to the Messianic quality of this verse, for the Lord uses it in relation to Himself. "Then saith Jesus unto them, All ye shall be offended because of Me this night: for it is written, I will smite the Shepherd, and the sheep of the flock shall be scattered abroad" (Matt. 26:31). The prophetic statement brings before us very vividly the ***death*** and the ***deity*** of our Lord. Not only this, but also the ***dictation*** of God, the ***dispersion*** of the flock, and the ***distress*** of the little ones.

The Sword

The sword is a figure of death and God issues the command for His Fellow to die. This was motivated by righteousness and love. "For God so loved the world, that He gave His only begotten Son" (Jn. 3:16). To impart salvation to us who were sinners, it was an absolute necessity for God to make Him "to be sin for us, who knew no sin; that we might be made the righteousness of God in Him" (2 Cor. 5:21). He was treated as sin deserved to be treated. Amazing, yet blessedly true! He was "stricken, smitten of God, and afflicted" (Isa. 53;4). In the death of Christ, we observe God's sovereignty, and man's responsibility involved. Israel was charged with His death, yet God planned it. As Peter addressed the nation, this truth was uttered on the day of Pentecost; "Him, being delivered by the determinate counsel and foreknowledge of God, ye have taken, and by wicked hands have crucified and slain" (Acts 2:23).

As the Lord Jesus moved about doing good and healing those that were oppressed of the devil, He brought infinite delight to the Father's heart, thus the sword slept. However, the moment He took the place of sin-bearer, that sword awakened out of its sleep to smite the Shepherd. How beautiful are the words of Anne Ross Cousin:

"Jehovah bade His sword awake;
O Christ, it woke 'gainst Thee!
Thy blood the flaming blade must slake,
Thy heart its sheath must be;
All for my sake my peace to make,
Now sleeps that sword for me."

God's Fellow

The One smitten was a Man, indicating the humanity of Christ. He was also the Father's *Fellow*. What does this mean, *Fellow*? "*Amiyth*" is from a primitive root meaning to associate, a comrade. It is used of an equal, an associate, one on an equal status. Only one Man could ever claim this position, God manifest in the flesh, the Lord Jesus Christ. Thus we see His absolute deity. It has been rendered, "The Man My equal," by DeWette.

Scattered Sheep

Resulting from the Shepherd's death was the scattering of the sheep. Israel is metaphorically spoken of as a flock. In A.D. 70, Titus besieged Jerusalem and overthrew it. Following the destruction of Jerusalem, because of the nation's sin in rejecting its Messiah, a worldwide dispersion of the Jews took place, and remains until this day.

The Little Ones

The prophet also adds, "I will turn mine hand upon the little ones." These compose a little remnant, those of His own. The word meaning, "those who appear as little, those who make themselves small." They are humble. Just as their Lord was persecuted, so they would experience the same. Believers in Christ are accounted as nothing in the eyes of a godless society. Pagan Rome put to death over six million saints, Papal Rome exceeded with over sixty million brought to the slaughter. The Lord forewarned His own "The servant is not greater than his lord. If they have persecuted Me, they will also persecute you" (Jn.15:20). Just as God programmed the death of Christ, in like manner, He programmed the tribulations that would befall His little ones.

How mysterious are the ways of God, yet we must remember this, that all is in His control, and all is ultimately for our eternal blessing and good. Just as the cedar walls of Solomon's magnificent temple endured the hammer and the chisel, as intricate designs were incorporated into the wood, then overlaid with silver and then gold; so God with us, uses trials as the carving tools to engrave a beautiful design, which in the glory shall be seen in the overlaying gold, to His glory and ours.

"Ye fearful saints fresh courage take;
The clouds ye so much dread
Are big with mercy, and shall break
In blessings on your head.

His purposes will ripen fast,
Unfolding ever hour;
The bud may have a bitter taste,
But sweet will be the flower."

The Mount of Olives

Zechariah, in the closing of his prophecy, points to future days relative to the coming kingdom, the mount of Olives cleaving in the midst as the King descends from heaven and stands on the mount. Living waters shall go out from Jerusalem; half of them toward the eastern sea; half of them toward the western sea. The LORD shall be King over the whole earth. "And the wealth of all the heathen round about shall be gathered together, gold, and silver, and apparel, in great abundance…And it shall come to pass, that every one that is left of all the nations which came against Jerusalem shall even go up from year to year to worship the King, the LORD of hosts, and to keep the feast of tabernacles" (Zech. 14: 14,16). The prophet ends by giving us a glimpse of the atmosphere of His millennial reign, with these inspiring words - "HOLINESS UNTO THE LORD."

O what a glorious day that will be,
When Satan is bound and is cast
Into the pit, for a thousand years,
Peace there will be at long last!

With pierced hands and feet and side,
Messiah as High Priest will reign.
From sea to sea, all will bow to Him,
The creation no longer in pain.

An abundant entrance will be ours,
To His kingdom in that day.
For if we suffer, we shall reign with Him,
As He rules in kingly array.

CHAPTER NINE
Ezra The Skillful Scribe

FIFTY-SEVEN YEARS have rolled their course. Zerubbabel, the governor; Jeshua, the high priest; and Haggai and Zechariah, the prophets, have all passed off the scene, and the grandson of Darius is now king. Conditions in the land have deteriorated. In clear violation to the word of God, many had taken heathen wives, and along with the mixed marriages naturally would come the participation in idolatrous heathen festivals.

The Worth of Ezra

However, God had a man in the shadows to correct such fallen conditions – Ezra by name. He was a most unique man, a man raised up of God for the occasion. Great men of God realize their own weakness, and in all their endeavors, count on God for help. Ezra fit that criterion. He could trace his genealogy back to Aaron, Israel's first high priest, but even though he was a priest by birth, yet he became a skillful scribe in the law of His God only by diligent work. Notice the Spirit's evaluation of the man. "He was a ready (skillful, diligent) scribe in the law of Moses" (Ezra 7:6). "For Ezra had prepared his heart to seek the law of the

LORD, and to do it, and to teach in Israel statutes and judgments" (Ezra 7:10). The same holds true today. Believers are constituted priests unto God, immediately upon receiving Christ as Lord and Saviour, but becoming skillful in the word of God is another matter. Salvation is by God's grace, but skillfulness in divine things comes only by hard work. Paul exhorted Timothy, "Occupy thyself with these things (the holy scriptures); be wholly in them, that thy progress may be manifest to all" (1 Tim. 4:15, Darby).

Men that are used of God in spiritually ministering profitably to the Lord's people are men that have spent many hours alone in the sanctuary with God and with God's Book. Like Ezra, they have sought for the knowledge of God and His word, putting forth much effort to acquire it. They have devoted themselves to the investigation of divine truths contained in the Book. Growing in grace, and in the knowledge of our Lord and Saviour Jesus Christ does not come by viewing nature, nor does it come from higher education; it comes solely from time with the Book.

The Sufficiency of the Book

Many problems that have devastated assemblies could have been avoided if only the shepherds had been men of the Book. Some Christians have turned to psychiatrists for help, simply because they were not Christians of the Book. The Holy Book is able to solve every single existing problem that might befall individuals or assemblies - if only the plagued ones were acquainted with it. As I stated, a personal acquaintance with the Book comes only through a diligent study of it. To spend only fifteen minutes a day with the Book is almost like an insult to God, It takes a normal reader, at the longest, about sixty hours to read the Holy Scriptures from cover to cover. That averages only ten minutes a day. Yet to our shame, many professing Christians, who have been saved for years, have never read entirely through the Book.

I knew a godly lady who read the Holy Scriptures through six times a year. She also worked eight hours a day in a factory office. She didn't ***have time*** to read the Book – she ***took time*** to read the Book! Another sister, I know very well, has handwritten the Holy Scriptures from Genesis 1:1 to Revelation 22:21. Her handwritten Bible is stored in the attic, and she is contemplating handwriting a second copy.

American Children

Recent statistics show that, "American children spend more time watching TV than any other activity, besides sleeping. In fact, by the time the average American child is six, she will spend more time watching TV than talking to her own father in her lifetime. This trend starts early, typically U.S. children begin watching television as early as six months, and are fervent viewers by the time they are two or three years old. By the time children are in school, they watch an average of four hours a day, 28 hours a week, and 1,456 hours a year. By the time they are through high school they will have spent 26,936 hours watching television."

Can you picture what kind of a Christian one would develop into, if this "children's attitude" was in them regarding the Bible? What kind of a believer would you see if that person gave themselves to the intense study of God's word four hours every day? Can you picture a believer reading the scriptures from cover to cover twenty-four times every year? That is what would happen if that person devoted four hours a day simply to reading the Bible. But there is more to godliness than simply reading the Bible. There is the meditating upon what has been read; there is the diligent searching out of the scriptures; there is the bowing in obedience to what has been read.

The man of the Book has little time for the frivolous toys that the world has to offer. His time is too valuable, too precious, to be wasting it on transient things that will amount to nothing in the spiritual realm, nor will they amount to anything at the judgment seat of Christ. Why is it Christians turn to sports, theaters, and other time-consuming activities? It is because they have lost their appetite for the wholesome word of God. When this is the case, they become spiritual Pygmies, and open to every susceptible spiritual virus and disease.

The Computer

The computer has also been introduced in our spiritual warfare to disarm us. Hours upon hours are being spent on the Internet - for what? It certainly is not for an education in spiritual things; not to develop a closer walk with God; not to increase one's spirituality. The whole affair simply wastes valuable time that could have been spent examining the scriptures. Job confessed, "I have esteemed the words of His mouth more than my necessary food" (Job 23:12). Do you spend as much time in God's banqueting house feeding on His word as you do at the table for breakfast, lunch, supper, and snacks in between? Or is your stomach more important than your soul? The U.S. Department of Health and Human Services says that one third of adult Americans are obese. They love to eat, they love their stomachs. This can be contrasted to the spiritual realm, where most suffer from frailty and leanness of soul. It seems today that many saints are plagued with spiritual anorexia. They certainly cannot exclaim like Jeremiah, "Thy words were found, and I did eat them; and Thy word was unto me the joy and rejoicing of mine heart" (Jer. 15:16). Their feeding on the word of God is minimal.

We have the strange concept that to keep our young believers we must keep them busy with activity, and with social events. However, the word of God is clear that the only preservation of a young believer is the word of God. "Thy word have I hid in mine heart, that I might not sin against Thee" (Ps. 119:11). "By the word of Thy lips I have kept me from the paths of the destroyer" (Ps. 17:4). Peter emphasizes the importance of the Book. "As newborn babes, desire the sincere milk of the word, that ye may grow thereby" (1 Pet. 2:2).

How rich are the words of the psalmist in his appreciation for the scriptures.

"O how love I thy law!
it is my meditation all the day.
I have rejoiced in the way of thy testimonies,
as much as in all riches." (Ps.119:97,14).

Ezra was a man of the Book, a skillful scribe in the law of Moses. In fact, Jewish history claims that he could quote the whole Bible by memory, which at that time included every Old Testament book except Malachi. The same memory ability is attributed to Nicodemus, who came to Jesus by night (Jn.3). Ezra was raised in an atmosphere that was famed for literature. The Chaldeans were famed for their study of the stars, and being a studious man he may have been tempted to follow the norm of his day. However, it was not the heavenly stars that he chose to occupy his time with intense study, but rather the Holy Scriptures. There are folks that invest money in expensive telescopes to study the universe, and there are people who are engrossed with geology and invest heavily to pursue their quest. Far better to spend one's precious time in studying the Bright and Morning Star, and the Rock of Ages. Ezra spent his time searching out, investigating, the Holy Scriptures. He was a diligent scribe.

Scribism seemed to rise when prophecy declined. Their work was to teach, interpret, and apply the law of God. Also attributed to Ezra was the fact that history claims him to be the founder of the Great Synagogue, and to him is credited the placing of the books of the Old Testament in order.

One Man

Have you noticed how often God uses one man to accomplish His purposes? Some of the greatest works accomplished for God have been done, not by multitudes, but just one person. Who did God use to deliver Israel from Egypt? – Moses! Who delivered Israel from the Philistines? – Samson! Who gathered the people together to crush the Midianites? – Gideon! Who was it that rescued the nation by slaying the giant? – David! Separate men, raised up and used of God. Ezra was such a man.

The basic purpose of his going was because he knew of a need in Israel. This worthy scribe had prepared his heart to seek the law of the LORD, and to do it, and to teach in Israel statutes and judgments. The word *statutes* means, *to engrave, to set down in writing,* and would involve precepts and rules to be strictly obeyed. *Judgments* means, *to set upright – to judge,* thus judicial writings. You will observe the area of Ezra's motivation – "his heart." He not only sought the law of the LORD, but he obeyed what he learned – he did it. His discoveries were turned unto deeds. This is the secret of advancing in learning. "If any man will do His will, he shall know of the doctrine" (Jn. 7:17). Following that exercise, he taught God's statutes and judgments. There is a vital lesson here. It is absolutely useless to seek to influence God's people to holier living through one's teaching, if the teacher himself is not bowing to the truth of God. Can you picture a minister of the word playing jokes on people and then standing before them and exhorting them to sobriety? The whole idea is obnoxious, to say the least! Yet I have seen it, much to my grief. If a servant of the Lord is toying with the world, and at the same time exhorting God's people to "love not the world," how can you expect his words to be taken seriously, and his advice followed? You can't, it is impossible!

A man may be an intellectual student of the Book, but if the truth of God never grips his own heart, causing total submission to God's ways, he will have no power. He may preach with eloquence, he may be dramatic, he may be an orator, he may be popular, but he will lack the vital essential, and that is, Holy Ghost power! Ezra was a man who lived what he preached, thus he was respected and his words had grip and power, and so were heeded. One could say of him, his affections were controlled by the Book; his walk was controlled by the Book; his words were controlled by the Book; consequently he could be called, *a man of the Book.* Men of such caliber are exceedingly valuable today.

God's Hand

You will notice that the hand of the LORD his God was upon him. God's hand is mentioned three times in relation to Ezra, all of them in chapter seven. The references are found in verses six, nine, and twenty-eight. In verse six he finds favor with the king; verse nine, a prosperous and safe journey; and verse twenty-eight, strength to initiate and carry out his plans. Thus we see supplication, safety, and strength. Not only is God's hand mentioned, but also Ezra's hand is mentioned in verse fourteen and in verse twenty-five. "The law of thy God which is in thine hand…the wisdom of thy God, that is in thine hand."

Ezra's Hand

The law of God being in his hand would convey to us that this scribe was familiar with the Book, and well able to apply its truths to the hearts of the ignorant. The wisdom of God in his hand reveals that this man possessed God-given wisdom, the ability to apply his knowledge of the Book profitably. A lack of knowledge has destroyed many people, it destroyed the nation of Israel. God laments, "My people are destroyed for lack of knowledge" (Hos.4:6). Paul informs Christians, "But of Him are ye in Christ Jesus, Who of God is made unto us wisdom" (1 Cor. 1:30). Christ is the believer's source of wisdom, it is through Him that we are made wise. We are wise through the scriptures. This wisdom is to be sought for. "If any of you lack wisdom, let him ask of God, that giveth to all men liberally, and upbraideth not; and it shall be given him" (Jas. 1:5). There is no excuse for ignorance in the believer's life. Why do some saints make terrible blunders? Why do they make horrible mistakes, that produce traumatic effects on their lives? It all goes back to the fact that they have not been familiar with the Book. Their lack of knowledge of the Book has deprived them of the wisdom that is from above. It is most sad to see, when the resources of wisdom lay near at hand, yet are never apprehended. To be lacking in wisdom, when it could be had, is a tragedy indeed. Ezra had the wisdom of God in his hand. We might also add that God had the heart of the king in His hand, thus Ezra found favor in the king's sight.

The Walk of Ezra

"Ezra went up from Babylon...and the king granted him all his request, according to the hand of the LORD his God upon him. And there went up some of the children of Israel, and of the priests, and the Levites, and the singers, and the porters, and the Nethinims, unto Jerusalem, in the seventh year of Artaxerxes the king. And he came to Jerusalem in the fifth month, which was in the seventh year of the king. For upon the first day of the first month began he to go up from Babylon, and on the first day of the fifth month came he to Jerusalem, according to the good hand of his God upon him" (Ezra 7:6-9). In our modern day of travel, we certainly are not familiar with four-month journeys. Neither are we familiar with journeys that could prove very dangerous due to bandits along the way.

No doubt this man Ezra had made very favorable impressions on the king. He would be a man that would give honor to whom honor was due. He would be a man whose life would speak deeply to a heathen's heart. In our day, let us consider men that God has governmentally positioned over us. We are told to pray for them (1 Tim. 2:1,2), to honor them (1 Pet. 2:17), to pay tribute to them (Rom:13:7), to obey them (Rom. 13:1) and not to speak evil of them (Acts 25:5). We are even obligated to honor our employer, that the word of God be not blasphemed (1 Tim. 6:1). Having requested of the king to go up to Jerusalem, the king granted to him his petition.

Not only did the king grant Ezra his request because of the scribe's character, but because the hand of God had moved the king's heart favorably toward Ezra. This is generally the outcome when a man's ways please the Lord. Solomon observed that, "When a man's ways please the LORD, He maketh even his enemies to be at peace with him" (Prov.16:7).

It is readily seen that Ezra was a distinguished man and one of great influence. Not only was permission given, but also the king was so interested in this venture that he issued a decree. The words of the decree are recorded in 7:13–26. He consented to let all those of Israel return to Jerusalem of their own free will. There was no pressure, no command, it was all on a voluntary basis. God desires willing servants, not pressured servants. God never forces us to worship, to pray, to preach, or to give of our substance. God values and uses only willing hearts.

The king was influenced, also some of the children of Israel, the priests, the Levites, the singers, the porters, and the Nethinims, were influenced – and Ezra moved! On the first day of the first month, over fifteen hundred left Babylon and arrived at Jerusalem four months later to the very day. A direct route would have been about 500 miles, but it is generally believed that they took the safer northern route which would involve a distance of about 900 miles. Even at that, an average of only 7 or 8 miles a day seems a slow pace. More than likely they rested at intervals along the tedious route for the sake of mothers and children.

Ezra's Faith

What great faith Ezra had in his God! "For I was ashamed to require of the king a band of soldiers and horsemen to help us against the enemy in the way: because we had spoken unto the king, saying, The hand of our God is upon all them for good that seek Him; but His power and His wrath is against all them that forsake Him" (Ezra 8:22). Ezra knew that the king would be willing to send a band of soldiers along with the little company to assure them of safety all the way. Ezra was willing, not only to maintain a testimony of faith before the king, but also to put his life and the lives of all that went with him into the hands of God, the God of hosts (armies).

In our modern day there are all kinds of human insurance policies. However, divine insurance policies have a far greater coverage. Notice some of the many benefits. "The angel of the LORD encampeth round about them that fear Him, and delivereth them" (Ps. 34:7). "For He shall give His angels charge over thee, to keep thee in all thy ways" (Ps. 91:11). "Let your conversation be without covetousness; and be content with such things as ye have: for He hath said, I will never leave thee, nor forsake thee" (Heb.13:5). "Wherefore, if God so clothe the grass of the field, which to day is, and to morrow is cast into the oven, shall He not much more clothe you, O ye of little faith?" (Matt. 6:30). Now these are wonderful promises, not to be taken lightly. Ezra was ashamed to ask of the king, for in doing so he would have lowered his testimony of faith in the king's eyes.

A Farmer's Experience

There was a godly brother who operated a large farm. He always trusted in the Lord to preserve his crops from hail damage. However, one year the government made it very attractive to apply for hail insurance, which he did. A neighboring farmer happened to be at the same place applying for hail insurance and noticing the Christian farmer, rebuked him, knowing that the Christian had always claimed that his God could protect his crops. The brother's heart was immediately smitten.

Ezra was ashamed to ask – his testimony was at stake, and with no human army to afford protection, the journey began. I have no doubt but that holy mighty angels surrounded the little camp as they made their way back to the city of God.

In passing, we may add that this was a "religious mission." The mission of Nehemiah was different. Nehemiah was a political official of the king, which required a military escort, for as far as the king was concerned, the mission was political. There was no request on the part of Nehemiah for the king's protection; it was the king who sent the army. (Neh.2:10).

Ahava

Nine days on their journey, and about eighty miles northeast of Babylon, they encamped at Ahava for three days (Ezra 8:15, 31). While there we read of Ezra, " I viewed the people, and the priests, and found there none of the sons of Levi. Then sent I for Eliezer, for Ariel, for Shemaiah, and for Elnathan, and for Jarib, and for Elnathan, and for Nathan, and for Zechariah, and for Meshullam, chief men; also for Joiarib, and for Elnathan, men of understanding. And I sent them with commandment unto Iddo the chief at the place Casiphia, and I told them what they should say unto Iddo, and to his brethren the Nethinims, at the place Casiphia, that they should bring unto us ministers for the house of our God. And by the good hand of our God upon us they brought us a man of understanding, of the sons of Mahli, the son of Levi, the son of Israel; and Sherebiah, with his sons and his brethren, eighteen; And Hashabiah, and with him Jeshaiah of the sons of Merari, his brethren and their sons, twenty" (Ezra 8:15-19).

Perhaps the sons of Levi, dwelling quite comfortably in Babylon, and having no inheritance in the land, had no fleshly reason for living in Jerusalem. In other words, it seems that temporal comfort meant more to them than sacrificing an easy life for God and His testimony. We are living in a day of luxury and self-pleasing where making sacrifices for God and His testimony are not the normal way of life.

Lives For God – David Livingstone

One's heart is touched reading of men who sacrificed their lives for God. David Livingstone was born in the Scottish Highlands and gave his life for God in Africa. He swam rivers infested with crocodiles, and faced cannibal tribes ready to murder him. After a trip on the Zambezi River, his wife became ill and died. He said that, as he placed her body in the earth, he buried his heart with her. Yet he went on for God, facing death many times. He died in an African hut while praying on his knees. His life a sacrifice, recorded in heaven.

J. Hudson Taylor – William Carey

J. Hudson Taylor, an Englishman, gave fifty-one years of his life for God in China. William Carey left England to labor for God faithfully in India. His wife went insane four years before her death, but he had the joy of seeing three of his four sons become missionaries in the Orient.

The Apostle Paul

Perhaps the most familiar missionary of all would be the apostle Paul. He sacrificed a great position as teacher in Israel, to become, "as the filth of the world and…the offscouring of all things" (1 Cor. 4:13). What a missionary report we have of him on the pages of scripture. "In labours more abundant, in stripes above measure, in prisons more frequent, in deaths oft. Of the Jews five times received I forty stripes save one. Thrice was I beaten with rods, once was I stoned, thrice I suffered shipwreck, a night and a day I have been in the deep; In journeyings often, in perils of waters, in perils of robbers, in perils by mine own country-men, in perils by the heathen, in perils in the city, in perils in the wilderness, in perils in the sea, in perils among false brethren; In weariness and painfulness, in watchings often, in hunger and thirst, in fastings often, in cold and nakedness" (2 Cor. 11: 23-27). We know little of sacrifice today.

The Levites

However, as Ezra views the situation, he sees the need of Levites in the work of God in the temple. He sends for the chief men and for Joiarib and for Elnathen, men of understanding. They were intelligent men with discernment, men who could teach. Ezra saw the importance of getting qualified men to get a job done. There is a principle here to learn. When the time comes for an assembly to present the gospel, who should they appoint? There is a strange notion among us that everyone should have their turn. That is interesting, for if that be the case, why then has the Holy Spirit imparted particular gifts?

Not that I am interested in baseball, but let me use an analogy related to it. Do you think that the team manager would say, "Well now, I think that it would be nice if the outfielder, then the first-base man, each had a turn on the pitching mound. We will just put the pitcher behind home plate and let him have a turn at catching, and put the catcher on the mound to pitch." Let me say, it would be considered folly, and they would never win a game. Yet in God's assemblies, some seem to think that all should have their turn at preaching the gospel, whether qualified or not. No, brethren, the Spirit has imparted gifts, and when the gift of preaching the gospel is detected in a brother, he is to be encouraged to develop that gift through preaching.

Ezra, having engaged qualified men, nine of them chief men and two of them men of understanding, he sent them to a nearby village called Casiphia to seek ministers for the house of God. Being competent men, they would be more likely to succeed in Ezra's mission than men of an inferior quality. Important work requires qualified men, even today. Seemingly both Levites and Nethinims, the upper and lower order of temple ministers, had settled there, Iddo being the chief man there. It has been surmised that Iddo headed a college there for the instruction of Levites and Nethinims, but this is only conjecture.

Having accomplished their mission successfully, the twelve men brought back with them "a man of understanding, of the sons of Mahli, the son of Levi, the son of Israel; and Sherebiah, with his sons and his brethren, eighteen; And Hashabiah, and with him Jeshaiah of the sons of Merari, his brethren and their sons, twenty; Also of the Nethinims, whom David and the princes had appointed for the service of the Levites, two hundred and twenty Nethinims: all of them were expressed by name" (Ezra 8:18-20). Thus Ezra sent the right men, to the right place, to the right person (Iddo), with the right words "I told them what they should say" (vs. 17). The Hebrew equivalent is, "I put words in their mouth."

Fasting

After successfully adding essential men to their company, they didn't hold a feast, but rather proclaimed a fast and afflicted themselves. There seemed to be an extreme consciousness of God with them. Solomon wisely said, "To every thing there is a season, and a time to every purpose under the heaven…A time to weep, and a time to laugh; a time to mourn, and a time to dance; (Eccl.3:1,4). This was an occasion of great searching of heart before God. They had taken a stand before the king, declaring the all-sufficiency of their God, His omnipotence and ability to keep them safely all along their perilous journey that lay ahead.

However, it is one thing to proclaim God, but quite another thing to prove God. They were now about to prove God in a very practical way, consequently they proclaimed a fast that they might afflict, or humble, their souls. Peter advises us, “Humble yourselves therefore under the mighty hand of God, that He may exalt you in due time” (1 Pet. 5:6). James counsels, “Humble yourselves in the sight of the Lord, and He shall lift you up” (Jas.4:10). So far, Ezra had seen nothing but success. He had been successful in his request to the king. He had been successful in gathering a following of over fifteen hundred men. He had been successful in obtaining Levites from Casiphia. What was the result of all this? He was humble!

In fasting (starving the flesh) and humbling themselves before God, they sought of God *a right way,* for themselves, for their little ones and their substance. *A right way* simply means *a straight way, a way made level by the removing of obstructions.* In other words, a prosperous journey. Ezra was interested in little ones – are we? Some brethren feel themselves too important for children’s work. What a biased attitude! Notice the words of our blessed Lord, “Suffer the little children to come unto Me, and forbid them not” (Mk. 10:14). One should not underestimate the importance of dealing with the souls of children. What a privilege to sow the living seed into little hearts, where it can abide and be used later by the Holy Spirit to their awakening and conversion to Christ. There are older sinners today that still remember the scriptures they learned through the exercise of a godly saint sowing the seed into their little hearts in their childhood. "Let us not be weary in well doing" (Gal. 6:9). The great man Ezra fasted, afflicted his soul before God and prayed for the little ones. God was entreated of them.

"Through a desert, waste and cheerless,
Though our destined journey lie,
Rendered by Thy presence fearless
We may every foe defy:
Naught shall move us
While we see Thee, Saviour, nigh."

Holy Vessels

Following their intimate meeting with God, Ezra then selected twelve priests that were just brought from Casiphia, and ten of their brethren with them, "And weighed unto them the silver, and the gold, and the vessels, even the offering of the house of our God, which the king, and his counsellors, and his lords, and all Israel there present, had offered" (Ezra 8:25). The offering came from three sources – first, the gifts of the king and his counsellors; second, the collection taken by Ezra from the non-Israelites; third, the voluntary offerings of the people of Israel (Ezra 7:15,16).

Considering the importance of the trust, Ezra charges the twenty-two men. "Ye are holy unto the LORD; the vessels are holy also; and the silver and the gold are a freewill offering unto the LORD God of your fathers. Watch ye, and keep them, until ye weigh them before the chief of the priests and the Levites, and chief of the fathers of Israel, at Jerusalem, in the chambers of the house of the LORD" (Ezra 8:28,29). The value was high, amounting to approximately

74,100 pounds of silver, and 11,400 pounds of gold. The truths of God could easily be compared to these vessels – both are precious and useful in the temple of God. The gold would symbolize truths relating to the deity of Christ, while the silver would remind us of His redemptive work. The vessels were entrusted to the chief of the priests, and their ten brethren, who were carefully chosen beforehand. Even so today, "ye are a chosen generation, a royal priesthood" and as priests, we have had entrusted to us precious divine truths (1 Pet. 2:9).

Alert Shepherds

Watchfulness was required, meaning *to be alert.* It carries the thought of sleeplessness. Shepherds who have had precious truths committed to them are to feed those truths to the flock and in doing so, to be very careful not to let any of those truths be diminished or lost. Paul warned the Ephesian elders with these terse words, "Take heed therefore unto yourselves, and to all the flock, over the which the Holy Ghost hath made you overseers, to feed the church of God, which He hath purchased with His own blood. For I know this, that after my departing shall grievous wolves enter in among you, not sparing the flock. Also of your own selves shall men arise, speaking perverse things, to draw away disciples after them. Therefore watch, and remember, that by the space of three years I ceased not to warn every one night and day with tears" (Acts 20: 28-31).

Since a scriptural assembly can rise no higher in quality than the shepherds, how essential it is that the shepherds guard tenaciously the precious truth of God. The priests journeying on to the earthly Jerusalem were plainly told,

"Watch ye, and keep them" (Ezra 8: 29). Not until they reached the city could they relax. Neither can shepherds relax today, as they journey on to the heavenly Jerusalem. We often hear the world say, *Take it easy*. Since when are we told to *take it easy?* I think the very opposite. What most of us need is more energy in the things of God and less casualness. Do we have the attitude that Jude enjoins upon us? "Ye should earnestly contend for the faith which was once (and for all) delivered unto the saints" (Jude 1:3).

Arrival at Jerusalem

Commencing the journey from Ahava, they arrived at Jerusalem with this testimony. "The hand of our God was upon us, and He delivered us from the hand of the enemy, and of such as lay in wait by the way" (Ezra 8: 31). Upon arriving they rested for three days and then weighed their guarded treasure in the house of their God. The weight had not diminished.

The lesson is this, that the passage of time should not diminish in any way the precious truths of God. Those truths should carry the same weight with us as when we first began. Alas, this is not always the case. How often one hears, "Oh, I used to think that way, but you know, times have changed and we have to change our methods to conform to society." Even in Israel's history they were warned about tampering with the plain truths of God's word. "Ye shall not add unto the word which I command you, neither shall ye diminish ought from it, that ye may keep the commandments of the LORD your God which I command you…Ye shall observe to do therefore as the LORD your God hath commanded you: ye shall not turn aside to the right hand or to the left" (Deut. 4:2; 5:32). Turning to the right hand would be legalism, while turning to the left would be looseness. Timothy had been entrusted with the truth of the gospel and ministry for the people of God. Paul warned him, "O Timothy, keep (guard) that which is committed to thy trust" (1 Tim. 6:20). Later he addresses the same issue. "And the things that thou hast heard of me among many witnesses, the same commit thou to faithful men, who shall be able to teach others also" (2 Tim. 2:2). Paul himself at the end of his journey could say, "I have kept the faith" (2 Tim. 4:7). He had preserved and held fast the embodiment of divine truth right to the very end. Peter saw the importance of holding fast the unchanging truth. "Wherefore I will not be negligent to put you always in remembrance of these things, though ye know them, and be established in the present truth" (2 Pet. 1:12). May we be preserved from ever having to confess, "truth is fallen in the street" (Isa. 59:14). The committed treasure weighed the same in the house of God as it did by the river side in Ahava.

Following the weighing of every single vessel, we observe the people offering burnt offerings and a sin offering unto the God of Israel. They were not unmindful of the Lord after the great and perilous journey was over. Let us apply a blessed truth to this. When we reach the heavenly city above, things are going to be weighed. Have we held the truths of God, or did we allow them to become diminished in our life on earth? Will we be accounted faithful? Will we hear those coveted words, "Well done, thou good and faithful servant: thou hast been faithful over a few things" (Matt 25:21)? It would do us all good to ever keep in mind, that we shall all stand before the judgment seat of Christ to render an account to our Lord how we have used everything that He has entrusted to our care. We shall give an account of how we used all our material possessions, how we used our time, how we used the spiritual gift imparted to us, and what attitude we maintained toward the Holy Scriptures. It will be a solemn event for us all. As previously stated, following the weighing comes the worship. What a glorious sight that must have been to see such a multitude offering twelve bullocks for all Israel, ninety and six rams, seventy and seven lambs, and twelve he goats for a sin offering (Ezra 8:35). After the judgment seat of Christ, we shall partake in the marriage supper of the Lamb and the worship to Him will begin – and never end! Throughout the eternal ages we shall praise Him in our redeemed bodies, possessing all the fullness of eternal life. What a glorious eternal day that will be!

Artaxerxes' Decree

In the decree of Artaxerxes we see the work that was appointed unto Ezra. Evidently the king sought the favor of Ezra's God as 7:23 reveals. "Whatsoever is commanded by the God of heaven, let it be diligently done for the house of the God of heaven: for why should there be wrath against the realm of the king and his sons?" Ezra had made a tremendous impression on this king by his godliness. Not only this, Ezra must have made it very evident to the king why he lived as he did – he magnified his God.

Your Light

Our Lord mentions the practical truth of this. "Ye are the light of the world. A city that is set on an hill cannot be hid. Neither do men light a candle, and put it under a bushel, but on a candlestick; and it giveth light unto all that are in the house. Let your light so shine before men, that they may see your good works, and glorify your Father which is in heaven" (Matt. 5:14-16).

Just what does it mean to *let your light so shine before men*? The light shining is not your good works, but rather your confession of Christ. Thus, when they see your good works, they associate such behavior with your confession of Christ. In other words, they will say, "That person acts so lovingly because they are now a Christian." Not only this, if they knew you before you were saved and you were a bit on the rough side, after conversion they would say, "I can hardly believe it! He used to curse and now he sings hymns! He formerly visited the pub, now he goes to a prayer meeting! He was mean, now he shows mercy. He was greedy, now he manifests grace. He was contemptible, now he is content. He was selfish, now he is sharing. We wondered what had happened to change such a creature. Then he explained it all, he had found Christ as his Saviour, thus the transformation!" That is what it means to let your light shine. As you witness and produce works of grace in your life, they glorify your Father which is in heaven. They will have to admit, "He has a great God!" Ezra's behavior gave weight to his confession of his God, and it spoke loudly to the king.

Intelligent Worship

The king decreed that, with the money given, they were to buy bullocks, rams, lambs, with their meat offerings and their drink offerings, and offer them upon the altar of the house of their God which is in Jerusalem (Ezra 7:17). Ezra would be restoring scriptural worship in Jerusalem. How fitting to apply these animals to Christ. In the bullock we see the largeness of our Lord, and also the fact that in His sojourn here, He was strong to labor. Considering the ram, we are reminded of the ram of consecration in Leviticus 8:22, pointing us to the consecration of Christ, totally devoted to His God. How beautifully the lamb portrays that One Who was brought as a lamb to the slaughter (Isa. 53:7). His meekness and lowliness comes before us. In Genesis 22 we see the Lamb in Prospect; In Exodus 12, the Lamb in Picture; In Isaiah 53, the Lamb in Prophecy; In John 1, the Lamb in Person; In 1 Peter 1, the Lamb in the Purposes of God; In Revelation 5, the Lamb in Preeminence; In Revelation 6, the Lamb in Power; finally in Revelation 7, the Lamb Providing.

"Lamb of God! our souls adore Thee
While upon Thy face we gaze;
There the Father's love and glory
Shine in all their brightest rays.
Thine almighty power and wisdom
All creation's works proclaim;
Heaven and earth alike confess thee
As the ever great I AM."

The king also made known in his decree, that those involved in the work of the house of God were not to have imposed upon them toll tribute, or custom by the king's lieutenants and governors beyond the river. This principle is practiced in many countries even today.

The wisdom of God was in the hand of Ezra to such a degree that the king acknowledged it. "And thou, Ezra, after the wisdom of thy God, that is in thine hand, set magistrates and judges, which may judge all the people that are beyond the river, all such as know the laws of thy God; and teach ye them that know them not. And whosoever will not do the law of thy God, and the law of the king, let judgment be executed speedily upon him, whether it be unto death, or to banishment, or to confiscation of goods, or to imprisonment" (Ezra 7:25,26).

Government

Not only was worship to be taught and practiced, but judicial government was to be imposed. Evidently, prior to the coming of Ezra into Jerusalem, there was a lack of proper worship and government. One cannot picture such a situation in the days of Zerubbabel, Haggai, and Zechariah, but let us remember, fifty-eight years had passed and the godly influence of these men was gone. They had served their own generation, and passed on. The deplorable conditions that existed as Ezra made his journey to the city, go to show how quickly things can deteriorate when godly men leave the scene.

Discipline

The degrees of punishment correspond with the degrees of punishment, or discipline, to be inflicted in a New Testament Church. First, death. Physical death inflicted in the Old Testament corresponds with excommunication in the New Testament. The sins enumerated for such punishment are found in Matthew 18:15-18, and 1 Corinthians 5:9-13. In the Matthew passage, the brother is put away for his rebellious attitude to the government of the assembly. His case is brought before the church, he is advised as to his sin of trespass against his brother. However, his refusal to hear the church constitutes him a rebellious person, thus he is put out of the fellowship of the church, not for his trespass against the brother, but for his rebellion against the church.

The sins calling for excommunication in 1 Corinthians passage are sixfold. "But now I have written unto you not to keep company, if any man that is called a brother be a fornicator, or covetous, or an idolater, or a railer, or a drunkard, or an extortioner; with such an one no not to eat....Therefore put away from among yourselves that wicked person" (1 Cor. 5: 11,13). Let us explain the list.

Fornicator – the word is *pornia*, where the word *pornography* comes from. It means, *unlawful sexual intercourse.* This includes all, whether married or not married. The word is comprehensive, embracing adultery. It includes incest, sodomy, harlotry, and perversion. The Hebrew word is *Zanah*, and is translated, *whoredom*, and *harlot* in the Old Testament. It is used in Genesis 38:24; Leviticus 19:29; Judges 19:2; Jeremiah 3:1-9; and Ezekiel 16:15, often describing the sexual sin of a married woman, such as the daughters of Moab (Num. 25:1,9), Amazziah's wife (Amos 7:14-17), and Jezebel (2 Ki. 9:22).

Covetous – *one eager to have more, especially what belongs to others, greedy of gain.* Gambling and playing the lottery would come under this category. Some have even considered playing the stock market a mild form of gambling.

Idolater – *a worshipper of false gods, even one who attends their sacrificial feasts.*

Railer *– mischief; abusive, a blackguard.* One who constantly seeks to defame another person.

Drunkard *– intoxicated.* One who has become a slave to strong drink.

Extortioner *– rapacious, a robber.*

Not only are such people to be put away from the assembly, those in the assembly are forbidden to eat with them. This particular word eat is found only five times in the scriptures and always refers to a social meal, never to the Lord's supper (Lk.15:2; Acts 10:41; 11:3; Gal. 2:12). Such wicked ones are forbidden assembly fellowship until fully restored to the Lord, and in the meantime, those in the fellowship are forbidden to socialize with them in any way. To do so will hinder their restoration to God and to the assembly.

Some sins in Israel would call for lesser degrees of punishment, such as banishment, confiscation of goods, or to imprisonment. This would correspond to "warning them that are unruly" (1 Thes. 5:14); withdrawing themselves from every brother that walketh disorderly, and not after the tradition which they received of the apostles (2 Thes. 3:6).

Thus Ezra was commissioned to set up an administration that righteousness might be maintained among the Lord's people. Every scriptural assembly has a government. That government is not democratic in form, nor is it dictorial, but it is theocratic, with a body of elders ruling over the flock in the fear of God. Those in the local church are to obey them and submit themselves to them, as they, the elders, watch for their souls (Heb. 13:17). Elders are to be just and ruling by example, in the fear of God. They will be called upon to give an account of their work at the judgment seat of Christ. Ezra was to see to it that the king's decree was fully carried out.

Ezra's Worship

Upon receiving the writing from the king, Ezra burst forth in praise to his God. "Blessed be the LORD God of our fathers, which hath put such a thing as this in the king's heart, to beautify the house of the LORD which is in Jerusalem: And hath extended mercy unto me before the king, and his counsellors, and before all the king's mighty princes" (Ezra 7:27,28). After arriving at Jerusalem "they delivered the king's commissions unto the king's lieutenants, and to the governors on this side the river: and they furthered the people, and the house of God" (Ezra 8:36).

Distressing News

Ezra chapter nine portrays a sad account. "Now when these things were done, the princes came to me, saying, The people of Israel, and the priests, and the Levites, have not separated themselves from the people of the lands, doing according to their abominations, even of the Canaanites, the Hittites, the Perizzites, the Jebusites, the Ammonites, the Moabites, the Egyptians, and the Amorites. For they have taken of their daughters for themselves, and for their sons: so that the holy seed have mingled themselves with the people of those lands: yea, the hand of the princes and rulers hath been chief in this trespass" (Ezra 9:1,2).

The freedom of intermarriage being practiced was more than just indifference to the law of God. Notice that the princes and rulers were chief in this trespass. They were the wealthier among the people. Poverty and hardship had come upon the remnant, and, being weak, they were quite unable to resist the attacks from the surrounding communities. God's law of separateness, in their eyes, was producing commercial ruin. Their brethren in Babylon were enriching themselves by trade from the heathen, while they in Jerusalem were being held back from foreign commerce, which to the aristocratic families was commercial suicide. By contracting foreign marriages, they felt that such would increase their business dramatically, thus bringing more riches into their accounts. Many marriages were thus established, not because of fond love, but because of filthy lucre.

Ezra, prior to his journey, had been exhorted by the king to teach the law of God to those who knew it not (7:25). After being in Jerusalem over four months (10:9), the princes made Ezra aware of the severity of the people's departure from God. One wonders why it took them over four months to make the situation known to Ezra. Perhaps they were ignorant of the law of God themselves, and through Ezra's expounding God's precepts to them, they became enlightened as to the truth, thus responding favorably.

The Unexpected

It doesn't seem that Ezra expected such a report. To him it was not only shocking, but devastating, so much so that he exclaimed, "When I heard this thing, I rent my garment and my mantle, and plucked off the hair of my head and of my beard, and sat down astonied" (Ezra 9:3). The path of separation had been broken down by mixed marriages. This involves more than meets the eye. Ezra knew very well what this would ultimately lead to. What the people had done was in direct violation of an oft-repeated command. "Thou shalt make no covenant with them, nor with their gods" (Ex.23:32). "Take heed to thyself, lest thou make a covenant with the inhabitants of the land whither thou goest, lest it be for a snare in the midst of thee" (Ex.34:12). "Neither shalt thou make marriages with them; thy daughter thou shalt not give unto his son, nor his daughter shalt thou take unto thy son. For they will turn away thy son from following Me, that they may serve other gods: so will the anger of the LORD be kindled against you, and destroy thee suddenly" (Deut. 7:3,4). "Take good heed therefore unto yourselves, that ye love the LORD your God. Else if ye do in any wise go back, and cleave unto the remnant of these nations, even these that remain among you, and shall make marriages with them, and go in unto them, and they to you…they shall be snares and traps unto you, and scourges in your sides, and thorns in your eyes, until ye perish from off this good land which the LORD your God hath given you." (Josh. 23:11-13).

Ezra knew that mixed marriages would ruin the next generation, that their sons would turn away from following Jehovah, and when that happened, there would be no more testimony to Jehovah in Jerusalem. Not only this, he recognized the fact that what the people were doing was the very reason for God's anger against them, expressed in the destruction of the city, and the captivity of the nation to Babylon over 150 years before. Now the people were repeating past history, the same history that ruined them as far as a testimony was concerned. The very ones whose duty it was to maintain godliness and separation in the land, alas, were chief in this trespass. They had gone astray first and had taken multitudes with them by their unscriptural example. Elders in local assemblies are exhorted to be ensamples to the flock, they are to lead by godly example, they are to be models. Where does departure often germinate, where does it commence? – in the leaders! In the natural realm, sheep always follow their shepherd. In the spiritual realm, sheep have a tendency to follow the example laid down by the shepherds of their assembly. If the shepherds go astray, the sheep are sure to follow. We are living in perilous times. It is distressing to see an assembly commend a man to full-time evangelistic work who does not have the same spiritual convictions of the godly men who have gone on before. What is the result? Such men with a lack of godly convictions create a tremendous influence over younger believers, and gradually the wall of separation is broken down. If this continues the ultimate end will be that scriptural testimonies, gathered unto the name of the Lord Jesus Christ, will be no different in principle and practice than Christendom. Ezra saw the danger in his day, do we see the danger in our day?

The Unequal Yoke

Solomon, as wise as he was, would have set a poor example for Ezra's time. He loved many strange (heathen) women, consequently they turned away his heart after other gods, and the Lord was angry with him (1 Ki. 11:1-9).

Regarding mixed marriages, or any fellowship with a godless world, the word of God is careful to warn us even today. "The wife is bound by the law as long as her husband liveth; but if her husband be dead, she is at liberty to be married to whom she will; only in the Lord" (1 Cor.

7:39). She is not allowed to marry an unbeliever. The Lord warns the Corinthians. "Be ye not unequally yoked together with unbelievers: for what fellowship hath righteousness with unrighteousness? and what communion hath light with darkness?" (2 Cor. 6:14). It has been well expressed by older brethren that unbelievers are constituted children of the devil and if a saint marries one, then they have the devil for their spiritual father-in-law. Marriage was instituted by God and God intends that those being bound together as one have not only the same temporal interests, but spiritual sympathies as well. The woman is to be a help to the man. What help can an ungodly woman afford a saint? How can she help him in a heavenward path, when her feet are on the broad way? When the troubles of life enter into their union, how can they both go to the same source for comfort and help, seeing that she is a stranger to grace and to God? The same applies to a Christian woman taking a child of the wicked one for her husband. What disgrace to the Christian profession, what denial of the Lordship of Christ! It was outlandish women meaning, *women outside the land,* that caused Solomon to sin. An unsaved partner in life will hinder the growth of the believer and perhaps even cause them to drift away from the Lord and fall into sin. Solomon is a classic example.

Such marriages are detrimental to the children of that marriage. Very often the young drift the way of the unconverted parent. The home is divided and sorrow results. We quote the blunt words of Richard Baxter.

> "Such unlawful unions have been usually advocated thus:– The godly party pretends to make no doubt but that the other party may be converted: 'God

> can easily convert men when He will; and if there be but love, persons are easily won over to the same mind with those they love.' *Answer* – (1.) Then it seems because you love an ungodly person, you will be easily turned to be ungodly. If so, you are not much better already. If love will not draw you to their mind to be ungodly, why should you think love will draw them to your mind to be godly? Are you stronger in grace than they are in sin? (2.) If you know well what grace is, and what a sinful, unrenewed soul is, you would not think it so easy a matter to convert a soul. Why are there so few converted, if it be so easy a thing? You cannot make yourselves better by adding higher degrees to the grace you have; much less can you make others better by giving them the grace which they have not. (3.) It is true that God is able to convert them when He will; and it is true that, for ought I know, it may be done. But what of that? Will you in so weighty a case take up with a mere possibility? God can make a beggar rich , and for aught you know to the contrary, He will do it; and yet you will not therefore marry a beggar; nor will you marry a leper, because God can heal him; why then should you marry an ungodly person, because God can convert him? See it done first, if you love your peace and safety."

W. Secker had a unique way of presenting truths which we will also interject at this point. His thoughts on raising children are a solemn warning.

> "Hannah vows, if the Lord will give her a son, by bearing him, she will return that son to the Lord by serving Him (1 Sam.1:11). A spouse should be more careful of her children's breeding than she

> should be fearful of her children's bearing. Take heed lest these flowers grow in the devil's garden. Though you bring them up in corruption, yet do not bring them up to damnation. Those are not mothers, but monsters, that whilst they should be teaching their children the way to heaven with their lips, are leading them the way to hell with their lives. *Good education is the best livery you can give them living; and it is the best legacy you can leave them dying.* You let out your *cares* to make them great. Oh lift up your *prayers* to make them *good*; that before you die *from* them, you may see Christ live *in* them. Whilst these twigs are green and tender, they should be bowed towards God. Children and servants are in a family as passengers are in a boat; husband and wife, they are as a pair of oars to row them to their desired haven. Let these small pieces of timber be hewed and squared for the celestial building. By putting a *sceptre* of *grace* into their *hands*, you will set a *crown* of *glory* upon their *heads*."

Ezra saw the importance of an unmixed marriage to raise the children properly and in the fear of the Lord. He saw the effectiveness of an equal yoke to continue the testimony in the land, and he realized the wisdom of an equal yoke to incur the blessing of God upon their land.

Bitter Fruit

The unequal yoke bears fruit and we find that bitter fruit in the report to Ezra. As already noted, the community had not separated themselves from the heathen, and were doing according to their abominations. Some had even taken heathen wives to themselves (Ezra 9:1,2).

The remnant had left the position of separation and were doing according to the abominations of the surrounding heathen, they had fallen into idolatry. With this would accompany festive activities of a most immoral character. Enjoined upon every believer is separation from the world. Christ said, "Ye are not of the world" (Jn. 15:19). That does not mean that we neglect the secular duties of life. Christians have to work with the ungodly, but they are obligated not to pursue the same principle, and spirit of the world. Its frivolous pleasures are not to find lodging in their heart. Saints are to walk the narrow way, the way that produces pressure and tribulation, for that is the meaning of the word *narrow* as found in Matthew 7:14.

Ezra's Woe

Nowhere in Holy Scripture do we have recorded a more violent display of remorse, grief and sorrow, than when Ezra rent his garment and his mantle, and plucked off the hair of his head, and of his beard, and sat down astonied (Ezra 9:3). So great was his distress and horror that he rent both his outer and inner garments. Jews had been known to shave their heads in time of grief, but Ezra went further, he actually pulled off the hair from his head and face by the roots! There he sat, a sight indeed, in a numbed state, totally stunned. One may wonder, why such an extreme? The answer can be found in the person's measurement of sin. Iniquity is ever a source of pain to the godly. The greater the degree of godliness, the greater the sensitivity to sin. Dabbling in sin deadens the conscience and makes sin less painful to the soul. However, a man dwelling constantly in the light of God's presence has a tremendous abhorrence of sin.

Ezra was such a man and the sins of the leaders and the people were like the pangs of hell surrounding his holy soul.

When we consider Ezra's reaction, what must it have meant to the holy, impeccable, spotless Lamb of God as our sins were laid upon Him? There is not an orator on earth that could expound it worthily. There is not a genius that could even begin to comprehend its awfulness to Him. There is not a heart that could drink its blessed truths to their fullness. What a tremendous work accomplished by our Lord. What a tremendous cost! "For He hath made Him to be sin for us, Who knew no sin; that we might be made the righteousness of God in Him" (2 Cor. 5:21).

"But none of the ransomed ever knew,
How deep were the waters crossed.
Nor how dark was the night
That the Lord passed through,
Ere He found His sheep that was lost."

First notice, Ezra rent his garment. This would express his personal grief. Second, he rent his mantle, an official robe. In doing so, he expressed his distress as representing the people. Third, he plucked the hair off of his head, symbolizing the loss of Israel's glory. Fourth, he plucked off the hair of his beard. Being a sign of manhood, the beard was regarded as a symbol of honor. By destroying his beard, he was solemnly declaring that the honor of the nation had been wounded by their departure from God's law.

There is quite a contrast between Ezra and Nehemiah. When both men received the same kind of distressing news, Ezra wept, Nehemiah became wroth; Ezra fell down, Nehemiah smote them; Ezra prayed, Nehemiah contended with them; Ezra humbled himself, Nehemiah cursed them; Ezra plucked his own hairs out, Nehemiah plucked their hairs out (Ezra 9:3,5; 10:1; with Neh. 13:25).

Ezra's Effect Upon Others

The effect of Ezra's grief had an overwhelming effect upon others. There was a trembling among the people. The word of God had entered their heart, producing conviction of sin. How rare today to see sinners trembling as sin, judgment, heaven and hell, and the sacrifice of Christ, are brought to their attention. How seldom, if at all, do you see saints trembling at corrective ministry. We are living in a day of hardness. The people of Jerusalem trembled and in doing so, sat in silence with Ezra.

What a sight that must have afforded to the eyes of the heathen. I have no doubt that it spoke volumes to them. Through this newly formed attitude on the part of the people they were in reality inviting the presence of God. "To this man will I look, even to him that is poor and of a contrite spirit, and trembleth at My word" (Isa. 66:2). Those gathered had sympathy for Ezra, sorrow for their sin, and great searching of their heart. Ezra gathered men in Babylon, he gathered men in Ahava, and now he is gathering men in Jerusalem. Good men attract the godly, and seek to gather God's people together. Ezra could have said, "Oh my, this place has certainly departed from the right paths, I'll have nothing to do with them. I can't associate myself with people that hold the truth in such light regard, even though this is the place where God has chosen to place His name. Now that I am here, I will just keep myself aloof and constantly complain about conditions." Not so with Ezra! He was a wise man, not a wrangling man, a helpful man, not a hindering man, a spiritual man, not a selfish man.

It is most unwise, if in a spiritually deteriorating assembly, to stand aside and constantly point out the faults of others, or even to purposely miss meetings. You have perhaps heard of the SMOs, they are the Sunday Morning Only people. One Irishman quaintly called them, Seventh Day Adventists, that is, they made their advent to the assembly every seven days, but seemed to navigate to other places, such as their place of employment, during the week. Ezra was overwhelmed at conditions, but one thing he recognized, that Jerusalem was the designated place where God had placed His testimony.

Between 2:30 and 3:30 P.M., at the time of the evening sacrifice, the great scribe rose up, after several hours, from his heaviness (affliction of self, fasting) and falling upon his knees spread out his hands unto the LORD his God. The open hand is a symbol of truth. He drew near to God in sincerity, expressing a genuine faith.

Ezra's Prayer

Years ago an old preacher was asked what he thought of a certain brother. The wise old preacher quaintly answered, "I cannot say, I have not heard him pray yet." How often public, audible prayer exposes the spiritual quality of the person praying. We will now have an opportunity to X-ray Ezra through his public prayer. It is not long, taking less than two minutes to read. There are no direct petitions to be found in his prayer, not even a one requesting the forgiveness of their sins. It is one great paragraph of confessing to God His greatness, and confessing to Him their sin. Ten verses of the Bible are dedicated to it, and it is translated into only 419 words in our language. Its wealth is immense. Ezra uses one expression when speaking *of* God, and three different expressions when speaking *to* God. He speaks of God as, the LORD my God, *Jehovah* my *Elohim*, my Triune God. Ezra is acknowledging a personal and intimate relationship with *Elohim* – my God. The word God is in the plural, indicating three Persons, the Father, Son, and Spirit. It is the plural of *Eloah*, "the Adorable One, the supreme object of worship." Ezra speaks of his supreme object of worship as Jehovah, the "One that always was, that always is, and that ever is to come." Thus seen as ever existent, eternal and unchangeable.

Ezra, in addressing God, uses three expressions; (1) Vs.6, "O my God;" (2) Vs. 10, "O our God;" (3) Vs. 15, "O LORD God of Israel." We find the same variety in our Lord's prayer. When addressing His God regarding Himself, He says, "Father." When He asks His God to preserve His own, keeping them holy in a defiled world, He says, "Holy Father." When He speaks of an unrighteous world who knew not God, His expression is, "O righteous Father" (Jn.17: 1,5,11,25). Let us be careful of the adjectives employed when addressing God. Never bring Him down to the level of a loved human by attaching *dear* to His name.

It was the time of the evening sacrifice when he prays to God. The sacrifice would indicate to us the efficacy of the redemptive work of Christ on the cross. He gave Himself as a sacrifice unto God, as a sweet smelling savour. It is the sight of His cross that lifts us up beyond despair. His sacrifice alone affords us the liberty into the presence of our God to obtain mercy and find grace to help in time of need.

The great man Ezra prays: "And said, O my God, I am ashamed and blush to lift up my face to Thee, my God: for our iniquities are increased over our head, and our trespass is grown up unto the heavens" (Ezra 9:6).

Like Daniel, Ezra includes himself in the sins of the people – "*our* iniquities, *our* head, *our* trespass." Instead of standing apart from the people, Ezra associated himself with them in their guilt and need of God's grace and mercy. This corresponds with what we have today in a New Testament testimony. 1 Corinthians chapter twelve reveals the fact that all in the local testimony are closely linked together, just as a human body with its many members. "And whether one member suffer, all the members suffer with it; or one member be honoured, all the members rejoice with it" (1 Cor.12:26). Ezra was part of the nation, thus in his prayer, he identifies himself with it.

The humility of the man is seen in his posture, he fell upon his knees, with his holy hands outstretched toward heaven. His voice would be heard by those gathered, yet he was not praying *at* them, but as the nation's representative, he was praying to God *for* them. Let us be careful in public prayer that we are not preaching at the audience, or simply trying to impress those listening with our knowledge. It has been said of Ezra, "To the particular offence which he is now deploring, Ezra is as innocent as an unfallen angel. Yet he blushes for shame, and lies prostrate with confusion of face. He is such a true patriot that he completely identifies himself with his people."

Ezra's Shame

Rather than being belligerent over the people's sin, Ezra blushes. He is truly ashamed, when he considers the grace of God to the nation and yet their ingratitude. Are we ashamed? You say, "For what?" For the grace of God to you, and His longsuffering all the days of your downward path in rebellion to Him. For the times you have failed Him since He graciously brought you up out of the horrible pit, and the miry clay, and set your feet upon the Rock. Well might all of us fall down in tears and confess like Isaac Watts.

"Alas! and did my Saviour bleed?
And did my Sovereign die?
Would He devote that sacred head
For such a worm as I?

Thus might I hide my blushing face,
While His dear Cross appears;
Dissolve my heart in thankfulness,
And melt my eyes to tears."

The first thing Ezra addresses is the enormity of their sin. He describes it as, "our iniquities." The word is, *perversity,* and carries the thought of distortion of heart, or actions; lawlessness from right to wrong; gross injustice. Ezra's next description is, "trespass." This carries the thought of *revolt*, or, *rebelling*; *Refusing subjection to rightful authority, or obedience to a law we ought to observe; Refusing allegiance to whom due; going aside; overstep-*

ping. Ezra certainly does not minimize their guilt. Godly men never minimize sin. The Lord Himself never once, looked lightly upon sin. Sin, if not dealt with by a sinner, will harden his heart, murder his conscience, warp his mind, blind his eyes, hold him tightly with its cords, and ultimately, like a lead weight, sink his damned soul down into the depths of a burning, and eternal hell! T. De Witt Talmage penned it this way.

> "Others may throw garlands upon sin, picturing the overhanging fruits which drop in her pathway, and make every step graceful as the dance; but we cannot be honest without presenting it as a giant, black with the soot of the forges where eternal chains are made, and feet rotting with disease, and breath foul with plagues, and eyes glaring with woe, and locks flowing in serpent fangs, and voice from which shall rumble forth the blasphemies of the damned."

Ezra acknowledges that their sin was about to swallow them up and that their guilt was so great that it had risen to the very throne of God.

Israel's Dark Past

He then traces their trespass to its source. "Since the days of our fathers have we been in a great trespass unto this day; and for our iniquities have we, our kings, and our priests, been delivered into the hand of the kings of the lands, to the sword, to captivity, and to a spoil, and to confusion of face, as it is this day" (Ezra 9:7).

Some have thought that Ezra is referring to the time when Israel came up out of Egypt, but it would seem that he is referring to the previous history under the kings, where most of them turned to idolatry. Of the Southern Kingdom (Judah) there had been twenty-one kings, of which thirteen did evil. Of the Northern Kingdom (Israel) there had been twenty kings, most of whom were idolatrous. Ezra acknowledges a dark past history, the history of a nation that never seemed to learn, even though God had disciplined them time after time.

God's Divine Grace

He then mentions to the Lord what His grace had wrought on their behalf. "And now for a little space (moment) grace hath been shewed from the LORD our God, to leave us a remnant to escape, and to give us a nail in His holy place, that our God may lighten our eyes, and give us a little reviving in our bondage. For we were bondmen; yet our God hath not forsaken us in our bondage, but hath extended mercy unto us in the sight of the kings of Persia, to give us a reviving, to set up the house of our God, and to repair the desolations thereof, and to give us a wall in Judah and in Jerusalem" (Vs. 8,9).

Counting from the first year of Cyrus (Ezra 1:1), the "little moment" spanned a period of eighty years. God gave them a nail in His holy place, meaning that God had given them a firm and sure abode. Even though a feeble remnant, yet they were a nation settled once again in the land, the desired result being that God would lighten their eyes. When the Lord drew near to those on the road to Emmaus, "their eyes were holden that they should not know Him." However, as they sat at meat with Him, "their eyes were opened and they knew Him." Later that day as the disciples were gathered together, the Lord appeared in their midst. "Then opened He their understanding, that they might understand the scriptures" (Lk. 24:15,16,31,45). Christians should be enlightened people.

Lightened Eyes

The allusion to lighting the eyes could be the cheering of spirits. David cried, "Consider and hear me, O LORD my God: lighten mine eyes, lest I sleep the sleep of death" (Ps. 13:3). David mentions those that were seeking God. "They looked unto Him, and were lightened: and their faces were not ashamed" (Ps. 34:5).

C.H. Spurgeon once said, "Lighten mine eyes, let the eye of my faith be clear, that I may see my God in the dark." Jonathan, weary due to the battle, came to where there was honey on the ground. Putting the honey to his mouth, his eyes were enlightened. He was encouraged, he was strengthened.

Ezra prays for strength and encouragement that there may be a little revival in their bondage. His expression, "We *were* bondmen," is actually, "We *are* bondmen," as the nation was still under the Persian monarchy and subject to its laws. He acknowledges the mercy of God bestowed on them: First, in bringing them to their own land again (vs.8); second, enabling them to rebuild the temple (vs.8); third, granting them security in the land (vs.8); fourth, influencing the Persian king to treat them so favorably (vs.9); fifth, for punishing them less than their iniquities deserved (vs. 13). Truly, our God is "plenteous in mercy: (Ps. 86:5,15;103:8). Ezra acknowledges the merciful character of God.

"O the love that drew salvation's plan!
O the grace that brought it down to man!
O the mighty gulf that God did span
At Calvary!

Mercy there was great, and grace was free,
Pardon there was multiplied to me,
There my burdened soul found liberty –
At Calvary"

A Wall

The next thing Ezra mentioned was God giving them a wall in Judah and in Jerusalem. The literal walls of Jerusalem were still broken down and not repaired until almost fifteen years later in Nehemiah's day. Ezra is not referring to those walls. The wall is an expression of safety, defense, and continuance. God had graciously granted them that in the favor of the Persian kings, and Ezra desires that God may continue to shelter and protect them.

Having said this, Ezra now recalls Israel's particular sin, spreading it out before God and in the ears of those gathered around him who trembled at the words of the God of Israel. "And now, O our God, what shall we say after this? for we have forsaken Thy commandments, Which Thou hast commanded by Thy servants the prophets, saying, The land, unto which ye go to possess it, is an unclean land with the filthiness of the people of the lands, with their abominations, which have filled it from one end to another with their uncleanness. Now therefore give not your daughters unto their sons, neither take their daughters unto your sons, nor seek their peace or their wealth for ever: that ye may be strong, and eat the good of the land, and leave it for an inheritance to your children for ever" (vs.10-12).

Ezra is not quoting any particular verse, but is making a statement that correctly describes many scriptures. He is mentioning the general picture of warnings found in the prophets. The filthiness of the Canaanitish nations is what brought the judgment of God upon them. In doing so, He used Israel as His battle bow, to destroy those nations, with the purpose of giving the land to Israel. Israel was not completely successful in their mission in driving them all out, thus later, they became thorns in her side. One of those thorns was idolatry and all the utter filthiness connected with it. The psalmist laments," They are corrupt, they have done abominable works, there is none that doeth good. The LORD looked down from heaven upon the children of men, to see if there were any that did understand, and seek God. They are all gone aside, they are all together become filthy: there is none that doeth good, no, not one" (Ps. 14:1-3).

The prophets had warned against unequal yokes, not only in marriage, but also in social life. They were not to seek their peace or their wealth. The command was rigid, unchanging, demanding, and divine.

Ezra closes his short, solemn, scriptural, and searching prayer by owning God's justice in visiting them with His disfavor. "And after all that is come upon us for our evil deeds, and for our great trespass, seeing that Thou our God hast punished us less than our iniquities deserve, and hast given us such deliverance as this; Should we again break Thy commandments, and join in affinity with the people of these abominations? wouldest not Thou be angry with us till thou hadst consumed us, so that there should be no remnant nor escaping? O LORD God of Israel, Thou art righteous: for we remain yet escaped, as it is this day: behold, we are before Thee in our trespasses: for we cannot stand before Thee because of this." (vs.13-15). As Ezra continues in prayer, you will notice that his description of their sin intensifies. At first he terms it, "our iniquities, our trespass" (vs. 6), but now he describes their sin as, "our evil deeds, our great trespasses." He acknowledges what would be the ultimate result if their sin was not judged, they would be consumed. That is, the testimony to His name would cease to exist.

Ephesus

One is immediately reminded of the threat of the Lord to the church at Ephesus. "Remember therefore from whence thou art fallen, and repent, and do the first works; or else I will come unto thee quickly, and will remove thy candlestick out of his place, except thou repent" (Rev. 2:5). The Lord does remove lampstands for various reasons. When a local testimony links up with the ungodly world for its own carnal "prosperity," they are in great danger of what Ezra feared, "wouldest not Thou be angry with us till thou hadst consumed us, so that there should be no remnant nor escaping?"

Finally, the weeping, humble and afflicted scribe leaves all in the hand of his God. They had, through the mercy of God, remained up to that day. God had marked their iniquities, how could they stand (Ps. 130:3)? Ezra gives his final tribute to God in his fervent prayer, "O LORD God of Israel, Thou art righteous."

As Ezra commenced his prayer he fell upon his knees

and spread out his hands. As he proceeded in prayer he was seen weeping and casting himself down before the house of God, as he felt more and more the vileness of the people's iniquity. It must have been an exceedingly moving sight to see this great man, sent by the Persian king, a godly man of profound knowledge in divine things, casting himself thus on the ground. It was in a public place, before the house of God, which would be the great court of the temple. So tremendous was the effect of Ezra's grief and humiliation, that the men, women, and children who gathered "wept very sore." The word for children could mean young men, but it seems here to indicate little ones, still under their mothers' care.

A Mother's Tears

As a lad, when sitting beside my dear mother in gospel meetings, invariably she would weep over me. Her tears were a message to my heart of greater weight than the preacher's words. Saints were sober after hearing the gospel in those days, and would file out of the meeting and go immediately to their homes. Today paints a different picture. The meeting may be unusually solemn. Sin, judgment, and hell fire may be faithfully proclaimed. Yet when the meeting is dismissed, what do we often see? Laughing, lightness, and not one tear for the dear unsaved hastening on to a burning hell. Ezra took the situation very seriously, soberly, and spiritually – he wept!

Shechaniah's Counsel

"And Shechaniah the son of Jehiel, one of the sons of Elam, answered and said unto Ezra, We have trespassed against our God, and have taken strange wives of the people of the land: yet now there is hope in Israel concerning this thing. Now therefore let us make a covenant with our God to put away all the wives, and such as are born of them, according to the counsel of my lord, and of those that tremble at the commandment of our God; and let it be done according to the law. Arise; for this matter belongeth unto thee: we also will be with thee: be of good courage, and do it" (Ezra 10:2-4).

Hope

Shechaniah, the son of Jehiel, was a godly man. He appears suddenly on the chronicler's page with words of hope and good counsel. "Yet now there is hope," he said. Considering the fact that a man like Ezra was now in Jerusalem; and considering that the people were manifesting true repentance, there was hope that the people would return to God and His path for them. He, like Ezra, included himself in the people's sins. There is nothing to indicate that he had taken a heathen wife, as did his father (10:26). This worthy man put God before his own family, he was not about to show favoritism. The glory of God was paramount in his life. He would be a man who would honor his father when honor was due, but he was also a man who would honor God above his own father. His father, with others, had sinned and the sin must be dealt with, regardless of relationships.

The Stolen Radio

Many years ago a young man stole a little radio from a local store. He was caught, and of course, being a rather small community, it was published in the local newspaper. The assembly had to deal with the sin. However, the lad's parents objected, and other members of the family threatened to leave the assembly if they put away their dear little relative. The discipline was carried out according to 1 Corinthians 5:11-13, and the young man was put away as a covetous person. The sad result was, thirteen of his relatives left the assembly. There are people that cannot stand the glare of an open Book. Controlled by their carnal emotions, they placed their relative in higher esteem than God and His assembly. The assembly may have suffered in loss of numbers, but thank God, the quality was not diminished, it remained the same. Shechaniah was a man that put God first.

According to The Law

This God-fearing man now proposes a scriptural action to put away the heathen wives and their children. He is careful to say, "Let it be done according to the law." In any assembly matters, all must be done according to the Book. We must have a "thus saith the Lord," regulating the actions of the government in any local church. Actions are not to be based on how I feel about it, or, "we've always done it that way," or, "this would work the best to our advantage." No! That will never do! God has definite guidelines, He has a plain blueprint for all the activities of a local testimony, and woe be to that testimony that governs itself by emotional feelings or businesslike tactics for personal gain. Departure from the word of God is characteristic of Christendom, but this should never characterize a gathered out company of the Lord's people.

Jehoshaphat and Ahab

It was a sad day when Jehoshaphat linked himself with Ahab to go to war. Ahab gathered about four hundred prophets to give their advice. They all pleased him with their reports. However, "Jehoshaphat said, Is there not here a prophet of the LORD besides, that we might enquire of him?" (1 Ki. 22:7). Micaiah was brought, but he was hated of Ahab because he had always prophesied against that wicked king. He spoke the plain truth. One could liken Christendom, with all its ritual, dogmas, and man-devised creeds to Ahab, and Micaiah to the unvarnished word of God. Christendom has little use for all the truth of God, for God's word condemns it. If we inquired like Jehoshaphat, "Is there not here a prophet of the LORD besides, that we might enquire of him?" we would say, "Yes, here is the Book, God's holy word!

Urgency and Support

In urgency, Shechaniah said to Ezra. "Arise; for this matter belongeth unto thee: we also will be with thee: be of good courage, and do it" (Ezra 10:4), thus encouraging the skillful scribe with their full support. Admitted was the fact that the matter belonged to none other than Ezra. The responsibility had been placed on him alone, to deal with the matter. There was no sidestepping the matter, it must be faced head on. One of the reasons that the responsibility lay on Ezra was because the king's commission gave him the authority, he was sent by the king to uphold the law of God and demand obedience to it. Another reason would be his character and ability qualified him for the work, also, being a skillful scribe in the law of God, he had the people's confidence.

Perhaps the greatest quality of Ezra that gave the people confidence in him was the fact that he not only knew the law of God, but that he lived it out in his own life. He not only talked well – he lived well. One old preacher said to me, "The man in the message is worth more than the message in the man." That is something worth thinking over.

Encouragement

Perhaps lurking in the back of Ezra's mind was the thought that the rulers of the people would balk at such a suggestion. This was immediately dispelled by Shechaniah's word –"Be of good courage, and do it." The first time that expression is used is found in Numbers 13:20. Moses said to the men who were to spy out the land of Canaan, "Be ye of good courage, and bring of the fruit of the land." The next occurrence is Deuteronomy 31:6. Moses speaks to Israel as they are about to enter the land – "Be strong and of a good courage, fear not, nor be afraid of them." Then turning to Joshua he says, "Be strong and of a good courage." Following this, as Joshua stands as commander in chief of the nation of Israel, ready to invade the land, the LORD Himself addresses Joshua thrice with these words, "Be strong and of a good courage" (Josh. 1:6,9,18). In verse 7 the LORD said, "Be thou strong and very courageous." Later, Joshua exhorts his captains, "Fear not, nor be dismayed, be strong and of good courage" (Josh. 10:25). Joab, encouraging Abishai in war said, "Be of good courage" (2 Sam. 10:12; 1 Chr. 19:13). David, in advising his son Solomon regarding the ruling of the nation, said, "Be strong and of good courage" (1 Chr. 22:13; 28:20). Isaiah uses the expression once (Isa. 41:6) and David twice in the Psalms (Ps. 27:14; 31:24).

The expression to Ezra, "be of good courage" is the

last in Holy Scripture. It is easy to see, by the use of this expression, that courage is needed in fighting the Lord's battles, in ruling God's people, and in carrying out God's discipline. Such work is not for spiritual weaklings. Christians are exhorted. "My brethren, be strong in the Lord, and in the power of His might. Put on the whole armour of God, that ye may be able to stand against the wiles of the devil" (Eph. 6:10,11).

Good nutrition promotes growth and strength. "As newborn babes, desire the sincere milk of the word, that ye may grow thereby" (1 Pet. 2:2). Study of, and obedience to the word of God is the secret of spiritual growth and strength. Without an intimate knowledge of God, and a good understanding of His word, a person cannot acceptably rule the people of God, nor can one profitably proclaim the gospel. Dealing with sin in the assembly is a serious business. There must be wisdom, there must be compassion, there must be absolute obedience to the word, and there must be spiritual strength and good courage. Ezra was exhorted to be of good courage.

Unity With an Oath

"Then arose Ezra, and made the chief priests, the Levites, and all Israel, to swear that they should do according to this word. And they sware" (Ezra 10:5). Those men of greatest position and influence were all in agreement and the nation followed in their unity. Ezra made them *swear*, that is, he made them *take an oath.* The word is, *shaba*, meaning *to be complete,* but used only as a denominative from *sheba*; *to seven oneself*. It carries the thought of *repeating a declaration seven times.* Whether this was actually done is not stated, but one thing is certain, the taking of an oath lent solemnity to the occasion, which in future days would prevent them from drawing back on what they had pledged to accomplish.

The Chamber

"Then Ezra rose up from before the house of God, and went into the chamber of Johanan the son of Eliashib: and when he came thither, he did eat no bread, nor drink water: for he mourned because of the transgression of them that had been carried away" (Ezra 10:6).

Johanan evidently had an external chamber of the temple assigned to him, and it was into this provided chamber that Ezra retired from the gathering. So immense was the burden on this man's soul that he went into seclusion, neither eating food, nor even drinking water. Fasts employing such strictness were very uncommon. Some, when fasting, merely abstained from meat and wine, others abstained from all food, but drank water. The severity of Ezra's fast betrays his extreme earnestness regarding the sins of his brethren. Let us derive a lesson from this, that, in dealing with the sins of others, there must be affliction of self. A spirit of vengeance, a spirit of pride, or a spirit of self satisfaction in putting away a wicked person from assembly fellowship will never accomplish the desired result, namely, the restoration of the sinning person. Personalities should never enter the picture when dealing with sin. Oh, for men of tender hearts when dealing righteously for God in putting away the offender. I remember when a servant of the Lord had to be removed from his work as an evangelist because his behavior was unbecoming. As the notice was made to the assembly that he was associated with, the saints broke down in tears. The occasion was sad, but the attitude was good.

Let us be careful, when dealing with sin.
Lest we too ourselves go astray.
Let the spirit be tender, the Book be our guide,
And for the erring one, cease not to pray.

Self-Affliction

Ezra, in fasting, was seeking closer communion, and greater power with his God. The disciples' failure to cast out a dumb spirit from a lad caused this question to their Lord, "Why could not we cast him out? And He said unto them, This kind can come forth by nothing, but by prayer and fasting" (Mk. 9:28,29). Ezra had proclaimed a fast and afflicted himself by the river Ahava, when contemplating his perilous journey to Jerusalem. Now he is found afflicting himself again in a side chamber in God's house as the seriousness and magnitude of the situation and its solution bears down heavily upon his righteous soul. The mourning man was a mighty man. How thankful any assembly ought to be if they have men of this caliber in their midst. Such men are rare in the society in which we live today.

It would seem that in the chamber of Johanan, Ezra would be consulting with the priests, the elders, and the princes of Israel as to the measures to be used in the carrying out of the agreement that had been solemnly made by oath. The piety manifested by his fasting and mourning would have a tremendous effect upon the company.

The Proclamation

"And they made proclamation throughout Judah and

Jerusalem unto all the children of the captivity, that they should gather themselves together unto Jerusalem; And that whosoever would not come within three days, according to the counsel of the princes and the elders, all his substance should be forfeited, and himself separated from the congregation of those that had been carried away" (Ezra 10:7,8).

The issue at hand was serious, consequently the proclamation was severe. It was made in the twentieth day of the ninth month, which corresponds to our December, which in Israel was a rainy season. It was in the spring of the year when Ezra and his company left Babylon, the same time of the year when Israel left Egypt under the leadership of Moses. It was the beginning of months, with bright scenes of hope before them. Ezra's journey, having taken four months, would bring them into Jerusalem in the heat of July. It was just a matter time until the princes brought the sad and sobering tidings to him, and now the season of rain had set in – a picture of heaven weeping. The case to be handled was certainly not done in haste. There might have been lengthy deliberations regarding the conditions and the dealing of those conditions in a scriptural way. Every avenue would be considered by these wise and god-fearing men.

The Warning

The great gathering was to take place in the capital of the nation – Jerusalem. Three days were allowed for all the people (probably able-bodied men) to make their presence known. Those who failed to do so would be punished. The limits of Judea at that time would have been the Mediterranean, 37 miles to the west; Jericho 15 miles to the northeast; Beersheba, 46 miles to the south; and Bethel, 12 miles to the north. Those from Beersheba would have to journey at least 15 to 16 miles each day to reach the city. The penalty was indeed severe, involving the forfeiting of all their substance. The word forfeited is devoted, which indicates that their substance would be taken and given to God for the service of the temple. Also, the person would be separated from the congregation, meaning that he would be deprived of all the rights and privileges of the community. In today's terms, he would be constituted a nonmember. There was a cost for disobedience.

Today, in the assembly we are told, "Obey them that have the rule over you, and submit yourselves: for they watch for your souls, as they that must give account, that they may do it with joy, and not with grief: for that is unprofitable for you" (Heb.13:17). Failure to obey the elders of the assembly causes them grief as they watch for your souls. Not only this, at the judgment seat of Christ, disobedience to the shepherds will result in the loss of reward. There are two great things that should keep saints in obedience to God's word; First, love to Christ; second, the judgment seat of Christ.

The Great Gathering

"Then all the men of Judah and Benjamin gathered themselves together unto Jerusalem within three days. It was the ninth month, on the twentieth day of the month; and all the people sat in the street (court) of the house of God, trembling because of this matter, and for the great rain" (Ezra 10:9). According to Hecataeus of Abdera, the court was a stonewalled enclosure, about 500 feet long and 150 feet wide, which would afford sitting room for 20,000 men. The number of the gathering on this solemn occasion is not revealed. Not only was the situation uncomfortable, but the weather was uncomfortable as well. As another has aptly put it – "How impressive and melancholy a spectacle! The vast multitude seated before the Temple of God, tired, troubled and trembling, beneath the dark canopy of heavy clouds, with rain falling down upon them in torrents!"

Ezra's Words

"And Ezra the priest stood up, and said unto them, Ye have transgressed, and have taken strange wives, to increase the trespass of Israel. Now therefore make confession unto the LORD God of your fathers, and do His pleasure: and separate yourselves from the people of the land, and from the strange wives" (Ezra 10:10,11).

How vital is separation to a fruitful testimony. There was to be a social separation (the people of the land), and a sentimental separation (the strange wives). What a great cost to the transgressors! Sin at first is sweet, but later it doles out its bitter wages. God was being honored, spirits were being humbled, and hearts would be broken. The sin was great – the cost was great. Christian Hebrews were exhorted, "Wherefore Jesus also, that He might sanctify the people with His own blood, suffered without the gate. Let us go forth therefore unto Him without the camp, bearing His reproach. For here have we no continuing city, but we seek one to come" (Heb. 13:12-14). The Corinthian saints were warned, "Wherefore come out from among them, and be ye separate, saith the Lord, and touch not the unclean thing; and I will receive you" (2 Cor. 6:17). In all dispensations, God calls for a separated people unto Himself. Ezra calls for two things always associated with true repentance: first, to confess their sin unto the LORD God of their fathers; second, to separate themselves from the people of the land and from the strange wives. They were to admit their sin, and abandon their sin.

Sin

If we only could see sin as God sees it, what a transformation would take place! To God, sin is exceedingly hateful. There is no tolerance of sin with a holy God. It has made the heavens unclean, it has totally ruined the human race, and the enormity of it was displayed at Calvary, for it cost God the abandonment of His unique Son in those dark hours when He was made sin for us. Sin is sweet to the human tongue, it nestles in every human heart, and it lurks in every human brain belching out its wicked thoughts. It is a viper, sucking the life blood out of the soul. Have we, even as Christians, been deluded as to the enormity of sin?

Repentance

Repentance is the first step in dealing with personal sin in the life. However, repentance is only proved by a change in action and ways, not merely by words of mouth. A repentant blasphemer's provoking turns to praise; a harlot becomes an honorable lady; a vile drunkard becomes a vibrant disciple; a sensual whoremonger becomes a sincere worshipper; a hypocrite becomes honest, a liar becomes truthful — true repentance is manifested by drastic change!

"Repentance means to leave
The sins we loved before;
And show that we in earnest grieve,
By doing so no more."

A Sensible Request

The reply from the congregation was sincere and sensible. "Then all the congregation answered and said with a loud voice, As thou hast said, so must we do. But the people are many, and it is a time of much rain, and we are not able to stand without, neither is this a work of one day or two: for we are many that have transgressed in this thing. Let now our rulers of all the congregation stand, and let all them which have taken strange wives in our cities come at appointed times, and with them the elders of every city, and the judges thereof, until the fierce wrath of our God for this matter be turned from us" (Ezra 10:12-14).

Questions

To deal with the problem in a matter of just a few days, or at that particular time, was an impossibility. It was proposed, and rightly so, that appointed times be set to deal with each case on an individual basis. Each case was to be investigated thoroughly before judgment was passed. More than likely there were brethren that had taken heathen wives to themselves that became proselytes and their children circumcised. Did not Moses marry a Midianite, and Boaz a Moabitess? Did the law condemn their marriages? Perhaps these questions would be brought before the court – godly wisdom was needed.

Objectors

The next verse has been misinterpreted by some. "Only Jonathan the son of Asahel and Jahaziah the son of Tikvah were employed about this matter: and Meshullam and Shabbethai the Levite helped them" (Ezra 10:15). The casual reader would be led to believe that only these men were employed in dealing with the many cases. However, the opposite is true, for in verse 16, we read, "And the children of the captivity did so. And Ezra the priest, with certain chief of the fathers, after the house of their fathers, and all of them by their names, were separated, and sat down in the first day of the tenth month to examine the matter." The examiners were Ezra and with certain chief of the fathers, not Jonathan and Jahaziah. In fact, it was these two men who gave opposition. The expression, "were employed about this matter," really means, "they stood up against this matter." The name Jonathan means, Jehovah has given, and the name Jahaziah means, Jehovah views. These objectors were certainly not living up to their name. Meshullam, who had married a heathen wife (10:29), and Shabbethai were persuaded to help them. The opposition had no effect upon the remnant; God; using Ezra, had commenced a mighty work.

The Court in Session

Sitting down the first day of the tenth month, the examinations began, and continued on until the first day of the first month. Some have suggested that three to four cases were handled every day the council met. There would be days, such as sabbath days, where there would be no meeting. In a population of almost 50,000 souls, only 113 mixed marriages had to be dealt with. That would amount to three hundred or more justifiable marriages to one unlawful marriage. This shows that the sin had not yet spread to great proportions. Better to nip sin in the bud than to overlook it until it grows into a strong tree in the camp. It is far easier to uproot a sapling than to fell a huge oak. As soon as the matter came to Ezra's ears, there was immediate action. As Solomon advised, "To every thing there is a season, and a time to every purpose under the heaven" (Eccl. 3:1). When Ezra reached Jerusalem, it was a time not *to keep silence*, but *a time to speak.* A time not *to keep,* but *a time to cast away.*

As the cases, one by one, came before the council, the names of the priests appear first. They had been invested with greater responsibility, thus theirs was the greater sin. The sin of a shepherd in an assembly is more serious than that same sin committed by one of the sheep. Fallen shepherds stand in danger of leading the flock astray. Aaron was a leader and in sinning, he plunged the whole nation into idolatry over his golden calf. Can you picture what would have transpired in Israel at this time if Ezra had been exposed of committing gross sins? There would have been no confession of sin among the people, no repentance wrought in their hearts, and there would have been no cleansing of the nation. "One sinner destroyeth much good" (Eccl. 9:18).

Elders and Judges Summoned

After the individual cases of the priests and Levites were judged and the sentences passed, the common people were called. No doubt this was done in an orderly way. Those from Beersheba would have a forty-six-mile journey. Along with the accused would come the elders of their city and the judges. These responsible men would be called upon to testify regarding the accused, the reason for this being that they would be familiar with the person and would be able to furnish the necessary information as to the character and conduct of that person. Every accused one was welcome to plead his cause if need be. The court was held in a respectable and spiritual manner. I am certain there would be tears. Mothers who were to be put away were given the children. Can you picture a husband, a loving father, saying goodbye to his wife and little family in the courtroom? It certainly must have affected Ezra and those who officiated with him. They were not hard men, but compassionate men; however, God's claims elicited a higher place in their hearts than their fleshly emotions.

Oh, the sorrows of sin! Think of the ultimate end of a sinful life – hell, where there is weeping and wailing forever. As the divorced wives made their way back to their relatives there would no doubt be bitterness of soul. I can picture a heathen father gnashing his teeth at the Jews for the rejection of his greatly loved daughter, being put away from her home, to return to her heathen parents, weeping with her little ones. I can picture the Jewish father, after his case was closed, returning to an empty house to weep out his folly in ever disobeying God and taking to himself a heathen wife. His love for her is now dashed to the ground as much as if she had been killed and buried. The sweet voices of his daughters and the embraces of his little son no longer will be heard or felt. Oh, the silence of the walls of his house, the stillness and loneliness of the night. The aftermath would be more intense than the trial. Whether or not these men ever remarried is not recorded.

Oh the folly of his sin,
Returned with weight that day.
Never to see her face again,
Nor hear his children play.

The names of the offenders were listed as a warning to all. Paul writes Timothy regarding the church at Ephesus. "Them (the elders) that sin rebuke before all, that others also may fear" (1 Tim. 5:20).

The Offending Priests

Of the priests we read. "And they gave their hands that they would put away their wives; and being guilty, they offered a ram of the flock for their trespass" (Ezra 10:19). What a lovely attitude to behold. Sincerity marks the guilty priests. Giving their hands simply means that they solemnly pledged themselves. They completely bowed to the judgment and followed the sentence through. There was no wavering on their part in obeying the Lord. "He that covereth his sins shall not prosper: but whoso confesseth and forsaketh them shall have mercy" (Prov. 28:13).

Annulment or Divorce?

Some writers have suggested that this act was simply the annulling of the marriage, that mysteriously they were not actually married who had taken heathen wives. But notice, the women are termed *wives*! Some have interjected Malachi 2:14-16 to support this theory. However, the text will not support such a notion. The term "put away" actually means *the dissolving of the marriage bond.* A careful examination of the Malachi passage is worthy of notice.

"Because the Lord hath been witness between thee and the wife of thy youth, against whom thou hast dealt treacherously: yet is she thy companion, and the wife of thy covenant . . . For the Lord, the God of Israel, saith He that hateth putting away: for one covereth violence with his garment saith the Lord of hosts; therefore take heed to your spirit, that ye deal not treacherously."

It is evident what God hated here was the treachery of these Jews in divorcing innocent wives. Divorce for adultery is not considered here. This was what Jesus referred to as "hardness of heart" divorce. It was not treachery to divorce an adulterous wife. God did not hate divorce for adultery, but He did hate adultery and instituted the death penalty for it, which would automatically sever the marriage bond.

It would seem that Ezra and his council were acting on the principle of Deuteronomy 24:1. "When a man hath taken a wife, and married her, and it come to pass that she find no favour in his eyes, because he hath found some uncleanness in her: then let him write her a bill of divorcement, and give it in her hand, and send her out of his house."

Removing Cancer

If the act of putting away a heathen wife seems too severe, consider the following. Heathen wives would seek to seduce their husbands into idolatry. The children being raised by the mother would invariably be bowing down to idols at an early age.

With cancer of this nature in the camp, it would soon spread until the returned remnant would be no better than their forefathers at the close of Israel's corporate testimony, prior to the destruction of Jerusalem by Nebuchadnezzar. A good surgeon, in an effort to stop the cancer in his patient, removes it, if possible, with the knife. The only way to prevent the whole nation from lapsing back into idolatry was to remove the strange wives. Ezra, in this sense, was not only a skilled scribe, but a skilled surgeon

Marriage – New Testament Teaching.

The question arises, what about our day, what is the attitude a Christian should manifest toward an unsaved wife or husband?

When the gospel came to Corinth, all were heathen idolaters. Married couples were saved, but in some families only the husband, or only the wife were saved, leaving them with an unsaved partner. What was to be done in such a case? The New Testament teaching is very clear. "If any brother hath a wife that believeth not, and she be pleased to dwell with him, let him not put her away. And the woman which hath an husband that believeth not, and if he be pleased to dwell with her, let her not leave him. For the unbelieving husband is sanctified by the wife, and the unbelieving wife is sanctified by the husband: else were your children unclean; but now are they holy" (1 Cor. 7:12-14).

The unbelieving one is sanctified. Just what does that mean? Simply this. The word *sanctification* means, *to be set apart.* When a sinner trusts Christ, he is judicially set apart for God. This is not the case in the unbeliever married to a believer. In their case, sanctification simply means that *positionally* they have been placed into a position of privilege. They are now exposed to the word of God, prayers are now offered for their salvation, they are exposed to the company of saints. Thus, they are sanctified as far as their *position in life* is concerned. They are no longer under the darkness of heathendom, but fully exposed to the radiant brightness of Christianity.

Children – Unclean, Holy

What does it mean when God says, "else were your children unclean; but now are they holy"? Since the word *holy (hagios)* and the word *sanctified (hagiazo)* come from the same root word, their meaning is similar. The child was unclean in the sense of being raised in an idolatrous situation, but now one of their parents has become a Christian. They are not to be sent away, they are bound to the parent, and under the umbrella of Christianity, they are set apart.

Jeshua the Priest

During the time of the trials, 113 offenders were convicted (Ezra 10:18-44). Twenty-five percent of the guilty were religious leaders. Among the names were the sons of a departed godly man who would have wept exceedingly if he had known. His name was Jeshua, the former high priest.

In Ezra 3:2 he is seen helping to build an altar. In 3:9, he is faithfully appointing workers and overseeing the work of laying the foundation of the temple. In 4:3, he appears again, defending the testimony against the adversaries. Coming to 5:1,2, he is deeply affected through the prophesying of Haggai and Zechariah, so much so, that he with others, begin to work on the temple.

In Ezra 8:33, his son is employed in weighing the vessels that were brought with Ezra's coalition. He must have been a worthy man to have been entrusted with the sacred vessels for weighing. However, how disappointing to see his name on the list of offenders. His name is indelibly engraved on the page of holy writ and can be seen in Ezra 10:22. His name means, *Jehovah is Bestower*, or, *the Lord gave,* indicating the godliness of his father in acknowledging the goodness of Jehovah in giving him a son. Whether Jesuah was still alive at the time of Ezra's appearance in Jerusalem is not certain, but seemingly he has left the scene. If so, he would have been spared the grief of seeing his God-given son depart from the faith.

Our Children – Joy and Grief

This is an echo in the lives of many Christians. How often Christian parents experience the great joy of seeing their children saved, and then added to the assembly. They can say like the apostle John, "I have no greater joy." However, as time goes on, they drift from the path of separation and cease to manifest an interest in divine things, bringing grief to the hearts of their parents. In some cases the reason for their drift is, they never have truly been born again, and true to the parable of the sower, "They on the rock are they, which, when they hear, receive the word with joy; and these have no root, which for a while believe, and in time of temptation fall away" (Lk. 8:13).

In other cases, young ones may be saved, but they have never received proper shepherding, thus as time goes on, they drift. Shepherds should be very keen in knowing the state of every sheep in their flock. Sometimes one is overtaken in a fault, meaning *a lapse or deviation from truth and uprightness.* That fault could be, missing meetings, or an interest developing in worldly things, or improper dress at the gatherings, or a bad attitude developing. Shepherds are to tend the flock, which includes not only exposition of the word, but a tender care over the particular needs of each sheep. A true shepherd will devote his life to the welfare of the flock. A godly shepherd will encourage young saints to read their Bibles. This encouragement can take various forms, such as asking them what they have been enjoying from the word lately, or asking them privately if they can help them with any questions that have developed in their mind while reading the scriptures.

An Older Teacher

On one occasion, while in a home during a conference, an older teacher from overseas asked the young folks gathered in the family room if they had any questions they would like answered pertaining to the scriptures. Why did he do that? It was because he was interested in their spiritual welfare and wanted to be a help to them. Socializing is pleasant, and taking young Christians out for a snack or meal is a manifestation of love and friendship, but it is not *feeding*, in the true sense of the word. Feeding the flock always involves the word of God which is the spiritual food.

Parental Responsibility

Is it not also the responsibility of parents to instruct their saved children in the paths and principles of God? Most certainly! Taking them to places of worldly entertainment will hardly encourage them in divine things. However, there must be interest shown in the innocent and pure things of life. We took our children to the zoo, to see the creation of God in the animal world; to the art museum, to behold history; to the health museum, to consider the human body. But we never took them to the various amusement parks, the circus, the theaters, the sport stadiums, or the racetrack. Such a list could hardly be termed innocent and pure.

Televisions and Computers

The television has ruined the minds of millions of people, especially young minds. Older preachers used to say, "No spiritual Christian would allow one in his home." A blunt statement, but I believe it to be accurate. The computer if used properly can be a very helpful tool, but if misused, it can become a harmful instrument. Parents are to be overseers of their children and a wise father and mother will take an intimate and earnest interest in their Christian child to see to it that they receive the best of spiritual medical care for strong spiritual development.

Divisions of Two Books

In closing, let us once again consider Ezra the skillful scribe. His book is divided into two parts, chapters one to six, the rebuilding of the temple under Zerubbabel, and chapters seven to ten, the restoration of worship under Ezra. The following book of Nehemiah is similarly divided, chapters one to six, the reconstructing of the wall, and chapters seven to thirteen, the reinstructing of the people. In the book of Ezra we are taught the correct attitude toward God, while in the book of Nehemiah we are taught the correct attitude toward the heathen.

Ezra and The Book

In the book of Nehemiah, Ezra takes a secondary place and is mentioned seven times in chapter eight; in chapter twelve he is mentioned as, "Ezra the priest, the scribe" (vs. 26). He is seen associated with the Book in chapter eight. As the people all stood together before the water gate, Ezra brings the Book. Standing upon a pulpit of wood, made for the occasion, he opens the Book and reads from it from morning to midday to an attentive audience. In doing so, he is publicly associated with six men at his right hand and seven men at his left hand. As the people stood up at the reading, "Ezra blessed the LORD, the great God. And all the people answered, Amen, Amen, with lifting up their hands: and they bowed their heads, and worshipped the LORD with their faces to the ground" (Neh. 8:6). Those assisting Ezra mingled with the congregation and "caused the people to understand the law: and the people stood in their place" (Neh.8:7). The Book was read distinctly, or, with an interpretation, which, in giving the sense, caused the people to understand.

Weeping Turned to Joy

Fourteen years prior to the reading of the Book at the water gate, Ezra was in the temple court weeping and casting himself down before the house of God. A very great congregation was gathered and they too wept sore, as the law of God was declared unto them. It was a solemn day of sorrow and mourning (Ezra 10:1). How different in Nehemiah chapter eight. Ezra is again seen with the Book, but he is not weeping as before, but the people are. However, they are advised, "This day is holy unto the LORD your God; mourn not, nor weep. For all the people wept, when they heard the words of the law. Then he said unto them, Go your way, eat the fat, and drink the sweet, and send portions unto them for whom nothing is prepared: for this day is holy unto our Lord: neither be ye sorry; for the joy of the LORD is your strength. So the Levites stilled all the people, saying, Hold your peace, for the day is holy; neither be ye grieved. And all the people went their way to eat, and to drink, and to send portions, and to make great mirth, because they had understood the words that were declared unto them" (Neh. 8:9-12). There is, "A time to weep, and a time to laugh; a time to mourn, and a time to dance" (Eccl. 3:4). "For his anger endureth but a moment; in his favour is life: weeping may endure for a night, but joy cometh in the morning" (Ps. 30:5).

Happiness

When things are right with God, there is a happiness to God's people. When the flame of love to Christ burns fervently in our hearts, then joy fills our souls. "Whom having not seen, ye love; in Whom, though now ye see Him not, yet believing, ye rejoice with joy unspeakable and full of glory" (1 Pet. 1:8).

What an expression! The joy is of such magnitude that no human mind could fully conceive it, consequently the tongue that is the instrument used to convey audibly the thoughts of the mind cannot give worthy expression. "Full of glory," is the second unique expression. First consider the word glory. It means *to make glorious, adorn with lustre, clothe with splendour, to render something excellent, to make renowned, render illustrious, to cause the dignity and worth of something to become manifest and acknowledged.* It is the superlative display of excellence. The word glory immediately projects our minds on to a future and glorious day when we shall be physically in heaven with Christ, Whom we have not yet seen. Who can give full expression to that day? Not one! We cannot begin to enter into what a glorious place heaven must be. However, one thing we do possess and that is the anticipation of that glory. We look for it, we wait for it, and we long for it. The prospect of enjoying the glory of heaven corresponds with the joy that we have presently. Our joy here is of the same kind that it will be there. The joy in heaven is but an expansion of the joy we possess on earth. This heavenly joy is only experienced through an obedient and steadfast walk with Christ. A frowning Christian is a poor testimony, a silly Christian is a disgrace, but a joyful saint is one of the most powerful testimonies that a child of God can offer to a sick, sinful, and suffering world. The words of John W. Peterson come to mind.

Born of the Spirit with life from above
Into God's family divine,
Justified fully thru Calvary's love,
O what a standing is mine!
And the transaction so quickly was made
When as a sinner I came,
Took of the offer of grace he did proffer,
He saved me, O praise His dear name!

Heaven came down and glory filled my soul,
When at the cross the Saviour made me whole;
My sins were washed away
And my night was turned to day
Heaven came down and glory filled my soul!

To Each Man His Work

Some have wondered why Ezra never made an attempt to rebuild the broken-down walls of Jerusalem, since he was such a godly man and a skillful scribe in the law of his God. The answer is simple, God appoints certain men for certain tasks. God had a man in the shadows for the work of rebuilding Jerusalem's walls, that man being the cupbearer to king Artaxerxes. When God's time came, Nehemiah left the court of the king, with all the authority of the Persian Empire, arriving at Jerusalem to accomplish the work that God had laid upon his heart. You will notice, as this man comes to the front, Ezra occupies a lesser place of prominence. There was no resentment, no pouting, but a spirit of support in the community. He is not mentioned until the wall was finished (Neh. 6:15), thus with separation complete he seeks to sanctify the Lord's people to a higher degree with the scriptures. In the local assembly, God has chosen men for different tasks, thus we have evangelists, teachers, shepherds, deacons, exhorters, and helps, each functioning in his own capacity for the good of the assembly. May God help us to appreciate saints today that resemble the character of the five men we have portrayed for consideration, and may the Lord raise up in the midst of His gathered out people more like them, that separation may remain with us, and that a greater knowledge of God's ways may be gained and manifested in our lives to His glory.

Thank you for traveling with me through the pages of this book. I trust that it has been a help. In closing let me add, how unique is the Book of Ezra. Its first verse tells of a great king and its last verse mentions little children.

Sequel to Summer of Lies

Barbara Baker

Print ISBNs
Amazon Print 978-0-2286-2283-3
LSI Print 978-0-2286-2284-0
BWL Print 978-0-2286-2285-7

BWL Publishing Inc.
Books we love to write ...
Authors around the world.
http://bwlpublishing.ca

Cover art by Pandora Designs

Dedication

Andrea, Evelyn, Lisa, Lyndi

Thanks for all the love and support.

Chapter 1

It's midnight here in Banff which makes it two AM in Toronto. Way too late to text friends. Figures. Nothing in my life has been working out these days.

I kick off the blankets and stare at the darkness of my new bedroom in Opa and Aunt Steph's house. Maybe someone's awake. I could use company. The cold floor squeaks as I tiptoe down the hallway and see a light shining at the bottom of the stairs.

Opa, in his plaid flannel pj's, hunches over the kitchen table. Four squished beer cans sit in front of him and a whole bunch of pill bottles. What the hell?

"Opa," I whisper. "What are you doing?"

He jerks straight in the chair and his hand knocks over the cans as he scoops the pill containers close to his chest.

I grab a cloth and wipe the stinky spill. "What's going on?"

"Nothing, Jillian. Nothing at all."

His shoulders sag. I move closer and give him an awkward side-hug. He stiffens.

"Are you sick?"

He shakes his head.

"Then what?" I wave my hand over the containers. "What are all these?"

"They belonged to your Oma. I'm supposed to take them to the drug store to get rid of them." Opa picks up a container, studies the label, sets it down, takes another. "Heart medicine. Arthritis pills. And the oxy." The almost full vial rattles as he shakes it. "They helped with the pain. She was in a lot of pain. All the time."

Wow. Oxy. Those are solid drugs. I look Opa in the eyes. He stares right back. Did he take one? How would I tell?

His lips quiver.

"Steph wants to clean out Oma's closet. I still go in and smell her blouses like she just took them off. I can't get rid of her things yet."

"Oh, Opa." My tears start even though I blink super fast. "It'll get better," I blubber. "You'll see."

How can I make him happy?

We sit there as the cuckoo tick tocks. Snot drips over my top lip and I wipe it away. Ugly crying. When does being sad get easier? It's been five weeks since Oma died, and it hurts more each day.

And her dying kicked the crap out of my life. Sorry, Oma. No offense but it really did.

Mom's at her new job in Germany trying to impress the boss with her worldliness and I'm stuck here to help Aunt Steph take care

of Opa. I try not to make this about me because I feel awful for him. I do. And I miss Oma a lot, but getting flown three thousand miles from home a month after I start grade ten because Mom's selfish, and Opa's sad, just doesn't seem fair.

And what about my dad? It still feels bizarre to call him Dad since I only found him a few months ago. I sent him a text when Oma died. He called and left a message. Said he was sorry.

Sorry? That's it?

I never called him back. It doesn't matter though. He's probably too busy being important in Denver. Guess I should be grateful he's still coming with his family next year to meet me. It took me forever to find him and he's in no rush to see me.

What's that about?

Apparently, his wife and two daughters need time to adjust to the fact I exist. Like finding out about him and him not knowing I exist didn't need adjusting too?

Why is the world always about someone else?

It's only been three days, but I miss home, I miss my friends and I miss my normal life.

Guilt creeps in for having selfish all-about-me thoughts.

Enough. Stop the whining and crying. My eyes will look gross tomorrow. Wouldn't that be great on my first day at a new school?

Besides, none of this brings Oma back. She'll stay in her box on the living room bookshelf until Opa's ready to bury her or scatter her ashes. Steph put Oma's picture on the front of the box, so Opa remembers she's inside. Like that's not morbid at all.

Opa hiccups and swipes at his eyes. I pick up the beer cans and put them in the back porch.

"Come on, let's get you to bed." I tap his chair.

"I'm not an invalid."

"I know you're not. I'm just trying to help. Let me."

He grabs all the pill bottles, but they slip out of his hands and roll across the table.

"You know what, I'll put them away. Come on." I tuck a hand under his arm, he pushes his chair back, gets up and we make our way to his room. "Good night. I'll see you for breakfast." A quick kiss on his whiskery cheek and I go to leave.

"If I wake up dead, don't you be sad. Promise me."

I freeze in my steps, take a breath and turn to face him. "Opa, please don't say stuff like that."

"I mean it."

"I know you do. That's why it scares me. I love you. And I don't want you to die too."

He waves both hands at me. "Get out of here."

I nod and leave.

"You're a good kid," he calls out before I close his door.

"Thanks."

I go upstairs and stand outside Steph's bedroom door. What will she do if I walk into her room in the middle of the night? Whenever we're together, she flips from being a drill sergeant to acting like I'm a new acquaintance and she's on her best behaviour to impress me. Neither one is working.

Guess I should cut her some slack. It's not like she planned on having to step up to play Mom … ever. Yeah, the huge family secret I fell into when I found my dad.

Aunt Steph's sister raised me for fifteen years. She's who I call Mom. But Aunt Steph's my biological mom which is why my dad was such a huge secret. Trust me, it's a lot to get used to.

And Mom, the one who raised me to my current almost awesome state, sent me here. 'It's only for a year," she promised but who knows these days, lying might be her new 'go- to'.

Before they dumped all this on me, Steph was just my cool aunt. Now that I know she's my bio-Mom things are a bit weird, uncomfortable weird. It's crazy and somewhat creepy having two moms. I'm not sure I'll ever get used to it so, I hope the year whizzes by, and I can go home to my normal life.

"Steph," I whisper as loud as I can and knock. "Wake up." I open her bedroom door.

"What the hell's going on?" Steph flops around in her bed like she's in a wrestling ring.

I flick on the light. Her hand flies over her eyes and she drops the F-bomb. Bucky, on his cushion in the corner, buries his head under his big black paws.

"Do you know what Opa was doing?"

"I don't know what I'm doing." Steph pulls a blanket over her head. "Turn the damn light off."

"Fine." I flick the switch. "Opa was in the kitchen with Oma's pills and beer. I think he was going to take them. He wants to wake up dead."

Silence.

Steph swings her legs over the edge of her bed. She hangs her head and lets out a huge sigh.

"Sorry you had to see that," she says in a quiet voice.

"What? He's done it before?"

She clasps her hands in her lap and looks up. "Jillian, he's a grown man. Grown *old* man. His wife died. She was his best friend. He's miserable. He's lonely. He's not himself right now."

"He could die if he took them all."

"I told him that. I also told him he might not die. He might end up a vegetable in a diaper for years."

"That's terrible. And mean." I slam my hands on my hips. "How could you say that to him?"

"Because he needs to hear it. There's no easy way out for him. I think," Steph pauses, "it keeps him from taking the pills."

I stare at her. How can she be so cold? He's her dad. And *she's* my real mom. She's got to have the tiniest heart. Maybe giving me to her sister to raise really was the best option. I should feel grateful instead of betrayed because she never wanted me.

"We have to do something," I say. "We have to help Opa."

"We do help. Trust me. You being here helps but we can't babysit him. He doesn't want it. And I really don't want to. It's not fair to anyone. Now go get some sleep. He'll be fine in the morning."

"Whatever." I close her door and lean against the wall.

This can't be happening.

Mom would know what to do. But I can't worry her. Steph and I made an agreement, so Mom won't freak if she hears about something going wrong here. We decided we will not tell her the bad stuff unless it's life-critical to me. This is life-critical but not to my life. Anyways, I do the time zone thing like I've done since she left and realize she's already at work. And to bother Mom at work is not worth it.

I tiptoe downstairs to the kitchen, get a bag, put all the pill bottles in it, and take them to my room. In my closet under a loose floorboard, I stuff the bag next to my journal. I've written some ugly stuff no one needs to read. I cringe when I remember what I wrote last night – *I hate you, Mom. If I can't get along with Steph, I have to go to an all-girl's boarding school, where they wear uniforms, in northern BC. Northern BC! Like being stuck in Banff isn't bad enough. How can Mom be so mean? To me.*

Really, I know I don't hate-hate Mom. I'm just super pissed at her. And because of her I have to figure out how to get along with Steph or I'll end up in the middle of bloody nowhere northern BC where I'll know no one at all. It'd be even worse than here.

Chapter 2

There's lots of chatter as kids wander down the locker-lined hallway. Everyone stares at me. And why wouldn't they? They've been back for over a month so it's easy for them to spot the newbie. When I registered, the secretary said it's a good school and I'd enjoy my classes. Right. Because she knows what I like.

I pull my shoulders back. Please let me make a friend. Someone who's not already tight in a group. Someone I can walk down the halls with and hang out with so I'm not the loner kid.

On my third attempt at the combination, the lock pops open. I shove my backpack into the bottom and grab my cellphone.

"Be sure to turn it off before class. Better yet, leave it in your locker."

I pull my locker door back to see a tall, skinny, blond guy with crooked glasses staring down at me.

"Pardon?"

"No phones on in class. No drugs. No smokes. Pretty much no fun allowed." He shrugs. "School rules."

"That's archaic."

"Yup. But you'll lose your phone if the teachers hear it." He raises his hands and waves them. "Huge hassle. Easier to leave it behind."

"Whatever."

I turn my back to skinny blond guy and flip screens to see if Steve texted. Still nothing. I check Find My Friend ® app. No Steve listed. What? He ghosted me. Already? I've only been gone a few days. What a jerk. I suck at picking a good boyfriend. Maybe my first clue should have been that Mom liked him. I shove my phone in my pack and grab textbooks. The locker door slams hard enough to make people look. Great. Now I'm the new kid with attitude. I lean my head against the door.

A whole year of this. It's going to be the longest year of my life.

"Barrett." Skinny, blond guy leans against his locker and points his thumb at his chest.

"Jillian."

"I can show you around," he continues.

"I have a boyfriend." I blurt out the words before my brain has a chance to tell me to shut up. My cheeks get hot.

"Sweet. But I was only offering to show you around. Not date you."

"I'm sorry." I look at him. "That was rude."

He nods.

Baggy, wrinkled t-shirt, jeans, dirty white sneakers. He's got a nice smile, not like hot or anything, just friendly.

"Homeroom for grade 10B," I say.

"Follow me."

He turns and walks through the crowd of kids. It takes me half a second to realize he's literally just leading the way. I walk quick to catch up.

"So, Barrett." I take a few half-steps to walk in sync with him. "How'd you know I was new?"

"You're kidding? Right?" He grins. "Small school. And I didn't recognize you. Plus, everyone knows your aunt and you kind of look like her."

I groan. Small towns suck. Big time.

"Homeroom." Barrett steps into the class.

A few kids are already seated. Barrett heads to the back, drops his books on a table and pulls out a chair.

Do I follow? Do I sit somewhere else? If I was at my school, I'd know these kids. I'd know where to sit. But here, what do I do?

I glance around. Act chill. Cause I am. Most of the time.

"Jillian." Barrett points to the chair next to him.

"You don't have to take care of me," I whisper as I sit down.

"I know." He leans forward and pokes the guy in front of him. They talk monosyllabic stuff while I take out my binder.

I stare at the back of the kids' heads.

Mom doesn't want me around. Steph doesn't know what to do with me being around. And Opa wants to kill himself. It all makes my gut hurt.

An older lady comes in wearing a blazer, turtleneck, long skirt combo. I check her legs and she's got on printed leotards. She looks like she walked out of Oma's closet. It makes me smile in spite of the unfamiliarity of the class.

The chatter stops when she stands in front of the room and looks up and down the rows, finger tapping in the air like she's mentally remembering everyone who should be here. She pauses when she gets to me, nods, smiles, and carries on.

When she's done taking attendance, she reviews last night's homework. Homework I'm already behind in. A few keener hands shoot up with answers and I write down keywords which sound familiar in hopes I can reference my notes at home.

After class, I ask Barrett where the biology lab is. He points down the hall.

"First left and follow the smell of formaldehyde. You can't miss it." He takes off in the opposite direction with a wave. My knight abandons me. Great.

It feels even more awkward being in a classroom of all strangers. At least when Barrett was there, I knew someone, sort of. I go to check my phone a thousand times and stop when I, once again, realize it's in my locker.

I catch a few kids checking me out. They're not fast or polite enough to look away, so I stare at them till they do.

The lunch bell goes, I grab my books and when I look down, I see blood on my crotch. You've got to be kidding? I tip side to side. Yup. Bit of a blood streak on the seat too.

I pretend to write notes and sort paper till everyone leaves before I pull off my hoody. Then I scoot my butt across the seat. Of course, it smears but most of it is now on the ass of my jeans.

Quick glance around the room. No one. I stand up, tie my hoody around my waist, rip sheets of paper from my binder and press the paper over the blood stain. After a few swipes, the seat is clean. I scrunch up the paper without getting any grossness on my fingertips and toss it in the garbage can.

I walk out of the room with my thighs pressing tight against each other. Quick trip to the can to add toilet paper to the leak and two wrong hallways to find my locker. I power walk to Opa's. I've probably ruined the blue jean seam on the inside of my thighs. Thank God no one's home. I'll deal with the

laundry mess after. On the way back to school, I pray my incident went unnoticed. I do not want that kind of attention.

Classes go on forever. A few people smile and one girl says hi. I think she's from math class. When school's done for the day, I hurry to my locker and this time don't take the wrong hallway. Bonus.

"You survived?" Barrett says as I sort books to take home.

"Yeah," I say. *Like it's been a total peach of a day.*

"Not so bad?"

"Easy for you to say." I laugh. "You're not the new kid."

"Meh. Not a big deal. Don't make it one."

I open my eyes wide like I'm in the presence of a super star. "Aren't you the wise one."

He shrugs and leaves.

What a guy. It's obvious he doesn't have a huge need to impress anyone. Part of me feels slighted he didn't hit on me. And that thought drops me back to the here and now. My phone. Steve.

As I swing out the front door to find a non-busy piece of grass to stop on, I see a familiar face way down the sidewalk. Seeing someone I know makes me smile. It's Steph's boyfriend's sister, Mika. She waves and her straight, long hair swings as she walks faster towards me.

How sweet is she to check how my first day went?

I go to wave back, pause halfway and yank my arm down when I realize she's not waving at me. Who's she trying to…before I finish my thought, Barrett rushes up to her. And they kiss. They *really* kiss.

My mouth hangs open.

Mika never said anything about a boyfriend when they were over for supper the other night. She just went on about driving the horse team and wagon in town and how great tourists are at tipping. Oh yeah, and how hard math correspondence is. Not. One. Word. About. A. Boyfriend. I know we're not BFFs or anything, but I'm hurt she didn't tell me about Barrett.

And why didn't Barrett tell me? Oh right, why would he? We just met. But he'd know Mika knows me. He says there are no secrets in a small town. Kudos to him, though, for snagging an older chick. My smartassedness makes me chuckle.

With all the Mika and Barrett distraction I forgot why I rushed outside and turn my phone on. Messages from Steph and Kyra scroll up. Still nothing from Steve.

What happened to him?

I catch a glimpse of Mika and Barrett heading into the Cascade Mall. I will deal with them later.

I text Steve again.

What's up

I check Find My Friend ® app. Still no Steve. I text Kyra.

Have u seen S

Dots flash across the bottom of my phone as I wait for the message. I've told her how to turn it off so people can't tell you're responding right away but she obviously doesn't care.

No

See him at school

Nope. How's Banff?

Fukin awful

Right after I hit send, I regret it. She'll feel bad because she can't fix my life and she's all about trying to make everyone's lives full of smiley faces and heart emojis.

Sorry not your fault ttys

Before I shove my phone in my pocket, I go back to Find My Friend ® app, delete Steve and text Mika.

Call me asap

I know better than to wait for her response. Mika hates technology. Her brother, Tom, got her a cell phone in case of an emergency and she packs it around to appease him but seldom turns it on.

There's only a couple of elementary kids and an adult ahead of me on the sidewalk going home. Figures. I'm not sure why I thought my new best friend would live next door.

Opa and Steph's trucks are both in the driveway.

"How was it?" Steph calls out in her way-too-cheery voice the second I open the back door and Bucky almost knocks me over as he rushes outside to pee.

Opa's moustache wiggles as he comes to greet me. "Hello, Doll."

I drop my backpack and give him a hug. It's good to see him grin.

He squirms out of my arms. "A good day?"

I put on a fake smile and nod.

He winks, pats my back like he's dislodging something stuck in my throat and heads off to the TV room.

"So. Tell all. How'd it go?" Steph leans against the kitchen counter still wearing her work clothes—the unfashionable lame green park warden uniform.

"Well." I roll my eyes. "Where to start? How about with not knowing anyone? Or with my period starting early?"

Steph covers her face with both hands.

"Yeah, great hey? First impressions."

"I'm so sorry." She peeks through her fingers. "That sucks."

I nod.

"I wanted you to have a good day."

"It was not a horrible, bad day," I say. "It was just not a great one."

Her frowny face makes me feel guilty for whining. It's not like she's in control of my body functions or responsible for me not knowing anyone at school.

"Some guy." I watch Steph's expression. "He has a locker next to mine and he made it his mission to take me around. His name's Barrett." Did her lips move, like she's trying not to let on she knows him? She's so expressionless at the best of times it's hard to tell.

"That was nice of him."

"That's all you can say? He knows you. He says everyone knows you."

Steph laughs.

I put my hands on my hips and take a deep breath. "So, how come you never said anything?"

"About what?"

"About Mika and Barrett."

Steph opens the fridge, ducks her head down and pulls mustard and ketchup out. It's all I can do not to grin as I let her suffer in silence.

"She's Tom's sister," I say. "You must have known."

"I'm sorry." Steph faces me. "It wasn't my news to tell."

"Mom says not telling is as bad as lying. You could have said *something*. Mika's like the only other person I know in this stupid town."

"That's not true."

I stick my chin out. "Yes, it is."

"You know Mrs. Bronigan."

"Right cause she's like...older than God."

"Okay. That's fair." Steph laughs. "What about Eddy? You know him."

Tom is so jealous about Steph and Eddy's friendship, but I don't dare mention that right now. She'd come down on me like a crazy person.

"Eddy lives in the woods with his dog." I shake my head. "Nothing weird about that."

"He lives in town in the winter."

"Well," I say, "that just makes him marginally less weird."

"Is your period making you cranky?" Steph crosses her arms. "If this is all about Mika and Barrett, I think you need to relax. They're dating. Big deal. It's not like she stole your boyfriend."

"Easy for you to say. Everyone has someone except me." I make a circle out of my thumb and index finger and wave it at her. "Zero. I have no one."

"Oh, come on." She cuffs my shoulder. "You have Steve. You said he might come for Thanksgiving. And you'll meet other kids, you'll see."

"You said he has to stay in a hotel if he comes." I walk past her. "But don't worry. He's not coming."

"What? Why not? I was joking. He can sleep on the couch," she calls after me, but I don't respond.

Once I'm in my room, I check my phone. Nothing. From anyone. I drop onto my bed and stare at the ceiling. No tears. Sad or

angry ones. Just kind of a blah, numb, nothingness.

***

Good Saturday morning to me. I survived the first week of school. Not a single text from Steve and Kyra isn't saying anything about his silence. Her messages are so vague when she's usually all about the details. What's she hiding? She's not going with Steve, is she? She wouldn't do that to me. It's girlfriend code. But something irks me.

I send her a quick text.

R u seeing Steve

I wait for the dots to start but they don't. She's always on her phone. What's she up to? If she is seeing Steve, worst BFF ever. She wouldn't, would she? I wait for the screen to change. It doesn't. Whatever. She's probably all awkward about me being stuck here and doesn't know what to say. It takes so much energy to keep being in touch when no one responds.

Out of sight, out of mind. Mom warned it would happen, but I was sure she was wrong. Kyra is my BFF and Steve is supposed to be my boyfriend. I hate it when Mom's right. I send her a quick email and tell her how fabulous life is in Banff. Bet she doesn't read the sarcasm in my words.

Mika hasn't called all week. I did not say a word to Barrett about seeing them kiss. I thought he might crack because he feels awkward, but nope. Apparently, he's good with me not knowing. Or maybe he doesn't know I don't know. Why is it so tough to figure out what's going on with people?

"Morning, Doll." Opa's voice pulls me away from my muddled thoughts. "Since when are you an early riser?"

"I'm usually not." I tap the top of his prickly head. "Want some coffee?"

"It stunts your growth." His newspaper rustles as he chuckles.

"Done the crossword puzzle yet?" I pour water into the coffee machine.

He grunts.

Rain drips down the window. The yellow and orange leaves look brighter when they're wet. Toast in hand, I grab a chair and sit next to Opa.

After adding two sugars to each of our cups, I slide his closer. "Want some help?"

"I cheat," he says.

"Pardon?"

"I cheat. Stoph says I need to do the damn puzzles to keep my wits sharp, so I do it to shut her up. Goes faster if I cheat."

"You're bad." I squeeze his arm. "I won't tell."

While I have breakfast, Opa half mumbles clues, scratches his stubble then pulls his cellphone out of his pocket. He

Googles answers, winks at me and fills out the squares.

“A six-letter word for bad, starts with ‘s’” he says.

“Shitty.”

“Works for me.” His chair squeaks across the floor and he gets up.

While he’s at the counter I see how hunched over he is. He’s gotten old. Or has he always been old, and I never noticed? As I debate him aging, Opa’s body jerks and he leans in closer to look out the window.

“Jesus Christ,” he shouts.

I almost fall off my chair.

“Get some towels. Now.”

Opa pulls Steph’s yellow rain slicker off the hook at the back door and does a stiff-legged jog side-to-side as he rushes down the steps and out the back gate to the alley.

I press my face against the window. What the heck’s he doing? And then he’s on his way back and there’s a little kid’s head, with the biggest smile, sticking out from under the slicker.

I run down the hall and grab towels.

“Get inside, you brat.” Opa pushes the kid into the back porch. “Shoes off. Put them on the mat. Give me those towels.”

Opa grabs them out of my arms. The kid, maybe six, seven years old, grins like he just got a handful of Halloween candy.

“Yes, sir.” He salutes Opa and lines his soggy shoes up beside mine.

"Jillian, Kyle. Kyle, Jillian. And don't get any ideas young man." Opa shakes a finger in Kyle's face. "She's too old for you."

"Easy." I tip my head at Opa.

Opa rubs the towel on Kyle's head like he's drying Bucky. When he's done, he grabs both ends of the towel, flips it over Kyle and pulls it back and forth, up and down his body. I bite my bottom lip to keep my grin under control. Kyle must think he's going through a mini car wash.

"Okay, think we got most of it." Opa rests both hands on Kyle's shoulders. "You good? Your mom okay?"

Kyle nods.

"And," Opa twirls his index finger in the air, "what's your story this time?"

"She told me to play outside. She's got friends over."

"She didn't bloody notice it's raining cats and dogs?"

"It's okay." Kyle stands straighter. "I don't mind."

"Jillian, turn around. Kyle, take those wet clothes off. I won't let her see your man bits." Opa shooshoo me away. After a few minutes, Kyle walks past me wrapped in the towel.

"You get dry clothes on. You know where they are," Opa says. "Then we'll have breakfast. Pancakes."

Kyle turns, salutes Opa again and runs to the study.

Once he's out of the kitchen I lift my hands in the air. "What's going on?"

"Same old crap. Different day. Can you make pancakes?"

"Sure."

"Well," he ushers me towards the stove with both hands, "get at it."

I salute him too, but with added sarcasm and wonder what just happened. While I mix the batter and heat up the frying pan, I hear Opa's voice on the phone.

"He's here." Silence. "Not going anywhere." Silence. Then footsteps.

The batter sizzles in the frying pan. Opa pats my shoulder and gets plates and silverware out.

"Everything ok?" I flip a pancake and it splats. Fried butter smell wafts up.

"They will be. Sorry, Doll." He nods. "Trust me, the less you know about this shit-show the better."

I stare at the golden-brown pancakes. What is Opa up to? He's not the befriending-a-wet-kid kind of guy. I mean, I know he loves me, he has to but taking care of people was Oma's thing. They tolerate Opa because she was nice to everyone. Opa says people are a pain in the ass and few are worth getting to know. Sometimes, he's got a point. The thought reminds me I'm pissed at Mika for not telling me about Barrett.

Kyle comes into the kitchen, hair slicked back and wearing a shirt which is way too long and grey sweats.

"Smells so good," he says. "I love pancakes. Can you make Mickey Mouse ones?"

"Sorry, I made plain, round ones. Next time." I wave the pot in front of him. "Want coffee?"

"I'm just a kid. I can't drink coffee."

"I know." I laugh. "I was trying to be funny."

"You're not very good at it," Kyle snorts. "I have a book of jokes. I could lend it to you."

There's one in every crowd. "What do you like on pancakes?"

"I can eat them plain."

I flip a couple onto his plate. "If you wanted something on them, what would you want?"

"Butter, syrup, Nutella." Kyle stares at me for a second and breaks into a huge smile. "Ice cream."

"Nice try." I pass him the butter and syrup.

Head down, he inhales the pancakes and only comes up for a sip of juice or to stab another one. Where is he putting it all? Opa leans against the counter. I'm not sure what his expression means. It's almost a smile but a funny smile like he's on the inside of a joke.

The doorbell interrupts Kyle's pancake marathon and his head pops up.

"GG?" he says.

Opa nods and heads to the door.

I stack the dirty plates. "Who's GG?"

"Great Gramma." Kyle shovels in his last bite and rushes to follow Opa.

Before he reaches the back porch, old Mrs. Bronigan and her walker thump into the kitchen. She's his great gramma? I am so confused. Opa and I will be having a bit of a chat when I get him alone.

"Hello, girlie. Nice to see you." Her red lipstick is fresh. And thick. "Thanks for helping out. Mums the word." She winks.

Kyle follows her and Opa into the TV room. I stand there like I've been dropped down a rabbit hole. What the heck is going on? The fact Opa and Mrs. Bronigan are partners in crime is pretty cute. Hopefully it distracts Opa enough he stops talking about waking up dead.

Chapter 3

Tom answers the apartment door. Faded jeans, blue t-shirt. Looks like he just showered. No wonder Steph slips off to see him every chance she gets. Me living with her probably makes getting alone time tricky and part of me is okay with inconveniencing them since, really, how inconvenient is it for me to be here?

"Hey, Jillian," Tom says.

"Hi." I clasp my hands in front of me. "Is Mika home?"

"She is." He opens the door all the way and Mika comes around the corner, stops mid-step when she sees me. She's still in pjs. Wow. So not like her. It's almost noon. And her hair is in a pony. My curly hair lives in a pony because it's the only way to keep it contained but I've never seen her wear hers in one. I shove a runaway, curly piece behind my ear.

"Jillian."

"Hey," I say.

Mika responds with nothing. Nope, I'm not kissing her ass. This is not my fault. The silence echoes out the hallway.

"Well, then. I'll see you gals later." Tom grabs his coat, squeezes past me and

rushes away like Steph's waiting outside for him.

Once the door is shut the quiet is uncomfortable and I force myself not to break it.

"What's up?" Mika heads towards her room and I follow. She closes a binder and some textbooks, scoops them off the bed and sets them on the floor. "If I didn't know better, I'd say you've been avoiding me."

I flop on her bed and stare at the ceiling. If I look at her, she'll be able to tell something's wrong, but I want her to apologize to me.

"So?" Mika sits beside me. I can feel her stare but focus on the light fixture. "Talk to me. You haven't called or anything all week."

"I texted. You didn't answer. What the hell, Mika?" I sit up. "Why didn't you tell me about Barrett?"

Mika takes a huge breath and exhales so slow as if she's trying to figure out what to say before she runs out of air.

"Because I didn't think you wanted to hear it." She stands. "You're so mad about having to be here, leaving your friends. I didn't know *how* to tell you."

"It's not your fault I'm stuck here. We're suppose to be friends. You can just tell me. You don't hide it."

"I know, but I feel bad for you. I love my job. I'm doing half decent with

correspondence classes." She looks away. "And Barrett and I…well, my life's so good."

"'Mika and Barrett sitting in a tree.'" I mimic the old kid's jingle.

She smacks me but her smile is huge. "My life is good and yours, well, you're not exactly excited about it."

I snort. *No denying that*. I haven't exactly hidden my feelings about being stuck in Banff. Mika makes me feel a tad guilty she thinks she can't tell me stuff because she's afraid I'll get upset.

Note to self—work on attitude or fake happiness to some degree. It's not everyone's fault my life is crummy right now. It's only Mom's fault.

"And then when Barrett met you, he was surprised you didn't know about him and me." Mika exhales. "He got all pissy cause I didn't tell you, like I was embarrassed cause he's, you know, younger. That was a fun conversation with him. Geesh. Touchy feely guys. So sensitive."

"Barrett? Sensitive?" I raise my eyebrows for two reasons. The idea Barrett's sensitive and the thought of Mika having a relationship conversation with a guy—that would have been fun to eavesdrop on.

"We started hanging out at the end of July. And then it didn't seem the right time to share my good stuff at your gramma's funeral. I'm sorry," Mika says. "No, I'm not

sorry. I'm not sorry I'm seeing Barrett. I'm sorry I didn't have the kahunas to tell you."

"You never will have kahunas." I laugh.

She slugs me in the shoulder. "Made you laugh."

Out of nowhere, my eyes start to burn. I look down at my hands and blink. Why do I cry at such stupid shit? I'm happy for her. Really, I am. Jealous—a bit. I feel out of place. But I don't feel alone. It takes a few minutes to control my tears, but I pull it off.

"Are you okay?" She taps my arm. "Are we okay?"

I nod.

"Want to go hang out?"

"Nah."

"Want to talk?"

I shake my head.

We just sit side by side for awhile. Quiet.

"Okay." I take a deep breath. "I've got to get back. Opa's got some kid and Mrs. Bronigan at the house."

"Kyle?"

"What? You know?"

Why does everyone know what's going on except me?

"I heard Tom talking. Your gramma took him in a few times when Mrs. Bronigan moved to the lodge. It helps Kyle's mom out, you know, when she's getting lit and he's better off somewhere else."

I stop at the doorway. My mouth is wide open, but I can't think of anything to say.

"Relax," Mika says. "Mrs. Bronigan's the only other family Kyle's got in town. His mom hates her, but she gets to see Kyle at your place during these…events and it keeps him safe."

"That's crazy. He's just a kid. She left him outside. In the rain. Who does that?"

Mika shrugs.

"Come on." I put my hands on my hips. "Spill. You know more?"

"Nope. That's all. Sorry. Is he a brat?"

"Not at all. It's just weird. Opa won't say anything to me but acts like it's no big deal."

"He's safe. That's what counts."

Mika gives me a solid hug. Makes me feel bad about all the nasty thoughts and all the daggers I threw at her in my mind. And all the mean stuff I said to my pillow.

I hug her back.

***

"What should I put in his lunch?" Opa says as I pour a bowl of cereal.

"PBJ sandwich."

"What the heck is that?"

"Peanut butter and jam."

"Well, then why don't you just say peanut butter and jam. You kids." Opa waves his hands in the air like he's chasing flies. "All your mumbo jumbo talk. What else?"

I wave my hands back at Opa's mumbo jumbo hand gestures. "A couple of cookies, juice box, apple."

"You don't have to do that." Kyle dumps a banana peel in the garbage. "I go to the lunch program. It's free for kids with no lunches."

"You won't be going there on my watch," Opa grumbles. "And you bloody better eat this. No trading for chips and shit."

"Language," I whisper in Opa's ear, but he pushes me away. What a guy. He pretends to be so tough. Just like Steph does. Genetic. Apple falling close to the tree and all that stuff Mom quotes when she's being introspective about people.

"I'll drive you." Opa shakes the lunch bag in the air. "Be ready in 20 minutes."

"What?" I fake a scowl at him. "He gets a ride? I have to walk?"

"He's company." Opa taps me under the chin, grabs Bucky's leash and they head out for their walk around the block.

"Sorry. He can drive you," Kyle says. "I can walk."

"I'm just giving him a hard time. Relax." I scruff up Kyle's hair. "Besides, you're good for him. You keep him out of trouble."

***

It feels less weird walking into the school today.

I check my phone for messages. Happy face from Mom. *Have a good day* from Steph. Nothing from anyone at home, not even Kyra. Sigh. I turn my phone off.

This week I will smile at school until my face hurts. I will be positive, and I will make new friends. Promise.

"Hey," Barrett mumbles from inside his locker. "How's things?"

"Okay." I unpack my books and sort out what I need for class.

My locker door moves back and Barrett's face peeks at me.

"Really?" he says.

"Really." I tuck the books in one arm and put my lock back on. "If I have to be here, I might as well make it less miserable for everyone else."

"Nice attitude." Barrett points down the hall. "Lead the way."

"By the way, thanks for telling me about you and Mika." I stare straight ahead and force myself not to smile.

"About that." Barrett waves a hand in the air. "I guess…"

"Never mind. It's no biggie." I punch him in the shoulder. "But don't hide shit from me again."

He salutes me and we talk about other stuff as we walk. Nothing heavy. Oma used to call it 'weather conversation'. People

wave. Probably at Barrett. But that's okay. I'll take it even if I ride on his shirt tail. Is that how the expression goes? Mom would know.

When we're at our desks in homeroom, Barrett says, "What's your option?"

"Steph said to take the Outward-Bound course. She said there's a bit of climbing."

"You climb?"

"Not well. But I like it."

"Great. I'll see you there."

***

After an intense math class, I head to the room off the gymnasium for the Outward-Bound class. Maybe 12-15 kids are already there. Barrett shoots his arm up and waves me over. I smile. What a knight. People will talk if he keeps it up. Mika might not like that. I walk over to the empty chair next to him.

A guy in a wool sweater, beige khakis and a buzz cut steps to the front of the class.

"Who's your friend, Barrett?"

Barrett does a finger-thumb gunpoint at me. What the hell? Tom and Steph do that all the time. It makes me want to pull my hoody over my head and back out of the room.

"Jillian Meier," Barrett says.

"Hello, Jillian." Mr. Amatt smiles. "Nice to have you join us. What's your experience level?"

I glance at the side of Barrett's head.

My tiniest voice squeaks out, “At what?”

“Sex,” a voice from behind shouts. I force myself to not look back as heat runs up my face.

“Settle down,” Mr. Amatt says. “Sorry. The only person who asks your sex level isn’t getting any. Right, Eric? I meant climbing, Jillian. What level of a climber are you? It’s the first section of the course. Have you done much?”

I take a slow breath to make my normal voice return.

“Not a lot.”

“How much is not a lot?”

“I did the Via Ferrate on Norquay.” I shrug. “The easy route.”

“That’s cheating,” loudmouth Eric pipes in again.

Mr. Amatt crosses his arms. “No, Eric, it’s not cheating. The cables and anchors are in, yes. But you still have to get yourself up and down.”

Eric sounds like he’s going to be a real knob.

“Anything else, Jillian?” Mr. Amatt says.

“West end of Rundle last summer. Backside. He had ropes but we didn’t use them because it ended up being a scramble.”

And it was the hottest freakin’ day to be hiking up a mountain. I learned climbing guides have this code—*the group goes as fast as the slowest person*. How humiliating.

I was the slowest person. I don't think I'll mention it to the class.

Mr. Amatt points at me. "You took a guided trip?"

"Yeah, with Greg..."

"Not Patterson?" Mr. Amatt interrupts. "Greg Patterson?"

I nod. Heat runs up my face again. There's no way Mr. Amatt knows I had a mini crush on Greg. I mean, Greg doesn't even know.

"Greg's back from Whistler," Mr. Amatt says.

A murmur of voices and a few giggles.

"Easy gals." Mr. Amatt shakes his head. "He'll be helping with the class to get his guiding hours in. Let me emphasize the *teaching* aspect of climbing is what he'll help with."

Louder giggles.

With slight head movement, I try to see where they came from. Steph says Greg is all about getting into a girl's pants. I don't think so. Besides, he never mentioned a girlfriend. When we were done the climb, he said, "great job", and shook my hand. He. Shook. My. Hand. Full stop. Never texted or called even though he had my number on the waiver. That hurt but I stopped thinking about him when Steve and I started dating.

I smile when I remember swapping spit with Greg. It was not kissing related. I ran out of water before we reached the summit of

Mount Rundle and Greg passed me his canteen. Like I said, we swapped spit.

No wonder the girls are giggling. He's kind of gorgeous, him and his soft, Aussie accent, messy hair and shy smile. On top of that, he's super nice. Not a combo I've seen in many guys.

How cool would it be if Greg finished high school here, right in this school? To pass him in the hallway once in a while…I shake my head. Get real. It was *my* mini crush on him. The feeling was not mutual. Besides, he's all about work and paying bills and taking care of himself. Mom would call him an old soul because he's being so mature even though he's young. An old soul in teenager guy skin.

Mr. Amatt sorts papers on his desk and hands them to the kid in the first seat.

"Pass them around. Overnight bivouac permission slips and information. No parental signatures, no trip."

"Can we bring a friend?" a female voice behind me asks.

"You're kidding, right?" Mr. Amatt says.

"Can't hurt to ask." She laughs.

"Pack your food, utensils and pots. You want to cook together go for it. You don't bring anything, you don't eat. Barrett, do you have the topper on your truck?"

"Yup."

"We'll get a teacher to drive it with the gear."

"Where we going, Mr. A?" loud-mouth Eric says.

"You think I'm falling for that again?" Mr. Amatt tips his head and gives the back of the class a stink eye. "Not likely. You'll know when we get there."

The bell rings. Chairs screech. I wait till the room clears a bit before I get up.

"What was that all about?" I say to Barrett.

"Ah, last time someone told someone where we were going and that someone told another idiot and there were all these people with beer and rye and," Barrett makes a pouty face, "big gong show. Trip got cancelled."

"Got it."

"Don't worry. It won't happen again. It's a good time without the booze. You'll see. And you and Patterson. Who's keeping secrets now?"

"There is no *me and Patterson*."

Barrett grins and nods. I slap his shoulder.

"Yeah."

***

Opa and Kyle sit at the kitchen table dipping cookies in glasses of milk. Bucky sits beside Kyle's chair, and from the looks of how close his mouth is to the table, I assume there's been some spillage.

Kyle licks his lips. “How was your day? Mine was awesome. Mr. Meier parked in the No Parking spot and the cops came. He didn’t have his license. Then they called Miss Stephanie. I got to sit in the back of the cop car. So cool.”

“It’s not a big deal. I didn’t see the bloody sign. It’s this big.” Opa makes the bottom of a square with his thumbs and pointer fingers. “You’d think they’d have better things to do than harass old men.”

“Well, then. I guess my day’s boring compared to yours.” I grab a cookie from Oma’s ceramic duck container. “You do know the rules for driving are meant for old men too, right?” I wink at Kyle and turn a serious face to Opa.

“Don’t you have homework or something better to do than pick on me?” He gives me a fake grumpy face.

Chapter 4

"Go to the dance tonight," Aunt Steph says. "Who knows. You might even have fun."

"I don't have anyone to go with."

"What about Mika and Barrett?"

"Right." I plant my hands on my hips. "Cause they want me along."

"You know they do. You're just being grumpy."

"Fine." I snort and leave the kitchen.

My pity party gets put on hold as Opa comes down the hallway. Did he hear us? I hope not. He's got so much going on with Kyle. Which is great. At least he's not sitting in the dark with a bunch of pill bottles and drinking beer.

"Guess I'm going to the school dance." I force a smile. Not too big and not too fake. "Gotta get ready."

"I'll drive you. You know, in case you kids drink." He winks.

"Opa, I'm not old enough to drink."

"None of us were." He laughs. "You have fun, Doll. Meet a nice boy."

"I'm so done with boys."

"Well then," he shrugs. "Meet a nice girl."

I poke him in the ribs. "I don't want to meet a nice girl either. I'm going cause Steph's on my case about staying home on a Friday night."

He leans in and whispers, "Bet she's got a hot date with Tom."

Steph shouts, "I can hear you."

***

It's like I stepped into Mom's old school movies. The gym has a giant disco ball in the middle of the ceiling and colourful lights flicker across the almost dark room. A lot of girls have shirts tied in knots above their navel. Flared jeans. Blue jean skirts. A lot of plaid. Maybe I should have paid more attention to the poster.

A couple I usually see making out at their lockers are doing it on the dance floor. Get a room. Three kids walk by. One girl waves, but doesn't gesture for me to join them.

I give this dance one hour and I'm out of here. I'll walk downtown or something equally lame. Kids lean along the wall beside the food tables. No sign of Mika or Barrett. *Why did Mom have to have an epiphany now about wanting to be someone important at work? We were fine with her old job. Couldn't she have waited a few years till I finished high school? Then I wouldn't have to try fitting in where I don't belong.*

I lap the dance floor again. If I was braver, I'd walk up to a group and hang at the edge. See if they invite me in. But I'm not that brave. Bet no one else feels as wallflowerish as me.

"Can I get you a drink?" A guy peeks around my shoulder. Spaced front teeth. Shaggy hair. I don't remember what class he's in.

I glance at the snack table and shake my head. "I'm good, thanks."

"Got beers in the truck." He nods his head towards the door.

"Really, I'm good."

He moves in front of me with his thumbs hooked in his front belt loops.

"Big city girl. Bet you're used to the good stuff."

"Pardon."

"Oh, come on." He grins.

I nod and pretend I get what he's saying. Weirdo. "Gotta go. Have a good night."

"Wait. Don't be so stiff. Vape?" He pats his pocket then nods his head towards the door again. "I'll share if you got nothing."

"Thanks, but no." I leave and feel him follow me until someone shouts "Eric". Ah, that's where he's from. The big mouth knob in Outward-Bound class.

"Next time Jilly," he calls out.

Not if I can help it.

As I walk by the girls at the ticket table, they look up and smile. I almost pause but

decide against it and head out the door, onto the sidewalk of Banff Avenue.

That'll show them, right? I don't need any of them.

But I do. Just one or two. We don't have to be BFFs or anything. Just a few to hang with. They don't even have to really like me. Just let me be a part of them. So I don't have to be 'the new girl'. The loner 'new girl'.

I head downtown. The shops, people and streetlights make me feel less alone. I zip up my coat and spend time judging window displays. Maybe I can fit in as a tourist.

The first Outward-Bound trip is next week. Then another one at the end of November. Not sure I'm psyched about sleeping outside in a snow cave though. Broaden your horizons. Get to know your surroundings. Blah, blah, blah. Thanks Mom. Thanks a lot.

Will winter be *any* better? There are lots of snowboards and ski sales advertised in the stores. Steph has gear in the garage. Maybe her stuff will fit me. I can decide which one I like better. Then guilt Mom into buying me new stuff.

After I've done both sides of the street, I check my phone. Text from Mika.

Where r u

Not into it have fun going home

And it's nine o'clock. Good enough. Maybe Opa wants to watch a movie. I'll

make popcorn. He can even pick one of his old cowboy shows. I jog the last dark block home.

"Opa." I flick on the light in the back porch. "Want popcorn and a movie?"

Silence.

That's odd. He never goes to bed this early. I tiptoe towards the living room where light from the TV flickers on the wall. There on the couch—Mrs. Bronigan at one end, Opa at the other, Kyle in the middle with huge headphones on. Mrs. Bronigan and Opa are asleep. My heart does a hurt pang for Oma. Kyle smiles like it's Christmas morning.

I grab two throws and tuck them around Opa and Mrs. Bronigan. Neither budge. I lift one of Kyle's headphones up.

"Want popcorn?" I whisper.

He nods and I give him a thumbs up.

I pull out a bag of microwave popcorn, unwrap it and toss it in, grab two bowls and juice glasses. A bang on the back door interrupts my snack arrangement.

"Forgot your key Steph?" I open the door.

"I want him." A tall, goth lady hisses inches away from my face. "Right now."

I step back from the booze stink. Her face scrunches up so much it's all wrinkles. I put my hand up to make sure she doesn't come closer.

"What are you talking about?" I say in a voice I hope doesn't betray my fear.

"You fucking know what I'm talking about. Get Kyle. Now!"

Something inside me forces me to remain expressionless but I tense up. Mrs. Bronigan's 'mums the word' rings through my head.

"I'm sorry. I can't."

Crazy lady puts both her hands up to shove me, but she trips. I grab her shoulders to stop her from falling down the steps. She takes a swing. Well, maybe not a swing. Maybe more a girl slap.

Of all the things Mom and I disagree on, her making me take karate is not one of them. I grab the lady's wrist. Slowly turn it behind her back. Not hard. Not like I want to bust her shoulder or anything. Just hard enough for her not to be able to slap again. With one hand in the middle of her back and the other tight on her wrist, I walk her down the steps to the sidewalk.

"What's going on?" Opa's shout scares me. And goth lady straightens.

"Jillian," he barks. "Go inside."

"It's okay." I turn the lady so she's facing Opa. "She's just leaving."

"Let her go." He points to the open door. "Go inside. Now."

"What?"

Opa tips his head down a smidge and gives me a look. He's never given me the

look before. I drop crazy lady's hand. Throw both mine in the air and stomp to where he's standing.

He points into the house again. "You burned the popcorn."

My mouth tightens. I know better than to talk back but dammit, this is not my fault. She started it. I walk into the house and Opa pulls the door shut. Hard.

The kitchen stinks as smoke seeps out the microwave. I lean my ear towards the porch. I can't make out what Opa's saying so I peek around the doorframe. He's pointing, shaking his arm at her. Goth lady waves a fist in the air and drops the F-bomb which makes it all the way through the closed door. Then she turns, marches out the yard and slams the back gate.

Opa stays on the deck and shakes his head as he watches her go. I hurry back to the sink, push the window open and grab a can of air freshener to spray away the popcorn stink.

"Everything okay?" I say without looking at Opa.

Silence.

I turn to him. He's bent over picking stuff off his sock.

"Opa, are you okay?"

"There are chips in the cupboard. Don't burn them." He walks up to me. "That was a nice hold. Next time snug it up a bit higher." He grabs my wrist, but not hard, turns me

around and slowly lifts my arm behind my back. “Bring it up until you have them on tiptoes. You’ll have all their attention then.” He lets go, pats me on the back and says in a quiet voice, “She’s his mom. She’s gone off the deep end again, but it’ll pass. It always does.”

“Okay.” I nod a few slow times.

“His old man is a schmuck. He’s in the wind somewhere. The bugger’s as useless as a tit on a bull.”

My eyes go big.

“You didn’t hear it from me.” He heads back to the TV room.

Well, I guess that clears up some of the Kyle mystery. *Tit on a bull*. I’ve never heard Opa insult someone that bad. And kudos to him. Another secret. He knows self defense. Maybe he’s the reason Mom makes me take karate.

Life. Adults. Family. God they’re complicated and full of surprises. When they’re together and apart.

Chapter 5

"We're going to do what?" I say to Mika and Barrett as I grab my coat.

The back door whips open and Kyle bursts in between them before either one can respond.

"Is Mr. Meier ready to go?" Kyle shouts.

"Whoa." I grab him by the shoulders to stop him from tracking through the house with his shoes. "What's the rush?"

"We're going shooting. He promised. GG brought her cane and her walker. She says she's gonna whoop some ass."

My face freezes in a surprised expression which I try to hide. "You're doing what?"

Opa clears his throat. I turn and watch him walk across the kitchen.

"Relax, Doll." He holds out an arm full of orange Nerf guns, a giant freezer bag full of Styrofoam bullets, and safety glasses hooked on his finger. "Just going to have a bit of fun."

Barrett, Mika and I laugh.

"Go easy on the old folks, Kyle," Barrett says. "They may have good aim, but they can't move fast."

"You listen here, you hooligan. I can run with the best of them." Opa wags his finger at Barrett. "I just need a bit of motivation." He waves the bullets.

Kyle and Opa head out and get into Mrs. Bronigan's car.

I turn to Mika. "Should she be driving?"

"She's got a license."

"That's not what I mean."

"They're fine." Mika sighs. "Quit being such a nerd."

"Thanks." I scowl at her and pull on my coat. "Are we doing anything as fun as them?"

"Mountain biking. You'll love it."

"Mountain biking? Like biking on a mountain? Sounds terrifying." I follow them out the back door to Barrett's truck. Three bikes hang off the tailgate. Mika jumps in the passenger side and scootches over to the middle. Barrett's old-school man truck shines so much I need sunglasses to cut the glare. I climb in.

Shag carpet on the dash. Giant cloth dice hang off the rear-view mirror. It's spotless inside too. And a lap seatbelt? Is that even legal?

"I've never mountain biked." I cinch the seatbelt hoping it's more effective when it's super tight.

Barrett leans forward as he starts the truck. "But you do ride a bike, right?"

"Who doesn't?"

I can ride a bike, but it's been years. *Another one of Mom's old lines almost makes me chuckle out loud. Like 'riding a bike, you don't forget how'.* Here's hoping it's true.

We drive down Banff Avenue, cross the bridge, and pass the Banff Springs to the Spray Trailhead parking lot. Barrett unloads the bikes and Mika plunks a helmet on my head.

"You know, just in case you crash." She passes me a pair of gloves. "And these will keep the gravel out of your palms."

"What are my chances of crashing?"

"Hardly any at all." She grins.

Barrett pushes an orange bike over to me and shows me how to adjust the seat.

"There are a few hills," he says. "Gear down before you start climbing. Don't power through a shift. It's hard on the chain. Stay loose." He shakes his whole body like he's doing a goofy dance. "When you're going downhill, gear up so the chain is tight and doesn't flap around. Look ten feet in front of your tire. You won't have to correct as often."

Exactly how far is ten feet? And why would the chain flap? I don't remember having to know all this when I learned to ride a bike.

"Got it," I say. So it looks like I understand everything, I get on the bike.

Barrett tucks pepper spray in his pocket. Mika has one hanging off her pack.

"Hey, where's mine?"

"We've got you covered."

We pedal across the parking lot to a gate which has a Bear Awareness sign beside it.

"Um, should we be going here?" I get off my bike.

"The sign's always up." Mika pedals around me, maneuvers her bike along the skinny trail beside the gate and onto the dirt road. "The sign makes the Park less liable."

I read the '*hike in groups beyond this point*' section and stop reading when the print gets smaller. *We're in a group. Not breaking any rules*. I climb on the bike again.

The wagon-trail road starts off flat and it's not hard to keep up with them. We chat as we pedal but stop talking when we climb a hill. Then it's flat again for a bit. More talking. Another hill. A much steeper one. No more talking. There are so many long, steep hills. Some don't seem to end until I almost lose a lung.

I can no longer pedal, breathe and talk on the flats so I listen. The road narrows. More potholes. On some sections there's only a skinny dirt trail. Barrett takes the lead, Mika follows. I try to keep up.

"Don't look where you don't want to go," Mika shouts.

What exactly does that mean?

I'd ask but my mouth is dry. I glance at the loaded buffalo berry bushes along the right side of the trail. The bike's front tire rolls right into them. I put a foot down, lift my bike back onto the trail and now understand the 'don't look where you don't want to go' statement. Lucky it was on the right side of the trail because the left side would have been a rocky landing down a steep bank.

Mika's butt disappears over the top of a hill. It's hard to get back on and crank quick enough to get momentum when you're halfway up a slope. Third try and I make it. My lips taste like slimy salt. So gross.

I can't hear them talking anymore. Either they're struggling too, or they're really far ahead and don't know they left me behind.

No more gears. Grannie gear is not getting me up this hill any easier. Snot drips off my nose but I can't take my hands off the handlebar, or I'll ditch it again.

Movement in the tall grass. Ahead. On my left. If Mika is trying to scare me, I'm not falling for it.

A bear head pokes up.

Oh, my God.

Big black bear steps onto the trail. In front of me. I crash. Rocks stab my butt and legs. I scream. Mouth open. Not a sound. Not helpful.

The bear rocks its head side to side. A black thing hangs around its neck. A blue tag

in his ear. His shoulders roll as he comes closer. I crab walk backwards. Like in dreams I yell again but no sound comes out.

The bear stops, lifts his head and sniffs. Long snout. Yellow teeth. Sharp. He snuffs again, lets out a hoarse bark and rushes forward. I close my eyes. I don't want to die. Not like this.

"Get out of here," I hear Barrett scream.

I open my eyes in time to see a riderless bike fly through the air. *Thunk*. Solid hit. Bounces off the bear and lands a few feet in front of me. The bike. Not the bear. The bear spins and crashes off into the trees.

"Jillian!" Mika runs to me. "Are you okay?"

I close my eyes and drop my butt onto the ground. After a few huge breaths I look at her.

"Good timing," I say. "Thank you."

With his pepper spray out, Barrett puts his other hand above his eyes and paces while he peers through the trees.

"You okay?" he calls.

"Almost shit myself. But I'm good."

Mika grabs me under an arm and stands me up. She brushes stuff off my clothes a little too hard.

"Easy." I step back and finish the job with a gentler touch.

Barrett picks up his bike, gets down and pokes at stuff on the frame. "Only a few scratches and a bent crank."

"I think we should head back," Mika says.

"He charged Jillian." Barrett stops in front of her. "We need to call it in."

"No, he didn't. It was a bluff."

"It was not. That was a full out charge."

"Barrett." Mika shakes her head. "He had a collar on and a tag. If we report it, the wardens will shoot him."

"What?" I stare at Mika. "Why would they shoot him?"

"He's been in trouble before. You're not hurt and the bear's gone. We'll stick together and warn anyone we see."

Barrett puts his pepper spray away and shakes his head.

"Come on." Mika grabs his arm. "No one got hurt."

He gets on his bike. "It's your call but you're wrong."

Mika stares at me. "Promise you won't tell Steph."

I look at her, at Barrett, then back to her. A bluff charge. A real charge. I have no idea which one it was. I'm just happy it didn't involve me getting chewed on by a bear. I'm okay. Besides, I'm sure Steph wouldn't shoot it. How would she ever find it, anyways? Barrett's being over cautious, trying to protect us, right?

"I won't tell, I guess." I shrug. "What's the big deal?"

"Someone gets hurt, it's going to be a big deal." Barrett gets on his bike and starts to pedal home.

The upside to going back, there are more downhills than up. They pedal at my pace, but conversation is minimal. The bruise on my butt throbs so I try to stand while I crank. It's awkward. I press harder on the butt cheek which doesn't hurt. Still awkward but not as sore.

***

My legs and back are stiff when I get out of the truck at Opa's.

"You're okay, right?" Mika says.

"Sure." I give her a half-smile. "Relax, I won't tell Steph."

She gives me a thumbs up, and they drive away.

Before I head up the path to the house, I wipe dirt off my jeans. It takes all I've got not to limp. My butt and hip hurt every time my right foot hits the ground.

Steph rushes out the back door. *Did she see me limp? Oh my gosh, does she know?*

"Gotta run. There's been a bear encounter up the Spray. Someone's hurt." As she hurries by, pulling on her ugly green warden parka, she calls, "Can you feed your Opa and Kyle, please. I don't know when I'll be back."

"Sure." I doubt she hears me though. Her truck screeches out the back alley.

Oh, my God. The Spray. The bear. Shit. What if it's the same bear? Dammit. I should have said something. But what good would it do now? It happened. Shit, shit. Barrett was right. We should have called the park wardens when it happened. If Steph finds out, she'll ground me for life. I grab my phone and text Mika.

Bear encounter Spray someone is hurt

I shove my phone in my pocket and head inside. Mika pisses me off. Why did I promise not to tell? What if we could have stopped this? Steph is going to be so mad. I mouth a silent prayer which seldom happens since they never seem to help—*please don't let the person be too hurt.*

When I close my eyes, the bear's snout, his breath—they're in my face. I open my eyes. I should not have listened to Mika. I should know better. When I can't figure out what's the right thing to do, Mom says go with my gut. My gut told me to listen to Barrett but my chicken-shittedness made me do what Mika wanted.

***

It's after 9 and dark outside. Steph isn't home yet, and the house is quiet.

I finally get a text back from Mika.

I know followed by a sad face emoji.

A sad face emoji? Like that helps anyone? Her response makes me even madder for listening to her.

Opa shows Kyle how to do laundry. Poor kid. He's just a kid. A kid who eats an incredible amount of food and is now learning how to keep house. Opa treats him like he's training him for the armed forces. That might not be a bad thing if his home life doesn't straighten out.

Tomorrow I'm supposed to walk him to school. It's only a few blocks out of my way but I wish they'd let me in on what the heck's going on. Steph and Opa treat Kyle as if he's family. Mrs. Bronigan pops in. She and Kyle disappear for hours. She brings him back and hangs out here before going back to the Senior's Lodge. No one says anything about when he's going home. Weird. Plain weird. I see lots of people coming in and out of Kyle's house all the time. Why doesn't he just go home? His mom's batshit crazy but she's his mom? Why doesn't she take care of him?

As I lock the back door and go to turn on the alarm, Steph jogs up the steps. Yikes. Dirt streaks run from under her nostrils and smear across her cheek. She looks sad. Not angry. I open the door.

"Hungry?" I say.

She nods.

I head to the fridge and pull out leftover chili. Without looking at her I ask, "Everything go okay?"

"Define okay."

"Was the person hurt bad?"

She turns on the tap, washes her hands then scoops water up and rubs her face. As the chili spins in the microwave, I grab leftover garlic bread and a beer.

"He'll need a lot of stitches on his forehead. Busted nose and he probably screwed his knee good. He put up a hell of a fight."

Dammit. Damn you, Mika.

The chair screeches as Steph pulls in closer to the table. I pass her the plate, but she grabs the beer first.

"The guy said he never saw it coming. A couple hikers heard him scream." She shakes her head. "He was in the wrong place at the right time. They're still trying to track the bear but it's too dark. They'll start again in the morning."

I fuss with tidying stuff up and biting my lip as she continues with the details.

"The bear just wants the berries. They're getting ready to make their plug," Steph says.

"What?"

"A plug. Imagine a giant tampon shoved up a bear's butt. It's one of the stages a bear goes through to get ready to hibernate."

"Gross."

"The guy's pepper spray was in his pack. He couldn't get to it. Whenever you're out, even on the river trail, take the chest harness

and canister," Steph points, "at the back door, on the hook."

I take a deep breath and sit across from her. She doesn't look up.

"We saw a bear today," I whisper.

Her head snaps up. Eyes wide open.

"We were mountain biking." I give as few details as possible and eliminate the crash and crab walk backwards with the bear coming at me because Steph's eyes look like they might jump out of her head. Yeah, yeah, I know. Elimination of details is borderline lying but it's necessary right now.

"Why didn't you tell me?" Steph snaps.

"Well, you kind of ran out of here. Didn't give me a chance."

"You have a phone." She stabs her finger on the table. "You could have called."

I clench my hands on my lap. "I didn't think it was a big deal."

"You see a bear on a popular trail, and you don't think you should tell me? Where are you from? Mars? We would have closed the trail to keep people safe and give the bear a chance to move on instead of hunting him down."

Her phone rings. Steph pulls it out of her shirt pocket and glances at the display.

"Hey, Tom." She nods. Then lifts her head and stares at me.

"I see. Okay."

I can't read the expression on her face. Her lips move into so many positions but

don't seem to know where to stop. She shakes her head and sighs.

"Thanks. I'll talk to her," she says. "Goodnight."

Uh-oh. I'm sure the *her* she refers to is me.

Steph puts the phone back into her pocket with super slow movement. I squirm in my chair. She's got the same look Mom does when I'm in trouble but don't know what for yet. Guess I shouldn't be surprised they can make the same face. They're sisters. Creeps me out she's doing the mom thing though.

"So." Steph drums her fingers on the table. "Mika fessed up. Are you going to?"

"Um, I'm not sure what you're talking about. I already told you. We saw a bear."

"Tom said," she stops and says nothing else like she wants me to walk into a trap.

I chew on my cheek. I have no idea what Mika said and I'm not sure what will lessen the shitstorm Steph'll unleash if I tell her all the details.

Steph finally says, "Mika told you not to say anything."

I gather her dishes and put them in the dishwasher, gauge it's fullness and add soap. Before I face Steph, I turn it on and wish it wasn't such a quiet machine. Steph remains expressionless.

"It was dumb of you not to tell me."

I nod.

"Don't do it again. Regardless of how much trouble you can get into, tell me first. Don't let me find out from someone else."

"Will do." My head nods way more times than it needs to but I'm not sure what else to do and do not want to say something like *tell you when I've done something that'll get me into trouble? Do I look that stupid?* I'm positive that would only increase her piss-me-off meter.

Steph stands and goes upstairs.

What? That's it? No way. She must be playing the guilt game. She'll come back after she thinks her talk has sunk in and rip me a new one. I'm glad I didn't give her attitude.

The stairs squeak. Bathroom door opens, closes. Shower starts.

Maybe it is over. She didn't sound mad. More factual with her 'don't do it again' and 'tell me first'. She didn't even yell. How sweet is that? Maybe she's not so bad at this mothering thing after all. Mom would have yelled, given me the silent treatment and then hashed it out over and over for days.

Or, hold on, maybe Steph didn't get all crazy mad because she doesn't care about me. Could that be it? No way. She has to care. Even though she didn't raise me, she's got to like me a little bit, right?

She's never been big on touch-feely emotions, she saves those for Tom. Like she thinks I don't know what they're up to. The

thought of them sneaking kisses is pretty cute.

So, what's she doing? Is Steph trying to be the cool Mom? No yelling. Deal with the facts. Set the ground rules for future situations. And move on.

That's it. Right?

Well, as Mom would say, I dodged that bullet. No boarding school in my imminent future. That's a win!

Lesson learned—I will not let Mika talk me into anything again if my gut says it's the wrong thing to do. And I will have to figure out if telling Steph is my go-to when I do something wrong. I'm not so sure it's a good idea. Not that I do a ton of bad stuff, I'm just not sure she needs to know when I do.

Chapter 6

"You don't have to walk me." Kyle pulls on his Spiderman coat. "I know the way."

"Opa would be so…" I pull on my parka and heave my pack on. "…he'd be disappointed if I didn't, and the bivouac starts today. I can use the exercise as a warm-up."

Kyle bounces down the back steps and gives Bucky a good rub before we head out the gate. At the alley he stops and looks towards his house. The curtains are closed. Lawn chairs are scattered in the backyard. Some are upright. Others are flipped over. Lots of booze bottles on the yellow-brown grass. I watch Kyle. His lip twitches and he takes a big breath, puffs it out.

"Let's go." I steer him towards the street. "You can't be late."

"Mrs. Meier used to walk me to school," he says. "We'd leave super early. I always got to school before the buses."

"Yup, Oma was never late for anything. Kind of her thing."

"Do you miss her?"

My heart stops and I try to remember the last time I thought about Oma. It's been a few days and that makes me feel guilty. Maybe it's because Opa's back to being a tease. He doesn't even grumble about walking Bucky when Steph can't take him to work. And he tried butter chicken and quinoa salad last week. That's a huge change from his meat and potato menu. Maybe because he's doing better, I miss Oma less.

Is that how it goes when someone dies? At first, you hurt so much you can't see the end of it, and then the hurt sneaks away bit by bit till you have to remember them for it to hurt again. I wonder if Opa feels the same.

"When I think about her, I miss her a lot." I cinch up my packs hip strap, so the weight doesn't pull on my shoulders.

"Then, if you don't think about her, you don't miss her?"

"I don't know," I say. "Do you miss your mom?"

Kyle kicks a few pebbles off the sidewalk.

"I guess." He looks up and gives me a huge smile. "You're lucky. You have two moms. I wish I had two moms. Maybe one would…" He looks at the ground without finishing.

"It's not that great." I give him a light punch in the shoulder. "They both boss me around."

"That's no fun."

I nod.

Kyle grabs my hand, sticks his other hand out in front, looks both ways and we cross the street. The driver of a blue Jeep stops and dives over to the passenger side. Saskatchewan plates. Did he drop his phone? Or spill hot coffee? That would suck.

Buses pull in next to the elementary school and the kids shout and race off for the playground.

"See ya." Kyle waves and takes off after them.

***

"Hey Jilly." Eric jumps in front of me in the hallway.

With the heavy backpack on I fall into the lockers like a klutz. I check around to see if anyone saw. A few smirks. A few disappointed headshakes.

I say in a low voice, "It's Jillian. Just Jillian."

Eric waves his hands in the air like an animated baboon. He's got this huge black eye. Wish I could have seen how he got it. Probably talking when he should have been listening.

"Ooooh," he says. "Excuse me, Just Jillian."

Not worth the time. I walk away.

"Hey, easy Cranky Pants. What's your problem?"

I don't stop to blast him with some smart remark mainly because I can't think of one. He hurries past me, turns and puts his arms out so I can't get by. I close my eyes and force myself to not react. *Why does there always have to be that one person?*

"What's your problem?" he says. "You on the rag?"

Barrett's voice comes from behind us. "Hey, they're loading gear in the parking lot." He grabs my elbow and gives it a tug. "Let's go."

"Thanks. I had it," I hiss as we walk away.

"I know you did."

***

I catch my breath when I see Greg and I shouldn't. It's not like we were a *thing*. I had the crush. But he's got to know I'm here. Everyone else in town seems to but I guess it's possible he doesn't since he's not in school.

His hair is longer and way curlier now. Still scruffy in a super sweet way. Kids pass him their gear. He lifts each pack like it's a weight, and some get stacked in Barrett's truck while others get handed back to the owner so they can lighten their load.

Kids high five, shoulder bump or shake Greg's hand. A girl lifts both arms and walks in for a hug but he puts one hand up to her

shoulder and sticks his other hand out for a handshake. What's that about? A broken heart? She puts on a huge pouty face that embarrasses me. Come on girl. Not subtle at all.

I take a deep breath, sort stuff in my pack while I glance for an opening to pass it to Greg when he's alone. He looks at me and turns away. No trademark wink or smile. What the hell? He doesn't recognize me? It's been a few months. Not years. I doubt I've changed that much.

"You ready?" Barrett grabs my pack and does the same thing Greg is doing. "Nice job. You left the make-up and toothbrush behind?"

"I can take it." I pull to get my pack back, but Barrett won't let go.

"I've got it." He heads to his truck and passes both our packs to Greg.

Really? Argh.

"Okay troop. Get in the bus," Mr. Amatt calls. His wife and the gym teacher, Miss Box, stand next to him with fake poster smiles. I can't imagine how unexcited they must be having to supervise the trip to make the adult-student ratio work.

I get in the line.

"We'll meet you at the parking lot." Mr. Amatt waves to Greg and Barrett.

"Where're we going?" Eric shouts as he plops down in the seat next to me. What's

worse than having to sit alone on the bus? Sitting with him.

"You'll see when we get there." Mr. Amatt smiles in the big mirror above the driver seat as he closes the door. "Let the fun begin."

Right. Fun. Exactly what this feels like. I watch Greg and Barrett pull away. It's not like I want him as a boyfriend or anything. Just a friend would be nice. Why's he being weird?

Banff Avenue disappears as we head to the Trans Canada. Eric slouches with his knees up on the back of the seat in front of us. I hold my breath waiting for the conversation to start. There's nothing. His chin nods towards his chest. And he's asleep sitting up. Little whistle noises. Okay. Well, that's not so bad. I glance at him and wonder how he got the black eye. It looks new. Does he play football? Soccer? Maybe he's just really bad at it. At least he's quiet.

I turn to the window and watch the trees whip by as we take the turn to Lake Minnewanka. Steph was right. We're probably going up Mt. Aylmer. The bus slows as we wind our way past the closed snack shack, around the picnic shelters and to the end of the parking lot. I poke Eric. His hand whips up to wipe drool off his chin.

When we get off, I find Barrett, grab his arm and pull him behind the bus.

"What'd you say to him?"

Barrett does huge googly eyes. "What are you talking about?"

"Greg. What did you say to him about me?"

He throws his hands up. "Nothing. I said nothing. We talked mountain biking. Whistler's got wicked runs."

"Really?" I tip my head. "That's it? Nothing at all about me? Not one word?"

"Sorry. You never came up. Did you want me to say something?"

"No. Not at all. I just thought..." I head back to grab my stuff.

"Can you go park the truck, please," Mr. Amatt says to Greg. "Then bring up the rear and gather any stragglers. We'll stop at the lake viewpoint to regroup before we do the final stretch to the Lookout."

Greg gives him a thumbs up and jogs back to the truck. I watch too long before I realize what I'm doing, feel my face flush and focus back to the group.

"So, here are the rules." Mr. Amatt hoists his pack on as if its full of Styrofoam. The carabiners clink like wind chimes when they bump into the rope. "Walk with a buddy, pepper spray accessible and no extra curricular activities till you get home."

A lot of laughs and elbow pokes.

"Not kidding." Mr. Amatt points his finger at the noisiest kids. "Stay on the trail. Pack it in. Pack it out. Patch a blister before you whine. And no whining. Ready? Let's go."

I lift my pack off the ground and with an awkward swing, try to get it on. One shoulder strap twists and I wiggle to straighten it out. Definitely not Styrofoam in my pack.

"I've got it." A girl shorter than me with straight, black hair and serious dark eyes fixes it for me. "I'm Akemi."

"Thanks." I shake my shoulders till the packs weight feels even. "Jillian."

"I know," she says.

I shake my head. "Small town."

"Small school. Sorry about your gramma."

"Me too." I look down, take a breath and clip the hip belt together, pull it snug until I get my eyes under control. How awkward would that be to start crying about Oma now? I bite my bottom lip.

"I probably didn't need to pack extra everything." Akemi's solid laugh helps me through the moment.

Mr. Amatt takes the lead onto the rocky trail at the edge of the lake. Kids fall in right behind him. Barrett and Eric jostle each other to get ahead. Mrs. Amatt and Miss Box count kids as they pass and space themselves out. I don't want to be the straggler, but I don't want to hurl a lung in front of everyone by going fast.

"Want to walk together?" Akemi says.

"Sure."

She hooks arms with me and away we go. I did not expect that. Not that it's weird.

Well, it is sort of. We just met. Kyra and I walk like this, but I've known her forever. Pulling away seems rude so I don't. Voices ahead and behind us are going-to-the-arcade enthusiastic.

Akemi glances at me. She's got a sprinkle of tiny freckles on the bridge of her nose. And her hair frames her face perfectly. If I take the elastic off, my hair will be in my face all day. Lucky girl.

"Have you bivouacked before?" she says.

"No."

"Me neither. I hope I don't freeze to death."

"I doubt that'll happen. Have you got a good sleeping bag?"

"Dad says it is."

We dodge smooth roots which crisscross the trail. After the bridge at Stewart Canyon, the trail gets steeper and rocky. Akemi trips. I almost fall on her with the linked arms but save myself in time and land in bushes. Lucky for me they aren't rose bushes.

"I hate this." Akemi brushes the dirt off her jeans. "I don't want to be here."

"Hey, don't worry." I tap her pack. "Happens to everyone."

"No, I mean I really don't want to be here. I want to be at home. In my room."

I steer her back onto the trail. "Come on, let's go."

"There's a huge gamer competition this weekend. League of Legends." She stops, looks over her shoulder at me. "I want to be in it."

"So why aren't you?" I lean into my pack and tuck my fingers under my shoulder straps to take some of the weight off my back and keep my balance better.

"Because Mom says I'm a nerd. I'm only doing this to keep her from blaming dad. He likes computers too. We're both nerds."

"Moms are the worst," is all I can think to say while I concentrate on my footing.

I wonder what my dad will think of me. I don't think I'm a nerd but maybe he will. The thought should bug me but it doesn't. It's not like he's a huge player in my life and I don't know if he ever will be. I think my messages and emails to him are chill, like I'm sort of cool. But I never know how adults interpret stuff. Maybe he thinks I'm obnoxious or a smart ass. I hope not.

"Do you have a boyfriend?" Akemi interrupts my dad thoughts.

"Trust me. Boyfriends are overrated."

"Boyfriends are overrated, no way. I can't wait to have one." She stops and faces me. "Hold on, you've got one, a boyfriend." She grabs my arms. "You're so lucky. Tell me everything, don't leave out any details."

"I had one. Past tense."

"What's it like? You've kissed, haven't you? I practise on oranges or grapefruits.

Google says that's the best thing to use. God, don't tell anyone I said that. What's it like? Was he super cute? Have you," she looks around like someone might hear her, "have you had sex already?"

"No." I turn her around and give her a gentle push to get her to keep moving. "No more boyfriend talk. Walk."

Thank goodness there's another steep hill and Akemi quits with all the boyfriend excitement. Yes, I wish I had one. Preferably one better than Steve. And no, I'm not telling Akemi that. I'm also not going to be desperate about finding one. If it happens, great. If not, well, I hope I don't have to deal with an *if not* for too long.

We start to cross a scree slope which runs straight down to the turquoise-blue lake. Through the trees, I can see a few fishing boats bob in the whitecaps. The avalanche path above us is rocky and the last of fall coloured bushes dot across it. Our path is only one boot wide, so I hug the hillside slope to avoid slipping and falling down to the water.

"Jesus Christ," a scream. With a quick look up, I see a person on a mountain bike heading towards Akemi. She jumps to the downhill side and falls. Biker keeps coming. I jump to the uphill side and scramble to keep my balance.

"Asshole," I yell as his tires spray stones at me.

He doesn't stop.

"Akemi, are you okay?" I rush along the trail till I'm above her then gauge my steps to get down beside her without rolling rocks. She's holding her head.

"Hey, are you okay?"

She looks up. Tears. Tiny sobs.

"Akemi." I get on my knees. "Are. You. Okay?"

"I'm sorry. I'm so dumb."

"What are you talking about? This is not your fault. He's the idiot riding like he owns the trail."

She swipes her eyes then presses on the ground to get up. I stand, grab the back of her pack and pull her up.

"I should pay attention."

"He came flying around the corner. It's totally his fault. Not yours. Does anything hurt?"

"My feelings."

I laugh. "Easy to fix those. Come on." In four-wheel drive mode we crawl back up to the trail.

Once on the path I pat her arms and legs. Her jeans are ripped on one knee and the skin showing through has more road rash than a cut. No blood.

"Did you see that jerk?" A super tall chick, a guy, and another girl rush up. "He almost hit us."

Akemi fusses to get her pack comfortable and avoids looking at them. What's going on with her?

"She had to jump out of his way." I point at Akemi.

"I'm fine." She gives me a look which I think says 'shut up'.

"You guys go ahead." I step aside so they can pass.

After they're out of ear shot, I poke Akemi. "Hey, what's up? You don't like them?"

"Drop it," she says and walks away.

"What? What's going on?"

"*They* don't like me." Akemi turns and glares at me. "*They* think I'm a nerd, too."

"But," I laugh, "you said you're a nerd."

She glares again.

"Come on. There are lots of computer geeks. It doesn't mean people won't like you."

"You don't get it." She takes off at a fast pace. "People said stuff about me. Then I might have lied a bit, I don't know, so they'd think I was more like them, so they'd like me."

"Why would you do that?"

No response.

We walk in silence. I try to think of a neutral, fun conversation I can start to distract her pissiness. Just as I debate between who's your favourite group and what's your favourite movie, I bump into her

and have to grab her pack, so I don't knock her over. She points down toward the rocks and water.

"Something moved," Akemi whispers. "Is it a bear?"

I grab my pepper spray, stick my head forward but can't see anything. "Where?"

She stabs her finger towards the boulders and poplars below us. Big waves slap the shore.

I shake my head.

"On the ground." Akemi backs up.

I stare through the tall, dry grass and brush until movement catches my eye. Right on the ground. Blends in so well. I take a step closer only because I know it's not a bear. It struggles to stand but flops down again.

"It's not a bear," I say. "It's a fawn."

With super slow steps, trying not to make any noise, I move closer. And that's when I see the mom a crosswalk distance past the fawn. She watches me. Her nostrils flare as she moves her head to get my scent.

I crouch so I don't look so big and put my hand up at Akemi, so she stops following me. Something's wrapped around the fawn's legs. The sun catches it and little rainbow lights flicker. Rope? Really thin, clear rope? No, it's fishing line.

"It's tangled up," I say in a quiet voice while I slip off my pack and get scissors out of my first aid kit.

Mom deer watches. Her open mouth twists side to side as she makes snuffy kitten mews. She doesn't come towards me which makes me think she knows I'm trying to help. And the fawn, well it's as cute as all fawns are with big brown eyes, white spots on its butt and long, gangly legs. Long and gangly with pointy, sharp hooves.

I look back to the mom. There is nothing she can do to help her kid. And if I don't do something, coyotes or wolves will have a feast tonight. The very thought makes me hold my breath.

"Take off your pack and come here," I say to Akemi in as calm and soft a voice as my shakiness allows.

This is a wild animal. It's not going to let me walk up and cut the fishing line. I glance at the hooves again. When I wrestle with Bucky, if he's getting rambunctious, I drop my weight on him till he can't move. That might work with the fawn. And I need to pin those legs down.

"I'm going to lie on the fawn and hold it's legs." I pass Akemi the scissors. "You cut the line."

"What? No way."

"Yes way."

She huffs but grabs the scissors.

"Wait till I tell you to come here."

With more slow, quiet steps I crouch towards the fawn. Its mom takes a step forward. I stop and give her a few seconds

before I move again. The closer I get to the fawn, the lower I squat. There's some blood on a back leg. The fawn tries to get up but flops down.

"Easy." I try to sound calmer than my heart tells me I am. "I'm not going to hurt you."

I doubt she understands but it makes me feel better. Just as I'm about to put my body over her, she flings a leg which is not tangled in the line. The hoof slashes my chin. Frick. I pull in a chunk of lip between my teeth. Doesn't kill the sting but it's a distraction.

"That's okay." I lie across her body and drop my weight on her. "You didn't mean to do that."

My elbow presses the fawn's head down and my knees pin her legs. She tries to get out of my hold but only thrashes a few times. Her heart thumps against my chest.

"Okay, Akemi, come on."

"Are you sure we should do this?"

"If we don't, something will eat her for supper."

"Let's get help."

"Akemi. Focus." I turn my head to her. "Use the scissors and cut the line."

The fawn wriggles and I try to be as heavy as I can while Akemi cuts the line. Voices come from above us. There's no crunching twig noises so they have enough sense not to get any closer. I glance at the

mom. Her mouth twitches as she lets out more snuffy sounds, but she stays put.

"It's so tangled. So tight," Akemi says. "These scissors are crap."

"Sorry. It's all I have."

I feel her move away.

"Akemi?"

A jackknife waves in front of my face.

Whoa. She comes prepared. Sweet. And it's way sharper than the scissors.

"I'm just about done," she says.

"Let me know before you cut the last one. And be ready to move back. Fast." I tense my body, ready to jump off. "He's going to want to go in a hurry."

"Last one."

Akemi steps away and I slide my hands to the ground, move my knees off the fawn's legs. With a quick push up, like a burpee, I bring my arms to my face to avoid any flailing hooves. The fawn doesn't move.

"Hey, go. Go see Mom." I wave my hands. And it's up, dashes left, right. Mom lets out a whistle-bleat noise. The fawn rushes to her and they boing away. No limp. Mom looks back once and then they're off.

I ball up the bits of fishing line on the ground and shove them in my pocket.

"Nice work." I high five Akemi.

"Thanks." She hands me my scissors, flicks her knife shut and shoves it in her back pocket. "That was cool."

As we head up the slope a few kids clap. The look on Greg's face does not match the happy I'm feeling or the sound of clapping.

"Way to rock it Akemi." A guy thumps her on the back. "Rad work. You the gal."

Akemi looks down. "It was nothing." But I hear it in her voice. She's happy. Cool.

Greg says nothing.

Akemi falls in behind the others. I'm just about to follow when Greg says, "That was dumb, Jillian."

He gets points for acknowledging he knows me but what the hell? I stop to process what he said before I turn and face him.

"Seriously?"

"You were lucky you only got a cut." His voice sounds bossy. So unlike him.

He takes his pack off and pulls out a monster first aid kit. "You need to clean it."

"It's fine." I walk away. "Doesn't even hurt anymore."

"Jillian. Stop." He uses an even bossier voice. "You need to clean it, so it doesn't get infected."

Well, that's true and I hate that he's right, so I go back.

He squirts peroxide onto a piece of gauze and hands it to me. "Soak it good."

"Yes, sir." I stick it on my chin and holy shit. Electric zings right through to the roots of my hair.

He puts a finger under my chin and tips my head up, peels back a corner of the gauze I'm holding onto. There's the Greg I know. That cute smile. Those eyes. Oh my gosh. My past mini crush makes my cheeks flush, and I look away. *So not cool.*

"I know I'm going to sound like an ass, and you'll get mad, but seriously Jillian, that was dangerous. You two could have gotten hurt. Their hooves are sharp. I've seen a video of a deer taking on a big shepherd by kicking it to death. If anything happened to you guys, Mr. Amatt would get reprimanded." He shakes a finger at me like Opa does when Kyle screws up. "Serious consequences. For everyone."

The sting is gone, but my embarrassment meter is off the wall. I press harder on the gauze. Doing good things shouldn't make me feel this stupid. Especially in front of him. It doesn't seem fair. No one died and I hardly got hurt. I'm still glad we did it, but I'll keep that to myself.

"Besides nature has a way of taking care of its own," Greg carries on as he puts his first aid kit back.

"Really?" I give him a dead-serious look as I figure out how to word my response without sounding like a little kid in trouble. "Nature didn't put that fish line there. People did. Not the fawn's fault. Not fair for it to get eaten alive because we're irresponsible."

Greg's chest puffs out and then settles. He nods.

Logical, practical, no-nonsense Greg. Stating the facts and agreeing with me in his quiet way. He heaves his pack on again.

"Let's go," he says. "Tell me what you've been up to."

"What?" I give him a huge, confused eye roll. "You ignore me like we've never met and now you want to know what I've been up to?"

He puts his hands on my shoulders, rotates me in the direction the others went and laughs.

"You have no idea the lecture John, Mr. Amatt gave me about not fraternizing with the girls."

"Fraternizing? I didn't ask you to fraternize with me. Just thought you might say hi."

"Sorry. There was a bit of drama at Whistler. I need to focus on teaching, or I'll lose this gig. I didn't know how to treat you like a cobber without everyone thinking we're a thing."

"We *are* friends." As I walk, I force my voice to be casual, casual and chill. "And we're *not* a thing."

"We know that, but you know how girls…and guys talk."

I feel a tug on my pack and turn around.

"Forgive me mate?"

"Okay." I let out an exaggerated sigh. "But don't do it again."

He puts his arms out and we hug with hands thumping each other's backpacks. It feels good. Comfortable good. I don't want it to end but he pushes me back, grabs my shoulders and turns me around on the trail again. And we're off. I'm glad Greg's behind me so he can't see the flush in my cheeks as I swallow the disappointment of my mate status. But mate status is better than nothing at all since people aren't exactly knocking me over to be their friend.

We come over the rise on the trail and see the group scattered along the edge of the lake viewpoint eating snacks. Akemi is sitting with Eric, and two others whose names I can't remember. Her hands are animated in the air until she sees me. Then she drops them and smiles like she's been caught. Whatever. It's good to see her get the attention. She needs positive vibes.

"Nice of you to join us. Akemi says you helped her and I'm glad it went okay. No more heroics, though." Mr. Amatt tips his head at me then turns to the group. "Let's tidy up. We have a few kilometers to go before we set up camp."

What? Already? My legs need a rest. I watch as everyone puts their stuff together and pulls their packs back on. I will not whine. I'll suck it up.

The next section of the trail is twisty with a super steep, rooty incline. No level ground to use my Sherpa-walk and give my knees a

break. Sweat burns my eyes. The more I rub them, the more they sting. No one talks. We trudge single file. All I see are feet because I don't dare look up or I'll trip.

The climb is endless. When I feel ready to snap from the weight of my pack, my tired legs and the boredom of the endlessness of it all, someone cheers. It's followed by more hoots and hollers.

I'm so glad I didn't bitch out loud.

We grab snacks and guzzle water. It takes a few tries for me to catch my breath so I can swallow without choking.

The almost level area of the campground is surrounded by tall spruce trees and has a steel firepit in the middle. A wider, smoother trail heads off towards the distant ridge.

"We'll put our sleeping gear in a circle ten feet out from the firepit. It'll be a small fire. No throwing any big logs on it," Mr. Amatt says. "Grab a spot, settle in and we'll start supper prep for anyone who needs a fire to cook."

Akemi chats with Eric and a few others but makes no attempt to include me. A tad disappointing. I thought I might have made a friend. Oh, well, not being around Eric is no loss. Kids stake out their spots and I drag my pack to an empty area.

"Hey." Barrett drops his gear next to mine. "How's it going?"

"Fine."

"Fine? Just fine? We're missing math and chem." He socks me in the shoulder. "Life is much better than fine."

"I guess." I spread out my thin foamy and unroll my mummy bag. "What's for supper?"

"Granola bars. Sandwiches. Apple."

"Me too. PBJ?"

"Nope. Cheese and salami."

Mother Nature calls and I excuse myself.

The trees are too spaced out, so I walk further into the woods for privacy. That's when I hear voices. I slow down to listen. Akemi? Her voice sounds tense. I walk faster till I see her. And Eric. He's got her in a bear hug and she's pulling her head away from his face.

"Hey," I shout.

Eric drops his hands and turns to me.

"Akemi, you okay?" I say.

"I'm fine." Akemi tips her head so Eric can't see her face and glares at me.

"Oh, Just Jillian." Eric runs his hands along the side of his body. "Jealous you're not getting any of this?

"Not at all." I roll my eyes. "Akemi?"

"Totally okay. Bye." She shooshes me off with the wave of her hand.

Okay then. Read that totally wrong. I guess she goes for the bad-boy type. I wouldn't have guessed she'd want her first guy to be that, but I hope her fruit kissing skills are paying off. I go in another direction

and walk further into the trees because I still have to pee.

When I get back to the group, a few people have sticks glowing above the fire. Burnt wiener smells make me jealous they're eating hot food.

After supper, Mr. Amatt whistles like a referee. Eric stands behind Akemi, drapes his arms over her shoulders as they stand at the edge of the group. The stupid jerk winks at me but Akemi will not make eye contact.

"We'll get an early start and try to reach the summit by noon." Mr. Amatt points to the black ridge against the night sky. "Depending on the weather we'll set up a few belays and see where everyone's at with their climbing skills. Sound okay?"

Nods, grunts, thumbs up.

"Your enthusiasm truly overwhelms me." Mr. Amatt shakes his head, but his grin has a hint of sarcasm. It might be why everyone thinks he's the chillest teacher. "When you're done with all food-related items, bring them over and we'll hang them in the canister and put out the fire."

Chapter 7

There are a few hushed voices in the dark mixed with the rustle of sleeping bags. No stars. No moon. I tighten the hood on my bag to keep the wind out and listen to the whistle noises from Barrett's breathing.

Akemi basically ghosted me in person. How rude. First, she chats me up, helps with the fawn. And then in steps Eric and I'm out. She's stuck to him like duct tape. Why? He's so full of himself. Mr. Amatt told the two of them to chill once, and his wife put her bedroll next to Akemi. Akemi moved and Mrs. Amatt followed. Funny to watch the pissed-off expressions on their faces.

Miss Box separates another couple from snuggling up. Makes me chuckle that no one thinks Barrett and I need supervising. I guess they think he's responsible. Besides, I'd never do that to Mika.

Greg keeps his distance from the girls. Some are insistent on being in his space and I feel sorry for him but can't blame them. He's hot. And he's nice. Hot and nice in the same package.

I'm glad Greg and I are okay. Being a friend is what he wants, and I work on convincing myself I'm good with it. Besides, boyfriends are too much work. Today. Maybe tomorrow too. It took a bit to get over Steve being a douche. I didn't really have a choice since I have no idea what happened or what I did wrong, but I hope there's another boyfriend in my future. Some day.

A few spits of rain hit my face. I pull the fly over my mummy bag and snug it up as lightning brightens the meadow and highlights the circle of bodies on the ground.

I'll never fall asleep.

What's Mom doing? Is her new job everything she wants it to be? I can't even remember the last time she called, and her emails are shorter, less often. Her out of sight out of mind rings true again.

Does anyone back home even miss me? Does Kyra have a new bestie? She's been so distant but it's not all her fault. I don't text nearly as much as I used to cause there's nothing much for me to say that doesn't sound like I'm always complaining. And I don't want to be that person.

Be positive.

***

A referee whistle pierces my dream and my first thought is—I can't believe I fell asleep. I wrestle to sit up. Where am I? I pull

the hood off my head and smell smoke. I turn to the firepit and it's dark.

A bright light sweeps over the group spread out on the ground. When I glance back, Mr. Amatt's waving a flashlight. A blue tinge floats inches off the ground.

"Grab your headlamps, pack your gear. Now." Mr. Amatt waves the light over everyone again. "There's a fire on the ridge."

"What?" voices shout. "Where?"

Mr. Amatt's long shadow arm points towards the mountain above us. Heads turn. More flashlights fill the darkness and point to the orange glow above the tree line. It's so close you can see the yellow turn to orange and large sparks fly off like a bunch of candles floating above the mountain's edge.

"The wind's bringing it this way. We leave in five minutes. Get moving."

Barrett shines a light in my eyes, and I put my hand up to stop the glare as I crawl out of my warm bag.

"Got a poncho?" Barrett says as he shakes his out and drops it over his head. "Put it over your coat. It'll keep you warm."

"Yup, somewhere." With my headlamp on, I dig till I find it, shove everything back into my pack and tie my foamy onto the bottom.

"You're walking with me. It's going to be tricky going down."

"I'll be fine."

"I know."

Mr. Amatt hurries the slowpokes along then sweeps his light across our campsite several times. I push my hood off to hear better and catch a glimpse of Eric shoving stuff in Akemi's pack. I want to think she needs me but it's obvious she doesn't.

"Everyone." Mr. Amatt ushers us closer. "We've got time. Watch your footing. Keep sight of the person ahead of you. Greg will bring up the rear. Don't rush. The fire crew will be busy enough without having to rescue one of us."

Headlamps flash across the trees as kids hurry to follow Mr. Amatt. Their shadows make me dizzy as they bounce across the beams and the blue cloud of smoke.

Barrett grabs my elbow.

"Let them go," he says. "We'll stay at the back and help Greg out."

"You think so?" I hear the whine in my voice, give myself an eyeroll as kids pass by and then we start down after them.

Within minutes, my palms throb from grabbing tree trunks to slow myself down. It takes practise to figure out where I want my headlamp's light to be on the trail so I can gauge my steps without tripping over roots and rocks.

Occasional shouts from below, encouragement and snapping of branches filter up the trail. Mr. Amatt didn't need to worry about anyone rushing. I can't even walk at a normal pace.

My back cramps from the chill and stress of being careful where I step. I relax my shoulders and focus so much on not being tense that my feet slip out and I land flat on my butt. Feels like my spine rams into my neck. Barrett pulls me up.

"I'm okay." I give myself a good shake to make sure everything is shakeable without pain. "I'm good. Thanks."

Onward. Doesn't it always seem longer to get home than it did to get where you're going? Especially in the dark.

"Help!"

I turn my head to figure out where the shout came from.

"Hey, someone. Help."

"Akemi?" I shine my light from where I think I hear her voice. Trees, tall grass, yellow poncho with a goofy duck on the hat. "Akemi." I rush over.

"My ankle. It hurts."

"Stay still." I press against her shoulder so she doesn't try to get up. "Where's Eric?"

I wave my light around to search for him. He's nowhere. What the hell? He just left her? Such a jerk move. No. He wouldn't just leave her here alone. No one's that mean. Maybe he doesn't know she's not behind him anymore. But he'd check for her, wouldn't he? I'm back to he's a jerk.

"What's going on?" Barrett and Greg hunch over Akemi with me. With all the

headlamps on her, she cups her hands over her eyes.

"It's her ankle," I say.

"Which one?" Greg scoots to her feet. Akemi points to her left boot and he pulls up her pant leg, presses around. "We're not taking the boot off. Let's get you up and see if you can walk leaning on me."

Barrett pulls her pack off. "I'll carry this."

Greg radios Mr. Amatt then Barrett and him help Akemi stand. She whimpers but doesn't scream. A good sign? While Greg explains to her how they're going to walk down, I help Barrett strap her pack onto his.

"That's a lot." I lift the weight up and then settle it against his again. "Are you going to be okay? I can take some stuff."

"You may get a turn," he whispers. "What the hell's she got in there? Her whole wardrobe?"

"Where's Eric?"

Barrett shrugs. "Looking after himself, I'm sure."

We stay behind Greg as Akemi hobbles beside him. It looks awkward since most times the trail is only wide enough for one person. The smoke sinks to the ground. A scary-movie forest floor. My quad cramps accompany creepy thoughts.

As the ground starts to level, a bright light on the lake flickers through the trees. A boat? For us? Hurray!

"Akemi, your chariot awaits." Mr. Amatt waves his hand towards the shore as the boat gets closer. "Does anyone else feel they can't make it the rest of the way?"

Lots of hands fly up accompanied with 'me', 'pick me'.

"They have room for five people." Mr. Amatt stares at the boat then turns to us. "You guys figure it out."

Eric rushes up and puts his arm around Akemi. She doesn't pull away. Long shadows reach the treetops in the boat's headlight. Eric leans over, kisses her then pulls her into a hug. Solid jerk material. What can she possibly see in him?

"Thanks bro." Eric unties Akemi's pack from Barrett's back, wraps an arm around her waist and helps her hobble-hop to the shore.

No one follows them.

Someone taps my shoulder. I turn and am blinded by Barrett's headlamp.

"You ready to go?" He nods towards Eric and Akemi. "Or are you taking the boat?"

"No." I give him a pretend cranky face. "I can walk out."

"I know you can." Big goofy Barrett grin.

Walking above the shoreline is easier than the steep path. The grade is a gradual slope, and the darkness isn't as dark as the light from the boat fades. But the walking never ends. I argue with myself about not going on the boat. It would have been so

much easier. Being stuck in the same place as Akemi and Eric was a huge don't-go-on-the-boat factor. Is that why no one else got on, too?

I trudge along visualizing the hottest shower ever, hot pepperoni pizza and snuggling in my goose down duvet for a long nap.

Chapter 8

"How come you're here?" Kyle grabs my hand at the school crosswalk. "Did you ditch your hiking trip? And what happened to your chin?"

"Ah, got kicked by a fawn, there was a forest fire, we had to evacuate, came home this morning, had a good sleep and shower, and here I am, just for you." I give him a super-happy-to-see-you-too smile. "How was your day?"

"I got in trouble at lunch. Mr. Meier put a chocolate bar in my bag." Kyle's voice is quiet. "I have a note he has to read. Do you think Mr. Meier will make me go home?"

"No, no way." I jiggle his hand. "Besides, it's my fault. I forgot to tell him the school has a no junk food rule."

A blue Jeep screeches to a stop in front of us. It looks familiar. The Saskatchewan plates again. A man gets out.

"Dad," Kyle screeches and runs to him.

What?

The guy jogs to Kyle, picks him up and twirls him in circles. Squeals and shouts. The closer I get to them the slower I walk. Kyle's

eyes are squished shut. Biggest smile. Around and around they go.

When he sets him down, he takes Kyle's hand.

"This is my dad," Kyle shouts.

I put my hand out. "Robbie Bronigan?"

"Yup. I'm sure you've heard the stories."

"Mrs. Bronigan's mentioned you a few times." I laugh. Maybe he's not as big a schmuck as Opa thinks. "I'm Jillian Meier. Kyle's been staying with us…" and I zip it. Shit. I shouldn't have said that. Dumb me. Talking before thinking.

Mr. Bronigan frowns for a second then smiles and shakes my hand. Squeezes it harder than necessary so I squeeze back and give myself an internal high five when he tries to hide his wince. Love it when guys are so full of themselves. Yay, karate and all that stuff I never thought I'd use.

"I thought I'd surprise Kyle and take him for dinner." Mr. Bronigan taps Kyle on the head. "Maybe we can go to MacDonald's."

"I love MacDonald's." Kyle jumps up and down. "Let's go!"

"Sorry." I take Kyle's hand. "You'll have to check with Mrs. Bronigan or Mr. Meier. I can give you their numbers."

His lips press together, and he nods.

"Come on, jump in. I'll give you a ride to the house and I can ask. I'm sure there won't be an issue."

"Dad can see GG and," Kyle's eyes open so wide, "maybe Mom's home. You can see Mom too. She'll be so happy you're here."

Mr. Bronigan's expression does not match the excitement on Kyle's face. He opens the passenger door for us, and Kyle jumps in.

"Come on Jillian. Hurry up. I want to go to MacDonald's." Kyle pats the seat next to him. "You can come too, can't she Dad?"

"For sure. The more the merrier."

I glance along the street. It's only a few blocks. I'll back out of going to MacDonald's when we're at the house. They can take Mrs. Bronigan and his mom. I climb in next to Kyle. "You know the way?"

"Yes, I do." Mr. Bronigan looks in the rear view and smiles.

"Maybe Mr. Meier can come too. He says he doesn't like junk food but if you buy it, he'll eat it. I know he will. And if Miss Stephanie's home she can come too."

Quiet, thoughtful Kyle rattles on. Makes me smile that he's this excited. Will I have the same feelings next summer when I finally meet my dad? I settle back in the seat and watch the street go by as they banter back and forth.

"Hey, wait." I lean forward. "You missed the turn."

"I'm taking a short cut."

"No, you're not. Stop." My voice gets higher, and I force it down, so I don't freak Kyle out. "Turn around."

"MacDonald's is over there." Kyle taps on the window towards downtown.

"Relax." The car bumps over the train tracks and towards the highway. "Just taking the scenic route."

My pocket rings. My phone. I dig for it. It's Steph. Before I can hit the green button, Mr. Bronigan reaches back, jerks the phone out of my hand, lowers his window…and there goes my phone, across the lane and into the ditch.

"Hey, what the hell?" I punch the back of the seat.

"Jillian." Kyle tips his head at me with a serious seven-year-old expression. "Mr. Meier doesn't like it when you swear."

I try the window. Locked. I pound on the glass as we pass people posing for selfies beside the giant Welcome to Banff sign. No one looks our way.

"Stop the car, now." I hit the back of the seat again. "I want to get out." I undo my seatbelt.

"Put your seatbelt on," Kyle says. "Maybe we're going to Disneyland."

"We're not going to Disneyland." I give Kyle a serious we're-in-trouble face. "If you don't stop this car right now…"

"You'll do what?" Mr. Bronigan says in a calm voice.

Well, isn't he right? My phone's gone. The windows are locked. Doors too. And even if they weren't, I'm not big on jumping out of a car, I peek at the odometer, at 110. Think. Come on.

Why is this happening to me? Mom, help. Please.

Kyle leans forward. "Where're we going?"

"We're going on an adventure. We'll have fun. Arcades, swimming pools and maybe even a circus."

"Hurray. Jillian, isn't this the best?"

Hwy 1A turn off flashes by. Where's he taking us? I doubt he wants me along. What's he going to do? To me?

The signal light goes on. Mr. Bronigan takes the Sunshine Ski Resort turn off. What? Uh-oh. He knows it's not open. There won't be anyone around. It's in the middle of nowhere. Dammit. I have to be ready. I clench and unclench my fists. I can do this.

After the first rock cut, he pulls the car off the road onto a dirt parking lot. Healy Creek's on my left. Road ahead offers no help. Woods. I can run through the woods. As long as I don't get lost.

Kyle looks out the window. "Do you have to pee, Dad?"

"No. You stay put, okay?" his dad says. "Leave your seatbelt on."

Mr. Bronigan gets out, comes around and opens my door.

"Out."

I press towards Kyle.

"No. Not without Kyle."

"Get out," he says. "Now."

"Dad, what're you doing?" Kyle undoes his seatbelt and tries to push past my feet to get to the open door.

"I said, stay put Kyle. Sit down," Mr. Bronigan barks. "Jillian is the only one getting out."

"Dad, please don't," Kyle's voice squeaks. "Don't hurt her."

"Kyle, sit down. Now."

Kyle whimpers but he sits. I clench my fists and make myself stiff.

"You. Out."

I shake my head.

"Now."

I shake my head again.

He grabs my bicep, hard. It feels like spikes digging through my coat into my skin.

"One way or another." He yanks my arm.

"Relax," I feign bravado. "I can't get my seatbelt off with one hand."

He relaxes his grip but doesn't let go. Kyle sniffles and watches me with glassy eyes.

"I'll be okay," I whisper. "Don't worry."

When the belt clicks, Mr. Bronigan jerks me out of the car and slams the door shut. His grip is so tight, only the tips of my toes touch the ground. I force myself to focus, get out of panic mode so I can figure out what to

do. Kyle thumps on the window as his face smushes against it. Muffled yell.

With everything I have, I twist sideways and fire a side kick at Mr. Bronigan's balls. He blocks it with his other arm and flips my leg to the side like it's a fly.

"You won't win," he snarls liquor breath in my face.

I yank my arm hard, so it pulls up and breaks the lock he has with his thumb and fingers—weakest point of a grip. It works. A quick turn and I run. But he grabs a handful of hair and jerks my head back. Spins me to face him and wraps his fingers around my throat. Squeezes. Lifts.

Gasp. Tuck chin. Try to swallow. Can't.

"Don't think I didn't expect that Miss Handshake Squeezer." He snickers. "I don't want to hurt you. So, cut it out."

I stop. Drop my weight. But have to stand on tiptoes to breathe. Opa was right. When your opponent is on tiptoes you have the advantage. Too bad I'm the one on tiptoes.

"I'm going to drive away." His eyes squint. "Do not leave here for 10 minutes. I'll wait at the exit. If I see you coming…don't let me see you coming."

"Don't hurt Kyle."

"I have no intentions of hurting him." He lowers his hand so I can stand flatfooted then walks me to the edge of the trees away from the road. "Stay put. I mean it."

Common sense helps me realize he's not going to hurt me if I listen. My *be positive* attitude kicks in.

He's Kyle's dad. Surely, he won't hurt him—at least not intentionally. And I can only hope he's not as drunk as he smells. I cross my fingers.

Opa and Mrs. Bronigan are going to lose it when I come home without Kyle.

Kyle's face presses against the window. I wave at him. Mouth "I'm okay." Because I am. Other than I'm a freaking long way from town.

They drive away. VWF 907. Saskatchewan plates. Blue Jeep. Four door. Needs a wash.

VWF 907. I wait. One, two, three, four, five. Fuck it. I walk towards the highway. Peer around the corner past the rock cut to make sure he's not waiting.

Amber alert. I need to get the cops to put out an amber alert.

At the highway, I stop and debate hitchhiking. Walk up the ditch to the shoulder. Almost stick out my thumb. What if some jerk picks me up? Someone worse than Bronigan. Besides, I'll get shit if Steph ever finds out. I walk down the ditch again. Walking builds character, right? Character is definitely overrated here and now.

Blue Jeep. VWF 907.

I trudge through the long brittle grass. What's the chance my dad's as big a douche

as Kyle's? Cars zing past. I sure hope he's not. Anyways, I won't find out till next summer and I've got more important things to focus on.

It'll be dark soon. But there are no bears on this side of the fence. That's a bonus. VWF 907. What was he wearing? Brown coat. Jeans. No moustache, no beard. What else? He's taller than me. All they have to do is Google him. He's probably even on Facebook. Or ask his grandmother.

I rub my hand along my throat.

And then it starts to rain. You've got to be kidding? And not a little rain. It's like it intentionally found me and turned the shower on. I pull my coat up high, hunch my shoulders forward till my coat tightens on my back. It helps keep me warm. A bit anyways.

How many steps left? VWF 907.

Liquor bottles, coffee cups, rolled up diapers. Seriously? Do people think there's a ditch garbage collector? Assholes.

Goosebumps run down my arms. The rain turns to sleet and soaks through my coat. Totally figures I'd pick today to wear a t-shirt. My toes squish in my runners. Not cool. I tuck my chin, but it hurts my neck, so I lift my shoulders to my ears.

Lights on the solar-powered Hwy 1A Johnston Canyon sign flicker orange. After that Vermillion Lakes. Then the Banff exit. It'll be really dark by the time I get to town. Steph will worry. Or she'll be mad. Hard to

guess which one but I'm going to go with worry.

A car pulls onto the shoulder. Red and blue lights flash. Fabulous. Uniformed woman gets out, pulls her hood up and walks towards me.

"You need to call an amber alert," I yell as I jog up the ditch to her. "VWF 907. Saskatchewan plates. Blue Jeep. Mr. Bronigan, he kidnapped his son."

"Whoa. Take it easy." She opens the back, passenger door. "Let's get you in first."

Bars and glass between us? I'm the bad guy? So glad Mom is not here.

Once she's in the driver's seat, I tell her my name and repeat my amber alert spiel and everything I can remember about Kyle's dad.

"Okay." She talks police lingo on the mike, gives Bronigan's name. The radio squelches.

I push back into the seat to get some heat from the dry material. My teeth chatter and I clench my jaw.

"I need to call Steph. Tell her what happened."

She looks in the review mirror. "Steph who?"

"My aunt. No, my mom."

Cop lady scrunches her eyebrows together.

"Long story. I live with her and she'll be worried. I have to let her know I'm okay or she'll freak."

"What's her number?"

"I don't know." I stare at the divider between us. "He tossed my phone out the window."

"What's her last name?"

"Meier."

"Steph Meier, the park warden?"

"That's her." First kudo for a small town. People know people when you need them to.

"She taught me to ride. She knows her way around a horse."

I nod.

The officer punches buttons on her radio while she maneuvers the car back onto the highway.

"Steph, Constable Brodie here. I've got your niece, or daughter. I have Jillian with me in the car."

Silence.

"Take it easy." Constable Brodie looks up in the mirror again. "She's okay. I just have a few things to check into."

More silence.

"No, she's not in any trouble."

Steph thinks I'm the one who's in trouble? What the hell? Totally something Mom would do but Steph? I thought she liked me, maybe even trusted me. Or did the bear incident lower me on her scale of good-teen status?

Constable Brodie turns towards me and gives me a serious wide-eyed holy-shit expression.

"On our way." The lights and sirens go on.

What the hell? What'd I do now?

"Your grandfather's been hurt. They're taking him to Calgary by ambulance."

I lean forward, put my hand on the plexi-glass.

"What happened? Is he okay?"

She shakes her head as the car accelerates. "Steph'll meet us out front of the hospital."

"What about Kyle? And Mr. Bronigan? You need to find them."

"Yup, they're on it at the station."

"I think he's been drinking. You need to stop him and get Kyle back."

She nods then looks up and says, "sometimes diabetics who are off their diets and meds can smell like alcohol. Let's not jump to conclusions. They're checking into him at the office."

I lean against the seat again. Opa, what happened? Did he find the pills? No. There's no way he'd snoop through my room. He's doing so good. How am I going to tell him about Kyle? And Mrs. Bronigan, what will she say? At least it's her grandson that has him. Not a random nutcase stranger. I cross my fingers and hope everything ends okay.

Over the tracks, speed bump by the bus station, we pull into the hospital parking lot. Constable Brodie does a hard right turn before the Emergency entrance. Almost throws me into the door.

An ambulance. A stretcher. Steph's hair whips in the wind. Tom's got an arm around her shoulder as she walks beside the stretcher being pushed towards the ambulance.

I go to grab the door handle but there isn't one.

"Let me out," I shout.

"Easy," she says. "Let me stop first."

After she parks the car, Constable Brodie gets out and opens my door.

"Steph!"

Steph turns, puts her hands up and catches me by my shoulders. I lean to the side to see the stretcher. Blankets are tucked up high and I can't see Opa's face.

"Is he okay?" I grab Steph's arms.

"What happened to your chin?"

I wave a hand across my face. "It's nothing. What happened to Opa?"

"We don't know. Mrs. Bronigan found him on the sidewalk at the bottom of the stairs. Unconscious. I'm going to follow them to the Foothills in Calgary. They're more equipped to take care of him there. You go home. I'll call when I know something." She takes my hands, looks around behind me. "Where's Kyle?"

"With his dad."

"What?" Her mouth opens so wide a silver filling on a bottom molar shines.

I take a huge breath and close my eyes. Mr. Bronigan squeezing my neck. Kyle banging on the window. The visual makes me clench my teeth but this is not the time to tell Steph about it. I sure wish I could though. It's not like it's my fault. He's an adult. A male adult. What chance did I have of getting away from him with Kyle? Intact?

"Hey, Steph, Jillian," Officer Brodie's voice interrupts as the paramedics close the ambulance doors. "I thought I'd let you know there won't be an amber alert. They've got it under control and it's a non-issue. Everyone is safe."

Steph stares at me. Then at Constable Brodie. Back to me. She lifts her hands in the air. "I can't believe you lost Kyle?"

"No." I glance at Tom for backup, but his eyes are closed. "I didn't lose him. His dad came. We were coming to tell…"

"I don't have time for this right now. You go home." Steph steps back. "I just put Bucky in the house. Take him for a walk. Don't lose him too."

Sucker punch to the gut. I chew my bottom lip because that hurt. A lot. And she didn't let me finish. She has no idea what Mr. Bronigan did or what I went through. And she dismisses me like I'm a little brat. Unbloody believable. Fine. Be that way. I know she's

stressed about Opa but seriously, what about me? Don't I count too?

I give myself a reality check. Grow up. This is not about me. This is about Opa.

Steph marches to Tom's truck. She doesn't even look back. It's okay if she thinks I'm irresponsible right now. I know I'm not. I didn't have any other choice. Right? I guess not getting in his car with Kyle would have been my other choice. Technically is he a stranger? It's a stretch but I'm going with no. Doesn't matter. None of it gets me to a different ending.

Opa is hurt. Kyle is gone. Steph is upset.

I want to run after her and tell her what Bronigan did. I want to tell her how scared I am for Opa. I want to tell Steph I need her on my side. But I don't. I watch her go. And then the shivers start. I press my arms against my sides to make them stop.

"She didn't mean it. She's scared and worried." Tom gives me an awkward side hug. "I'll get Mika to come over and I'll call later to make sure you're okay."

"My phone's…," my voice squeaks. I can't tell him Bronigan chucked it out the window or I'll have to fill in all the details and he'll tell Steph and she'll get mad and it's not worth it, not right now. "I lost my phone."

He tips his head and his eyes squint. He cares. I can see it. And then he gives me a solid hug. I don't want him to let go. He feels safe. But Tom stretches his arms out and

gives me a sad-not-happy smile. His face is the friendliest one I've seen all day. And then he walks away.

"Hey, Jillian." Constable Brodie tips her head at me. "I'll give you a ride home."

I nod because I don't want my voice to sound like a whiny little kid. When I'm in the back seat again, Constable Brodie talks about how people react when they're stressed. How she knows Steph didn't mean what she said. And how it's possible to misinterpret Mr. Bronigan and Kyle's relationship as an outsider. Right, like I misinterpreted his fingers around my throat. I bet everyone will believe him. He's the adult. Somehow, it'll end up being my fault. Wrong place right time. Whatever. I'm not going to say anything. I don't have any energy left to defend myself. Even the fact I feel like I have to defend myself exhausts me.

I stare out the window at the streetlights. This day has been too much. God, I hope Opa is okay. How can so much go wrong in one day?

"Thank you." Opa's windows are dark when she pulls up and I can hear Bucky barking. "Thanks."

Constable Brodie waves and drives away.

Shivers run from my neck down the back of my legs. A hot bath. Right after I let Bucky out to pee, I want a super hot bath. Bucky

almost takes the door off the hinges, ignores me and races for the gravel pad where he does his thing.

As soon as he's done, he runs back and rams his nose in my crotch. I rub his soft, warm head, kneel and bury my face in his neck. He tolerates it for a few seconds before we go inside.

With the lights on and Bucky curled on his bed, I don't feel so alone. I hang up my damp coat, stand behind Opa's chair at the kitchen table for a few seconds then trudge upstairs to my bedroom.

Bubbles. I'll have bubbles in my bath. That'll drown Steph's disappointment in me. I know she doesn't know everything that happened, but did she have to say, "don't lose him too"?

Poor Opa. What happened? What was he doing? He didn't find the stash of…I race up the last steps to my room to check the closet for Oma's pills. My door is stuck. What's going on? I lean my shoulder into it and push. Clothes and coat hangers and books are all over the floor.

With super slow head movements, I check down the hallway, peer into the bathroom. No one. Bucky's behind me. He's not acting weird, and he'd growl if someone was here. I step over books, pick my favourite teal shirt off the floor and toss it on my bed.

Opa? No. He would never do this. I rush to the closet and pry up the floorboard. The bag of Oma's drugs and my journal are there. Thank God. I press the board back in place. Whoever did this, didn't find the oxy. But Opa, no way. He would never go through my room.

What do I do now? Should I call Steph? Tom? What would they do? They're already busy.

I look at Bucky and he grins.

"Who did this?" I stare at him.

He wags his tail.

"Right, you weren't even here. You were with Steph."

I run to check the other rooms. They're okay. All of them. The doorbell rings. Bucky bounds down the stairs with his happy-to-have-you-ringing-our-doorbell bark.

I check the security cam and see Eddy. Even though he's Steph's weird living-in-the-woods-in-the-summer friend, it's great to see his uber friendly smile.

"Someone was in my room and ripped it apart. I don't know who." I blurt it out before I take a breath. "No one's here. Steph's on her way to Calgary with Opa."

Eddy kicks off his shoes and moves me to the side. "I know. She called and asked me to check on you."

"You have a phone?" The idea Eddy uses technology surprises me because what man living in a fort in the woods would?

"Yes Jillian, I have a phone." He heads upstairs.

"No, sorry. I thought you didn't…"

"Relax. I know what you thought."

"No, no that's not it. I'm sorry."

"It's not a big deal." He turns around and winks. "It keeps people on their toes when they don't know everything about me."

"That it does." I chuckle in spite of what's going on. I sure underestimated him.

"Holy shit," he says when he sees the mess in my room. "Steph never said anything about this."

"She put Bucky in the house—probably didn't come upstairs. And it's just my room. Everything else is okay."

The doorbell rings again. Bucky carries on with another one of his cheerful greetings and we follow him downstairs.

A quick peek at the door cam again, and I open it.

"Hey," Barrett and Mika step in and she gives me a huge hug. "Tom told me. How's your grampa?"

"I don't know."

Barrett and Eddy shake hands. Eddy tells him about my room. And the phone rings. Grand fucking central station.

Mika puts her hand up. "I'll get it."

"You have surveillance." Barrett heads toward Opa's office. "What's the password to the computer?"

"It's taped to the bottom of the mouse," I say.

He stops mid-stride, turns his head and gives me a goofy look.

"Not my idea."

And the doorbell rings again. I don't believe this.

Akemi. What does she want?

"Hi," I say but don't open the door enough to welcome her in.

"Hey." She gives me a toothpaste big smile. "Can we talk?"

"I'm kind of busy right now. Maybe another time."

She grabs my elbow and gives it a tug. "Please. It'll only take a minute."

"Fine."

I step out onto the deck and let the door close as she hobbles a few steps back.

"So," I point to her foot, "it's not broken?"

She shakes her head but doesn't look up. "A slight sprain. Nothing serious."

"Good. Glad to hear that."

"Don't tell the cops. He could go to juvie this time."

"What are you talking about?"

Akemi stares at me then points to the house.

"I don't have time for this," I say. "What's going on?"

"Eric."

I shrug. "What about Eric?"

She grabs both my arms. I swing them up and yank away. People grabbing me today. Enough already.

"He didn't mean to do it. Your grandfather, he tried to stop Eric. Eric didn't mean to push him so hard."

It takes a few seconds to make sense of what she said.

"Eric was here? He pushed Opa?" I hiss. "Down these stairs?"

"It was an accident. Honest. He didn't mean to hurt him."

"What the hell?" My eyes bulge. "Why was he here? Is he the one who trashed my room?"

Akemi looks down again and rubs her runner on the deck.

"Why would he break into our house?"

"He didn't break in," she whispers. "The door wasn't locked."

"Oh, and that makes it okay?" I grab her arm and shake it. Hard. "Opa's in the hospital. Unconscious. Because of Eric." I tighten my fingers on her coat.

Her eyes get glassy as she blinks faster. "I'm sorry. I'm really sorry. Eric wanted to, I don't know, warn you. Scare you." She tips her head and gives me a sappy smile. "So, you wouldn't ride my ass about him."

"What are you talking about?"

"I might have told him you didn't like him. That you didn't think we should be a thing. Because I thought," she takes a breath,

pauses, "I thought maybe he likes you, I think he does… more than me. It was stupid. I've never liked a boy before. I don't know what I'm doing. I'm sorry."

"You made up a bullshit story to make yourself look good? Is that your go-to? Lying?" I drop my hands to my sides and clench my fists. I don't think I've ever hated anyone before. It takes a lot not to palm-strike her in the face. "Get. Out. Of. Here."

"Jillian, come on. Please." Akemi clasps her hands together. "Please don't say anything. I don't want Eric to get into trouble. It was an accident."

"Eric deserves whatever he gets."

I go inside and slam the door so hard everyone in the kitchen stares at me. Mika balances a plate of sandwiches. A cop's in the hallway next to the living room. They must have let him in the front door, the door only strangers and salesmen use. Barrett walks towards me.

At the same time, Barrett and I say, "It was Eric."

I look at Barrett.

"It's on the door cam. Your grampa was coming up the stairs and Eric was leaving the house." Barrett sighs. "He pushed him. Your grampa fell down the stairs. That's why Constable…" he turns to face the policeman.

"Erickson." The policeman looks at his phone and taps out stuff. "I'll be in touch." And he disappears out the front door.

"Steph called. She said she tried your phone, and you didn't answer," Mika adds in a quiet voice. "They put your grampa in a coma to stop the swelling. I don't know, she said something about it's better if he's in a coma for now. She'll call back later."

Not even relevant to what Mika said, all I can do is say, "My phone's gone."

The kitchen lights are so bright. I squint. The floor tips and I take a step to keep my balance. But the floor's gone.

Chapter 9

The silence. Is that what woke me? With my eyes closed I try to figure out where I am. I don't feel like I'm on my bed. I rub my hands on whatever it is I'm lying on. The couch maybe? Did I fall asleep watching TV?

I open my eyes. So many faces stare at me. Mika, Barrett, Eddy. They all start talking. And it's too loud. Mika pushes Barrett and Eddy back.

"Give her space," she says and then her face is right above mine again. "Are you okay? You fainted. What's wrong?"

Her lips move and I try to figure out what she's talking about. Faint? Why would I faint? I sit up and the room gets blurry, so I lean back against the couch till everything stays still.

The day flashes like a slideshow through my head. Fire, hiking in the dark, shower, I remember how good the shower felt, school, Kyle, Kyle's dad pulling me out of the car, squeezing my neck, the cop, Opa on the stretcher, Akemi, Eric. I close my eyes. Eric hurt Opa. I rush to stand but Mika holds my shoulders down.

"Easy. You stay put. I'm going to get you something to eat."

It's all my fault Opa is hurt. No, it's not. It's Mom's fault. She sent me here. If I wasn't here, Eric wouldn't have been in the house. He wouldn't have rushed out and pushed Opa. Opa would be okay.

Yes, this is definitely Mom's fault.

A phone rings. I go for my back pocket and remember Kyle's dad chucking mine.

Mika passes me the house phone and I push myself up to sit.

"Hello."

"Are you okay? Why did you pass out? What's going on?" Steph talks so fast. "What happened?"

I take a few quiet breaths before I answer so I sound calmer than I feel. She doesn't need me coming apart right now. She's got enough to worry about with Opa.

"I forgot to eat. It's no big deal." I don't want her knowing everything or anything about what happened. Not yet. Not until I figure out how to explain it all. I'll dump this on her when everything turns back to boring. Or maybe never. "How's Opa? Can I come see him?"

"There's no point. He's unconscious and he'd never know you were here."

"But at least I could see him."

"There's not much to see."

"I could keep you company," I suggest.

"I'm not really good company right now."

"I'll call Mom and let her know what's going on."

Silence.

"Steph, do you want me to call her?"

"No. Not yet." More silence. "She can't do anything from over there. I'll call her after I talk to the doctor again."

"O… kay." Mom will totally lose it. No, she won't, not if she doesn't know what's happening. Steph's right. There's no point stressing her out until we hear what's going on. Oh, snap. This is too much. Is not telling Mom the same as lying? No, no it's not. Right?

"Tom's on his way there," Steph interrupts my thoughts. "Can you throw a few things in an overnight bag for me? He has a list."

"Sure." I sigh. "You're positive you don't want me to come?"

"I'm sure. Are you okay? You're not going to faint again, are you? Make sure you eat something. Who's all there with you?"

"They're all here. Barrett, Eddy, Mika. I'm going to tell them to leave. I'm kind of done. I'll eat and go to bed."

"No way. Humour me. Someone is going to stay with you. I don't want to have to worry about you too."

"Fine."

There's silence on the line.

"Steph?" I say. "Are you okay?"

"Yea, I just wanted to say," she pauses but I don't interrupt. "I just wanted you to know."

"Know what?"

"I'm not very good at this," she says in such a quiet not-Steph voice.

"Good at what?"

"I'm not very good at being there for you. I'm not used to, you know, having to think about you and your feelings." She takes a big breath. "I shouldn't have barked at you. I'm sorry. I'm learning. You're going to have to help me out, figuring this out, this you and me thing."

"Hey, stop. It's all good. You need to focus on Opa." I blink fast then keep my eyes open wide as I stare at the floor so no one can see my face. "Take care of him."

"You're growing up too fast, Jillian."

Who is this lady I'm talking to and what have they done with my Steph? The hard-ass Steph who doesn't get flustered or emotional ever.

With a quick attempt to change topics I say, "Tell Opa I love him."

Silence.

"You tell him, for me, okay?" I've never heard the *love* word come from Steph's mouth.

"I will," Steph whispers. "Goodnight."

With both hands I push off the couch. Mrs. Bronigan has joined my group of babysitters in the kitchen. Perfect. I'm not

really crazy about her being here. It's not her fault but it throws everything that happened right in my face again and I'd just as soon forget about her idiot grandson.

I hang up the phone and sit on the empty chair at the table. Chicken noodle soup and crackers. Delicious sodium fix. I inhale supper and ignore the fact everyone is talking in low voices around me. When I finish, I look up.

"Robbie's a good man." Mrs. Bronigan shakes her finger at me. "He's had a tough time with life. I tried my best, but his folks were hard on him. I know he won't hurt a hair on Kyle's head." Her tone says there's no debating the issue and I'm not in the mood for it anyway.

Sure, he's a good man. That's why he hauled me out of the car, lifted me off the ground by the neck and squeezed. The fact I tried to kick him in the balls, well, he's a man, he was holding me against my will, he took Kyle, he totally would have deserved a nutcracker.

I wave a hand at Mrs. Bronigan. "As long as Kyle's okay."

Uncomfortable chit-chat. No one knows anything new. No one talks about Opa. After I can't stand the awkwardness anymore, I get up and put my dishes in the dishwasher.

"You know what?" I lean against the counter. "I'm done. It's been a day. Can you guys like…leave. I need to get some sleep."

They look back and forth at each other.

"I'm okay. Really. I'm just tired."

Heads nod. Everyone grabs their coat. They let Mrs. Bronigan and her walker lead the parade out the back door. Mika at the end.

She taps my shoulder and whispers, "I can stay." She nods. "I don't mind."

I shake my head and smile. "I'm good. Really."

It takes them forever to get out the back door. And when they've left, I bolt it, set the security alarm, and tidy the kitchen.

The backyard light flashes on.

"Seriously, Mika," I mutter as I turn the alarm off and open the door. "I said I'm good."

Oops, not Mika. Bucky rushes up and sticks his nose in Tom's open hand.

"Sorry. I thought you were Mika." I step into the kitchen.

Tom looks around the backyard then to me. "Is everything okay?"

I nod. "I told them to go home. I'm beat."

He pushes Bucky into the house and hands me a folded piece of paper and a small plastic bag.

"How's Opa?"

"There's been no change." Tom shrugs. "But they say that's good. At least he's not getting worse."

I close my eyes, inhale, exhale. Fuck Eric. Akemi. This is all their fault. And mine. Mine for being here. For being stuck in Banff.

Tom puts his hand on my shoulder. “He’ll be okay. He’s a tough old fart. You’ll see.”

“I hope so.” I check Steph’s list. Guess she plans on staying in Calgary for awhile.

“I’ll be back in an hour or so.”

I step back and wave the list in the air. “I’ll have it ready.”

“Why don’t you open the bag and see what’s inside.” Tom does the finger-gun thing. “Steph got it for you. We hope they transferred everything properly.”

“Transferred what?” I peek in the bag. “What?” A new phone. In a super cool case with horses on it. I hug Tom. “She didn’t have to. Thank you.”

“All your stuff should be there. Like the old one. Just new.” He smiles.

I give him another hug, and hug longer than I should. After today, it feels good to feel safe. He rubs my back.

I have to be positive. Maybe Steph doesn’t blame me. I can’t believe she got me a new phone when she’s so stressed. I ramp up my she-likes-me meter.

“Tell Steph thanks. Okay?”

He nods. “And you call if you need anything. Promise?”

“I will.”

When he’s gone, I repeat the lock-up process and go pack Steph’s suitcase. I flick

past the thong underwear in her drawer and stuff in a few granny panties. So much more hospital-visitor appropriate. T-shirts, jeans, socks, toothbrush, deodorant. I shove in her lip gloss and face cream. There's no make-up on her shelf, so I zip up her suitcase and put it at the top of the stairs.

Time to clean the mess in my room. I start with angry energy sorting and hanging up clothes, but it wanes, so I sit on my bed.

The doorbell rings. I don't move. It can't be Tom already. Whoever it is will go away, right? A loud knock follows a bunch of knocks. Bucky thumps down the stairs with his happy bark again. How can he tell who it is? I clomp down with the suitcase bumping my leg.

I turn off the alarm again, hang onto Bucky's collar and swing the door open. "I'm fine. Please go home."

Greg steps back and puts a hand up like a school crossing guard.

"Sorry. I thought you were someone else." I pull the door open to let him in.

"Guess I'm glad that greeting wasn't for me." He scratches Bucky's head and steps inside. "I heard what happened. Are you okay?"

"No secrets in this town."

He pulls his other hand from behind his back and waves a Tim's bag in the air. "Hungry?"

It takes a few seconds for my brain to figure out what's in the bag and when it does, I realize I'm still hungry. And the thought of him stopping by to check if I'm okay, how sweet is that? Mini heart melt.

"I am."

We chow through the sandwiches with snippets of chit-chat about Oma's weather conversation topics. And it's totally okay. In fact, it's comfortable. My face isn't even warm. Look at me, all grown up with a cute guy in the room and I'm not blushing. And we don't have to talk to fill the space. Quiet is okay. Odd? Very odd. But I like it.

Greg licks donut icing sugar off his fingers and watches me. Uh-oh. What's going on? Bring back the comfy feeling. Now my face feels warm, and I stare at the table, brush crumbs in a pile.

"So," he says in a quiet voice. "Are you sure you're okay?"

I nod but don't look up.

"Want to talk?"

No. Yes. I look up. It's like I haven't talked in forever. I press my hands on the table and the words start and I don't have any filters on. Right from picking Kyle up after school, his crazy-assed Dad, me walking back to town, the rain, Opa on the stretcher, trashed room.

I take a breath. And a drink of water. Swallow. Fight the tears because I don't want to cry. Greg'll feel awkward like he has

to fix it and there's nothing he can fix. It happened.

He taps the top of my hand.

I get to Akemi's visit. Greg doesn't say a word. Just nods and frowns. I ramble on to the end. And when I've put it all out there, I release the biggest sigh.

He pushes back in his chair and tips it on two legs, lets out a low whistle.

"Wow. That's some day."

"You think?"

"But your grampa will get through this. I've heard a lot about him," Greg nods, "and he's a fighter."

Now that the whole story is out, I feel ashamed. Why didn't I do more? I should never have let Kyle get in his dad's car. We should have walked home and met him there. Then I would have been here, and Eric wouldn't have come into the house. Opa wouldn't be hurt. Why do I always do the wrong thing first?

I shake my head to stop everything from bouncing around because it's making it hurt.

A phone rings. It takes a few seconds to register it's my new cell phone.

"Steph."

"Hey," she says. "How's things going?"

"Good." I take a quick inhale. "How's Opa?"

Silence. Then, "No change but the doc says the brain swelling is stable."

"That's a good thing, right?"

"Sure is. Did you get a chance to put some things together for me?"

"Yeah."

"Mika will spend the night with you."

I glance at Greg. "That's okay. She doesn't have to."

"I'd feel better if someone was with you tonight, you know with everything going on with Opa."

"I'll be okay," I say.

"She's staying. She'll be over later. You have a quiet night. Bye." *Click*.

I stare at my phone. Hmm, what happened to the Steph who shared a feeling on the last call? Where'd she go? Is she embarrassed she let an emotion slip out? Oh well, at least Opa is not worse. Damn. I forgot to thank her for the phone.

Doorbell. Again.

Bucky rushes up to Tom who kneels on one knee and gives him a good head wrestle. Once they're through the greeting Tom stands and Bucky goes to his bed. Tom eyes Greg up and down a few too many times and mentions Mika will be over later. I nod.

Greg makes a huge production of getting his coat on, waves and says, "Bye," then heads towards the front door. Odd. Was he wearing his shoes in the house? That's not like him. And why's he going out the front door?

Tom grabs Steph's suitcase.

"Call if you need anything," he says. "Promise?"

"Yes, I will. Let me know if there is any change."

After Tom's gone, I lock up again and listen to the cuckoo tick tock.

"Hey."

I almost jump out the kitchen window.

"Sorry," Greg says.

"You scared me."

"I noticed but I didn't know how not to scare you." He points to the back door. "I don't think he likes me."

"Meh, he's just being Steph in male form."

Greg takes off his coat. "Do you want to watch TV?"

"Sure." I lead the way to the living room.

"Sweet. Super Mario Cart." Greg grabs the game off the floor. "Let's play this instead."

Really? Super Mario Cart? Kyle tried to teach me but I'm not a gamer. Seems such a waste of time jumping and chasing coins and stuff for what? To win? Oh well, I can fake enthusiasm.

Greg pops the game in, sits on the couch and passes me a controller.

I'm not sure what made me think this might be romantic but the thought passes. Completely. I grab the controller, sit beside him, and lean forward like I am going to kick his ass. Of course, I have to bubble a lot to

keep up, so there's no ass kicking. Kind of like Greg's rescuing me from more than the game. My awful day fades.

And when I laugh out loud at my ridiculous hand flailing attempt to get Luigi to jump higher, the sound startles me. I laughed. Wow. I laughed.

"You win." I toss my controller on the coffee table. "I can't see straight anymore."

Greg shoulder checks me. "Valiant attempt Luigi."

He laughs and we both push back into our corners of the couch, my feet tucked under the cushion.

"Thanks," I say. "I needed that."

He nods.

"Hey, what happened at Whistler?" I poke him with my foot. "You said something on the hike, something went wrong."

"That. Yup, my bad. This chick that was on one of my climbing trips, I thought she was a mate, but she wanted," he puckers up his lips and kisses the air, "she wanted more. I was the guide. Not her boyfriend. It got awkward and when I told her, her parents got involved and made a fuss. They said I was the one who hit on her."

"Eww. That's so not your fault."

"I wanted to do a good job. You know, make a name for myself with guiding. *Not* flirting. I'm careful now. And it's hard, cause who wouldn't fall," his hands raise, and he frames his face with his thumbs and index

fingers and gives me the sweetest smile, “for this.”

“Ah yeah.” I throw a pillow at him. “The rugged, silent type. You can’t blame her.” And you can’t really. He is cute and sweet and the accent melts my heart every time. Wish I had guys jostling to date me. That would be super cool.

He tosses the pillow back.

“Why can’t gals be like you?” he says.

“Like me?” I sit up straight, a bit defensive. “What’s that supposed to mean?”

“You know, a good mate. We’re able to hang out,” he waves his arm across the room pointing at the TV and me and himself, “and have a good time without making it complicated.”

Well, that hurts.

I nod and smile because there’s no way I want Greg to know he deflated my heart and ruined any thought of my mini crush evolving into something with him. My positivity meter takes a huge hit.

He leans towards me and our feet touch. “What do you think?”

“Yeah, yeah,” I say too fast and recover with, “I get it. Totally. Mates.”

I throw my hand up for a high five and suck my feelings for him into a casual smile, so he thinks I’m good with it all. Greg whips his hand up, fist clenched. We do a few light knuckle pumps before we high five.

How can I be mad at him for not crushing on me?

I'm just a mate. Bonus points though. I'm a good mate. But not girlfriend material. It sinks in and tries to get comfortable in the pit of my stomach. My brain has a debate with my heart. Friends. Come on. Good friends are hard to find. Especially guy friends.

"Thanks," I say.

Greg shrugs. "For what?"

"For saying I'm a good mate."

"You're such a good mate, I'm going to take you to see one of my favourite spots." He gets off the couch.

I look at his profile, not quite sure what a good mate response is to his statement or what a favourite spot of his would look like.

"It's such a find and you can't tell anyone."

Still not sure what he's talking about I grin.

"Don't worry. It's not where I bury the bodies."

I stand up and straighten the couch cushions. "You're borderline creeping me out."

"Not to worry. It's just a cool spot. You're the type of mate who'd appreciate it. I'll pick you up tomorrow around noon."

And the doorbell rings which is kind of good timing for once because I'm curious where we're going, a bit excited I get to hang

with him again but don't want either feeling to betray our mate status.

"Mika?" I step back a bit surprised to see her again, but I shouldn't be because Tom and Steph said she was coming back.

She steps into the kitchen.

"Hey, Mika," Greg says from behind me.

"And what have you two been up to?" She lowers her head and gives me a have-you-been-up-to-no-good look.

"Just chilling." I laugh because the idea of necking with Greg was a fleeting option hours ago till he crushed it with the whole *mates* thing. "We were playing Mario Cart."

"Is that what you're calling it?" She puts her hands on her hips and gives us the mother look.

"Really. Just Mario Cart." I put both hands up. "What are you? Steph and Tom's enforcer?"

Greg grabs his coat. "Time to go. I'll let you two sort this out. See you tomorrow." He gives me a side hug and kisses my ear, faces me and winks. I know he's doing it to irritate Mika. What a brat. And along with that, I work hard to contain my happy thought because he just kissed me…albeit on the ear. Is that a mate thing? If so, I can get used to it.

"Get out of here." I cuff his shoulder.

After the door closes and we watch Greg walk through the back gate, Mika turns to

me, eyes round, mouth open, about to say something.

“Relax.” I turn the alarm on. “We’re mates.”

“He’s from Australia. You don’t know much about him. Besides, he’s a high school drop out.”

“Burn.” I lift a hand in the air like she lit a match to my palm. “So are you, my friend.”

“Yeah, whatever.” She let’s out a huge breath. “I didn’t have a choice. But I’ll get my diploma.”

“Maybe he didn’t have a choice either.” I give her a hug. “Chill, okay? He just wants to be friends.”

“He wants to be friends? What about you?”

“Doesn’t matter.” I fake an I’m-okay-with-not-being-girlfriend-material smile. “It was nice of him to stop by, see how I was doing.”

“I’m just looking out for you.”

“I know you are.” I give her an extra squeeze. “But you don’t have to.”

“Try and stop me. Now, you’re going to bed. And I’m staying.” She presses her hands on my shoulders, steers me around and pushes me towards the stairs.

Chapter 10

Greg said to pack a lunch and wear hiking shoes. No idea what he wants to show me, but I've had enough hanging around the house. Steph says there's been no change with Opa. I need to do something, anything to keep busy and stop worrying. Crazy images of Eric, Opa on the ground, the ambulance…they all rush around in my head to get the most attention. It's exhausting.

The doorbell stops my funk. Thank goodness. This thinking stuff gets me down. I grab my pack and head to the back door.

I open it. "Hey."

"Better bring an extra coat," Greg says. "In case the wind picks up."

I fold a thinner parka and stuff it in my pack.

"Where're we going?" I set the alarm and push Greg out the backdoor, so Bucky doesn't sneak out.

"Not telling," he says.

My stomach does a bit of a flip. We're friends. And since there's not a line of kids wanting to be my friend, I need to respect this. Why all the mystery though?

He throws his arm around my shoulder, and it takes a few steps to get our feet to walk in time. It feels cool to be a mate. I've never done this, walking down the sidewalk with a guy's arm over my shoulder, and there's no kiss in my future.

Main street passes by as we drive out of town towards Calgary and then Greg turns off on the Minnewanka Road.

"We're going up Aylmer again?" I say.

"Nope."

I stare at the side of his head till he glances at me. Straight lips. He shakes his head and focuses on the road again.

"Do I want to be going here?"

He nods.

"Okay. Trusting you."

He nods again as we pass cars and take the turn off to Johnson Lake. Since it's in between summer and ski season, there are only two other cars in the lot.

I point at the stool he ties to the back of his pack as he whistles the theme from Aladdin. "A movie in the woods?"

"Nope."

"Come on. A clue?"

He shakes his head again, grabs my elbow and we head down the trail and over the wooden bridge. I've been here dozens of times with Oma and Opa when I was little. We'd go on picnics or fishing. Once I skated on the lake during Christmas holidays.

"Care to guess?" Greg says.

"This place is a tourist photo op. Where's your camera?"

He laughs.

The trail is hard packed and not wide enough for us to walk side by side, so I follow him. A cool breeze off the lake mixes with the fall rot smells. Almost like Oma's compost corner after she cleaned out her planters, which reminds me, no one has done that yet.

Greg interrupts my thought with, "There was this guy, in 1910, Billy Carver. He was a hermit, and no one knows much about him."

"Okay." Are we going to meet him? If it was 1910 the guy's over a hundred years old. "We're going to his grave?"

"Nope."

Greg stops and turns to me. "Close your eyes."

I step back. "Ah, no."

"Come on. It'll be worth it."

He's a friend. He wouldn't do anything, would he? I squint.

"The wow factor will be higher if you close your eyes," he says.

"You know it's not my birthday, right?"

"Yup."

"Okay." I close my eyes. Greg puts a hand over them, like I'd peek. His hand smells like coconut. Then he puts his other hand in the middle of my back and moves me forward.

I put my hands out in front of me, in case he runs me into a tree, and drag my feet over the ground so I can feel for rocks or roots.

"Are we there yet?"

Another laugh.

Branches snap under my hikers.

The drama queen in me, which I totally blame on Mom, flashes a crazy visual through my head—me, lost in the woods, running naked, trying to find the trail. I shut the thought down fast. No one needs to see that.

Greg moves his hand off my eyes, puts an arm around my shoulder and says, "Now you can look."

Not sure I want to see what he's showing me but enjoying the weight of his arm on my shoulder, I only open one eye. A building. An old, small, log hut. I open the other eye. Green and grey lichen hang off the sloped roof. A door frame for a short person and there's no glass in the window. I slip out from under his arm and tiptoe to peek inside the dark room. An old pail, a large pan and a broom handle lie on the pocked wood floor.

I turn to Greg. "This is the hermit's house?"

He's grinning like its Christmas morning. "The Hermit of Inglismaldie lived here. Billy Carver."

I duck in the doorway and step cautiously on the rotted floor. A circle of light falls from a huge hole in the roof and

highlights the hanging cobwebs. Green, white and even a teal-coloured fungus covers sections of the logs like wallpaper.

Goosebumps run up my neck and I glance around as if someone is watching me. When I look out the window, the blue of Johnson Lake sparkles through the trees and there's Greg sitting on a three-legged stool with an empty one next to him.

I come outside, lift my hands in the air and shrug.

"My thinking spot," he says.

I take a slow look around the ramshackle cabin, the woods, and towards the lake. Another chill runs down my back. A tree creaks. Both our heads turn in the direction of the noise. It's tiny echo fades and then it's quiet.

Greg taps the stool next to him.

When I'm as comfortable as I can be sitting on a tippy three-legged stool, he passes me a granola bar. We munch in silence. I'm not sure what to think or say. This is right up there with odd. Most guys take girls shopping, to the board park or a movie.

Who takes a girl to a hermit's house in the woods and calls it a thinking spot? Is this Greg's version of a social studies class? Is he working on getting his diploma like Mika and has to write an essay or something? Feels weird sitting in the woods with a very nice guy who's not interested in making out.

I face the cabin so Greg can't see my smile from thinking about us kissing.

I'm not his girl. I'm his friend.

I need to get over it and be happy because this is sure better than being alone. Weird and odd...but better. The fact he thinks this place is cool makes it important and I feel sort of special he's sharing it with me.

"He lived here for 37 years. Alone. A guy from Anthracite, Mr. Gee Moy, brought him supplies so he didn't have to come to town," Greg halts my thinking and I face him. "Carver didn't have a police record. He worked in the mine once in a while to make some cash. He'd walk to the mine, work for twelve hours and then walk home."

"The Bankhead mines?"

"Yup."

"That's a long walk."

"Yes, it is."

Again, the goosebumps tickle my back. Not creepy, cold goosebumps. Anticipation goosebumps? But for what? I glance around. Nothing. Just the old cabin, us and the trees. I'm not sure if I expected something to step out into the open but something's here. In the air. Around us. I take another bite of the bar and press my arms tight into my sides.

"You feel it?"

I tip my head to Greg but say nothing. Can he read my mind?

"You do, don't you?"

"Feel what?" I pretend I don't get what he's talking about, but I do, and it creeps me out a bit more.

"That." He stretches his arm in front of him and waves his hand in a circle.

I watch the motion he's making. Will he conjure up a Billy Carver ghost from the ground?

"First time I came, I felt it too." He looks at me. "Then after the Whistler girl fiasco, I came back to Banff and spent my free time getting shit-faced."

I know my eyes are wide open, so I turn away. Greg doesn't seem to be the 'get shit-faced' kind of guy. He's not old enough to drink legally yet. Not that it means he doesn't drink, lots of kids do. I'm just surprised he got shit-faced…a lot.

"After a bitching hangover, I came out here to get my act together. To think." He laughs. "Hence, I call it my Thinking Spot. I've even camped out a few times. You get the feeling now, wait till you spend a night here."

"We're spending the night?"

"No, I'm just saying." He slaps his hands on his jeans and stands up. "I've never shown this place to anyone. I thought you'd think it's cool."

I nod. He hasn't brought a girl here. Sweet. Every time I think I'm okay with being his mate, something tells me that girlfriend would be nice too.

So I don’t have to talk right now, I take another lap around the cabin, peek inside, try to imagine being alone here. All year. Winter and summer. Winter would be so long. Could the rusted old stove keep the cabin warm? Really warm? I know I couldn’t do it. Even without a lot of friends in Banff, it’s nice to have Opa and Steph to go home to. And even sometimes when one or the other of them is in a mood, it’s better than coming home to no one.

We walk through the woods away from the cabin for awhile, pass under the powerline and go to the ridge.

“Mr. Moy used to come up from down there.” Greg points to a flat green space below us where cars zip by next to it on the Trans Canada. “I’ve never found how he got up the slope. It’s so steep.”

The sun hangs across the valley over the top of Mount Rundle. After a few minutes Greg leads the way back through the woods to the cabin again and we eat our lunch. He’s got all the food groups in a container with little compartments, and I have a PBJ and juice box. Makes me feel like a little kid and Mom’s ‘old soul’ expression comes back to me.

“We should start heading back.” He stuffs one stool under a blanket of branches and sticks the other one back in his pack. “It’ll be dark soon.”

What an odd afternoon.

"Remember, it's a thinking spot." Greg squeezes my shoulder. "Don't be showing it to just anyone."

"Got it." I nod. "Thanks a lot. I needed a, I don't know, I needed a chill afternoon. With no stress."

***

I watch him drive away and wish I'd asked him in. We could've made a pizza for supper. The idea of being alone in the house. Geesh. I give myself a solid eye roll. Grow up girl. Carver did it for 37 years in the middle of nowhere and I'm whining about a night alone, in town, in a house with food, a real bed and a security alarm.

Bucky gives me a quick crotch jab which recaps my whoa-always-me moment before he goes outside to pee. You're not really alone when you have a dog, right?

My phone *bings* in my pocket. It makes me jump. How dumb is that? Back home it went off all the time and I even chose to ignore it once in awhile. Now it goes off and it scares me. I'm such a dweeb.

Opa is waking up. I'll be staying with him. Walk and feed Bucky. Please. Steph

I respond with a *K.*

Yay. What a relief. My guilt-meter dials back a smidge. Everyone says it's not my fault but what else can they say when they're trying to make me feel better? The reality is,

if I wasn’t living here, if I didn’t have to be in Banff, Opa would never have been hurt. Eric would be causing trouble somewhere else instead of waiting to be charged with assault.

So really, it is my fault. Hence the guilt trip.

Pizza and TV. And then maybe I can convince Bucky to sleep in my room. Steph will never know.

Chapter 11

Opa is supposed to get moved to the Banff Hospital on Friday. The doctor says he's crushing the odds but is still wobbly and needs a cane to get around. When he comes home, he may need someone with him all the time. Steph says we'll figure it out which means she'll figure it out and tell me how it's going to be. I'll do whatever to help him get back to normal.

I walk down the hall to my locker and notice kids look at me and turn away fast when they see me notice them. What's that about?

As I turn the combination on my lock, Barrett shoulder-checks me.

"Hey," I say. "What's going on?"

"Nothing."

"No, I mean why is everyone staring at me?"

"Small town."

I pull my locker door half open so I can still see him. "They all know?"

He gives me his goofy grin and shrugs.

"Fabulous."

"Don't worry about it. Them talking about you means they're leaving someone else alone."

"Great. And I should feel good about that?" I grab my books and slam the door harder than I need to. Now everyone stares at me. It's going to be one of those days.

Barrett swings his arm around my shoulder and steers me to homeroom. I lift my chin. Everyone likes Barrett. Maybe if they see us being friends, they'll cut me some slack.

But then Akemi steps in front of us. I slip out from under Barrett's arm so we don't run her over.

"I hate you," she hisses and stomps away.

After I wipe her spit off my face, I close my eyes and try not to feel everyone staring. Barrett squeezes my shoulders and pulls me along with him again.

"Bigger bark than bite," he whispers.

I roll my eyes.

It's the longest day. Akemi passes me in the hallway more than she usually does. I wish she'd stay out of my face. If I was ballsier, I'd tell her Eric is a dipshit and deserves what he gets. And that it's totally not my fault she's a lousy judge of boyfriends. But I'm not that ballsy so as soon as I see her, I avoid eye contact.

When class finally ends, I trudge home. She's there, at Opa's back gate. Waiting. I take a deep breath and when I'm a car length from her, she turns and walks away. She

doesn't even look over her shoulder. I shove the gate open and race up the back steps.

What did she do?

The door is locked. When I open it, the alarm *beeps*. Bucky gets off his bed, arches his back in a dog stretch and pads towards me.

There's no way she's been in the house. Is there? No. Bucky would be going nuts. I'm psyching myself out. No, she's trying to psych me out. Right? I grab Bucky's leash and take him around the block to make sure Akemi's not hanging around when a car slows behind me. I pull Bucky over to the side of the back alley to let it pass.

"Are you hungry?" Steph calls out and Bucky lunges at her truck.

Who'd ever have thought she's the friendliest face I'd want to see?

"Early supper." She waves a paper bag. "Burgers, onion rings, and fries."

I smile, tug on the leash, and jog the half block back to the house.

"How've you been?" Steph digs in the bag as I get plates and glasses out.

"Good." I keep my back to her not sure my face has a convincing *good* expression on it.

"Your Opa is a rock star. The doctors can't believe how fast he's improving. He'll be home in a day or two. He doesn't want to stay in the Banff Hospital, so I've got to deal

with Home Care and figure out how to get help in for him."

"What can I do? I can help."

"If you can be here, you know, like when you're not in school, if you can stick around home until I figure something out that'd be great."

"Well, let me check my calendar." I pull out my phone. "Yup, nothing on it…*forever.* I'm available." Part of me groans cause how boring is my life and the rest of me is glad I can do something to help with Opa. I'll tidy up his room and bathroom tomorrow and straighten out the TV room for him, get his old movies sorted out and put the games away.

After we've eaten Mika comes over and she and I head into the living room. We're just into a game when Steph walks in, staring at her cell phone like the worst news is scrolling across her screen.

I throw the game's controller at Mika and jump off the couch. "Is Opa okay?"

"It's not Opa." Steph looks up. "A helicopter went missing this afternoon."

"What helicopter?" I lift my hands in the air. "Where?"

Steph stares at us. "Tom's in it."

Mika bolts off the couch. "What?" she screeches.

Steph inhales. She glances at her phone and her eyes dart side to side before she stuffs it in her back pocket.

“Mika, can you truck two horses from the stables up to the Fireside parking lot?” Steph heads to the kitchen.

“Sure. Why? Is that where he is?”

“You girls ride up toward Edith Pass.” We follow Steph to the back porch and grab coats and boots.

“The chopper was looking for missing hikers in the pass when they lost contact.”

“Is that where Tom is?” Mika says again.

“I don’t know. Anything you see, call me.” Steph throws a backpack at me. Her eyes are round as frisbees, and they don’t blink. “There’s a first aid kit inside. Keep your eyes out for two hikers. Guy and gal.”

“What about Tom?” Mika barks. “We have to find him.”

“They have another chopper in the air.” Steph stomps her heel to get her boot on. “You guys go as far as you can on horseback. Stay in touch.” She waves her phone at us.

Mika puts her hands on her hips. “I want to help find Tom.”

“You are helping. If you guys start looking for the hikers from the bottom of the trail, more people can focus up higher and look for them. Right?”

Her hands drop to her side and Mika gives a slow nod. Steph squeezes her shoulder then takes off down the back steps.

"He'll be fine." I shove Bucky into the house, ignore his whining and jog after Mika. "You'll see."

"The helicopter crashed," Mika snaps.

"You don't know that. They lost touch. It doesn't mean it crashed."

Mika stops. I bump into her and have to flail my arms, so I don't fall.

"Reality check, moron. When helicopters aren't in touch it's because they crashed." Mika turns and marches to her truck.

There's not much I can say to that. It can't hurt to be optimistic though, can it?

***

Mika drives the truck and trailer like an old lady and hugs the shoulder. Her knuckles are white. I'm sure she's scared about Tom. She's got this can't-talk-right-now aura going on. I'll be the quiet passenger who's a bit fearful of my destiny.

When we pull into the Fireside parking lot and she backs the trailer up to the bank, I breathe. Step one done as per Steph's instructions. Getting here was stressful. Riding horses, much easier. I set the backpack on the floor of the truck, grab my big parka, pull it on and then my gloves.

A helicopter buzzes overhead and I hear hooves kick the inside of the trailer. I jump out to help Mika settle the horses down.

She passes me the reins of the saddled pinto. "Her name is Pinto."

"Wow, how creative."

"Keep the reins loose. She likes to have her head."

I want to say 'yes ma'am' to lighten her up but I doubt she's in a receptive mood, so I stroke Pinto's neck before I climb on. The stirrups are too long. I get off and shorten them while Mika shuts the trailer door, climbs on a big bay gelding and we're off.

The wide, smooth trail runs across the base of the hill before it snakes through the poplars. I follow Mika as she opens her horse into an easy canter. Every time I snug up the reins, Pinto throws her head around. It freaks me out to have the lines so loose but it's better than her having a fit.

When the going gets rougher with more roots and rocks across the trail, Mika slows to a fast walk.

"Keep your eyes open," she calls back.

Like riding with my eyes closed is an option? I laugh to myself.

We ride forever. Up. And more up. Pinto's sides heave. No conversation with Mika. Just staring into the trees and bush. A few times, helicopters fly overhead. Pinto must be too tired to care anymore because she doesn't spook.

"Crap," I hear Mika say as she stops her horse.

I ride up beside her and she points to the fork in the trail.

"Should we call Steph? Ask her which one to take?"

She shakes her head. "This goes up to Cory Pass. That goes around to Mount Edith."

I stare at the two trails because the information she's given me means nothing.

"And?" I get off Pinto to stretch my legs.

"You go right. Only ride till the end of the tree line. It gets too rocky after. I'll go this way." She points to the left trail.

"We're going to split up?" I glance at her hopefully hiding the what-the-hell feeling I have. "Do you think we should?"

"We'll cover more ground. Check your phone." She pulls hers out of her coat. "Do you have service?"

I nod.

"Keep your eyes peeled." And she takes off.

When I get back on, Pinto wants to follow Mika's horse.

"Make her mind," Mika shouts.

I snug up the right rein and make Pinto turn a few circles before steering us towards the other path we're supposed to take. After ramming her ass into a tree, Pinto stops fighting me and steps out.

Even though Mika didn't talk on the way at least she was there. I peer into the woods. Pinto slows down as soon as she realizes

I'm not paying attention. I squeeze my heels and she picks up the pace.

"Jillian!" The shout is followed by a crazy-ass loud whistle.

"Mika." I pull in the reins and twist around in the saddle to look down the trail.

Another whistle.

A quick kick with my heels and Pinto spins, trot-jogs back. Her shoes ping off rocks as I press my ear in the direction I think the whistle came from. At the fork I steer us up the trail Mika took.

It's hard to urge Pinto any faster with all the twists along the rooty-rocky trail.

"Jillian!"

Pinto picks up the pace and I lean along her neck to avoid branches smacking me in the head. When Mika's horse sees us, she whinnies and dances around the tree she's tied to. Mika's on the ground kneeling next to someone. The blue-jeaned butt of another person is bent over beside her. Is it Tom?

I jump off, tie Pinto next to Mika's horse.

"Check your phone," Mika shouts. "Have you got service?"

"No."

"Me either. Grab the first aid kit."

I shove my phone back in my pocket and glance around on the ground, on Mika's back and by the horses. Where's the pack? I tap my shoulders. No shoulder straps. And then I remember I left it in the truck. On the floor. The helicopter, the horses spooking, I went

to help Mika and forgot the backpack Steph told me bring.

"I forgot it," I whisper. "In the truck."

"What?" she screeches. "How could you forget it?"

"Sorry." I walk up to them feeling like the kid in class who gave the wrong answer to the easy question.

The guy on the ground has dried blood on his face. It's not Tom. Blue butt person is a freckle-faced lady wearing a ball cap tugged down on two long, red braids. Guy on the ground clutches his arm against his chest and his wrist looks weird. There's no way it should hang like that.

"I can't believe you forgot it. Ride back till you have reception," Mika says. "Tell them where we are."

I look from the pigtail lady to Mika and the guy on the ground, up the trail, then down the trail.

"I don't know where we are," my voice squeaks. I kneel beside the guy to look at his wrist. "He needs a splint, so it doesn't move and do more damage."

"Well, wouldn't that be easy if you had the first aid kit?" Mika glares at me.

Geesh. Relax girl. I made a mistake. Bitching me out is not helpful. To anyone.

"My bad." I close my eyes cause she's right. Stupid, stupid me. I open them. "I can't pull a first aid kit out my ass. I'm sorry I forgot

it. But I *can* help him before he damages his ligaments and nerves."

Mika stares at me like she's trying to make sense of what I said. At least her mad look is gone.

"I learned it in first aid. Splinting will help stop tissue damage. And it'll hurt less." I pull the string out of the hood of my parka. "Get a few small sticks. Smooth straight ones."

"Sure." Mika nods and says to the woman, "Lorna, find a few sticks."

Lorna gets up like a zombie. She looks at me. Red eyes. Red crying eyes.

I hold up my index fingers about six inches. "This long. Straight and smooth as you can find."

She doesn't move.

"Please," I say. "Now."

I look back to the guy. "A splint will make it feel better." Blood oozes out of a cut above his eye. I dig through my pocket, pull out a pack of Kleenex and fold two up into a thick square and press it on the cut. "Can you hold this with your other hand?"

"His name is Phil," Mika says.

"Phil, I'm Jillian. What happened? Have you seen a helicopter?"

"No, they didn't. I already asked," Mika says. "Phil was taking a selfie. On a boulder." Mika tips her head up towards me and rolls her eyes. "A one-armed handstand and he slipped."

"Yikes, that sucks." I smile at him to make him feel less foolish.

Lorna comes back with a handful of twigs. I grab the two thickest and straightest ones.

"This'll hurt a bit."

"Doubt it." He shakes his head. "I can't feel anything from my shoulder down."

I look up at Mika and frown. This is not good. He might be going into shock. I turn to Lorna. "Do you have any clothes in your backpack?"

"No. We have some food left but we put everything on. It got so windy, and he started shivering."

"Hang on Phil." I stretch his wrist, so it lies straight across his chest and then check his expression to see how much I hurt him. He watches what I'm doing without a grimace. "Mika, put your hand under here."

I support his arm as I pull it off his chest. Still no change in expression. I tuck the sticks down his coat sleeve leaving a couple of inches out past his thumb then wind the string around to keep it tight, unzip his coat half-way and tuck his arm in so it works like a sling. When that's done, I lift a tiny corner of the tissue on his head. Congealed blood. Good.

"How's it feel?" I look at Phil. "Can you sit up?"

He sits.

"Can I have your cap?" I point to Lorna. She gives me a weird look. "It's for Phil. Keep the Kleenex on the cut."

Wrist is snug, ballcap holds tissue in place. No blood drips out but he's shivering. I sneak a glance at everyone to see who's got the most clothes on. Nothing extra. We need to get him out of here fast before he goes into shock. There's more helicopter noise above the trees. I can't see it which means they can't see us.

"They're looking for Tom," Mika says as she runs up the trail.

I get it. She's freaked about Tom missing. What to do, what to do?

In seconds Mika's walking back towards us. How can I make this better? Think. Think. What if…

"Mika, you and Lorna can double." I nod as I talk out my plan, so she sees it's logical without arguing. "Phil rides Pinto. He needs to get out of here." I lift my head higher, give Mika a slow wink and point to Phil, then shiver but make sure the other two aren't watching.

Mika doesn't say anything. She looks back and forth between us and the horses.

"What about you?" she says.

"I'll start walking. Call Steph when you have service. Tell her to have an ambulance at the trail head for him."

The sound of a chopper again makes us all look, but we still can't see it.

"They must be close. I wish you knew how to drive the truck and trailer," Mika says. "I'll take them down. You go up the trail a bit. See if you see anything. Anyone. Maybe you can help find Tom. I'll come back and get you."

What? Go further up? Alone? I force a smile and nod. I don't want to, but she won't go with Phil and Lorna if I argue.

It doesn't take much to get Phil on the horse because he doesn't seem to feel any pain. And that bothers me.

"Are you okay up there?" I say to him.

He nods.

I tie the reins together and point to the saddle horn. "Hold onto that."

He nods again.

"Stay awake so you don't fall off."

Another nod.

Mika gets on her horse.

"Grab Mika's hand," I tell Lorna. "Bend your left leg and I'll help lift you on behind her."

Lorna looks at me like I asked her to step inside a rocket.

"It'll be okay." I point at Mika. "She's an expert with horses. You'll be fine."

Her expression does not exude confidence, but she bends her leg and I ease her up until she can swing her other leg over. I pass Mika Pinto's reins.

"See you in a bit." I give them an exaggerated slow wave, and they ride away.

Chapter 12

Doubt, fear and panic fight to be first as they race up my throat. No Mika. No Pinto. I'm in the middle of the woods. Alone. I hesitate to take the first step away, but I make it and then another one. My cowboy boots slip on the hardpacked clay while my eyes dart in as many directions as possible which make my eyeballs hurt from the exercise.

The trail gets so steep, and I slip more often. I force myself to go 20 steps before I get to take a break to catch my breath. Then 18 steps. My chest pinches if I take big breaths, so I pant.

Another helicopter and I can see its tail rotor go over the peak in front of me. It looks like the trail runs right up to the base of it. Maybe Mika was right. Maybe I am close and can really help.

As long as they don't need a first aid kit.

I give myself another silent "you dumb ass" kick for having forgotten it. It's not like there was a huge list of things to bring. "Take the backpack. It's got a first aid kit in it," Steph said. Simple, right? You'd think.

I tell myself to let it go.

The trail is now covered in scree and it's like walking on marbles with smooth-soled shoes. I use four-wheel drive more often and am glad I'm wearing gloves to grab onto the rocks.

The trees thin out and it's multi-shades of grey all the way to the peak of the mountain. No sign of anything, anyone or, specifically, a helicopter.

There's movement, something large, hairy. I stop. It's not a bear which is a huge relief. It's a dog. A large husky-like dog walking back and forth across the path above me. It looks familiar somehow. But from where?

Hesitant with a dash of curiosity, I walk with my hands out low in front of me. They keep me steady on the steep trail and if the dog decides to jump me, I'm ready. I stop to laugh. Ready for what? Like I can take on a wild dog? The air must be thin. I chuckle some more. I'm such a doofus.

There he is again. It's almost as if he's waiting for me. I scan everything above him. Does he have a pack? Is he trying to get me in the open so the rest can jump me? I don't see any other dogs. He turns and walks away up the trail. I follow at a respectable distance.

What's he doing way out here? Was he in the chopper? Or did he eat the guys who crashed? No, I don't think so. He's not being

aggressive like he's protecting his kill. Total opposite. Every few minutes he stops, glances over his shoulder at me then carries on almost like he expects me to follow. Why? Does he know where the helicopter went down?

There are many car-sized boulders. More dogs could hide behind them, but there's no other movement. And then the husky is gone too.

What the hell? Where'd he go? I was so sure he was taking me to the helicopter.

I rush up to where I saw him last, stick my neck out like a chicken, and see the ground dip into a deep gully. Is that where he went? Is the chopper down there? Caught by one of those wind shears Steph talks about?

Scrambling over the rocks and trying to find a safe way to get down takes time. It's harder than climbing straight up the trail because I'm so focused on not making the wrong step. If I get hurt, there's no way Mika can ride this far. My armpits get as warm as my face.

I shield my eyes from the sun and watch for the husky. My foot slips. My hands fly forward to break my fall and the palm of my right-hand slams into a sharp rock.

"Frick." I squeeze it with my other gloved hand till it stops pulsing. *Be careful. Pay attention.*

Between trying to keep the sun out of my eyes, watching where I step, and

concentrating on everything ahead of me in case something moves, it takes forever to cover any ground.

At the edge of a steeper drop off, I inhale. My nostrils squeak as my breathing slows. With both hands shading my eyes as the sun sets, I rotate my head across the field of boulders and random trees which grow at crazy angles. What I wouldn't give for a street sign right now.

The husky strolls across again, stops, looks over his shoulder. Enticing me to follow? I catch my breath when a man walks up behind the dog.

"Tom!" I run and slip and slow down but move towards him as fast as I can. "Tom."

When I look up, he's hunched over, walking towards me. We'll meet halfway. No, I don't think so. He's limping. Moving even slower than me.

I rush the last few steps to him. The right side of his face is covered in blood. I go to grab his arms, but the hand with the elbow pressed into his ribs lifts to stop me.

"Oh, my God, are you okay?"

He nods and his eyes look over my head. I glance back to see what he sees.

"Where's everyone?" He looks at me, like right through me. "We need help."

I glance at my boots then back at him. Put on a fake smile. "I'm the help. For now. Didn't you see the helicopter? They'll come back. Mika found the hikers and she took

them to the truck with the horses. She's coming back to get me." I ramble on in hopes my good news makes him smile. But it doesn't.

"She can't ride this far." Tom shakes his head. "The chopper didn't see me." He lets out the longest exhale.

"But Mika'll come back for me."

"Did you leave a trail? A few Inukshuks or arrows?"

Again, I look down. Why didn't I think of that? I lift my head slowly and shake it.

"Do you have a phone?"

I pull it out of my pocket glad to be able to do something right. "But there's no bars."

"Maybe it'll get reception up there." Tom points to a ridge. "Come on. You stay with Ray. I'll try to get a call through."

"Ray? Ray who?"

"The pilot." Tom turns and limps off and I follow.

Steph's gorgeous pilot friend? That Ray? Two of her favourite people were in the chopper. I could never figure out why Steph was with Tom when Ray is so frickin' gorgeous. Not that Tom isn't, but Ray is *way* bad-boy cute. I wonder if Steph knows he was the pilot. Hopefully he's not hurt too bad.

I curse as my cowboy boots slip on the rock but Opa's in my head saying, 'only wear cowboy boots when you ride a horse.' And then he'd go into the story about how he wore climbing boots once and a bear

spooked his horse. Opa slipped off and his foot got stuck in the stirrup. The horse dragged him and it buggered up his knee forever. Aunt Steph always says Opa has 14 favourite stories and to nod and smile when he goes on repeat. I hope Steph got someone to visit him this afternoon.

Head down, I bump into Tom. That's when I see the mangled remains of the chopper. A massive boulder seems to hold up the pilot's side. Huge chunks of metal, pieces of the rotor, and broken glass pock the ground.

Propped up against a rock, a silver blanket is tucked over a human shape with the top of a helmet sticking out.

Tom hobble-rushes towards it. My feet won't move. My eyes go from each piece of debris to the next. My mouth sucks in cool air. Tom walked away from this? He's not walking great but he's walking.

"Jillian," he shouts and it brings me back to the here and now. I hurry over to him. "We're going to get help, Ray. Hang in there."

I stretch up on tiptoes and peek over Tom's shoulder. Oh, snap. There's so much blood all over the helmet. So little recognizable face. Gauze soaked with blood. Hunks of skin peeled back. I sink behind Tom and hope Ray didn't see my reaction.

The blanket ripples on his shoulders.

"Your phone." Tom reaches a hand towards me.

It takes a second to realize he's talking to me before I pull it out and check the screen again. "Still no bars."

"You stay here." Tom grabs it. "And talk to Ray. Keep him awake. I'm going to climb higher." Tom waves my phone at the ridge in front of us. "I'll see if I can get a signal."

"What? No, I'll go. Let me." My words trip over each other. "You're hurt. I can climb faster."

"Do you know where to tell them to look?"

I stare at Tom and hope my brain tells me I know. But I don't.

"Listen Jillian." Tom steps close and puts a hand on my shoulder. "Talk to him. So he knows you're here." He shoves my phone in his coat pocket. "You can do this."

"Where's the dog? Can he stay too?"

Tom tips his head and looks at me through squinted eyes. "What dog?"

"The husky." Has Tom hit his head? The dog was right in front of him.

He gives me a half smile and limps away.

Is that a yes? Or a no?

I look over at the blanket covering Ray. First aid classes in school were never this real. We didn't deal with blood or really injured live people. Just Resusci Anne.

"Tom," I mouth but it's too late. He's gone and I'm here. With a huge breath and then another one, I find a spot next to Ray's back and sit so I don't have to look at his face.

"Hey, Ray," my voice squeaks. Another breath. How freaked out is Ray? He must know he's in bad shape. What if he dies? While I'm here. What do I do then? I glance towards the ridge and see Tom limp and fall and get up. "Ray, it's Jillian. Remember me?"

Nothing. I lean as close as I dare without touching the blanket. There's a gurgle sound like when you bend a garden hose to stop it from spraying.

"Tom's getting help." What do you say to a guy who's only got half a face left? I don't want to imagine what shape his body is in under this cover. "Ray, remember the bear? The one who chased Steph and me. You got there in time."

Two gurgles.

"We were so lucky you came. And when the bear hit the rudder with his paw, I thought we were all going to die." I stop breathing as soon as the word die leaves my mouth. Stupid me. What am I doing? He's probably thinking he's dying right now and here I'm talking about it. Dumb, dumb. "Did Steph ever teach you how to ride? She said she would. Did she?" I ramble on about anything not dying-related.

"Uh huh."

I freeze. It's his voice. That's got to be a good sign.

The wind makes my neck hairs prickle, so I scrunch my shoulders to keep warm. The husky, he's back, watching us.

"Can you see him? The dog." I turn to Ray.

Silence.

"Hey Ray, Tom said you have to stay awake." I lean in closer. The mashed-in face doesn't freak me out so much now that I know there's a voice there still. "Ray?"

"Colllldd."

"What?"

The silver blanket wiggles. I press my hand on what I think is his shoulder. His shivers vibrate through to my fingers. Darn it. I check for Tom. Nope. The sun is behind the peak. I look under the blanket to see what Ray's wearing. He's curled up on his side. Fetal position. He's wearing a parka, jeans. Looks like Tom put splints on his leg, wrapped duct tape around his coat. Broken ribs? I glance around for anything I can use to cover him.

"I'll be right back." I run over to the smashed cockpit. Careful not to cut myself on the jagged metal, I peer inside. Blood spatters everywhere like when you flick a loaded paintbrush at an easel. Cables hang from what's left of the ceiling. Floor mats. Big rubber floor mats. I tug on one, but it doesn't

move. Nothing's on top of it. I look closer, spot the silver nobs on the corners and turn them. It's heavy so I tug on it to get it out and drag it back to Ray.

"Hey Ray. I have a floor mat from the chopper. I'm going to put it on top of the blanket. Maybe it'll keep you warmer. If it hurts, if it's too heavy, let me know."

"'Kay."

As if I'm putting it on a balloon I don't want to pop, I put it on the upper part of his body.

"Is that too heavy? Should I take it off? Does it help?"

No response. No wonder. How do you respond to so many questions when each one might need a different answer?

"Is it okay?" I say.

Nothing.

"Ray?"

As much as I hate to do it, I slide two fingers along the side of his neck and press into his skin a bit. I hold my breath. And there it is. A faint pulse. Also, the shakes. He's cold.

I stare at the ridge for help but there's no one there. I stare at the husky. The heat from him, that might work.

"Come here boy." I stand up. Husky rests his head on his front paws. If it was Bucky, I'd drag his ass over here and tuck him in behind Ray. This dog, he'd probably eat me first.

I have to keep Ray warm.

“Ray, I’m going to slide in behind you.”

Silence.

I unzip my coat and take it off. As slow and quiet and easy as possible I lift the mat and blanket off, put my coat over Ray’s shoulders and back, slip in behind and settle the covers over us. Weird. Not weird. I scootch close till I’m against his back and cuddle him.

“Is that warmer?”

Nothing.

I press in harder and stay still.

Ray sighs.

It’s a good sigh, I think. I sneak my arm over my coat and pull it higher on him.

Another sigh.

I lie there for I don’t know how long and start to notice I’m not pressed against cold anymore.

“Ray?” I say.

“Yup.”

Phew. Closest I’ve been to a guy in all the wrong ways but I’m doing it. I’m keeping Ray awake and warm. Now if only Tom would come back.

“Got any plans for the weekend?” I smile as I realize how cheeky I’m being. I mean seriously, I’m spooning a guy I hardly know and making light conversation. How mature am I?

Ray’s body shakes. Not a shiver shake. It’s like he’s trying to laugh.

"Me neither. Thought I'd hang out on the side of a mountain with a guy under an emergency blanket and a floor mat."

Another body chuckle shake.

"They'll come. Steph'll make them find us." I convince myself as much as Ray.

"Yup."

"What're you going to do when we get out of here?"

Body chuckle shake.

"Fine, don't share. I'm doing all the blabbing. Hardly think its fair you're not holding up your end. Not to worry though. When I get home, I'm going to soak in a tub, a super hot, bubbly-up-to-my-chin bath. It's my favourite go-to after a long day."

My face gets warm. I'm telling a barely conscious guy about having a bubble bath. And the guy is like a man, old enough to be…I don't know, he's got to be as old as Steph so yeah, he's old enough to be my dad. God, when's the last time I thought about him—my dad? What was his last message about? I can't even remember. Or when it was. What a dumb time to be thinking about him.

The heat under the covers gets uncomfortable and the rubber smell of the mat permeates my nostrils.

"Ray?"

"Uh huh."

"Warm enough?"

"Yup."

"You know, you're not a huge conversationalist."

Body shake chuckle.

Tom, where are you? Where's the help? I don't want to lift the cover and let the heat out, but I think it's nighttime. My butt feels cold. It must be sticking out so I scootch closer to Ray. Can they get us in the dark? What if we have to stay like this all night? I shouldn't even have thought that. Now I have to pee. Tom where are you?

Will Ray make it? What if he doesn't and I end up hugging a dead guy? Gross. Stop it stupid brain. He's going to make it. Quit with the worst-case scenario shit.

***

My eyes fly open. It's so black. Because I haven't got a clue where I am, I stay still and scrunch up my face to hear better. Nothing. The smell of rubber, the pressure of something on my face and body, the feeling of someone cuddled in front of me makes it all come back.

"Ray," I whisper.

No response.

I lean up on my elbow and the cover lifts, letting in a bit of grey light.

"Ray?"

Still nothing.

I run my hand up his back and press my index finger against his throat. His pulse is steady and stronger than before.

"Jillian!"

Mom? I mean Steph. Never in my life have I been so excited to hear her yell my name. I push up the blanket and floor mat. Careful to move without cooling Ray off, I slip out and settle the covers back on him.

"Over here." I jump up and down.

Out of the grey gloom, a line of people heads towards us. Best day ever. Ray's alive. The husky arches his back in a big stretch, turns his head to me, to the people coming, and walks away in the opposite direction. Just like that. I don't get it, I don't get him—the dog.

Steph breaks away from the group and runs towards me. Incoming bear hug and I hug her hard, even hang on longer because I feel heat coming out of her and I don't want to let go. She pushes me back and holds onto my arms, stares at me up and down and up.

"Are you okay? Oh, my God, I was worried sick. How are you?"

"Fine now." I smile.

This mom side of Steph is cool, and I don't want it to end but in seconds she lets go and takes a few steps over to Ray, crouches and pulls the mat and blanket off his head.

"Hey," she says. "Need some help?"

Five more people drop their big packs and circle Ray. I step back to get out of their way. Within minutes I have to hug myself to stay warm as they pull out blankets and first aid gear.

Steph comes back to me and gives me a solid side hug. She pulls a coat out of her pack and hands it to me. Best present ever.

"Have they found Tom?" I zip it up and press my arms across my chest. "Is he okay?"

"He managed to hike out. All the way. A guy picked him up on the highway," Steph says. "Stitches in his head and torn ligaments in his knee. He'll be fine. Let's go. They've got this. A chopper's coming soon and they'll sling Ray out."

Man, if I was him, I'd take the ground route back to town. It'd be bumpy and long but flying again, not sure I could do it after crashing.

"I want to stay till they come."

Steph puts her hands on my shoulders. "We'd be in the way. Let's get you home."

"Just a minute." I hold up a finger, step over to Ray, crouch and slip in close. "See you later."

Slight head movement.

"Next time, you do the talking." I laugh and go follow Steph.

"Hey, Opa's supposed to be home." I call out. "Who's watching him?"

"Eddy."

"What? You're kidding?" Nothing against Eddy, but Opa is kind of old school and he just got out of the hospital. I'd have thought he'd kick Eddy's ass out of his room and tell him to go get a job.

"I know what you're thinking," Steph says. "But Eddy has a way with people."

I shake my head and keep walking trying to visualize Opa lying in bed and Eddy bringing him a tray of food. Maybe Opa's pouring him a beer instead.

"Eddy helped your Opa fix a flat tire, gosh, it's got to be almost 20 years ago." Steph stops and turns to face me. "Then he brought Oma's favourite African Violet back to life and he became one of their favourite people." She starts walking again.

The horses neigh and I see them dance around the trees they're tied too. My body moves towards them like I'm on autopilot as my sleep-deprived brain tries to make sense of Eddy hanging out with Opa. Oma, Opa, Eddy sitting around the kitchen table sipping coffee. What an odd visual. First Opa rescues Kyle from whatever goes on in his house. Now Eddy. Life is totally full of surprises.

Chapter 13

The light in my bedroom is so bright. Am I late for school? *Is* there school today? I have no idea what day it is and when I roll over, my body hurts. Everywhere.

What happened? Dirty jeans, shirt, socks, and a towel are on the floor. And then the replay starts—the news of the crash, the ride, finding Tom and Ray, the night keeping Ray warm.

Is everyone okay?

I pull a hoody over my pjs, shove my phone in a pocket and head downstairs.

Voices mumble from the kitchen. When I peek around the corner, my stealthiness proves to be unstealthy. Eddy, Opa, Greg, Mika, Barrett and Steph stare at me.

"I thought you were going to sleep all day." Steph gets up and goes to the cupboard, grabs a coffee cup. "Want some caffeine?"

I nod and hug myself. Did I wash my hair before I went to bed? I run fingers through it, and it feels damp. I bet it's sticking out all over like I got caught in a windstorm. No

one's eyes do anything weird so maybe I don't look like crap.

Besides, who would care. Greg and I are mates. Mates aren't judgey when the other mate looks rough. And no one else has any reason to care what I look like.

I inhale and step into the kitchen, walk over to Opa, drape my arms over his shoulders and kiss the top of his head. He's got troll hairs poking up. I'll have to trim him up soon.

"Morning, I'm so glad you're home."

"It's not morning. It's the middle of the bloody afternoon." Opa thumps my arms hard. He didn't lose his strength and he's still a *tough love* enforcer. I give him another kiss.

"Stop that nonsense," he grumbles as he thumps my arms again.

Chair legs scrape across the floor as everyone moves over and I pull out the empty one to sit next to him. Steph slides a cup of coffee and a bowl of cereal towards me and the room bursts into noise.

"You're a superhero." Mika leans over to high five me.

"No she's not," Barrett says. "She's a rock star."

"A rock star?" I shake my head.

He fist-pumps the air. "You were in the rocks when you rescued him."

"I hardly rescued him." I look from one person to the next, to the next, and next, and

then Greg who's got his sweet smile on. I didn't rescue Ray, but it feels so good to be here with all these guys. Who knew I'd ever think that? It almost feels like this is home. Sort of.

As I answer questions, my phone vibrates. Weird. Who'd be texting? Everyone I know is right here and Mom seldom texts, something about data packages and it's too expensive. Whoever it is can wait.

After they quit with all the questions and it's quiet, I ask Steph, "How's Ray?"

She nods and her lips tighten. "He'll be fine."

That's not her *he'll be fine* look.

"No, really, how is he?"

She locks eyes with me. "It'll take a bunch of surgeries to, you know, fix his face up. And he hurt his back. Bad."

No one says anything so I do. "Paralyzed?"

"That's only one of the scenarios." She wraps her hands around her cup. "After the swelling settles down, they'll know more."

I exhale. He's alive. Is he the type of person who can deal with being alive and paralyzed?

My phone vibrates again. Curiosity almost makes me pull it out, but I don't and focus on Steph's response.

"Ray's tough. And he's stubborn," Steph says like she reads my mind. "If anyone can do it, he can."

Awkward silence.

Greg stands followed by Mika, Barrett and Eddy.

"Work." He slips into his parka, walks behind me and kisses the top of my head. "I'm really glad you're okay." He waves and leaves.

Heat rushes to my cheeks and I stare into my cup. What? I'm embarrassed and giddy. We're friends. This is a totally stupid reaction. Besides, he did it in front of everyone. It means nothing. Possibly good mate status allows kisses on the top of the head. I'm cool with that if my damn blush would chill.

Mika, Barrett and Eddy say goodbye and are gone too. No more kisses.

Steph, Opa and I look at each other and Steph points to the fridge where a green folder with paper sticking out is stuck on the door. "Green Sleeve. It's for Opa. If he ever has to get medical treatment, of any sort, he needs to take this with him."

"Because?" I say.

"It tells the doctors his DNR orders."

I lift my hands in the air. "DNR?"

"Do not resuscitate."

"Opa, you don't mean that. Of course you want them to resuscitate you."

"Nope, not a chance." He pounds his fist on the table. "Let me out of this hell hole. I've been here long enough. It's time to move on out."

I scrunch my eyes at Steph.

"Sorry. It's his choice." She pulls her head back so Opa can't see and gives it a tiny shake. "We have no say in it."

"But he just got home. He won't be going back."

"I hope not but if he does," Steph says, "don't let him leave without this."

"I sure don't want anyone bringing this body back to life for any reason." Opa laughs. "It would be a bloody waste of money on our health care system. Next time I'm checking out for good."

"You don't mean that," I say.

"Enough." Steph puts up her hands. "I'm not talking about this again. Let's leave it be."

I make a sad face at Opa and he sticks his tongue out. What a guy. I'll change his mind. I'll talk him out of it when it's just the two of us.

"Hey, how's Tom?" I turn to Steph.

"He's whining about the pain and not being able to get anywhere fast so he's obviously on the mend." Steph slaps the table and stands. "I promised to bring him a burger and greasy fries. You'd think he could mix up his take-out order. Do you two want some?"

"What about my heart?" Opa says. "Do you want to kill me?"

"There's nothing wrong with your heart, Dad." Steph cuffs his shoulder lightly.

He winces, grabs his arm and gives her an exaggerated painful expression. It's so good to see him being a goof again.

"Sure." I nod. "Onion rings, bacon and cheese on the burger. And fries."

Steph's eyes go round.

"Come on. I missed a few meals." I get up and put the cups in the sink as Steph heads out the back door.

"You scared me," Opa says.

"I'm sorry. I didn't mean to. It happened and I just wanted to be able to help." I squeeze his shoulder. "Besides, you've scared me a few times too. Fair's fair."

He nods.

"I think we should trim your hair?"

"Again? I only have a few of them."

"But they're getting away on you." From under the kitchen sink, I grab the kid cape, clippers and scissors Oma used to use. "I'll be quick."

"Leave my bloody ears intact."

"I've never nicked an ear."

After I brush Opa off and he settles in front of the TV I remember my phone and the message.

Please call. I'm worried. Are you okay? Dale

Dale? My dad? That Dale? What the hell? It's been weeks since I've heard from him. He sent a short email when he heard I had to come live in Banff but nothing solid about feeling bad about it. Steph must have

told him what happened and that's why he's worried. I wish she wouldn't do that. It's hard enough having to wait till next summer to meet him and his family without her getting in his face and making him worry about me.

I'm good I text. Hmm, maybe it needs more. I add *When should I call?*

Before I have a chance to put my phone in my pocket it vibrates again. I unmute it and read the new message.

Can you call now?

Yikes. What do I say? What's he going to say? I don't do *under pressure* well with him because I've never had to. I want to be prepared. If Steph told him, I'm sure he'll understand things are a bit crazy right now. That'll work.

Got a few things going on will call later TTYS

That'll stall him. Right? I'll ask Steph why he's calling. She'll know what I should say. At least she knows him. Well, she doesn't exactly know him now. Not anymore. She knew him enough to sleep with him sixteen years ago and hasn't seen him since.

***

"You really need to call your dad," Steph says as I walk into the kitchen. "He messaged me last night."

The smell of coffee and pancakes and bacon perk me up way more than the

thought of talking to my dad. And it's a weekday. What's with the big spread? We usually do large breakfasts on weekends when no one has to rush. I glance at Steph. She's eating and reading the paper.

Don't get me wrong, it's not like I don't want to talk to Dale, to Dad, frick, I don't even know what to call him yet. I'm not sure what the big deal is that it's so urgent.

With a plate loaded with crispy bacon on top of pancakes, I head to the table.

"Why's he being so…like a dad? What did you say to him?"

"I didn't tell him anything. He asked if I could be sure to ask you to call him. End of story."

"Come on." I poke her with the end of my fork. "You know more than that."

She shakes her head and still doesn't look up.

"Yes, you do. That's why you're avoiding eye contact."

"Call him." She lifts her head long enough to see me then back to the paper. "Just call him."

"Fine." She's kind of freaking me out with her serious voice. I haven't done anything wrong. What the heck is going on?

"Promise?"

"I promise."

***

"Hi. Dale. Dad." I stumble over my words. "I'm sorry it took so long to call you back. How are you?"

"I'm coming to Banff."

Well, isn't that an abrupt way to start a conversation.

"I know," I say. "You're all coming out next summer."

"No, I'll be there on Thursday."

"What? Like three days from now?" I choke and swallow at the same time. "That Thursday? Are Jules and Jessica okay?"

There's a pause before he says, "Everyone's fine. You and I need to talk."

I stare at the ceiling. There is nothing on *my* agenda I need to talk to him about. What's going on? Does he have cancer? Is that what's going on? People never tell bad news on the phone. Well, most of the time. When Oma died, Steph told us on the phone. What if my half-sisters have something? What if one of them is sick? Will I get it? Could I have it? Stop it. Why am I making this about me?

"Jillian?"

I jump. "I'm here. Are you sure everything's okay? I mean, I'm okay. You don't have to come because of me. I'm good."

"Everyone is fine. I'll see you Thursday afternoon. After school."

"Uh, okay. Sure, I guess. Seriously I AM OK."

"See you Thursday."

Click. Silent air space.

I stare at my phone. Well, isn't that the weirdest call. Steph has to know something, and I'll have to get it out of her before Thursday.

***

Without Kyle as a distraction on the way to school, I spend the walk thinking of how to avoid Akemi. She glares every time she sees me. I should be used to it but it still makes me feel bad. Not for Eric. He frickin' deserves whatever he gets. I feel bad she picked him for her first boyfriend and now she's mad at me because he might go to juvie.

How'd I ever think she was nice? Maybe because I wanted a friend, someone to hang out with at school, and she talked to me. How can a shy gamer be such a bitch? And it's not like she's got tons of friends herself. I never even see her with anyone at school.

I'm tired of not fitting in but I don't want to come across needy and drive people away cause I'm trying so hard to make friends. I don't even care if I'm not part of the in crowd. I just want to have someone, besides Barrett, a friendly face in a hallway of kids who ignore me. It's tough though. Most of them have gone to school together

all their lives. They don't need me. I'm the outsider.

As I walk down the hallway, I see kids around my locker. And they're not there to hang with Barret. With a smile on my face, I walk toward them.

"She's here," someone says and they back away without looking at me and leave.

On my locker is a large pink poster with a glossy picture of two teenagers kissing. Below it, in black marker, it says *Running away with Greg. Need funds*. A Styrofoam cup is taped to the bottom of the poster. What the hell? I glance around. Why? With both hands I rip the paper off.

"What's shaking?" Barrett shoulder checks me.

I wave the poster at him.

"You and Greg?" He pulls his head back and gives me a puzzled look. "Really?"

"No!" I roll up the poster, smack Barrett with it and shove it into my locker. "I'm going to get her."

"She wants you to, so chill. Don't react."

It's hard to breathe. It's hard to not lose it right here in this stupid hallway in front of these stupid kids. I hate this place. I hate them. All of them.

"Hey." Barrett pulls my locker door away and looks at me. "Really, Jillian, relax. She's not worth it."

"Easy for you to say."

"No, it's not. I've been there. It sucks. But you're better than that."

Breathe in. Breathe out. I grab my books.

"There you go. You've got this." He swings his arm over my shoulder and turns me towards class.

"Aren't you embarrassed to be with me?"

"Nah, you're with Greg." He winks. "Remember?"

"Jerk."

What would I do without Barrett in this stupid school?

Classes go on forever. I'm jittery when I go to the Outward-Bound class and almost trip getting over to sit next to Barrett. Akemi doesn't show. What a relief. Mr. Amatt discusses the next trip to the Columbia Icefields, crevasse rescues, building snow caves and trekking on the icefield.

"But keep your marks up. You have to have a passing grade in all subjects and no truancy or suspensions," he says. "Got it?"

The bell rings, classroom erupts into chatter as chairs scrape on the floor. My pace slows as I get closer to my locker but there's nothing on the door this time. Thank God. On the way home I pull out my cell phone.

A text from Greg.

wfzy

What the heck's that mean? An Australian acronym for what? He couldn't

know about the locker scene, could he? And if he did, he'd know I didn't do it. Wouldn't he? He's so sensitive about girl drama.

I punch in his number. After a few rings it goes to voice mail.

"Hey, it's me. What's with the cryptic message?" I know I'm talking super fast like I'm guilty. "Call me."

My feet slow down, and I drop my shoulders, try to find a calm aura in case Steph or Opa are home. They can't know what happened. After all that's gone on, I don't need them worrying about this. I'm sure Steph is freaked enough that Dale is coming. I am, so I can't imagine what she's going through. She hasn't seen him in forever. Oh, and they both have their own lives which don't cross paths. Except for me. I'm what's making them cross.

I check my phone in case I missed Greg's call. Nothing. Please don't be mad at me. I don't want him to ever worry I'd cause trouble.

How did this get so complicated?

Chapter 14

As soon as I'm at the end of the school's hallway, I glance towards my locker. No one's there. Nothing's stuck on my door. As I work the combination, I get slammed into it.

"Easy." I turn thinking Barrett hip-checked me harder than he planned to but it's not him. It's Akemi. I roll my eyes and face my locker.

"After school. You know where." She drills her fingertips into the back of my shoulder so hard my face hits the edge of the locker. It takes everything not to whip around and shove her back until I remember what Barrett said. *Don't react. It's more effective.*

"You and me." She pokes again. "We're doing thls."

With one huge breath and a quiet exhale, I face her. "Leave. Me. Alone."

"Be there." She shoves my shoulder once more. "Or I'll find you."

"What is your problem?" I hiss.

"I don't have a problem."

I wipe her spit off my face as she stomps away. Other kid's eyes dart anywhere but at me. To hide the heat which creeps up my

face, I get my books out and pretend to flip through my math text.

What do I do now? Sensei always said, *don't be there, don't put yourself in a situation you have to defend. If you can't avoid it, be smart, act fast, be first*. So, I won't be there. Right? How long can I avoid her? Till I move back to Toronto? That's so many months away. Maybe she'll get bored and stay out of my face.

"What's shaking?" Barrett says.

I pull back my locker door. "Akemi wants to fight."

He scrunches up his face. "Whaaat?"

"I know. Stupid, hey." My eyes close and I huff toothpaste breath into my locker.

"No way." He shakes his head. "You're not going to."

"She can't make me, can she?"

He shakes his head again and we head to class. This time he doesn't put his arm around my shoulder. Why? Now he's embarrassed to be with me? Or is he worried? If he is, it worries me even more. Maybe my *avoid her* plan needs work.

It's like the whole school whispers when I pass and when I sit in my desk, I hear my name, and look to see sorry smiles or faces turn away so we don't have to make eye contact. Not cool. Why is Akemi doing this?

When the final bell rings I force myself not to run to my locker, shove homework into my backpack and head for the front door.

There's less chance she'll do anything with others around. A bunch of kids hang a few feet away from the bus stop in a cloud of vape mist and smoke. I tuck my head and walk across the school's soccer field. My heart slows enough I can breathe normal, and I give myself silent kudos.

"Jillian!"

I don't look back and keep walking. Running footsteps thump behind me. More than one person running. I pick up my pace.

"You deaf?"

Her hand grabs my shoulder. I jerk forward to get it off and twist around.

"I told you," Akemi snarls.

Kids circle. Unbelievable. This is ridiculous. I swallow and try to settle my heart before it jumps out my mouth.

"Really?" I shake my head and try to keep a bored expression in case she's bluffing. "Why are you doing this?"

Akemi glares—blood shot eyes, so angry, intense. Meaner than this morning. What's going on with her?

She tucks a hand in her jean pocket. "Eric's getting sent to juvie jail in Brooks. I'll never get to see him."

"That's not my fault."

"You could have stopped it." Her hand comes out of the pocket in a fist. "You could have told your grandfather to back off."

"Eric put him in the hospital. He deserves what he gets." I raise my hands,

palms up, facing her, in case she's clutching something in her fist. "And you deserve a lot better than him. You really do." I finish the sentence in my head with *he's such a douche. How can you not see that?*

Akemi flicks her wrist. A knife blade flashes. But she's holding it all wrong. Her wrist is sideways. What the hell's she doing? Regardless, I tense. And she steps forward.

I whack her arm to the side, step in and lock up her elbow. My other hand grabs the back of her neck and I push her head down till she bends over. I should drive my knee into her chest and knock the wind right out of her, but I don't want to. I don't even want to be here, doing this.

The warm pulse in her neck thumps in my palm. She wiggles. I tighten my hold. Kids clap. A few chant 'fight, fight'. Assholes. What is this? Like seriously.

And then I see red feathers pop out of a slice in my coat, near my bicep. Blood drips onto Akemi's back. My blood. She cut me. The bitch.

"Leave me alone," I whisper. "Fuckin' leave me alone."

I push her away. She turns to face me. Her expression, I can't read it but know enough not to turn my back, so I grab my bleeding bicep and glare at her. My hand slips in the blood and I squeeze harder.

Akemi looks at my arm. Her mouth opens, and she steps back. Feet shuffle

behind me. Her shoulders lift, sink, she sticks her chin out, turns and walks away.

A voice inside me says *atta girl, you got this*. I sure don't feel like I do when the blood oozes between my fingers. The thing is, I don't think she stabbed me. She wasn't holding the knife right. This is my fault. I didn't push her arm away hard or fast enough and the knife nicked me.

Even in self defense class the rubber knife would get me. Stupid me. Sensei would be so disappointed. And how am I ever going to explain this to Steph and Opa? They will totally freak. I focus on getting off the field, across the road and head towards home.

Squealing tires make me jump to the edge of the sidewalk. Barrett's truck screeches to a stop in front of me as he parks at a crazy angle and jumps out.

"What the hell?" he shouts.

I close my eyes. Black spots race inside my eyelids.

"Why'd you fight?"

"You think I wanted to?" I give him super stink eyes.

"Whoa Jillian. That's a lot of blood." He grabs my shoulders and steers me towards his truck. "I'll take you to Emerg."

"No, I can't. Steph'll find out."

"I don't think you'll be hiding that from her. If it's bleeding that much through your coat, chances are you need stitches."

I slump into the passenger seat. Barrett unrolls a wad of paper towel, lifts my hand, presses it against my coat sleave and pushes my hand on top again.

"Squeeze hard."

Houses, traffic lights, and people blur like slow motion trying to speed up. I force my eyes to open wide. The paper towel is red before we reach the hospital.

Barrett guides me through the emergency doors.

"I think she needs stitches," he tells the nurse behind the counter.

She pulls up a clip board. "Name?"

I answer the questions until she says, next of kin, your mom, dad.

Barrett steps closer to the counter. "Stephanie Meier." He whips his phone out and gives Steph's number.

Great. I can't wait to see her reaction. Just when we're doing good, this'll definitely screw it up. She's going to be so pissed. Look out boarding school in bloody nowhere northern BC.

The nurse gets up carrying the clipboard, comes around and tells us to follow her. She pulls a curtain aside and pats the bed.

"What happened?"

"School fight," Barrett says. "Knife…"

I give him a serious glare and he shuts up.

"Maybe…maybe when I ran through the gate, maybe a piece of wire stuck out. I didn't feel it. Just saw the blood." When I sit on the bed, black dots float down when my eyes are open. I focus on watching them fall.

"Let's get you into a gown, see what we're dealing with," the nurse says. "Maybe you should step out for a few minutes." She pushes the curtain aside for Barrett to leave.

"I'll be right here." He points to a square on the floor on the other side.

I nod. My phone vibrates in my pocket, but I ignore it. Small town. Bad news travels fast. It's probably Steph ripping me a new one.

As soon as my coat is off, blood oozes. The nurse helps pull my t-shirt off. When she wipes the blood away, I see the opening and it's wide, deep. Shit. Okay, now I see why it throbs. She grabs a pad of gauze and tapes it over the cut, then slips a gown on me.

"Lie down." She holds a hand behind my head and pushes on my shoulder till I'm horizontal.

The room starts to spin. A lot.

"Are you okay?" Barrett whispers from the other side of the curtain.

"Sure." I keep my eyes closed so the room stays still. More voices. A hand lifts my arm and the gauze peels off. Stings like no other. My stupid phone vibrates again. Yikes. Steph must be so mad.

"That's a nasty cut," a lady says. "We'll give you a bit of freezing before we stitch."

I open my eyes.

"You'll need a double layer of stitches to close it. No bicep curls for awhile." The doctor says a bunch of other stuff and when she shoves the needle in, hotness rushes through my bicep, runs up to my shoulder. Crap. Hurts as much as the throb.

"Where is she?" Steph's high-pitched voice calls from behind the curtain. Fingers crossed she's more upset than mad. This might be one of those times she pulls the life critical situation card and calls Mom. That would be bad. For all of us. Especially me.

Barrett's voice, Steph's and another voice which sounds familiar. Who is she?

"There you go. I'm done. 12 stitches. There should only be a thin scar." The doctor lady puts all her stitching stuff on a tray and places a small sling over my head. "Keep your arm up for a few days. And you've got company. I'll be back." She disappears around the curtain.

Steph and Constable Brodie step in. Fabulous. Steph's arms are across her chest and her lips are ruler straight.

Constable Brodie opens her notebook. "So, Jillian, we meet again."

I sigh as my phone vibrates in my pocket. What are the chances they'll let me off if I have an important message? I don't

tempt it because their bossy expressions look…bossy.

“Care to tell me what happened?” Constable Brodie points to my arm.

“It’s nothing. An accident.” I glance at Steph and give her a suck-up sweet smile. “Really.”

“You accidently got cut?”

There is no way I can tell them what really happened. I’ll be grounded till forever. And Akemi, if she’s mad at me now, what will she do if I get her in trouble? And what will all the other kids at school think if I rat her out?

“I’m kind of clumsy.” I shrug.

Constable Brodie taps her notebook and I hold my breath.

“Why don’t you explain *this* accident for me?” She holds her pen in the air. “Tell me what happened.”

I glance at Steph. Come on. Read my expression. Can’t you help get me out of this?

“Uhm,” I say and stop. I can’t make this worse. I know Akemi didn’t cut me on purpose. She’s pissed, I get that. She wants to make a point for idiot-face boyfriend. But I’m positive she’s not that mean to intentionally hurt me. She just sucks at picking a decent guy to date and was showing off to scare me.

I know she’ll get suspended if I tell them she had a knife. I do not want that hanging

over me. No one will ever want to be my friend if they think I'm a snitch. Not getting out of the way properly was my fault. Steph has to believe me. But for now, I need a plausible scenario. I take a deep breath and exhale to give my brain a few seconds to get creative.

"I was running through the gate at the soccer field, my cramps were bad, and I wanted to get home before...you know, I leaked everywhere." They both look at the floor. This is good. "I think I must've cut my arm on a wire on the way through." I tip my shoulder sideways in mock re-enactment. "It must've snagged me, cut through my coat."

Constable Brodie looks at me then Steph and back to me.

Steph steps to the bed and turns to face her. "You know, she's had a day. Can I take care of it? I'll...we'll, we'll call you."

Constable Brodie scrunches up her lips, taps her notebook harder, looks at me, looks at Steph. When she tucks her book into her coat pocket I breathe and realize I hadn't been.

Thank you, Steph. I owe you big time.

"I'm going to let this go. For now," says Constable Brodie. "Steph, we'll talk later."

Steph nods and after the constable leaves, the nurse comes back and hands Steph a clipboard, points at places to sign.

"No exercise for a week. Keep it completely dry for 48 hours. Wrap it in

plastic, elastic bands at the ends to keep it as dry as you can when you shower. Here's your appointment to get the stitches out." She hands me a card.

I roll my t-shirt into a ball with the unbloody parts on the outside then slip my good arm into my coat and try to do up the zipper with one hand. Impossible. Steph zips up my coat, says nothing, turns and leaves.

"Gee thanks," I whisper because I know better than to let her hear me.

I give Barrett a pathetic smile. "Thanks."

He nods and I walk fast to catch up to Steph.

Worst day ever.

Steph doesn't say a word all the way home and I don't push it. She'll get madder so what's the point?

When I open the kitchen door, Opa looks up from the table. The look on his face, I've never seen it before. And his eyes are red. Drinking? Did he find the pills? He's not a crier. And there's something else in his face, a hint of the ashamed look Mom pulls when she wants to make me feel guilty.

"The school called and said you are suspended for two weeks," Opa barks. "Are you happy now? Is this the hill you want to die on? What were you thinking, fighting? That's for boys, not for girls."

My mouth opens. I don't freakin' believe it. I stop a crazy girl from wanting to fight and get suspended for it? What the hell? I bet

Akemi made it all about her being the victim and me being the bully. What kind of bullshit story did she tell the school? There's no way she's getting away with this. I'll tell the principal first thing tomorrow. Then we'll see who gets suspended.

I look from Opa to Steph and back to Opa. He won't even look at me. Where is he? Where's the guy who's my biggest fan? Why isn't he on my side?

And right then, it hits me. I can't go to the principal. I can't tell him my side. I've already lied to the cop and Steph. What will they think if I pull this out my ass now? Oh, I know what they'll think. They'll think I'm a liar making crap up to save my own butt.

I don't believe it. I'm going to have to suck this up and take the suspension. Fuck. That blows. Totally blows. If I change my story now, no one will ever believe me again.

"You need to eat," Steph says in the quietest voice ever.

I look at her. Her words register at the same time I realize I'm standing there with my mouth unattractively wide open. I close it and try to figure a way out of this mess.

"I'm not hungry." I walk past avoiding eye contact with either of them.

"Go put clean clothes on and come back to eat." Her tone says, saying 'no' is not an option.

While I change, my phone vibrates again. I remember the number of times it

went off in the hospital, but I never checked because I thought it was Steph. Four messages from Mika.

Wth r u ok
Talk 2 me
R U OK
Barrett filled me in chat l8tr

Im ok just got home no biggy Send.
Oh, an after thought.
Thx 4 checking

An omelette with green stuff in it and two slices of toast on the side are at my place at the table. Steph hands me a glass of milk. Guess she forgot I'm lactose intolerant and it's probably not the time to remind her. I take the glass and sit down.

Opa and Steph are busy eating. Not talking. Not looking at me. Is this their silent treatment? Fine. Whatever. Before I know it, my plate is empty. I rub the last piece of crust along the inside to get the leftover bits of egg.

Still, no one says anything. I hate the silent treatment. Drives me mental.

"Thanks," I say. "I was hungry."

"They're sending your homework assignments to your email and cc'ing me. I'll print it out." Steph pats the corner of the table. "It'll be here in the morning. We sure

don't want you growing up to be an academic loser on top of everything else."

Ouch. That hurt. A lot. I wish she would yell and get it over with instead of throwing cheap shots. It makes me feel like she tolerates my existence but doesn't care about me or my feelings. At least when Mom yelled at me, I knew she cared and would get over it in time.

"I'm tired." I grab the glass of milk to take upstairs and stop behind Opa's chair. I want to connect with him. I want him to know it wasn't my fault, but his aura feels impenetrable, so I don't tap him on the shoulder. "I'm going to bed."

"Night." He waves his hand in the air without looking at me.

It hurts worse to know he's mad at me even more than when Mom is really mad. I want him on my side, so I walk back and give him a one-armed hug from behind. His shoulders stiffen. He doesn't pat my arm, so I let go and head to my room.

Don't cry.

The whole time I lie awake trying to fall asleep, I feel the thump in my arm and listen for Steph to come and talk. But she doesn't. Damn it. She got over the bear incident so fast. She never said a word about Opa's accident being my fault. Is this my third strike? Like Mom says, three strikes, you're out and this is my last one. What if Steph can't handle me anymore?

I felt like I fit in, like I was a part of hers and Opa's lives and then I have to go and wreck it. Will she send me to the boarding school? How awful would that be? I'd have to start all over again without Mika or Barrett or Greg. No Steph or Opa.

At least if she came up and gave me hell, I'd know she's mad but hasn't given up on me. I'd know she gives a shit. Come on Steph. Give a shit about me. Let's talk this out. I can make you understand what happened.

***

My room is full of sunlight when I wake up. Uh-oh, I missed my alarm. I'll be so late for school. When I sit up, a sting rips through my bicep and it all comes back. I lie down again.

Suspension. Two weeks. Great. And I have no idea where Steph's head is at with all of it. Oh right, and Dad, Dale—what am I going to call him? He'll be here tomorrow. What's he going to think? I have no idea what Steph told him, or what she told Mom.

I make a mental note to send Mom an email to talk her off the cliff. Or maybe I should send her the truth, tell her everything that's happened since she sent me here. Maybe we could move back to Toronto. Or, worse case scenario, she'd drag me across

the world to be with her. Neither choice excites me right now. Which is weird because going home to Toronto was what I wanted weeks ago. Maybe I'll hold off on the email till I feel Steph out. Right. That's the best option for now.

The living room is empty, Opa's bedroom door is shut and no one's in the kitchen. Not even Bucky. A white sheet of paper sits in the middle of the table. My homework assignments and Opa's scribble in the corner saying he'll be back for supper. Is he avoiding me? The thought hurts my feelings. I'm sure he took the Handi Van and is at physio and then off to visit Mrs. Bronigan. I go with that assumption to give my guilt a break.

I dial Mika's number and it goes straight to voice mail. Bet she's working. I send Barrett a text thanking him again. Yup, this is me procrastinating doing homework.

I nap and do schoolwork, nap some more, tidy up the kitchen and living room, wonder how Opa is doing—longest day ever.

Steph has a package of hamburger in the fridge, so I take out Oma's crockpot. I'll surprise them and make spaghetti sauce. Earn whatever bonus points I can.

Bucky rushes through the door and rams his nose up my butt as I'm tasting the sauce. He's a dog but hey, at least *he's* happy to see me. I bend over and grab his ears for a tussle.

"How was your day, boy?" I kiss him between his eyes.

"Smells good," Steph says from the back porch.

She's talking. Hurray.

"Spaghetti and meat sauce." I set the spoon on the lid.

"Is your Opa home?"

"Nope. He left a note—said he'll be back by supper time."

"Before he gets here, tell me what happened."

I'm sure my mouth is open and would catch a fly if it was summer. She's using a new approach. Sneaky like. Catch me when I don't expect it.

I stir some more and then put the lid back on.

"I really don't think she meant to do it," I say. "She's so mad at me and she got carried away. I don't know. And part of it's my fault I think."

"Start at the beginning, and I'll decide."

Steph's got this quiet face going on, a hint of sad but she doesn't look mad, so I give her a modified version of the whole thing skipping parts like how Akemi scares me, the poster fiasco, and how I try to avoid her since Eric hurt Opa. I give Steph facts only. Tangible stuff she can process.

She nods when I'm done. Her expression does not change. I could have been telling her how I brush my teeth.

Opa clumps into the back porch.

"Spaghetti sauce," he calls out.

Steph nods at me and leaves the kitchen.

What? That's it? Or I'll hear more after Opa is in bed? It's so stressful not getting the yelling over with and having to wonder when or if it's going to happen. I want it to. I want her to get mad at me. I'm mad at me for getting myself into this mess. If she's invested in our relationship at all, she has to get mad.

Supper is tasty, if I do say so myself, and I did. They mumble. I think it is in agreement but it's hard to tell. Opa peeks at me. His smile tips up, he winks quick and turns back to his plate as if he didn't want Steph to see him.

The house stays quiet like when you turn the TV down low to talk to someone on your phone. I bring my homework to the kitchen table, so I don't feel so alone in my room. Steph passes a few times, looks over my shoulder once but doesn't say anything.

The doorbell startles me so bad I flick my pencil across the room. Bucky gets up and growls. The hair on his neck and shoulders stands up.

"Lie down." Steph points to his bed and goes to the door.

"Jillian," she calls.

As I get up, I lean forward to see the doorway. Steph's body is in the way so I

can't see who's in front of her. How wonderful would it be if Greg was here? But no, even though Steph isn't his biggest fan, she wouldn't make him wait outside and Bucky wouldn't growl.

When I get closer, I stop. "Akemi?"

Steph pushes me in front of her, across from Akemi and a small man who stands at the bottom of the stairs.

"Akemi has something to say to you." I feel Steph's hands on my shoulder.

Silence. I glance up at Steph.

"You disgrace family. You say you sorry," the man barks. "Say it, now."

Akemi stares at our feet.

"It's okay," I whisper. "I'm good."

She looks up. Round, angry eyes. What the hell? I'm giving her slack and I get stink eyes?

"I'm sorry," she says.

How can her voice sound so sucky sweet when her glare says she's mad as hell?

I nod.

Akemi turns and walks down the stairs. The man, her grandpa maybe, makes her go in front of him as they head down the sidewalk to the gate.

"No internet, no phone, no fun," he says. "You study, learn lesson."

"I need the internet," Akemi whines, "to do homework."

"You do it old fashion way. Go to library. Read book."

Steph chuckles, steers me back into the house and closes the door.

"The move you did, you know, to push her aside, you learned that in Kung Fu?"

I shake my head. "Karate."

"Right. Karate." Steph puts her hands on her hips. "And you thought your mom made you take those classes so you couldn't be with your friends."

I shrug. She nods and almost smiles before she walks away. I get this huge sense it's over. That Steph's okay. That we're okay. Thanks to whoever or whatever brought Steph over to my side.

While she unloads the dishwasher, she says, "Dale will be here tomorrow afternoon around 3:30-ish."

"Okay." I close my books. "Mind if I ask what you told him?"

"Nothing."

Her back is to me, so I roll my eyes.

"No, really, what did you say?"

Steph turns, a plate in each hand. "I told you, I said nothing. At all. He wants to talk to you." She waves the plates in the air. "I have no idea what about. And any of this, what happened here," she points a plate at me, "is up to you to tell him. Not me."

"What?"

She turns back to the cupboard and puts the dishes away.

No way. Is it possible she didn't say anything to him? What game is Steph playing? Why didn't she tell on me? There's no way I'm saying anything about this to Dale…to Dad. It's the first time I get to meet him. I can't just dump this on him. Steph, what are you up to? Why can't I figure you out?

Chapter 15

Even though the homework list is endless, and I alternate between Math, doing the laundry and cleaning my room (like anyone is going to see it) the clock almost doesn't tick. I take the sling off and put on a long-sleeved shirt, but the stitches start to throb, so I put the sling back on.

Opa's physio lady stops in and is super cheery and smiley. I try to tap into it and end up pacing in search of something else to clean. When she leaves Opa comes into the kitchen and pours a coffee. I feel his eyes on me, so I look up.

"She's mean." He points his thumb towards the back door. "Hurts more when she leaves than before she came."

"But you're getting stronger? Feeling better?"

"It'll take more than some punk to keep me down."

He wraps his knuckles a bit too hard on the top of my head when he passes to go to the TV room. I grit my teeth and let the sting subside and grin because he's not upset with

me anymore. He could ease up on his signs of affection though, but I won't complain.

***

"You have..." Steph shouts.

I open the bathroom door and yell, "What?"

"You have company." Steph sticks her head up the stairs and peers through the railing.

He's here. My dad is here. Oh, my God. He heard me yell like I'm a little kid. I'm such a doofus. Geesh.

I run fingers through my hair and flip it over my shoulder to even it out. Nope. That looks dumb. I pull it into a high pony. Frick. Lifting my arm pulls the stitches but I breathe through it. With teeth clenched I wrap a scrunchy around my hair. Better. The pink hoody over my shirt hangs off my shoulders, sleeves looped together so my sling isn't so obvious. Clean jeans. Matching socks. I inhale then breathe into my hand. Toothpaste breath.

You'd think I was going on a date, not meeting my dad for the first time. Worrying about what to wear is a break from stressing about seeing him. Oh, my God! I'm meeting my dad for the first time ever.

With complete focus on the last few stairs, I put a smile on my face and walk into the kitchen. Opa and Steph with their coats

on, stand side by side. Bucky has his nose buried in Dad…Dale's, Mr. Cuthbertson's hand. That's totally a good sign, right?

"Jillian, this is Dale Cuthbertson. Dale, Jillian," Steph says. "I'm taking Dad and Tom out for supper and a movie to give you guys space."

Dale looks like his picture, the first time I found him on the internet. He's even wearing a business casual suit. Handsome for an old guy. Hair's a bit shorter, same strawberry blond as mine. Guys probably don't say strawberry blond though, do they? Green eyes.

"Hi." I step forward and stick out my hand, pull it halfway back and put it out again.

He has a solid, warm shake. I almost give a hard squeeze to show I'm tough but don't. First impressions. Let's make it my best. There's enough crap he'll hear about me in time if he sticks around.

No one talks. My eyes go from Dale to Steph and Opa to Bucky, out the window, around the room. Steph comes over, steps on my toes and gives me a robot side hug. I grin and slip my toe out from under her foot. Opa tips his head and winks. And away they leave, just like that.

The cuckoo clock ticks. I smile, a lot longer than I need to.

My, "How was…", is interrupted by his, "Can we go for a walk?"

"Sure." I go to get my coat way too fast.

"I've been sitting most of the day." He lifts both hands up and twists his back till it crunches. "I'd like to see some of the town before dark and it's better than staring at each other and trying not to say the wrong thing. Or to see who farts first." He pauses.

I laugh.

"Am I trying too hard?"

"No. It's easier knowing it's not any easier for you."

Dale nods. "We'll go for supper after. Maybe it'll be less awkward sitting across from each other by then."

"Sure. Where do you want to walk?" I push Bucky's nose back into the house and lock up.

"How about up to the Banff Centre so I can check out the house I lived in."

Wow, Banff Centre house. His parents must be rich.

"The town's changed a bit," he says as we head down the sidewalk. "New hotels, houses, new restaurants. Do you like it here?"

Loaded question.

"It's okay."

"I bet your grampa likes having you here."

"Some days probably not so much." Shoot. How's that for an almost too close to honest response? I'll have to think before I

talk, or I'll have to explain more than I want to.

"Can I ask what happened to your arm?" He points at my parka's flopping armless sleeve.

"Long story. It's nothing really. It'll be fine in a few days."

He nods. Darn. I can't tell him, but I don't want him to think I'm being sneaky or give him the idea I'm trouble.

It's quiet for too long.

"How was your flight?" I look up at him.

He's smiling. Good. He doesn't look upset. Or if he is, he's hiding it. Maybe he really is taking in the sites.

"It was okay. I was able to get a lot of work done. The drive from Calgary was like I remember. Flat, bald-ass prairie."

I stare ahead and grin. He's funny. Not stiff like I expected him to be.

"Brown-yellow prairie grass meets the snow-tipped Rockies. I've always enjoyed how the mountains pop out of the landscape. It never loses its effect."

"Yeah, it's pretty cool."

Wolf Street gets steeper as it connects to St. Julien Road and the mansions on the way to the Banff Centre. A few houses up, he stops and turns to face a driveway with a big garage made of rock attached to a black iron gate. Above the rock I can see the Tudor style house with red brick pillars. Super massive building. There's a national park

plaque in front of it. I watch for cars and go over to read what it says.

“You’re related to the Harmon’s?” I turn to Dale as he takes pictures.

“No. The town rented it for us.”

“It’s huge.”

He nods, inhales and lets out a long sigh which whistles a bit.

“Can I take your picture?” he says.

I point at the house. “With that in the background?”

“Sure.” *Click*. He puts his phone away and we continue walking. “Bet you’re wondering why I’m here.”

“It’s crossed my mind a few times.” I laugh. “Quite a few times. I thought Steph called you to…”

“To what?”

“Nothing. I thought she called and that’s why you’re here.”

He tips his head at me and gives me a puzzled look. “Is there something I should know?”

I shake my head. We walk in silence again and I’m about to ask him to continue with why he came when he starts to talk.

“That house, we only lived in it for a year. Mom wanted to settle down to give my brother and me roots before we graduated. Dad thought he could, but he was wrong. I don’t know how many times we moved, for him.”

I'm not sure where this is going, so I walk and listen and hope he gets to the 'why he's here' part.

"Dad liked to be in the thick of things, current trends, new innovations and saving the earth. Helping Banff manage their environmental issues was too small for him. There was never enough action for him to sink his teeth into. He tried though. He tried to like the quiet and calm."

We walk past the Eric Harvie Theatre.

"We did our high school Christmas play there." He points at the rock building. "Joseph and the Amazing Technicolor Dreamcoat."

I look up at him. "Wow. A musical. That's huge. You sing?"

"No. I was a guard. I stood in the background holding a spear." He stops, stands with his feet apart, one hand behind his back, the other holding, I assume, a pretend spear.

"Nice." I look at the ground. Not sure I'd be bragging about that to a lot of people.

"I was the best guard they had. And I was the only guard they had." He taps his chest. "Dad came to the play and after it was over, he said acting might not be my forte. He never beat around the bush. All-out honesty, all the time." He exhales with a puff.

I can't tell if it's cause he's sad about what his dad thought about the guard role or something else.

"Now they've got the Mountain Film Festival on," he says. "Have you seen it?"

I shake my head.

I'm not sure where any of this is going. Funny thing though, it feels okay. I know where he lived for a year of his life. I know he has two daughters and me. I know he's married. That's it. But I don't feel like I have to fill the air with chatter.

When we stop to look over the bank at the Bow Falls and the Banff Springs across the river, he grabs his phone again and takes a bunch of pictures, a few with me pointing, smiling.

He steps off the road and onto the trail. "Dad has dementia."

Dementia. Losing your mind. Old people disease. "Sorry. I didn't know."

His hand swipes across his eyes. Oh, no. Is he a crier? Mom says real men don't cry. In our family, no one ever cries, except me.

"At first it was nothing. He'd lose his car keys, forget where he parked, normal Dad stuff. Then he forgot where he lived. He drove onto the interstate to go home, and Mom corrected him which made him angry and irrational."

"Is he okay?"

Dale shakes his head and is quiet for a bit.

"He went downhill fast. He doesn't know me anymore and only sometimes recognizes

Mom. He knew my brother when he finally showed up. Mom put him in a home because she couldn't trust him. He'd get up and walk out of the house."

I stare at the ground. I'd hate it if Opa didn't know me. He forgets stuff sometimes. I feel sorry for Dale. It must be awful to watch your own dad do dumb stuff because he can't remember what the right stuff is to do.

"Does he know he has it?" I say.

"At first he knew something was up. He'd get mad at himself. Now, I don't think he does. He's happy and loves where he is, and most times he's nice to the staff like nothing changed."

"Well," I pause. "Maybe it's not so bad for him if he doesn't know."

Dale nods.

"I mean it's tough on you guys because you know. At least he's not in pain or anything."

"Yup, you're right. He's a 69-year-old man in a perfectly healthy body with no memory of who he was and can live for…for a long time like this." Dale coughs.

More silent walking.

A dog walker with the ugliest mutt who's wearing a red coat passes us. Bucky would be so embarrassed. The river slaps against the rocks as we get close to the pedestrian bridge.

How do I make the conversation cheerier? I don't want to look at him in case

he's still teary. How embarrassing would that be? There's nothing cheery about people losing their memory. Maybe I'll wait, let him continue or change the topic.

He stops and turns to me. "Where would you like to eat?"

"Uhm, anywhere. I'm not fussy. I eat anything except maybe spinach and I'm not crazy about purple cabbage either," I ramble on. He probably thinks I'm nervous but I just feel embarrassed for him if he has to get emotional again. "But I can eat it if I have too."

"No spinach, no cabbage—good to know. How about we go to Le Beaujolais?"

"It's gone. It's a beef barbecue steak place now."

"Steak is good."

***

Eddy is at the front of the restaurant dressed in a black suit. He hands us menus.

"Eddy," I grin. "You look awesome."

"What, these old things?" He spins around. "I bet you didn't think I had a wardrobe, did you?"

I laugh. "What're you doing here?"

"What's that?" He points to my arm.

I lean in and whisper, "Another time," then pull back and give him an exaggerated smile with blinky eyes.

He winks.

"So," I wave my finger up and down his suit, "what's this all about?"

"I need to make some cash. Shena's not doing so good."

"Oh no, what's wrong with her?"

"She's getting old. It might be her time to, you know, check out."

"I'm so sorry." I give him a solid hug.

He taps his finger under my chin, lifts it up so I look into his eyes. "She's had a good life."

Eddy steps aside and sticks his hand out to Dale. "It's been a while."

Dale nods and shakes Eddy's hand. It doesn't have a lot of seeing-an-old-friend enthusiasm, though.

Eddy seats us at a table with views of Banff Avenue and Mount Rundle.

After Eddy leaves, Dale says, "Who's Shena?"

"His dog."

"A dog?" He looks up from the menu. His eyes have an odd expression like he's surprised we're talking about a dog.

I hide behind my menu. He's not an Eddy fan? I wasn't either at first but Eddy's the best, when you give him a chance. Or maybe Dale knows Eddy and Steph are tight. Maybe that bugs him.

Dale tells me about ditching school to ski or go fishing. It takes forever for the food to come and the chit-chat is exhausting. As I

watch Dale cut his steak, I'm glad I ordered pasta.

There's still no talk as to why he's here. A few times the silence creeps me out and I ask about his daughters, Jules and Jessica. Does he think its weird our names all start with J? It's not like it was planned because, well, he didn't know about me. Mom, Anita mom, not Steph mom, named me after some track and field icon. Nothing unusual about that but what a coincidence all three of our names start with J.

After Dale puts his plate and utensils to the side, he wraps his hands around his coffee cup and leans forward. "You are a patient young girl."

"Pardon?"

"You've tolerated me for how long?" He looks at his watch. "Over two hours and you haven't bugged me about why I'm here. You let me ramble on."

I shrug.

He runs his finger up and down the cup's handle.

"I want to get to know you and I want my family to know you." He gives me an Oscar smile. "With all that's going on with Dad, and it's happening so fast, losing his memory, it got me thinking, what if it happens to me? You'd have no memories of me."

I scan the dining room for Eddy. When I look back at Dale, he's watching me.

"I want you to know the girls, Helen and me. I want you to have opportunities to go to schools, university, get the best education you can, make the best future. We can do that for you. And in the process, we can make those memories happen."

Make memories happen? Like a things-to-do list?

"Would you stay with us for Christmas break? Spend the holidays and check out Denver. Our house is pretty big. It's not like we'd be tripping over each other." He leans forward and rests his arms on the table. "Helen and the girls are so excited to meet you and show you around."

My mouth opens, closes, opens. And I close it in a tight smile.

"You don't have to answer now." He reaches over and pats my hand. "Think about it. Maybe you could move there if you like it."

Whoa! What? Move to Denver? I'm scared to say anything because I'm not sure how my voice will sound so I stir around the last of my noodles.

"Are you okay?" He taps the table with his fingers. "Did I scare you? I pushed it, didn't I? It was too fast. Helen knew I'd rush in. She said I'd make it sound like a job opportunity instead of a vacation. I realized what a void you must feel in your life because I've never been in it, and I want to

fix that. I want to make it right. I want to make your life better."

"Better?" I swallow the surprise I feel from his statement and take a breath before I say, "I'm okay. I don't need better."

"I'm sorry. That's not what I meant. I meant…I'm not getting this right, am I? I don't want to pressure you. I only want to offer you an opportunity to travel and get to know us." He pushes his arms out straight and presses his palms on the table. "I'm messing this up, aren't I?"

"No. I'm…I don't know. I didn't…I'm not sure." Now who's got dementia? I can't even finish a full sentence.

Dale puts his hands up like he's waving a truce. "Let's not ruin this. Think about it. Let's get you home." He gets up and comes over to pull my chair out. "I'm going to Lake Louise tomorrow to do a bit of sightseeing. Would you want to skip school and join me?"

Yikes. Is this where I tell him I'm suspended? Will he renege on the Christmas in Denver offer?

Do I even want to go to Denver? It would eliminate the whole Akemi issue for awhile. Give me and the other kids at school some space and time to get over it. Who knows, maybe I'd make friends. New friends. Mika and Barrett have each other. Greg, well, my mate Greg, I would miss him. A lot. But he works. Maybe going to Denver is just what I need.

"I have to ask Steph if I can go with you tomorrow."

"For sure. I don't want to cause trouble between you two."

There's no more mention of Denver. Dale points out the changes he sees on Banff Avenue, tells a few funny stories and I'm back home. He doesn't even come inside.

"Text me about tomorrow. If not, could I see you after school?"

I nod, offer my hand for a handshake, stop halfway and put out one arm for a hug. He grabs my shoulders and squeezes. *Well, isn't this embarrassing?*

"It was nice to meet you. Finally." He smiles and leaves.

"Bye," I call out.

He waves and disappears out the back gate. Just like that. I stare at the empty sidewalk.

Why don't I feel all bubbly and giddy and over-the-moon happy? I just met my dad, and we had a nice time. I thought this would be the end all, the big a-ha moment and that crapola mushy stuff people say when life works out and all the pieces fit.

I MET MY DAD.

And I don't feel any different.

I'm happy I met him. He seems nice. He wants to get to know me and make me a part of his family but I thought I'd be more excited. Ecstatic almost. I'm not. I feel meh, been

there, done that, now it's over. What's that about?

***

"So?" Steph lifts a glass of water and leans against the stove. "How'd it go?"

"He wants me to go to Denver for Christmas to meet them all. Check the place out."

Steph looks at Opa who looks back at her. I watch their awkwardness.

"And his dad has dementia," I say to give them an out. "He doesn't recognize anyone anymore."

"That's tough." Steph makes a frowny face. "But hey, a trip to Denver, cool."

"You think?"

She nods and looks at me for a few seconds before she walks to the sink.

"Go. Explore. Moab is fabulous. I saw it on TV. Beautiful place." Opa waves his pencil in the air like a plane. "Travel."

"Moab? That's quite a drive from Denver," Steph says. "And you and Mom always travelled. You were never home."

"That's when we were old farts. I mean when I was young, I wished I travelled and experienced the world. I never did any of that." He turns back to the newspaper and his crossword.

Over the top of Opa's head I scrunch my eyes at Steph. She shrugs. What's up with

him? Is that his way of saying he wants me to go so I can do what he didn't get to do when he was young?

"What do you think?" I say to Steph.

"It's up to you. It's a great opportunity. You can get to know them and explore Denver. Who knows," she pokes my shoulder, "maybe you'll like it. Have you eaten?"

"Yup. Did you know Eddy's working at the new steak place? He's got to make money to take Shena to the vet. Says it might be her time."

"Oh no." Steph's mouth twists. "That'll kill him. He's had her forever."

"He seems okay with it."

"Of course, he'd seem okay. He's a guy." Steph points to Opa. "Hey, Dad, maybe we can help Eddy out with some cash?"

Opa gives her a few slow nods.

"Did you have an okay time with Dale?" she says.

"Yeah. He seems nice. He showed me where they lived."

"Oooh, the mansion." She twirls an index finger in the air.

"What's that mean?"

"It was the elite of houses back in the day."

"I couldn't really see much. The gate was closed."

"Trust me, it's…" she stops, gives me a goofy smile, "never mind." And she heads for the living room.

Opa scritches away on his puzzle.

I stand there and wait for Steph to come back. She doesn't. Well, aren't they over-the-moon excited I finally met my dad? Guess it's not a big deal for them either. Maybe I'm making too much out of it.

Wait. No, I'm not. I met my dad for the first time ever. I'm fifteen. It should be a big deal. Why isn't it?

"I gotta call Mika." I give Opa another chance to say something. He doesn't so I stomp up to my room.

"Hey, elephant," Steph shouts.

Quick text to Mika.

Met dad

I stare at my phone but I'm not sure why. Mika sent a crazy GIF of a girl dancing when she found out I got suspended and she's terrible at checking messages unless she initiates them.

A map of Colorado fills my computer screen. I slip my arm out of the sling and zoom in on Denver. Not even a million people. Still, it's bigger than Banff. Skiing, hiking, museums, breweries—I'm not old enough to drink. Scenic pictures flash by with mountains and lots of colourful street festivals.

I sigh. Denver. Do I really want to go? It's only for Christmas break and Steph thinks

it's a good idea. I thought she might try and talk me out of it. She's tough to figure out. Just when I think we're good, we get along and she likes me she goes neutral, and I don't know where I stand.

Well, it's my decision, and I will make it.

Quick text to Dale.

What time tomorrow? Steph says it's ok

A teensy lie. I'll do homework tonight and Steph'll never know.

Does 8:30 work?

Cu then

An email from Mr. Amatt pops in my inbox.

Jillian—due to your recent suspension from school you'll be unable to attend the Columbia Icefields campout next week. When you are back at school, you'll be able to attend future outdoor activities. J. Amatt

No way. So not fair. I shut my laptop and grab my phone to scroll through messages. Greg never got back to me. Maybe he missed my text.

How's things got time to chat

And like my texts with Mika, I don't wait for a response. I only hope I get one.

***

Dressed in warm hiking clothes, I take a last peek in the mirror to make sure I look good. It'll do. Not too flashy, not too shabby.

There's an envelope on the kitchen table with Eddy's name on it. Opa and Steph must be helping him with the vet bill. I glance at Bucky's empty bed. He must be at work with Steph. I can't imagine how hard it is to put a dog down. Steph would even cry I bet. Probably the only thing that would make her cry. Poor Eddy.

Right at 8:30 the doorbell rings.

"Hey." I smile at Dale who's decked out in a business suit. "I better change. I thought we'd be walking, maybe hiking."

"I'm really sorry Jillian. Something came up at work and I have to fly home today."

"Oh," is all I manage to say.

"I hate to disappoint you when we're only getting acquainted, but I can't fix this from here. I have to get back to the office. You'll come for Christmas, right?" He grabs my shoulders and gives them a squeeze. "I'll email you the ticket. Let me know what your last day of school is."

I nod.

"Helen and the girls are excited to meet you."

An almost handshake turns into a super awkward hug, and he's gone. I stand there with my hand on the doorknob. What the hell? Here today, gone tomorrow. I hate it when Mom's old sayings get in my head. I close the door and stare across the empty kitchen.

Are Helen and the girls really excited to have me come to Denver? Or did he say it cause he feels guilty he had to bail right after he met me?

Was it something I did? Said?

I move to the kitchen table and tap my textbook as I recap last night. He was nice and everything. I thought we had a good first get-to-know-each-other time. But he sure doesn't seem to have a huge amount of *have to have you in my life* vibe going on. In fact, now it feels like he felt obligated to come meet me because of his dad's dementia. It made him feel guilty about not knowing me, not having any memories to share.

Well, at least now we have *one* memory to share.

Didn't I make any kind of impact? Or is he having the same *meh* feeling I had? Like does this really matter? Do we need each other? Or is he really such a busy guy, he has to go back to whatever else is way more important than me?

I didn't see this coming. I know how I felt last night but I'm his daughter, for Pete's sake. Why is he not more interested in getting to know me? I've been patient waiting to meet him. Hell, he's the one who said they'd come next summer. A whole year after I tracked him down with that one little email.

Oh, my God, the memory of the shit-show my message to him caused makes me

cringe. Mom and Steph, Oma, Opa—they were horrified. And then Oma died. I hope I told her I didn't blame her for keeping the secret from me. I'm sure I did, didn't I? I'd hate to think she didn't know before she died.

Back to me. Back to here and now. Does he really need more time to get used to the idea he has a daughter he didn't know about? I was so excited when I found him, and I was sure he'd be all over wanting to hook up and meet and fill in all the years we've missed.

Establishing a relationship with him is a whole lot more work than I expected. In my dreams he was going to swoop in and take care of me. In my dreams he thinks I'm amazing and loves me to pieces. Kind of like Opa does when he's not mad at me. I can't even imagine using the *love* word and *my dad* in the same sentence. Will I ever be able to?

If I do give him the benefit of the doubt, if he is a super busy, important guy and couldn't stay, I'm lucky I got a chance to meet him. Yes. That's what I'll go with. I'm probably making more out of it than I need to. After all, he did come to meet me. I'll let go of the *what about me* pity party.

Breathe. Move on.

I'll visit them in Denver and make up my own mind. I'll be the one to decide if I need them in my life. Heck, I'll decide if I *want*

them in my life. It's only for ten days so how hard can that be?

With my now lukewarm cup of too-sweet coffee, I give my heart a break and focus on a math problem, check my quiet phone too many times, and the train speed versus the car speed versus where they're going blurs and I stare out the window.

The doorbell makes me jump. Dad…Dale, I still don't even know what to call him, changed his mind?

When I open the door, Eddy is leaning against the railing.

"Hey, shouldn't you be in school?" He points to my sling. "And now, tell me about this?"

"Steph didn't tell you?"

His dreadlocks slap against his parka when he shakes his head.

"Bad judgement, slow reaction, a few stitches and a suspension."

Eddy's eyebrows lift.

"It's not a big deal, really." I grab the envelope for him. "Do you want me to come with you to help with Shena?"

"I don't want her stressed. She knows something's up so it's best I do it on my own. Thanks though, for the offer."

I stare at the floor. "I'm really sorry. It sucks."

"Relax. It's okay. How'd it go with your old man?"

"I thought it was good. We were supposed to go sightseeing today, but he bailed. Said he had to fly home, something about work."

"Hey, it happens. Don't beat yourself up about it."

I snort.

"Did you wow him with your awesomeness?"

"Whatever." I roll my eyes like he told the worst joke ever. "Hey, can you give me a ride?"

"Where to?"

"Johnson Lake."

Eddy pulls his head back and squints. "Can I ask why?"

"I need air. Somewhere to walk."

He nods. "Bring your pepper spray. Some of the bears aren't hibernating yet."

I pull on my hikers, throw gloves, my phone and bear spray into a backpack and grab my parka.

Eddy holds the screen door while I lock up.

Shena props her head on the console between the front seats. The passenger seats in the back are pulled down flat and there's an old sleeping bag on top for her. After I've done up the seat belt, I rub her between her eyes. She closes them. Her breathing gurgles. As soon as Eddy's in the driver's seat, she nuzzles her nose under his elbow.

I stare straight ahead and force my eyes wide open, so I don't cry.

The drive is quiet. No radio. No chatter. Just Shena's gurgle breathing.

There's one white passenger van in the Johnson Lake parking lot which is great. I won't have to worry about dodging crowds on the path.

Shena lifts her head when I grab my coat and pack. One last stroke through her husky head, I blink fast when I see her cool blue eyes and duck out of the truck, so Eddy doesn't see my face. I can't make it any worse for him.

"Thanks." I slip my coat on, adjust my sling with my backpack and wave.

"I'll be back by eleven-thirtyish," he says. "I'll text."

"You don't have to. I can walk back."

"Right, and have Steph bust my balls." He waves and is gone.

I watch his truck until it turns the corner. Poor guy. Poor Shena. Tears leak out. Life. Geesh.

And then the alone hits me. The all alone. And it's not just because I'm here and there literally is no one else around, it's the feeling like no one cares if I'm here or not. Well, except for Eddy and that's only because he wants his balls left intact.

Do Steph and Opa care if I go to Denver? They did the look thing with each other when I told them. And Steph did the

smiley face and said go. Does she *really* want me to go? If so, is it because she wants to get me out of her space for awhile or is it because she genuinely wants me to check it out and get to know them all? *Or* is she keeping her real opinion to herself and it's none of the above?

Adults are so freakin' complicated.

I wish she'd tell me what she really thinks so I don't have to figure out what's going on in her head. She could also toss in an *I love you* once in a while but that's way out there—I'm sure it will never happen.

It's exhausting trying to figure out what's going on inside people's heads.

I stop the turmoil and watch the reflections of the trees, mountains and clouds on the lake. The clouds move across the water without making a ripple. It makes me smile despite my confused state of not understanding grownups thought processes. I guess if I'm going to be alone at least I'm alone here with a picture postcard perfect view.

I head towards the hermit's cabin. The smell of dead leaves and dry ground, the quiet. Who'd have thought I'd ever enjoy it?

When I see the wood swing hanging from the tall pine trees across the lake, I walk a bit further and pick a skinny animal trail which runs away from the lake and the main path. Greg made me close my eyes but I'm sure we started somewhere close to here.

Careful to step over deadfall and avoid branches poking my face, I continue along until I see the powerlines. Damn. I've gone too far. Totally missed the cabin.

Backtracking and following faint trails I search along the ground for anything that doesn't belong. A moss-covered, knee-high chopped, tree stump and then another. Lichen hanging off an old pile of logs, neatly stacked. The woods get darker, and I squint to see ahead. Back and forth. Spider webs tickle my face and I swipe them away. I'm almost ready to go to the lake shore and try again when I spot a solid mass of darkness. The cabin roof against the trees.

To think, Billy Carver lived here all alone. How did he do it? And why? I can't imagine not having any people around. It'd be so lonely. He would have died in the cabin if those guys hadn't found him. Because of them, he died in an old folk's home. Would he have wanted to die here, at home, alone?

It's so primitive.

The rusted stove and pots are stacked outside now, underneath a tree. Someone must have moved them. I guess they can't read the National Park sign that says don't touch, it's a historic site.

Maybe I can find the trail that Mr. Gee Moy used to bring supplies from Anthracite. The one Greg wanted to show me. With a quick check on my bearings, I head towards the powerlines again taking the most

significant trails I find. They all have deadfall across them which I climb over or, if it's too blocked, find a way around.

I pass under the powerlines and head for the ridge where the hoodoo tops poke above the cliff edge. There the sun hides behind the clouds which hook on the top of Mount Rundle.

After a few times walking back and forth along the ridge, I admit I can't find an easy way down the hoodoos. I don't know why I thought I could if Greg couldn't. Guess I just wanted to impress him with my wilderness cleverness, increase my mate status point score.

The clearing where the buildings and greenhouses used to be, are filled with trees. The trail must have washed away, or Mr. Moy was half mountain goat. Or did the hoodoos get steeper over the years?

I find my way back to the cabin and pull out Greg's tippy stool from its hiding place.

A thud stops me from unwrapping my granola bar. I tip my head in the direction of the sound. Another thud. Far off branches snap. I kick my backpack in front of me and grab the pepper spray.

Hopeful it's deer or elk and not a bear, I stand with my back to the cabin and peer through the woods for movement.

Something red. A coat. A person. A person in a red coat on the main trail. I duck down. Why? Not sure.

"Winner, winner chicken dinner," guy in red coat shouts.

What's going on? The guy bounces up and down. Hunched over, I put Greg's stool back where it belongs.

"I found it first. I win," he yells.

Who is this nutcase? And what did he win?

More branches snap followed by loud voices. I crouch lower.

It's a parade of people. I can't tell how many. Loud chatter for a few seconds and they move off down the trail.

Well, that was exciting.

Footsteps. Coming my way. I stand, pull on my pack and pretend I'm looking around the old cabin.

"Jillian?" Greg says.

I turn.

"It *is* you." He comes to give me a hug but stops when he sees my slinged arm. "What happened?"

Avoiding an answer, I point in the direction the others went. "Are you with that group?"

"They're university students from a Natural History class. We did a couple nights bivouac."

"And you didn't show them the cabin?" I hip-check him. "I thought you were mad at me, that weird message you left. And you never answered my calls."

"I didn't leave you a message. A butt dial maybe. I've been out of service for a couple of days now." Greg points to the sling. "Now tell me about this?"

We start walking out to the main trail.

"Long story. Remember Akemi from the Aylmer hike? The gal that hurt her ankle. We had a…disagreement. It involved an encounter, sort of. I got a few stitches. And I got suspended." I glance up and give him a goofy smile. "But guess what? I met my dad. I might go to Denver."

"Whoa." He stops and the carabiners on his pack clink together. "I've only been gone a few days. How about you start at the beginning?"

I give a short version of what went on. Greg whistles but doesn't say anything.

"When're you going to Denver?"

"Christmas holidays."

"We'll have to teach you to ski or snowboard first." Greg drapes his arm around my shoulder as we walk up to the parking lot and I have to tell the giddiness in my gut to settle down. "Denver is a winter mecca. I can teach you to shred."

My phone *bings* and it's a message from Eddy. *On my way.*

"I found it first Greg," a lady in pink camo calls out. Greg takes his arm off my shoulders.

"I told you you'd find it." He unlocks the white van, opens the back door and his

group put their gear in. “Do you need a ride to town? We have room.”

“No, Eddy’ll be here soon.” I fight the I-miss-your-arm-on-my-shoulder feeling.

Greg looks around the parking lot. “Are you sure?”

I nod.

“I’ll pray for snow,” he calls out the window. “Skiing or snowboarding, which do you want to try?”

“Whichever is easiest.” And he drives away. I’m so glad he isn’t mad.

***

Eddy’s truck stops beside me.

“Hey.” I get in and notice the back passenger seats are up and Shena’s blanket is gone. “Want to come for lunch? You can help Opa cheat at his crossword puzzles.”

“You’re a doll, you know that?” he says. “But I’m good. Thanks.”

We pull out of the parking lot as spits of rain hit the windshield. Perfect timing.

“It was quiet.” Eddy clears his throat. “I know she knew what was going on.”

I swallow and stare at the wipers as they smear the rain into the dusty windshield. We ride in silence. Part way to Banff, big, fat flakes splat on the window and the wipers push them away. The peaks are gone.

"You sure you don't want to come in?" I say as I open the door. "It'll only take a few minutes to make lunch."

"Next time. I have to work in a couple hours and plan to catch some shut eye first."

I close the door, scrunch my neck into my coat to keep the snow out and wave. Eddy drives down the back alley and disappears onto the street. Will he get another dog? He'll be so alone. Maybe Steph can go talk to him.

After I shake the wet off my coat and hang it up, I step into the kitchen.

Opa looks up from his crossword. "What's there to eat?"

"You going to cheat?" I poke him on my way to the fridge, but the doorbell makes me do an about face.

"Kyle," I say way too loud and pull him into the back porch to give him a huge hug. My good arm soaks up the snow on his coat.

He takes his toque and coat off and shakes them around before he hangs them up.

"You got a buzz cut." I rub my hand over the bristles on his head.

"My fault. I fell asleep chewing gum. It got so stuck Dad said it was easier to shave my head than get it out."

"It looks good."

"No, it doesn't. Mom says everyone will think I had head-lice. She says Dad's too lazy to use an ice cube to get the gum out."

He points at my sling. “What happened to you?”

Just then, Opa calls, “Hey, brat. Get in here.”

Kyle ducks around me and rushes to Opa who noogies him on the top of his head.

“Ouch.” Kyle giggles and pulls away.

“So, you’re back with your mom?” I say.

Over the top of Kyle’s head, Opa gives me a *mind your own business* look.

“Yup. Dad says I’m too much work and I miss school and my bed and you guys.” Kyle comes over. “Can you walk me to school?”

I check the clock. If we walk fast, I can get him there before the bell rings. “Isn’t your mom taking you?”

“She’s sleeping.”

“Let’s go but we have to walk fast.”

Opa winks at me.

“You be good, kid.” He shakes a finger at Kyle. “No hooligan tricks at school.”

“What’s a hooligan?”

“It’s an old guy with a lousy sense of humour,” I say.

Kyle chatters about sleeping in the car and in a smelly place with a broken window and the great prizes in Kid’s Meals. He stomps in the snow-trimmed puddles. When we get to his school, he grabs my hand.

“Will you come in with me?”

“Ah, sure. Why?”

“What if the teacher forgot who I am?”

“I’m sure she didn’t. Let’s go see.”

Kyle pulls my arm towards the door. We take off our boots in the mudroom and lots of kids come up to say hi to him. Kyle's smile is the best.

"They didn't forget you," I whisper. "Bet the teacher didn't either."

At the door to his class, a lady in a track suit and silver whistle around her neck taps kids on the head as they go into the room.

"Kyle, welcome back. I'm so glad to see you." The teacher looks at me, gives me a full-on inspection without hiding it. "And you're?"

"Jillian. Kyle's neighbour."

"Is his mom coming?"

I shake my head.

"Can you please tell her I'd like to talk with her about homework Kyle has."

"Sure."

She taps Kyle on the head. "You go take an empty seat."

"Bye." Kyle waves at me, ducks under the teacher's arm and into class.

***

Mrs. Bronigan sits beside Opa in the kitchen. Her crooked fingers wrap around a coffee cup.

"Thanks, dear. It's nice of you to walk Kyle to school," she says with a red lipstick smile.

"His teacher wants to talk to his mom about homework."

Mrs. Bronigan and Opa look at each other.

"Okay, I passed on the message." I head for my room. "I've got homework."

I think my life is a shipwreck and Kyle's just a little kid with a mom who doesn't even get him ready for school and a dad who says he's too much trouble. Makes Denver and Akemi and my life seem chill.

My phone *bings*. Mika? Greg? Maybe Dale? It still surprises me how odd it is that a text message startles me. I could almost forget my phone at home. Almost. The only thing keeping it in my pocket is the fear I will one day miss something big and be the last to find out about it.

Thanx for everything. Ray

He must have got my number from Steph. I haven't thought about our night on the mountain in a few days. In fact, guilty, I haven't thought how he's doing since Steph said he's tough. Sorry Ray.

How r u?

I was transferred to the Banff hospital today. Lots of physio and my face almost looks like a face again, sort of. Each day is a bit better. Please stop by when you can. I'd like to thank you in person.

U bet what time r visiting hours

After lunch, any day you can come.

Ok

Chapter 16

"Morning." I squeeze Opa's shoulders.

The kitchen sink and counter are full of dirty bowls and flour. What the hell, Steph? She gets on my case about cleaning up after myself and leaves me with this mess. Not fair.

I slip my arm out of the sling and rinse crap off the bowls before putting them in the dishwasher. The stitches don't pull as much when I extend my arm. Cool. I'll ditch the sling today.

"You're going to be late for school," Opa interrupts my internal rant about Steph's mess.

"You know I'm still suspended. You have another week of me being around 24/7."

He stares at me. His eyes go funny like he's not sure he believes what I said. When the phone rings, Opa's chair screeches on the floor as he gets up.

"You get the phone," I say. "I'll make breakfast."

While I pop in two slices of bread, Opa shouts, "What?" He presses the phone hard on his ear. "You want money?"

I tap his shoulder and gesture to see if he wants me to talk to whoever is making him mad. He lifts the receiver in the air and drops it in my hand.

“Hello, Jillian Meier. Can I help you?” I watch Opa shuffle back to the table. He seems wobbly. Maybe the mini-blizzard made his arthritis flare up again.

“Hey Jillian, is your grampa okay?” Eddy says. “He didn’t recognize my voice and he sounds pissed off.”

I glance at Opa’s back.

“I don’t know.” I face the wall and lower my voice. “I think he’s good.”

“Can you tell Steph and him thanks for the loan. That’s why I called. I’ll stop by later this week after work to pay them back.”

“Sure, I’ll tell them. How are you doing?”

“I’m fine. Don’t you worry about Eddy.”

“But I do.” I take a deep breath and wonder how sad he is. “Take care. Bye.”

As I hang up, the smoke detector blasts. Opa jumps and knocks his chair over. He moves one way then the next and almost falls in his rush to go nowhere. I put my hands on his shoulder as smoke wafts from the toaster and point to the detector before steering him into the TV room.

Back in the kitchen smoke seeps out the oven door too. What the hell is going on this morning?

I shove a boot against the bottom of the back door to keep it open then hurry to check

the oven. A cookie tray of black circles. Steph was making cookies? And she left without taking them out? I turn the stove off and grab the tray with an oven mitt, set it outside on the snow-covered step and come back to wave a tea towel under the detector. It takes a lot of shaking until it finally stops screaming.

Opa shuffles back into the kitchen as I stare at the open oven door.

"Where are my cookies?" he snaps.

"Your cookies? I thought they were Steph's. I thought she forgot about them."

"Steph's no Susie Homemaker. They were Oma's recipe. What'd you do with them?"

"They're burnt." I point out the open back door.

"How'd that happen?"

"The oven was on. They were in it."

"Well, you better be careful. You could burn the house down." He shakes a finger at me and walks back to the TV.

What? This is my fault? Even when it's not my fault? What's with him today?

With more noise than necessary I clean the kitchen, make another batch of toast and coffee and take it in to him but he's not in his recliner. I tiptoe to peek in his room. Sound asleep on the bed, snoring like a bear. After I close the door without making it squeak, I take the food to my room to work on more boring homework.

The house is so quiet. I can almost say I'm looking forward to this suspension being over so I can be with people again. Not that Opa and Steph aren't people, but to be at school where there's stuff going on all the time. Even though I'm not a part of it, it's like white noise, a less lonely feeling.

Oh right, then there's Akemi. Will I just ignore her? Avoid her? Or will she get in my face? I have time to figure that out.

After my butt is numb and I can't get comfortable anymore, I stack my books on the corner of my desk and change into jeans and a fuzzy wool sweater.

Opa wears headphones in the TV room and waves his hands at the screen. The Wheel of Fortune contestants must be getting the wrong answers.

I lift one of the earpieces and say, "I'm going to visit Ray at the hospital."

"Get the mail and beer. Pilsner."

I roll my eyes, let the headphone snap back and noogy him on his bald spot.

***

"Hey, Ray." With my back to him, I pull off my parka and practise making a normal face at the wall, so he doesn't see how surprised I am at all the stitches and shiny, swollen skin on his face. I turn, smile at the nurse standing at the foot of the bed and say,

"How's it going? The food any good in this place?"

"There's my hero. No, my heroine. Naw, that sounds too corny." He points to me and the nurse lifts her head from her charting. "Let me introduce you to Super Girl."

"Hardly." I try not to blush, but it doesn't work.

"Well, I'd say you are. Ray told me all about your night on the mountain," says the nurse. "He'd be in a lot worse shape if you hadn't been there. He's a lucky man."

The heat continues to run right up to my hairline. Good God. Will I ever outgrow blushing?

She pats me on the shoulder on her way out.

"Well, that was embarrassing," I say. "What are you telling people?"

"Only the truth." With both hands, he lifts his legs off the bed like it's a big deal and pulls a walker closer.

I force myself not to stare at the bulges on the left side of his face.

"Time for me to do a lap. Join me."

Ray hunches over the walker and swings his legs to the side each time he takes a step. I look straight ahead so he can't see how difficult it is for me to see him walk. Wow, between walking and his face healing, he's got a lot to deal with. There's no way I'd be as cheerful as he is. But then I'm not the one who could have died.

"Do you have to do lots of exercises? When Opa came home, his therapist was always on his case."

"I do twice as many, every chance I get." He stops, straightens and takes a few deep breaths before he picks up the walker and carries on. "I have to. I need to, or I'll lose my license."

I nod.

"How about you?" He nudges me. "Have you saved any more people? What have you been up to?"

"No. No more saving people for me. I have to pick up beer for Opa on the way home."

"Pilsner?"

"How'd you know?"

Ray laughs, which makes me relax. When we reach the coffee room Ray heads for the chairs lined up along the big windows that face the street across from the bus depot. Cascade Mountain and Norquay have fresh snow on them.

"A beer please," he says after he's settled into the chair.

"Sorry, it's coffee, tea, looks like orange juice or a bottle of water."

"Surprise me."

I grab two waters.

Ray points to Norquay. "Are you going to ski this year?"

"Apparently snowboarding is easier to learn so I'm going to try that."

As we sip and stare out the window, a small group of people come out of the bus station and load onto a big van.

I glance at Ray's profile. "Where do you think they're going?"

We chat about tourists, the best sites, winter and how cold it'll get—light conversation without talking about the tough stuff.

"Call me butt face," Ray says.

"Pardon?" I look at him. Has he lost it?

"Do it, call me butt face."

"Okay, butt face."

He leans forward, slaps his knee and laughs, a lot.

I stare at him. He is losing it.

"Sorry. It's an inside joke. Let me explain it." He sits up and taps his bulgy cheek. "They grafted skin from my butt onto my face."

"Oh, I get it." I don't laugh but it makes me smile that he does. "Puts a whole new spin on 'kiss my butt'."

"Yes, yes, it certainly does do that."

"Ray," someone across the room calls. A guy decked out in the infamous ugly warden green uniform heads towards us.

"I'll say bye." I stand. "Looks like you have company."

"Thanks for coming, Jillian." He struggles to get up. I don't help him, and I don't stop him. "I really appreciate it. And

thank you for everything. I couldn't have made it without you."

"Exercises." I shake a finger at him to ease the impact of his last words…for both of us. "Double time. You keep doing them double time so you can get out of here."

"You know what?"

"No. What?"

"The first next flight I make in a chopper, I'm taking you with me. You're kind of my good luck charm and it'll be a thank you token to you." He sticks his hand out and we shake on it.

I smile and don't say how about maybe your second or third flight. Not that I don't trust him, but just in case he's rusty and I'm not as lucky as he thinks.

Chapter 17

My eyes fly open. Red then blue lights flash across my dark bedroom walls. I lift my head off the pillow and hear muffled voices. Steph's and someone else's who I don't recognize.

What's going on?

I pull a hoodie over my pjs. The bottom of the stairs is lit up and someone, in a dark uniform, stands next to Steph. I press against the wall as I head down. Another dark clothed person backs up with their hands on the end of a stretcher. I jump the last few stairs and rush towards Opa's room.

"Steph," I shout.

She rushes to me, puts her hands on my shoulders so I can't go forward and pulls me into the kitchen.

"What's going on?" I stand on tiptoes to look around her.

"We're not sure yet. It's possible he had a stroke." She hands Opa's green folder from the fridge to the ambulance guy. "Or maybe it was a heart attack."

I try to pull away, but her fingers dig into my collar bones.

"Listen to me," Steph says in a quiet, super-serious voice. "Go upstairs."

"No!"

"Jillian, go upstairs and get dressed. Please."

Tom moves behind Steph.

"Tom's going to drive us." She looks over her shoulder at him. "We'll follow the ambulance to Canmore. They can do more tests there."

I look at Tom. His dark eyes tell me nothing. Back to Steph. She doesn't blink and as usual I can't tell what she's thinking. They're rolling Opa out and putting him in an ambulance. Poor Opa. He's been through enough. How can Steph be so calm?

She releases her grip, turns me towards the stairs and gives me a push.

Back in my room with the light on, I notice my closet door is open a crack. Weird. I always close it. Walking over to the door like someone might be watching me, I pull the door open slowly. No one. The floorboard is up at the corner. I never leave it like that because I don't want anyone reading my journal. I yank the board off.

Oma's pills are gone. Oh no. Opa, you didn't?

"Jillian!"

"Coming."

As I hurry to get dressed, I try to figure out the last time I saw them, the last time I wrote in my journal. A few days ago? Could

Opa have found them? Would he really take them? He must have. They're gone and he's been confused and jumpy for a couple of days.

Stupid me. Why didn't I check? I should have found a better place to hide them. I should have taken them to the pharmacy and got rid of them, but I procrastinated, kept thinking I would. And now, look what happens. Stupid, stupid. How am I going to tell Steph?

Why would Opa take them now? He was doing so good.

I race down the stairs as Steph locks the front door. When she sees me, she turns away. Her eyes are red. Steph's crying? This is bad and I'm only going to make it worse. Maybe if they pump Opa's stomach or give him naloxone he'll be okay.

"I think Opa took Oma's pills." I blurt it out a bit too loud.

Silence.

"All of the pills," I say in a quiet voice. "They're all gone."

"Not now, Jillian."

"But what if its not a stroke? What if its an overdose? They need to know that."

"It's not an overdose," she snaps.

"How do you know? You're not a doctor."

"I took the pills."

"What?" I glare at her. "You went through my room?"

"This isn't the time."

Tom holds the back door open and gives me a pathetic attempt at an *it's okay* smile-nod.

"Let's go," Steph says.

What the hell? Why'd she go through my room? God, I hope she didn't read my journal. She'll know way more than I've told her about Akemi, about everything.

I want to be relieved Opa didn't take them, and I am, but I'm also pissed at Steph. Who does she think she is? I bite my tongue hard to keep from spewing out words I can't take back. How dare she invade my space. I'm not some little kid.

Oh, for God's sake, this isn't about me. I get angry with myself and repeat '*get over it*' in my head until I can focus on Opa and what's going on here and now minus my hissy fit about Steph snooping in my room.

No one says anything as the lights of Banff Avenue flash by. I chew on my lip till we're on the highway and the cab is dark.

"Did you call Mom?"

Steph shakes her head.

I stare out the windshield. Why didn't she call Mom? Strokes are serious. Heart attacks are serious.

As if she channelled into my thoughts Steph says, "I'll call her when we know what's going on. There's nothing she can do and there's no point upsetting her if it's nothing."

Tom pats Steph's knee. I lean back in the seat, worry about Opa and how upset Mom will get. I can fix that. I'll send her a quick email, let her know Opa's on his way to the hospital but not to worry, we're with him. I dig in my coat pocket and realize my cell phone is on the night table in my room. Well, doesn't that figure. Probably for the best. Steph's right. Again. A benign message with no facts would worry Mom.

Steph changes the radio channel to CBC. No more country music. Another *not good* sign. When headlights shine in, I see Tom and Steph's profiles. It's like they're playing Temple Guard in karate. They're both expressionless. Sensei would walk around the dojo and get right in our face to see if he could get us to smile. Steph and Tom would win.

***

The silence in the waiting room isn't as bad as it was in the truck because there's stuff going on. People slouched in chairs, shoes click on the floor, nurses, doctors, buzzers, and a lot of bright lights.

Every time an official-looking someone heads in our direction, Steph sits up straight. When they pass, she slumps, and Tom squeezes her hand. Is Opa awake? Have they done the tests?

He'll be okay, right?

For hours I try to sleep sitting up then drape across two chairs. When the ache in my back hurts too much I walk a bit, stand and touch my toes to stretch it out. When my movements irritate Steph, she pats a seat and I sit again. If I had my phone I could play a few games, listen to music, or text someone who cares.

Grey morning light comes in the window. Dark clouds hover along the base of the Rundle Range and run into the fresh snow. It's the only brightness to the morning.

Tom balances a tray of coffee cups and carries a brown bag to us. An Oma, who's been sitting across from me and knitting the longest blue scarf, looks up and smiles. Who's she waiting for? Her husband? She looks too old to have an Opa. Maybe her grandkid is in here getting fixed up.

Warm sugar smell drifts into my nostrils when I open the bag. Cookies and glazed donuts. Yum.

"We have lots." I hold the bag out to the Oma. "Would you like one?"

"Thank you, dear." She folds her knitting on her lap. "That would be nice."

I tip the bag towards her, and she plucks out an oatmeal raisin cookie. My favourite.

"Thank you." She pulls a tissue out of her pocket and nibbles on the cookie.

Just as I am about to finger through the bag to snag a donut, a tall lady in a white lab

coat with an iPad tucked under her arm calls out, “Stephanie. Stephanie Meier.”

Steph jumps up and walks to her. I look at Tom. He puts his hand out and I stay put. I lean forward and try to read lips, but I have no idea how. Steph nods a few times.

That’s a good thing, right?

But then she puts her hand over her mouth and turns away so I can’t see her face. Her head tips and her shoulders lift and drop. The lab coat lady pats her back.

That’s not good.

I stare at the floor, close my eyes and mouth a little prayer for Opa to be okay in case someone is listening. He has to be okay. When I open my eyes, Steph’s shoes are in front of me.

“We can see him,” she says in a quiet voice. “But he’s had a stroke and he has an aneurysm, an aortic aneurysm.”

“But he’ll be okay, right?” I say. “They’ll fix it.”

Steph crouches down and rests her hands on my knee. She shakes her head. “No, they can’t. It’s too close to his heart. He’s…it’s just time, he’s…” Her tears start and she stands.

I jump up and grab her. “No, he has to be okay.” I hug her hard.

Tom’s arms wrap around both of us. Steph’s body shivers as we all rock back and forth. My heart hurts so bad.

"Come with me," someone says and Tom steers us towards a door.

Steph clears her throat. "I need to call your mom." She pushes Tom and me forward to follow the lady. "I'll be right there."

"No, you have to come." I grab her arm.

"I have to tell your mom." Steph's face is blotchy, her eyes don't know where to look and her voice, it's shaky. "You go sit with Opa." She squeezes my shoulder. "So he's not alone."

Alone. I don't want him to be alone. I don't want him to die. And I really don't want him to die alone. Or with me in the room. Why does he have to die? What do I do? Or say? Well, that's just stupid. I don't have to say anything. Tom puts his arm across my back, and we follow the lab coat lady.

"Why doesn't he have tubes and stuff?" I point at Opa who looks so tiny under the light blue blanket. "He needs them to get better."

The lab coat lady, who I guess is his doctor, looks at Tom, gives him a lame smile as if I'm not smart enough to understand. Tom moves next to me, and we both stare at Opa.

"It's what he wants, Jillian," Tom says in a husky voice.

I can't look at him. If he cries too, I'm done.

Deep breath.

"He has a do not resuscitate order. We can only keep him comfortable," says the doctor. "It's what he wants us to do in this type of situation."

"That's wrong. You have to do more for him. You have to give him IVs and stuff. That'll help him get better, so he'll be okay." I slip my fingers around Opa's cool hand and give him a tiny squeeze. His face doesn't change so I squeeze a bit harder. Still no change. "He'll want to get better…for us. I know he will."

Silence.

My fingers rub the top of his hand. It feels soft, thin, like after you peel off an onion's first layer. Has it always felt like this? I can't remember. I don't think I've held his hand since Oma died. Mom needs to get here. She will make them listen. She'll make them keep him alive.

I lean in and whisper, "Opa, can you hear me?"

Nothing.

"Come on, you can do it."

Eye flutter.

"Did you see that?" I jump up and remember to let go of his hand. "His eyelids, they moved. I saw it."

"It's involuntary muscle movement. It's not him," the doctor says as if she's explaining to a toddler why she can't have a candy.

"How do you know?" As soon as I hear the words come out, I turn away. "Maybe you're wrong. Maybe he's trying. He knows it's me."

No one says anything. Fine. I know I'm right. I have to be.

I hold Opa's hand again. "I know you can do it. Come on. Do it for me. Prove she's wrong."

There's a loud sigh behind me and it's all I can do not to whip around and tell the doctor lady to fuck off.

"Jillian," Steph's voice interrupts my silent rage. "Are you okay?"

I nod but don't turn around. "When's Mom coming?"

Steph doesn't answer so I glance back at her.

"She's not coming. The flight's too long and connections and layovers are complicated. She wouldn't make it in time."

"What do you mean? She has to." I stomp my foot and regret it right away. "It doesn't matter. Opa's tough. You said so yourself. He'll make it if she's here or not."

"No, he won't," Steph's voice squeaks. "Not this time."

I watch her expression. Tom puts his arm around her, and she buries her face in his chest. They have to stop it. All their negative vibes. Opa doesn't need that. He needs people who believe in him. People like

me. Not ones who've already given up on him.

I rub his hand harder, realize that's not helpful, and ease off till I'm just a feather rubbing the small ridges of his veins. *Please don't die*. I bite my cheeks so hard and as the tears sneak out, I fight them back.

Positive. Be positive. He needs me to be positive for him.

A chair scrapes on the floor and I feel it behind my knees. Doctor lady gives me a sorry smile and presses her hands on my shoulders till I sit down.

"He does know you're here, dear. He really does." She pats the top of my head. I can't look at her. My eyes are on fire, and I don't like her, and I can't believe they think he's going to die.

My Opa's going to die. My sadness hurts so bad I can't swallow.

***

We sit. We stand. We take turns by his bed. Shuffle across the room to the window and back. Watch nurses come and go. Their quiet voices, smiles, and small head nods.

"Anyone need anything?" Tom says.

"Jillian, you go with Tom." Steph lifts her head and looks at me from across Opa's bed. "You go get some air. I'll stay."

In robot mode, I stand. It takes a few minutes before the room stops its slow-

motion movement. Steph gives me an 'atta girl' fake smile and I give her a half-wave.

Once we're outside the room and the door closes, the noises are noisy, almost cheery because it's not quiet. Out here it's easy to forget what's going on in Opa's room. People pass and smile. There's chatter at the nurses' desk. I take a deep breath and exhale in the normalcy of it all.

"Jillian," Mika calls from the end of the hallway.

I watch her hurry toward us. She throws her arms around me and hugs me hard. So not a Mika move. I hate this. This they-think-he's-dying stuff. The moment of walking away and forgetting what's going on for a few minutes is gone.

"He's going to be okay." I wiggle out of her hug.

Mika gives Tom a 'say what' look which she doesn't hide from me. I can't see what expression he gives her, and I don't care. If I believe it enough it will come true.

"I grabbed you a few things, your toothbrush and clothes and your phone." She passes me a faded Christmas bag. "Whatever you need, just tell me. I can get it for you."

"Hey." Barrett comes up from behind Mika and gives me a light hip-check. "How're you doing?"

I shrug because I don't trust myself to say anything.

Tom looks at his watch. “Why don’t you guys take Jillian out for something to eat. She’s missed a few meals.”

Before I can protest, Mika and Barrett link arms with me and haul me towards the exit.

“Call me,” I turn my head back to Tom, “you call me if anything happens. I have my phone.”

He finger-guns me as the three of us step out into a mini blizzard. The cold air feels so good on my nostrils as the flakes cool my cheeks. I stop and let it happen, let the weather take me away and inhale it.

“We’ll be snowboarding in no time,” Mika says. “Barrett and Greg say they’re going to teach us.”

I sigh. “Yeah, that should be fun.” I mean it and I feel a tad guilty meaning it.

***

Steak sandwich, fries, Caesar salad, apple pie.

“Where did you put all that?” Barrett points his fork at my empty plates.

I smile. “Didn’t think I was hungry.”

Mika and Barrett laugh, and it sounds comfortable. I’ve missed them. Why haven’t we hung out? Is it because of my dad? Do they feel weird about that? Or is it my suspension? It’s been days since I’ve seen them.

Barrett fills me in with what's new at school but says nothing about Akemi and the incident. I'm okay with that. I have to deal with it at some point, just not now. Mika's cramming for her GED exams so she can get her high school diploma and Barrett is tutoring her. She'll ace it, I know she will. She's determined to be a park warden. Why? I have no idea. The uniforms alone would put me off and the whole living in the bush and using outhouses for the summer are not my thing.

Mika tells me a story about a runaway horse and sleigh incident at the stables.

"The new guy was learning how to drive the team in the field. We gave him the best horses. They're a solid team. Fireworks don't even spook them." She waves her hands in the air and is so animated. "A blue healer dog jumped out of a guy's car, ran straight for the horses and started nipping at their hooves. Dumb dog. The driver started blowing his horn."

I get the gist of her story. Just watching her relive it and Barrett encouraging her, I could tell she's told it a few times. I feel my face relax. They're such a cute couple. I laugh when they laugh, and it surprises me. They go on about their recent high jinx which really aren't substantial in themselves but listening to them talk lets me sit back and unwind.

"We should go." I step back into my world and sigh. "Steph and Tom need a break too."

Barrett and Mika both nod. The laughter and easy smiles disappear. My reality sucks the life out of relaxing in a normal moment.

"You bet." Barrett slides out. "I'll go brush the truck off."

"Hey." Mika grabs his arm. "You're doing that, so you don't have to pay."

He pulls away and laughs before he heads out of the restaurant.

"What a guy," says Mika.

"Yeah, but he's your guy." I pull out my empty pockets to show her I've got nothing. "Will we have to wash dishes?"

"You guys are the worst." She pulls out her wallet and I follow Barrett.

"You're going to be okay." He grabs the passenger door then looks straight at me. "Either way." He nods.

I can't say anything because the sad and hurt is back and I don't want to cry and make it all awkward, so I stare at the snow on the pavement and shrug.

"We're here for you." He taps the top of my head with his snow brush's bristles.

"Hey." I bend down and scoop up a handful of snow and chuck it at him. "You're a jerk."

***

Mika, and then Barrett, give me hugs at the hospital entrance.

"Call, okay?" Mika grabs my shoulders and gives me a gentle shake. "For anything, anything at all."

"Do my schoolwork?"

"Don't push her kindness." Barrett winks.

I wave and watch them walk away necks scrunched in their coats. Barrett swings his arm onto Mika's shoulders, and she does a double step, so they walk in sync.

His truck heads out the exit and I stare at the road, the cars, the falling snow, sideways sometimes, then straight down. There's over an inch on the ground now. White and smooth. Traffic noise is soft. A few people walk past me. Is someone they love dying? Who are they here to see?

"Okay," I whisper and head inside. "I can do this."

***

Opa's door is open a bit. The room is dark. I put my hand out to push it slowly in case Steph is sleeping but she's not. She's hunched over the bed with Opa's hand in hers, holding it to her face.

"You can let go," she whispers. "We'll be okay."

I squeeze the edge of the door hard.

"Mom's waiting for you." Steph's back shakes. "Go be with her."

How can she tell him to go? To die. How can she not let anyone help him? I step back into the hallway.

It's going to happen, isn't it?

I swallow my sob. Opa's not getting out of here alive. It's not fair. I blink. The hallway goes blurry. With my head down I walk back to the exit. I can't listen to Steph. If she falls apart, I can't help her. My heart is broken. I can't deal with hers, too.

"Jillian?" Eddy's soft voice makes me look up.

I walk faster to him. His arms raise and I plunge my face into his ski jacket. The nylon cools my cheek. With every sob, his arms tighten, his chin presses on the top of my head.

"She told him he can go." My body shakes. "She wants him to die."

"No, no she doesn't." He rocks me side to side. "She wants him to know it's okay if he wants to go."

"I have to get out of here."

"Yup, I get that." He pushes me out at arms length. "But she needs you, Jillian, and you're going to need each other."

"Steph need me?" I zip up my coat. "No, she doesn't. She doesn't need anyone."

"Trust me. She does, she really does need you."

What's going on here? I'm the kid, remember? What about me? Why do I have to be a grown-up? Especially now. How can

I possibly be of any help to Steph? How can we help each other?

But Eddy's right, I can't leave her. Alone. No one should be alone when someone they love is dying. There's that 'I' word. It makes my eyes water and I blink fast to stop the tears. I need to step up. Toughen up. I need to be there for Steph.

I slip into the dark room and watch Steph's shoulders rise and fall with each quiet sob. The monitor blips green and beeps. I close my eyes and wish for Mom to be right behind me. Seems she isn't here for any of the big stuff these days.

"Steph," I whisper.

She lifts her head as I walk up behind her.

"Can I get you anything?"

"No thanks."

I grab another chair and put it on the opposite side of Opa's bed. After I sit down, I watch Opa's face, stare hard at his chest to make sure it still moves but it's hard to tell with only shadows of light, so I lean closer.

He's been there for me in his quiet way all my life. The only one in my fan club. Oh, except for the Akemi incident. He turned on me then. Thought I was guilty and didn't even ask my side. Was that the start of this? His stroke? Did I cause it? Was me being around, all the crap that's happened with Eric and Akemi—was it too much stress for him?

I glance at the part in Steph's hair. Now is not the time to ask her.

When did Opa get so small? Why didn't I notice? He knows how much he means to me, right? When's the last time I told him I love him? Gosh, I hope it wasn't back when Oma died. I hate that I can't remember.

The *love* word is almost taboo in this family. Why? Mom puts LOL on her emails. I told her it means *laugh out loud,* but she insists it means *lots of love*. It's the closest she gets to using the 'l' word so she gets points for that.

Steph exhales.

"We'll get through this." I reach over and tap her hand which rests on Opa's. "We will."

She looks up and I bite my cheek when I see her sad face. So not Steph. Her toughness never disappeared when Oma died so why is it gone now?

We both turn back to stare at Opa.

Eddy was right. I hope I can be here for Steph and have enough left for me. When Oma died, everything was crazy busy—getting here, the funeral, Mom getting things organized for her new job. It all happened so fast there was not much time to cry until after everyone's life went back to normal and ours didn't. Steph never missed a beat. She went straight back to work even though Tom tried to convince her to take time off. Was she being tough for Opa? For me? Or was going

to work her way of not having to deal with her own feelings?

I take a slow, long breath in, hold it and let it slip out my mouth without a sound.

Steph and I take turns moving around. Tom stops in but Steph sends him home to take Bucky for a long walk. He doesn't try to talk her out of it.

When Opa's face scrunches up and doesn't relax, Steph calls the nurse.

"It's a pain reflex. I'll increase the morphine." She checks his pulse before adjusting a little lever on the tube that hangs from a bag and runs into Opa's arm. "It'll keep him comfortable. It won't be long now."

I stare at Steph. What does that mean? He's going to die right away? I'm not ready. I don't want to be here. I don't want to leave either. Oh, Opa, can't you find your way back to us? Please.

The hours sneak by. *It won't be long* drags on. I want a shower. I want to lie horizontal and sleep until I'm not tired. Mika sends a broken heart icon. She must have talked to Tom. Barrett sends a sad face and Greg asks if I need anything.

Thanks I'm good I text them all.

It's dark. And my neck hurts. I lift my forehead off Opa's bed. Something woke me. What was it? Steph slouches in her chair. Is she asleep? And right then I realize the beeping is gone. The red dot isn't flashing.

"Steph," I whisper too loud, and she startles in her chair. I point to the machine that used to beep and flash.

"I love you." Steph squeezes Opa's arm. "Say hi to Mom."

A nurse comes in, turns on a dim light and walks behind Steph.

"I'm so sorry. You two take all the time you need." She pulls the cord on the machine. "Can I get you anything, anything at all?"

Steph shakes her head.

The room is quiet. I breathe without making a sound, so I don't disturb the silence. Why can't I cry? I wasn't with Oma when she died but I cried when I found out she was gone. Is not crying normal if you're there when it happens?

I glance at Steph. Her eyes are closed. No tears. I love Opa. I should be crying. He's gone. Why can't I? Maybe this is too much for me. Maybe I'm going crazy.

"Is there anything you want to say?" Steph whispers.

"I don't know." I can't think of anything brilliant to say. "Goodbye, Opa." And right then the tears start like I gave them permission. No sobs. Just a rainstorm down my face.

We sit. I stare at him and listen to my pulse thump in my ears. I check to see if Steph can hear them. She's busy tapping

Opa's arm. Her lips move but no words come out.

"I love you Opa," I say out loud.

"We sure do." Steph nods. "Okay, enough of this. You and Mom behave. Don't cause any chaos wherever you end up." She lets out a squeaky, not-funny laugh and gives Opa's arm one more squeeze before she tucks it under the sheet.

Chapter 18

The doorbell rings. I bet it's more mystery casserole with cooking instructions on index cards taped to the top. They mean well. Steph and I will be eating them for weeks. I've had enough sniffling gramma hugs to last me forever so when I hear footsteps on the back porch, I press against the kitchen wall to avoid having to answer the door. Bucky barks.

"You." I shake a finger at him. "Thanks a lot."

He flops his head on his paws. I put on a smile and open the door.

"Mika." She waves a brown paper bag with dark grease spots on it. "You're the best." I take it from her, open the bag and inhale burger and fry smells. "So much better than zucchini casserole surprise."

"That's what I thought." She pours a coffee and grabs a chair at the kitchen table. "How are you doing?"

"Oh, you know, answer the phone, stack the meals in the freezer, help Steph with funeral arrangements and the eulogy. Opa would hate the fuss. Steph's on a mission,

so I do what she asks. I'm looking forward to being back in school, to get back to normal. Whatever that's going to look like." I try to sound like none of this is a big deal because it helps me not to cry. Like Opa dying isn't ripping my heart apart. Crying is so exhausting that I'm trying this approach to see if it makes it easier.

Mika nods.

"This is so good," I say with a mouth full of bacon cheeseburger. "Thank you."

"Norquay opens tomorrow. The guys want to see if we're snowboard worthy."

"Gee, I don't know." I scrunch my eyes. "Is it too soon? What if people give Steph grief like I'm being disrespectful?"

"Greg checked with Steph. She said you need to get out of the house and gave her approval to go."

"Greg asked Steph?" I hold a fry in the air. "Seriously?"

Mika nods.

"Okay, then I'm in."

***

Steph hands me a $100 bill.

"What's this for?" I pluck it out of her fingers.

Is this get-over-grief money? Where should I shop first?

"Ticket, boots, board, rental, lunch."

"Oh, for snowboarding." I stare at the money. "Right, I forgot. Does it cost this much?"

She gives me an eye roll which is funny because it looks like it hurts her to do it.

"What?" I lift my hands in the air. "How would I know how much it costs?"

"Dress warm and use these." She grabs my other hand and drops a pair of black wrist guards into them. "They'll keep you out of the hospital."

***

Greg steers me through the rental shop while Barrett does the same with Mika. When Mika and I pass, we make googly faces to say '*what the heck have we gotten into*'. By the time we're done with the boot and board fitting, I'm sweating buckets in all the layers I have on and can't wait to get outside.

"Okay." Greg and Barrett stand in front of us with their boards upright.

They show us how to strap in one foot and move forward in a broken duck-legged walk. It's awkward and I slam face first on the ground three times before I realize I can't clip the edge of the board with my free foot.

Once we're up more than we're down, they show us how to push off and set the loose foot on the stomp pad so we can glide across the snow. My arms flail which helps

me stay upright but probably irritates the healing scar a bit too much.

“Way to go.” Greg taps my helmet when I slide almost ten feet without falling.

“You’re a natural.”

I hope my neck tube hides the heat creeping up my face. Mates. We’re just mates. It feels good to hear I’m doing okay.

After several laps of gliding in the practice area, and a few laughs when Mika or I land on our butts, we hike up the beginner hill. My armpits are wet. I hate the word armpits. Did I put on deodorant? If I didn’t, do I have enough on to hide the stink? Do I stink when I sweat? The onslaught of silly thoughts makes me laugh out loud because I don’t care. I haven’t had fun in forever.

Once we’re level with the top of the magic carpet lift, Greg takes off his board and digs it into the snow, so it stands upright. He straps in my loose foot, turns me so I face downhill, and my board is horizontal across the slope. He grabs my hands and pushes me till my heels press on the back of my boots.

“Heel edge.”

I nod and glance at Mika. Look at us, we’re almost snowboarders.

Greg pulls me forward. I grab his shoulders to stop from falling on top of him.

“Toe edge. Don’t use it until we start linking turns. It’s a brutal body slam.”

"Got it." I rock back onto my heels.

"Bend your knees. Head up." He squeezes both my hands. "I'm going to teach you to pendulum."

He pulls me across the hill to the left then back to the right and back to the left. My calves cramp.

"Pendulum." He smiles.

"Sweet."

We get to the bottom and hike back up. It's exhausting but I don't fall and after many trips, I fist-pump Mika.

"This time," Greg holds my shoulders to keep me from moving, "do it on your own."

"You think?"

He nods.

Visions of running into someone or taking out Greg run through my head as I wiggle my board forward and start to slide downhill. After I go too fast, I shift my weight to go the other way. Easy peasy, lemon squeezy.

"Atta girl. Head up." Greg zigzags backwards on his board (show off) in front of me. "You've got this."

After three successful pendulums, I feel myself going too fast and can't switch weight in time to change direction to slow down. I lean forward, windmill my arms. I feel myself falling and close my eyes, so I don't have to watch my face first body slam. Hands tighten on my waist and push me backwards. Butt

slam on the snow followed by a helmet smack.

What the hell?

It takes a few blinks to keep my eyes open. Greg pushes himself off me and hovers above on his hands and knees.

"Sorry." He hops up and stands on his board. "A face plant would have hurt worse. I took one for the team."

"Thank you. I guess." He puts his hands down to help me, but I push them away and do it myself on the third try. "My fault. I didn't change direction fast enough."

After successful pendulum runs Barrett shouts at Greg, "Let's take them on the magic carpet."

Greg gives him a thumbs up.

"A lift? Really? We're ready?"

"Yup."

We all unstrap a foot and step-glide across the snow to the lift. Greg and Barrett make it look so smooth while Mika and I clunk behind.

The guys take off their boards and tuck them under their arms.

"I'll run beside you," Greg says as he pulls me to the lineup. "Relax and the carpet will pull you up. At the top, put your foot on the stomp pad, slide off and push out of the way. I'll help if you need it."

"Got it." I take a deep breath and wonder if I really do 'got it'.

Please don’t run into anyone. And don’t crash. I can do this.

Greg reaches his hand out and I grab it as I watch the carpet roll up the hill.

“Whenever you’re ready,” he says.

I inch the front of my board onto the rolling carpet. It grabs the base with a small jerk and pulls me along. I got this. Greg lets go of my hand and walks beside me.

A group of boarders slide through the practise poles at the far side of the run. I envy their success, until one crashes.

Opa will never see me do this. I’ll never spend a day on the ski hill with him. I inhale and hold it. Would he be proud of me? Was he ever proud of me?

“Okay, get ready,” Greg calls. “Smile first.”

“What? Smile?” I shout.

“Cameras everywhere.” Greg points to a black monitor above the lifty’s shack.

Smile. Right. Smile.

“Now glide down,” he says, “and push out of the way.”

The lifty gives me two thumbs up. Gosh, don’t fall now. Way too much attention. My board slides down and when it stops, I push to follow Greg across the slope. And I do it without falling.

The four of us sit in a row across the top of the run to do up our bindings again. I wish we could stay here for awhile and pretend we’re the cool kids hanging out.

"We'll stay on this side." Greg points to the edge by the snow fence. "Controlled pendulum all the way to the bottom."

"Yes sir." Mika salutes him.

"Smart ass." Greg laughs as he shuffles his board until he's in front of me. "Nice and easy."

I nod, glance at Mika and Barrett and then to the bottom of the run. Eight pendulums, maybe nine. I shouldn't hit anyone, right? My butt can't take many more slams.

One pendulum. I exhale. Got it. I struggle to do this facing down the hill and Greg's doing it backwards. Not fair. Two pendulums. No incident. As my board picks up speed, I lean the other way, almost biff it, then recover and breathe. Three pendulums in and it almost feels natural.

As I get the hang of the movement, the speed, and breathing, and not panicking, a board runs across the top of mine. My arms flail as Mika slams into Greg and they both hit the snow. It's all I can do not to tumble on top of them but with horseshoes up my bruised butt, I swing my arms in the opposite direction, totally miss hitting them and with windmill arms manage to stay upright.

Breathless and upright.

As I slow down, Barrett slides in front of me and offers his hands. I shake my head. He grins. There's laughter behind me so I

know Greg and Mika aren't hurt and I continue to the bottom to wait for them.

"Nicely done, champ." Barrett thumps my back. "You'll be cruising the black runs in no time."

"Sorry," Mika pants. "Lucky I don't need a license to ride this thing."

"To the Cascade Chair." Greg points to the lift as the air freezes and thaws my nostrils with each breath. "Olympic boarders in the making."

"We'll go up in twos," Barrett says. "Fewer moving parts to navigate around when we get off."

Mika and I look at each other.

"Is getting off that big of a deal?"

"Not at all." Greg lifts his free foot, exaggerates setting it on his board, does a knee's bent crouch, one arm straight out in front and the other out behind above the board. "Slide down the ramp."

We watch skiers and boarders get on ahead of us and when it's our turn, Greg offers his hands and pulls me forward to the red line.

"Relax your legs. The chair will do the rest."

And away we go on the lift. Greg swings the bar down in front of us and shows me how to rest my board on the footrest, so the weight of it doesn't pull on my leg.

"Excited?" He taps his board against mine.

"Terrified." I watch a person in a blue snow suit pendulum beside the tree line where there are fewer people. "I'll come down over there. It's not so busy."

"Good strategy. It has a great fall line."

"Pardon?"

"Boarders need to stay on the part of the run with the best slope, so they keep their momentum. Skiers can push with their poles or skate on flat spots. If a boarder hits a flat spot, it's tough to go again. So," he waves at the steep part, "stay in the sweet spot."

He points to a few who wiggle back and forth to get going. Some gain speed, one guy ends up unstrapping and walking.

"Take your board off the footrest and hold onto this bar." Greg swivels in his seat so he's almost sideways and grabs the rail behind the seat, with his board straight out in front of him. "Smile for the camera." He points at another video camera on the lifty's shack. "When you feel the ramp under the board, stand up and glide down."

I glance at him, at the top of the lift and back to him.

"You'll do great." He taps my helmet.

Contact, up, arms out, knees bent, Greg offers his hands, but I shake my head and have an uneventful glide down.

"Push out of the way," Greg calls as he scoots across the slope.

Just like before the four of us sit across the hill to put our boards on.

"Whoa!" Greg jumps up and goes straight down the run at a stupid fast speed.

"What the hell?" I look at Barrett and Mika. "He's not going to help me?"

Barrett points and I watch Greg barrel towards a little kid snowboarder who's yelling and heading straight for the trees. I hold my breath. He's going to crash and it's going to be ugly.

Greg cuts the kid off, grabs him by his ski jacket and lifts him off the ground while he's still moving. A few turns and he stops, puts the kid down, and bends over like he's having a one-on-one chat about the dangers of boarding out of control. I exhale. Greg the old soul, making sure no one gets hurt. Old soul…and a hero.

"Sweet," Barrett shouts. "Okay gals, I'm all yours. Let's get to the bottom without any of that." He jerks his head in Greg's direction.

With Barrett in front of us boarding backwards, he watches Mika and me. Wiggle, accelerate, lean one way, more speed, switch, too fast, too slow, wiggle. Controlled fall, more of an excuse to rest. My calves are on fire.

"Hey," I call out to Greg when I get closer, "do you have a cape?"

When I stop, he lifts his hands. "A cape?"

"You know, like Superman, for superhuman rescues."

He bows. When he stands up, he tosses a snowball at me. Determined to catch it, my

movement makes my board slide. No longer focused on the snowball I pendulum to the bottom.

I conquer linking turns in the afternoon, do a lot of runs without any help and spend less time on my butt. Pretty proud of that and my butt is appreciative too although my legs feel like used rubber bands by the time we finish.

“After Christmas, we’re going the top.” Greg points to the top of the freakin’ mountain where a few tiny, black specks zigzag their way down the steepest run.

“Too bad I’ll be in Denver.” The reality that Christmas is only a few weeks away and I’m not going to be here, disappoints me. What’s that about? “Sorry, I’ll miss it.” And I am sorry. Really sorry. This is the first day I’ve laughed and been with friends and sweated so much in forever. It feels amazing.

Don’t get me wrong. I miss Opa and I get so sad. There are times I have to remember Oma’s gone too and it’s hard to share the sad because Opa’s hurts more right now. Maybe that’s why I really notice when I’m happy because it’s such a fabulous change not to have to deal with Steph and the funeral stuff and people in my face telling me how sad I must be. No disrespect, Opa. I’ll always miss you. You know that.

After we return the rental gear, Greg swings his arm over my shoulder, Mika

grabs my elbow and Barrett hugs her waist. I imagine what we look like if I was walking behind. Best friends forever. I smile.

***

Bucky rushes to the door when I turn on the light in the back porch.

"Hey there." I rub his head. "Is Steph working late?"

He doesn't answer as he pushes his nose against the door to get out.

"Not into talking?" I give his bum a nudge, so the cold air doesn't have time to sneak in. "I had a great day if you're interested." Talking to a dog—I shake my head.

The contents of the fridge breathe leftover mystery casserole. Far in the back there's a container of spaghetti sauce. When did we eat it? I peel the lid off and sniff. It can't be more than a few days, can it? It's been in the fridge so it should be okay, right?

Crusted garlic bread broiled in the oven, sauce on top and voila, my version of a sloppy joe.

"Smells great," Steph calls from the porch as Bucky pads across the floor with his snowy feet.

I grab paper towel, toss it down and step on it to drag over his wet prints.

"What's cooking?"

With an exaggerated wave of my hand across the counter, "Fine dining at the Meier's."

"Looks great. I'm starved." Steph loads her plate. "How was boarding?"

"Painful." When I sit, I use my hands to lower myself. "And a lot of fun."

"Great. I'm glad you liked it. Winter last forever here and if you don't have an outside activity you like, it can feel endless."

I nod and smile. Her voice is chill. Calm. We just have to get through the funeral on Saturday. I hope that doesn't start another rush on casseroles being delivered.

"How was your day?" I say.

"Nothing earth shattering. I was stuck in the office doing paperwork all afternoon."

We chat about snow shovelling schedules, a trip to Calgary to buy winter gear, non-funeral and non-Opa topics. It's the most comfortable conversation we've had in awhile. She says nothing about schoolwork or going back next week. That's a first.

When we're not talking, the quiet is okay. I'm not alone and a surprise thought runs through me. This feels like home. When the heck did that happen? I can't tell Mom. Or maybe I should. Maybe she'd be okay with it. Or she'd be super jealous. Not sure.

Chapter 19

"Is this okay?" I wave my hand over my blue pants, sweater and pale pink blouse. Respectful with a bit of silver bling in the sweater.

"You look amazing. So grown up." Steph smiles. "More like my little sister than my kid."

"What?" I tip my head. "You've never called me that."

"Called you what?"

"Your kid."

"Oops." Steph puts a hand over her mouth. "Sorry. It slipped out."

"Is that a good thing? Or not?"

"Good for me," she spins me towards the door, "but whatever you want it to be. After the funeral, I'm sending all the flowers over to the senior's lodge. Do you want to keep the ones from your dad?"

"That's okay. Send his over too. They may as well brighten up someone's day."

"Have you called him?" She bends over to pull her boots on. "He was pretty intense when he phoned. And your mom, have you called her?"

"No and no. I've been a bit busy." I give her my best-daughter-of-the-year smile. "I emailed them. I'll call them when things quiet down. Promise."

***

Kyle and Mrs. Bronigan are the first people we meet inside the funeral home. She shuffles over with her walker.

"Don't you look lovely. He'd be so proud of you two." She squeezes us into her itchy sweater and big boobs.

"Hey, kid." I put my hand on Kyle's shoulder. "You look spiffy."

"Can I still come over? You know, even though Mr. Meier is gone. Can I still come over to visit and hang out?"

"Always." I nod.

Mika, Barrett, and Greg join us. And then I see Akemi walk through the doors. What the hell? She sees me see her and looks the other way as an older man directs her towards the visitation room.

"Not today," Mika says in my ear. "She's not worth it." She links arms with me and pulls me towards the glass doors where Eddy, dressed in his working-at-the-steakhouse suit, hands out Opa's obituary cards.

Eddy shakes hands with Greg and Barrett, smiles at Mika and gives me a hug.

"How you doing?" he whispers.

I nod because it's all I trust myself to do.

"You got this. Follow me."

Eddy leads us to the front of the room and points to our chairs next to the big picture of smiling Opa which sits next to his red toolbox. Steph thought Opa would get a kick out of his ashes in the toolbox, sitting next to Oma in her fancy box on the bookshelf at the house. I didn't question Steph's choice. Dead is dead. It doesn't really matter what container ashes get stored in. It kind of creeps me out though that now there will be two boxes of dead people in the house.

As Opa's favourite song, "Edelweiss", plays I glance around the almost full seats of white-haired and balding people in dark clothes until I see Ray. He nods at me and I wave, take a deep breath and face the front.

The funeral guy says a bunch of stuff about Opa and the sniffling starts behind me. I'm okay though and that surprises me. Maybe it's because what he's saying is kind of generic. He was a good guy, lived in Banff for over 40 years, blah, blah, blah. I don't feel that burn in my throat that usually lets me know the tears are on their way.

After he's done, he introduces Steph. She goes to the podium with Tom and makes a huge production of opening her papers. Her shoulders lift. Tom puts his hand on her back and Mika squeezes my arm.

"Dad loved a good joke. He could tell them with a straight face. Most of the time." Steph looks up. "He loved his beer, good conversation, and he was never one to turn down a nerf gun battle with his favourite peeps."

I blink faster. Dammit. I feel the burn. Even though Steph rehearsed in front of me, so I'd know what she is going to say, it's still hard to hear. I mouth the words and it helps me not to cry.

"One of his favourite peeps came to live with us a few months ago." Steph looks at me. "Having his granddaughter, Jillian, around made Dad missing Mom a bit easier."

Oh, my God. She changed the script. What's she doing? I stiffen and bite my cheek. Greg squeezes my knee.

"Jillian made Dad's eyes twinkle again. Her energy and love reminded him of Mom."

What? She picks now to use the 'l' word? My tears start. Mika takes my hand.

"Jillian's antics kept him living in the moment." Steph's eyes shine. "She was good for him. It was good to have her around shaking up our routines even if it drove us a bit crazy." She smiles at me before looking back to her paper. "Dad loved old movies and popcorn. He could make it through the popcorn but not the whole movie."

Mika slips a tissue into my hand, and I dab the snot running onto my top lip. Figures I'd wear make-up today. Darn you Steph. I

would have been okay if you hadn't screwed it up.

When Steph finishes, she invites people to come to the front and tell stories and they do, in hoards. Ski stories which end at Opa's house with Oma making supper while they share bullshit stories of steep slopes and near misses with avalanches, to biggest fish tales, and shutting down dance halls. I swallow often and am thankful for the funny stories so I can laugh. If I don't look at his picture, I can almost stop the tears.

After they run out of stories, Steph starts the slide show. Opa and Oma smile across the screen, birthdays, beer fests, Opa and his old, carved hiking stick, Yellowstone, Bryce Canyon. I smile and realize for the hundredth time how lucky I am to have had them in my life.

And knowing Opa liked having me around makes my sad a little more manageable.

***

One last check in the mirror. I don't want to be all 'look at me, look at me' but I also don't want to look, you know, not good. My school suspension is over, and I took a few days off after the funeral. Now I'm excited and nervous to go back. Even if it's God awful, there's only a few weeks left before

Christmas break. I can handle it. I know I can.

Barrett said to chill. He says the kids at school have more on their minds than me. That hurt a bit, but it also made me laugh. I'm not the focus. Yay.

Head up, casual smile on, I walk to my locker. A few kids glance at me without looking away fast. Some wave. Are they pity waves? Whatever. I'll take them. I wave back. Maybe Opa dying trumps the fight with Akemi. Shallow, I know, but I'll take it if it makes my day easier.

"Hey." Barrett pulls my locker door open wide and grins his goofy grin. "You came."

I roll my eyes. "Like I have a choice."

We head to our first class and Barrett drops his arm onto my shoulder. It's not in a boyfriend girlfriend way, just a friend's arm. He chats about our snowboard adventure and the big dump of snow in the forecast. I sigh. He's the best stress distractor.

I watch for Akemi every time I go down a hallway but don't see her. I'm grateful she's not in my face. She doesn't even show up for the Outward-Bound class. The entire school day is uneventful. Why did I get so stressed about it?

"How'd it go?" Steph says as I tap the snow off my boots at the back door.

"It was okay."

"Atta girl. I knew you could do it."

"What do you mean, do it?"

"Sorry. I meant I knew you'd go and it would be okay. That's all." Steph closes her eyes and then opens them. "God, there's got to be a guidebook on how to talk to teenagers so I'm not on trial every time I open my mouth."

"There are." I wink.

"There are what?"

"Books about talking to teens."

***

All the eyes in the Chemistry class stare at the door and whoever knocked because we need a break from this brutal practise test. Why do teachers torture us before Christmas break? Mr. Stutz walks across the front of the room and points at us to focus on our papers. I studied. I really did. I just can't figure out these last two questions.

"Jillian." Mr. Stutz points to whoever is standing outside the door.

I look around and then point to myself. Me? This Jillian? He nods. I glance at Barrett. He shrugs and gives me a thumbs up.

Oh, no. Steph. I knock the table as I rush to get out of my chair. She can't die too.

The school's secretary waits for me in the hallway.

"Is Steph okay?"

She gives me a funny look then says, "Mr. Little would like a few words with you."

"Why?"

With a wave of her index finger, I follow her to the principal's office. What the hell have I done now? I think back on the last few days. Nothing. Other than possibly failing this Chem quiz, I have come to school and gone home. That's it. So, what's going on?

"Jillian." Mr. Little stands and waves his hand at the empty chair across from his desk. "How are you today?"

"Fine." Temple Guard training helps me keep my face expressionless.

"I'm sorry to hear about your grandfather passing away."

I nod.

"How are you doing? It must be difficult losing him and being here instead of at home."

"It's okay."

"Are you sure?" He leans forward, puts his hands on his desk and taps his fingers. "We're here for you Jillian. If you need anything, we can help. We have all types of counselling. We can even bring in a grief counsellor if that would help. Anything at all you need to get through this tough time."

"No, I'm good thanks."

He doesn't say anything. Just looks at me, looks over my head, then to papers on the corner of his desk, back out the door. I'm not sure what's going on and he's not my go-to guy if I did want to talk about Opa, so I sit and wait it out.

Mr. Little clears his throat. "Well, unfortunately, I've heard from a student, a concerned student, that you're acting out a bit. The school doesn't want a repeat of the last incident." He makes solid eye contact. Not mean or anything, just an I'm-talking-to-you serious look. "We're still trying to get the real story on that incident, and we've learned there are a lot of details you failed to mention—to anyone. Get what I'm saying?"

I bite my cheek. What details? Who told them? Does he know about the knife? I'm not a snitch. I didn't say anything. So who did? Wait. I'm acting out? About what? Not Opa. What the hell? Akemi, if you're behind this, you bitch. Why though? What's her game? Temple Guard face back on. Slow, quiet breaths so he can't tell my brain is trying to process what he isn't saying.

"I don't know what you're talking about," I say.

"You don't think you're possibly being a bit aggressive—pushing students, slamming doors? It's probably not even intentional and totally understandable given what you've been through. If we nip it in the bud, we can get past this and help you move on. Counselling could help you figure things out."

"I'm not pushing or slamming. And I don't have anything I need to figure out." I cross my arms and sit straighter. So much for staying emotionless. "Who says I'm a bully?"

"I didn't say you were being a bully, just acting out."

"Aggressively." My turn to give him serious eye attitude which gives me courage. I take another quiet breath to stop myself from saying anything stupid. "You said I'm acting out aggressively. That's being a bully. And I'm not a bully."

"Take it easy."

"Really? You accuse me of being a bully and I'm trying to figure out who would say that."

"I never said anything about being a bully." He clasps his hands together. "And I can't tell you who mentioned it. What I can say is that it's a concern and we need to deal with it. I need you to modify your behaviour, possibly get some counselling and stop intimidating students."

"Oh, I'm intimidating. And aggressive." I chew my bottom lip so I don't go off sounding like a crazy person. "What *exactly* am I *supposedly* doing?"

Denver can't come soon enough. I can get away from this crap. Akemi can find some other chick to harass.

"Jillian, listen, I'm here to help. I'm not the enemy and you don't want to alienate others. It's not good for you or the school."

"Oh, now I have enemies? Or is it just one person?" I tip my head. "Is there anything else I should know?"

"Hold on. Let's take a breath." Mr. Little puts his hands up. "There are a lot of balls in the air right now. We need to manage the ones we can control and hopefully catch the others before they fall."

What the hell do balls in the air have to do with me? Is this one of those lame adult comparisons I'm supposed to be able to interpret?

Mr. Little looks at me. I shrug because I have no idea what to say.

"Kids can go through a tough time in high school. It's normal." He nods. "You've had a really rough month but we're all here for you. You just have to let us know how we can help." He gives me an Oscar-winning finale smile.

"Okay, I will." I stand. "Thanks."

I turn and walk out of the office. With each step I expect to hear him call me back, but he doesn't. It takes all I've got not to hit or smack or scream as I walk down the hallway. The shrill bell makes me jump and I go straight to my locker. Screw my books in Chem. Screw the quiz. Screw this school. I don't bloody believe it. I'm a bully. I'm aggressive. Who'd say that about me? And why? It's got to be Akemi. She's playing me so she comes up looking golden.

"Hey, what's up?" Barrett hip-checks me. "Everything okay?"

I glare at him as hot air rushes out my nostrils.

“Whoa.” Barrett throws my Chem books into my locker, grabs my backpack with his and tosses my parka at me. “We need chill time. Let’s go.”

“You have class.”

“So do you, but you need air. Now. Come on.” He steers me through the crowd and out the front door where great big fat flakes float down.

“I think we should go boarding,” he says.

At the house, when I grab my gear and some cash, the phone rings.

“This is an automated message to advise you…” there’s a pause, “Jillian Meier” another pause, “was not in attendance for English 10 on December 8. Please contact...” I hang up.

“Your folks are going to get a call too,” I say. “You’ll get in trouble for skipping.”

“It’s snowing. They’ll expect more than that call this winter. If I was flunking out, they’d rag on me. But, you know, I’m kind of a super star.” He winks.

On the drive to Norquay, Barrett doesn’t ask any questions. He rambles on about some epic powder day he had a few years ago, his best day ever apparently.

Will I ever have an epic day? If I practice hard here, I won’t look like such a newbie in Denver. The pissed-offness seeps out of me at each switch back in the road and it leaves an empty spot inside which I can’t describe.

The wet, fat snowflakes fly off the windshield and by the time we're at the ski hill base, it's a whiteout. Great. Sort of matches the mood I can't describe. And it makes me grin. Ironic hey? Maybe winter will be my favourite season.

"Who doesn't love powder?" Barrett hands me my board and we head to the chairlift. "You'll love it."

The excitement in his voice is too cute. Who gets this jacked about a lot of snow?

"Sure," I say and hope I spend most of my time upright. I've been able to sit on hard surfaces without wincing for a few days and want to keep it that way.

At the top, we sit side by side in the snow to strap our boards on. When he's ready, Barrett grabs his knees and stares into the mini blizzard. His cheeks dimple. He really does love this stuff. I brush melted flakes off my nose.

"Let's shred." He makes a sweeping wide turn, stops and looks up at me.

I stand and a huge spray of snow showers me from behind. My arms flap to keep my balance.

"Skipping school?" Greg laughs.

"Something like that." I smile because I'm pretty darn impressed I didn't fall, and a bit thrilled he's here too.

"Nothing better than a pow day." Greg carves a few short turns before stopping beside Barrett.

Way too much attention.

I wave them away, so they'll go to the bottom, but with hands on hips, they both shake their heads. Really? Come on. Big sigh. They're being sweet. Irritatingly too sweet. I can't stand the pressure. *God please don't let me fall.* I wiggle my boots to move forward.

My board slides. Not too fast, super smooth and the fresh snow piles on and covers it as I link a few turns. Wow, I look back almost certain I'll see myself down on the snow but I'm not. I'm still going. I'm still doing it. Another turn. Look how I didn't take them both out. I wave and continue to the bottom. They clap and whistle as they race by me.

When I hit the flat, I undo one foot and slide to the lift line.

"Where's Barrett?" I scoot in next to Greg.

Greg points up the lift at the single riding on a chair ahead of us.

"Okay." We both slide forward and get on the next one.

It only takes seconds, and our parkas and snow pants are white.

"So, what's going on?" Greg says. "Why are you ditching school?"

I turn to him and shrug, pull my neck tube higher so there's less exposed face to give away any expression.

"Mate, come on." He pokes my shoulder. "You're not a skipper. You don't break the rules."

"I do too."

He shakes his head.

"Crappy day. Principal's a jerk."

"What about?"

"He thinks I need counselling because of Opa." I exhale louder than I need to. "And someone reported that I'm acting out. Being aggressive."

"So, you're like a bully or something?"

"Nope." I shake a glove at him. "He assured me he didn't say I was a bully."

"Hmm. Sounds odd." He makes a goofy face and I give him a short version of my conversation with Mr. Little.

"He's just doing his job, checking off the boxes. It's not your fault, Jillian. Just an unfortunate combination of shit happens and someone with an axe to grind. Are you okay?"

"Yeah." I laugh because, really, I know I'm not a bully.

I got pissed because I'm sure Akemi is trying to pin something on me, and Mr. Little believes her. She's the one who could use some of that counselling. Maybe work out why she does crazy shit when she's mad. It's not my problem. Anymore. I'm not wasting energy on it.

"Race you to the bottom," I call out to Greg as I push off the chair.

Run after run, I feel better, more balanced, and less tense. Life is sweet.

"Want to come for supper?" I ask Barrett and Greg as we walk back to the parking lot. "We have way too much mystery food which needs to be eaten."

"Free food?" Barrett says. "You're on."

Greg gives a thumbs up and heads to his car.

"I might have to skip class tomorrow too," Barrett says as the wipers scrape through the layer of snow on the windshield.

"Apparently powder days rule for more than just you."

He gives me a *say what* look.

"You know, Greg took it off too."

Barrett stares straight ahead. I see his cheek lift and lean forward to check him out. He forces his lips into a straight line.

"What'd you do?" I pinch his shoulder.

"Nothing."

"You told him something happened, didn't you?" I sit back in the seat and let the fact Greg came because Barrett said something sink in. "You're a jerk. You know that? In a dorky kind of way."

"I know."

***

"Hey, what's going on? I've been looking for you." Mika walks through the back gate

as we get out of Barrett's truck. "Where've you been?"

There's a tone in her voice I don't recognize. She sounds jealous. Does she think there's something between me and Barrett? No way. She knows I'd never do that.

"Crap day at school," Barrett says.

"Oh, the Chem quiz?" She turns to him. "I told you to study more."

Barrett shrugs and throws his arm around her shoulder. "We went boarding to relieve some stress."

"What's the big deal? It was only a practise test."

She tips her head and gives me a squinty-eyed look Barrett can't see. What's with her? Her eyes open wide, and she breaks into a smile when Greg parks beside Barrett's truck. So, she was jealous. She thought I was alone with Barrett. But why is that a big deal all of a sudden? I'm going to have to talk to her, make her realize I'm not that girl. I wouldn't hit on her guy.

"I brought pizza," Greg calls out. "I figured we'd let you save your mystery food for another day."

"How can I help?" Mika says as she comes into the kitchen.

I look at her and almost say something before the guys come in but decide against it. Why ruin the mood? If she was jealous,

she's being dumb or insecure. We can figure that out another time.

"Plates," I point to the cupboard, "and I'll get more chairs."

"Where'd my invitation go?" Steph shouts as she holds the door open for Bucky and waits for the guys to hang up their stuff.

"Probably in your junk mail," I say. "Hope you don't mind. It's a pow day. Thought we'd celebrate."

"A pow day?" She scrunches her eyes so her little wrinkles run into her hair. "You didn't go to school?"

"We did go to school." Barrett salutes her seriousness. "But we went to the hill after till the lift closed."

Steph nods. She's got a questionable look going on, so I turn away. Barrett sort of didn't lie. We did go to school. We did stay till the lift closed. Omission of details is not lying, right?

"There's tons of pizza." Greg points to the boxes on the counter.

The kitchen is noisy and has a light man-sweat and pizza smell about it. After we inhale the food, I notice Steph leaning against the counter, arms folded wearing a grin like she's got a secret she's not going to share.

"What's going on?" I put my plate in the dishwasher.

"Your Opa would love this."

Whoa. She used the word twice in one week.

I glance around the kitchen. "Love what?"

"The noise, you and your friends, hanging out here." She stops, her chest lifts and she looks at me. Her eyes are glassy. Oh, no.

"Hey." I give her a side hug. She turns it into a full-on boobs-against-boobs squishfest.

Chairs scrape, arms wrap around us and pull us into the middle of the room. The cuckoo clock ticks. Steph shudders against me for a few seconds and then she pushes her way out.

"But he'd have been upset with you." She shakes her finger at me and tries to sound angry. "Snowboarding. Really? He'll be rolling over in his toolbox."

I don't even know what to say. It's a funny visual, Opa's ashes swirling around in mini cyclones inside his toolbox. Should we be making jokes already?

"Shredder's rule." Barrett fist-pumps the air.

"Skiers live longer," Steph says.

And the seconds of sadness disappear into a loud snowboard versus skier debate and Greg is the only one who sits on the fence as a skier and a boarder. I try to picture Steph skiing. Maybe one day, we can go together. I can show her how good I'm doing.

Steph looks up from wiping the table. "Your ticket to Denver is here."

Wow. That shut me down. Fast. Denver. I want to go. I do. But so soon? When I've got all this, here.

"Great." I fake a smile so no one can tell how I feel about it.

"You leave the last day of school before holidays. It'll be tight getting you to the airport on time."

"My first Christmas in Denver," I say the words out loud to hear them, test them out, make them real.

"At least you're going somewhere fun," Mika says. "Tom and I are going to Lethbridge to see Mom. Who goes to Lethbridge for any reason?"

"Stop. I've heard all about it." Steph laughs. "It's only for a few days and I know you two will both survive."

Mika snorts. "Right. Mom demands an audience. She'll tell absurd stories about what she's doing. Then she'll make stupid promises and disappear on her broom."

"Ouch. That's harsh." I wince.

"You think I'm joking?" She laughs but it's not a funny ha-ha laugh. "She's my reality."

Mika has never said anything about her mom. I guess she's never come up which is weird because a lot of my life is about too many moms. Now is not the time to ask for details. She sounds hostile. I'll have to

remember to talk to her about that too when we're alone.

I look at Steph. "You'll be all by yourself on Christmas."

"Hey." She lifts her hands and twist dances across the kitchen floor. "The party will start here."

"What party?"

"Any party I choose."

"Hey, come have Christmas with my family. They can handle crazy," Barrett says. "We celebrate Christmas Eve and Christmas Day. An endless supply of food."

"What do I look like?" Steph sticks her chin forward. "A wimp who can't do Christmas alone?"

I nod.

"Well, I'm not. I'll be just fine. You watch me." Steph dances like a Hawaiian lady towards the back porch then waves her hands towards the door. "Now pitter patter, get out of here so Jillian can do homework."

"Thanks for everything," I yell after them. "Love you guys." What? I look around fast. Where did that come from? I check out the door to see if anyone heard, but all I see are their backs heading to the gate and hands waving in the air. Phew. That was close. What was I thinking?

"Homework. Now." Steph points at the table. "Too much fun isn't good for you."

"Since when?"

"I don't know. Your Opa used to say it when he was trying to be funny."

"Oh." I nod. "So, you're going to blame him for your lack of funny?"

"I am funny."

"No, you're not."

We tidy the kitchen and it's good, it's really good. I'm going to miss Steph. She is funny cause she's not funny. I hope she's okay alone. Her first Christmas without Oma and Opa. The house will be so quiet. I sigh. My first Christmas without them too.

Stop it. New adventures ahead for me. A new family to figure out. I'm a part of three families. Look at Kyle. He's got two broken ones and he's just a kid. It'll be fine. Steph'll be fine. And I'll be fine.

Chapter 20

At school, I smile a lot at everyone so no one can say I'm aggressive or acting out and hang with Barrett when we have the same classes. Akemi is like a ninja. Every time I see her, there she is, gone. I've got a spiel prepared for her if I can get her alone *and* if I don't chicken out.

"Unit test again. You must have forgotten to study for the last one, so you get to do it over." Mr. Stutz shakes a stack of papers at us. "Make me proud."

My brain hurts. As I head to my locker at the end of the day, I see Akemi at hers, so I walk over before she sneaks away.

"Hey." I lean against the locker next to hers. "How are you?"

Her eyes go big and round. She glances up and down the hallway as kids pass by. I step in front of her to block her view.

I give her a nice trying-not-to-intimidate-her smile. "Are you looking for someone?"

"No."

"I just wanted to say if you want to concoct bullshit stories about me, that's your business. It's pretty lame though. You

should," I pause, "deal with your anger issues before they really get you into trouble."

Her eyes dart everywhere.

"I'll let Mr. Little know we had this chat, okay? Merry Christmas." I walk away. I just walk away. And I'm in awe of me.

Next stop, principal's office.

"Can I talk to Mr. Little, please?"

"Sorry, Jillian, he's not here right now." The secretary stacks colourful folders on the counter. "Can I help you?"

"Sure, yeah, can you tell him something?"

She grabs a pen and pad of paper.

"Please tell him I had a non-aggressive, unconfrontational," I smile at her until she starts writing, "chat with Akemi. And it was good. You know just in case Akemi comes back to say I was aggressive or intimidating. You heard it from me first." I tap the counter.

"Got it." She nods.

"See ya." I turn, congratulate myself one more time and head to my locker.

"Wow, someone looks happy." Barrett swings his backpack on.

"Yup, taking care of business."

"Cool." He checks the hallway. "And you didn't leave any bodies. Nice work. Do you want to come pick up Mika from work?"

"No, thanks. I've got too much homework."

"Later." He gives me a thumbs up and is off.

***

"Go put this shirt on," Steph says as I come into the kitchen for supper.

"Pardon?" I take the shirt from her and shake it out. So much orange, green and pink neon splatter paint all over it like a kid with a fat brush made a white shirt into an art project. "I don't think so. It's not really me."

"Humour me. Go put it on."

The look in her eyes says she means it but not in a mad way.

I wave the shirt in front of me. Butt ugly. "Fine."

"We leave in ten minutes."

"Leave for where? What's going on?"

Steph puts her hands on her hips. "Quit asking so many questions and go put that shirt on."

"No one better see me in it," I mutter as I head to my room.

When I come back down, she's got her parka on and a hand on the back door. Bucky wags his tail at the possibility of another walk.

"You watch the house," Steph says to him as she tosses me my coat.

"What's going on?" I zip it up to my chin so none of the shirt shows.

"We're going out."

I groan.

"It'll be fun."

"It's not going to be fun if I have to wear this coat all night."

When we're in the truck she hands me a blindfold. "Put it on."

"No way. You're creeping me out."

"Again," she shoves it at me and gives a fake glare, "humour me."

"You're weird." I put it on. "Happy now?"

"I sure am."

No one better see this.

"Are you kidnapping me, so I can't go to Denver?"

"Nope."

"Then what's going on? I feel like a dork."

Steph laughs. "You sort of look like one."

"Thanks."

The truck slows and stops but with the blindfold on I've got no idea where we are. I turn to face Steph in case we're at a stop light and there are people in the crosswalk who know me. The truck takes a bump. The bridge? Another stop and then a sharp left turn.

"We're going to the hot pool? Why do I need the ugly shirt? And a blindfold?"

"It's not ugly and we're not going to the pool."

The truck stops.

"Don't take it off," Steph says. "Undo your seatbelt."

"I'm really going with being kidnapped."

"Don't flatter yourself."

My door opens. She grabs my arm and helps me out.

I slide my foot forward on concrete. "Now?"

"No."

Steph moves behind me and puts her hands on my shoulders. "Just walk normal. I'll tell you when to stop."

"Easy for you to say. You're not walking in public wearing a blindfold."

Cars pass by. One honks and I almost jump out of my skin.

"Easy," Steph says.

Popcorn smells.

"We're going to a blindfold-only movie?"

"Nope. Stop. There are one, two, three stairs." She grabs my hand and puts it on a handrail.

I slide my foot forward until it hits the first stair. I never want to be blind. What a helpless feeling.

"Okay, done the stairs." Steph steers me to the right. "Walk."

Nachos, French fries, maybe burgers.

"We're going for a mask-only supper?"

"Nope."

A rush of warm air, loud music and clanging sounds, more food smells. Brighter lights flash through the mask.

"Take it off," Steph says.

With both hands I pull the blindfold off.

"Surprise!" Greg, Mika, Barrett, Tom, Eddy, Mrs. Bronigan and Kyle stand in the doorway of the bowling alley grinning at me like crazy people. They're all wearing the same lame shirt and its super fluorescent in the neon light. They've accessorized them with glow in the dark neon bracelets, googly glasses, and necklaces.

I stare at them then turn to Steph, mouth open, close and open.

"Surprise," she says with the cutest smile. "A Merry Christmas send off."

Kyle waves two glow sticks at me. "Want one?"

"You bet." I take it from him as a blush moves up my neck to my cheeks.

"I booked two alleys. You kids take one and I'll challenge these amateurs." Steph puts her hands out and herds Tom, Eddy, Kyle and Mrs. B to the bowling shoe corner.

Steph did this? Steph organized this? For me? I have a heart-melt moment. Neon bowling is kind of juvenile, but everyone looks so freakin' happy.

"Come on." Mika grabs my hand and drags me over to get our ugly shoes. "Let's kick these guys' butts."

I take off my coat and follow the line of fluorescent glowing people, grin a stupid going-to-have-a-good-time grin.

"Girls against the boys." Barrett jumps and taps the soles of his feet together. "Bring it on."

Mika and I look at each other, roll our eyes and laugh.

Above each lane is a Christmas tree outlined in lights and the giant disco ball hanging from the middle of the room continually splashes colour across everything and everyone.

Before I go to our alley, I whisper in Steph's ear, "Thank you. You're the best."

"What?"

I mouth *thank you.*

She nods. Oh, no, she's getting glassy eyes. I give her a fake punch to the shoulder and go to get a ball.

Greg enters all our names as Christmas music blares. His first throw he does this tiptoe step and then a full turn before he lets the ball go. Hands on knees, he leans forward. They all fall except the middle pin which wobbles but recovers and stays standing.

"Nuts." Greg slams his fist into his palm at the same time Mrs. B. hobbles back with the hugest smile. I look down her lane and there are no pins standing. Impressive.

Balls spin, high fives celebrate strikes, exaggerated head hanging for gutter balls, the constant noise and lights and the fun, so much fun. My cheeks hurt. I lose track of who's winning but the board and Barrett are all over making sure the score is right. Mika and Barrett make a big production of being

better. Who knew Barrett was so competitive?

Greg grabs me in a tight hug complete with a twirl when he gets his first strike. I tell myself not to make a big deal out of it, but it sure feels good, and I wish it lasted longer.

“Food’s here,” Kyle shouts as trays of chicken wings, nachos, sliders, onion rings and other deep-fried stuff I don’t recognize arrives followed by a dessert tray full of chocolate deliciousness. Everyone rushes to fill plates.

After I’ve eaten enough grease, I pick a peanut butter marshmallow square and go over to Steph.

“This is so much fun.”

“I’m glad they kept it a surprise.”

I nod and we both watch our people.

When our time is up, we return our shoes. I’m hopeful someone sprays something in them cause the foot stink is rank.

“Thanks for coming.” I hug Mika first. “I’ll miss you guys.”

“Just remember to come back,” Barrett says as he joins in the hug and the rest follow. I’m stuck in the middle of another hugfest and it feels great.

As Steph drives out, the white lights, snow and black sky above makes the Banff Springs Hotel look like the magical castle pictured in so many postcards.

“That was the best,” I say.

Steph nods. Something tells me to be quiet, so I watch all the Christmas lights, blow-up Santas and smiling snowmen pass by. Banff Avenue is even more lit up. It feels like Christmas should be tomorrow. I want to meet Dale's family. I do. I keep telling myself I really do. I can't believe I'm thinking this—I'll miss Banff and everyone here.

***

"Are you all packed?" Steph leans against the kitchen counter with her hands wrapped around a coffee mug.

"Yeah. I texted Dale about packing a snowsuit. He said they have lots and I'm about the same size as Helen. Can you believe it, I'm her size?" I lift my hands in the air. "Anyway, it makes a lot more room without having to take that stuff. Do you think my gifts are okay?"

"They're perfect. Quit worrying. Besides, if they don't like them and have any kind of manners, you'll never know."

"I just want it to go okay. I want them to like me."

Steph sets her cup down and walks towards me with that here-comes-a-hug look. I'm not wrong. After she stops thumping my back and lets go, I say, "What was that for?"

"Because you're worried about whether they'll like you or not. How could they not like you?"

I roll my eyes. "Some people aren't Jillian fans."

"Name one. I'll deal with them."

"Stop. You know what I mean."

"I do know what you mean and you need to relax. Enjoy being with them. And have fun without me."

"That'll be easy." I wink.

"I'll be out front after school. Leave your bags in the back porch.

***

Lots of lockers are dressed up as Christmas presents and a few girls in sequined Christmas dresses with tree-light necklaces almost blind me. It all makes me smile. Merry Christmas greetings fill the hallway. Even to me. I get caught up in the fun until I see Akemi. As soon as she notices me, she looks the other way. Whatever. I will not let her lack of Christmas cheer ruin my mood.

During class, teachers are as unenthused to be here as we are. I can feel a tension like there's a huge party happening right after the next 40 minutes of boredom passes.

Barrett, in his goofy Santa hat, hands me a candy cane at the end of the day. “Have a great holiday.”

“I will.”

“That doesn’t sound convincing,” he says. “Try again.”

I put on an exaggerated happy face and wave the candy cane. “I will have a great holiday, Santa.”

“There you go. And I’ll stop in on Stephanie and irritate the hell out of her so she totally forgets you’re gone.”

“You’re the best. Thank you.”

“Besides, I need to live through you. I’ve never flown anywhere so have the best time ever and I want to hear about it when you get back.”

All I can do is nod, give him a hug and leave to meet Steph.

“Later, Spaghetti Face,” Barrett calls out.

I turn around. “What?”

He laughs and it’s okay. How does he always know what I need? My eyes don’t burn anymore.

Bucky shoves his head over the seat and sticks his cold nose on my face.

“You going to miss me?” I flap his ear. “You will, won’t you?”

“I’ve got all your stuff.” Steph points her thumb to the back seat beside Bucky. “And we’re ready to roll.”

After we’ve driven through town and onto the highway in silence, Steph says, “I’m

going to be okay. Do not waste time worrying about me. Got it?"

"Got it."

"No really, I mean it. I'll shed some ugly tears. That's normal. I'd be super weird if I didn't."

"You are weird."

"I am not." She pushes my shoulder hard enough I bump into the door. "Be sure to give Dale and his family a chance. Get to know them. Who knows, you may really like them."

That's it for the heavy talk. We point out favourite sites along the way and chat about nothing and everything to avoid stuff that will make either of us cry.

At the airport, Steph checks in with me and we walk to security together. Neither of us talk. My mind is in so many places. I'm nervous as hell about how it's going to go. What we'll do. How they'll act. Am I good enough for them? I practice different types of smiles.

"Jillian!"

Greg? Steph and I turn to see him jogging towards us.

"What's wrong?" It's hard to maintain a casual hi expression as my insides get giddy, he's here and curiosity works overtime as to why. Temple Guard training saves my ass. Mates. We're mates.

"Nothing. There's nothing wrong." He smiles. "I forgot to give you these the other night."

He waves a small Canada flag on a stick, spins me around and tucks it through the straps on my backpack.

“Americans like Canadians. Now they’ll know you’re one.”

“Thanks.”

He hands me a small booklet. Basic License, Alberta Driver’s Handbook.

“Study it on the plane. When you get back, you can take the test and I can teach you how to drive.”

I stare at the manual and nod because I’m not sure what look Steph must have on her face, and I don’t trust myself to look at either of them. The idea of driving a car is super cool. The idea of Greg teaching me how to drive that car is even super cooler.

“And this.” He pushes an envelope into my hand. “So you don’t forget us.”

I tuck the manual under my arm.

“Open it.”

I peel it open and pull out three pictures. One of the four of us leaving Norquay with our arms linked.

“How?” I stare at him. “How’d you take this?”

“Remember I told you they have cameras everywhere? I searched their site and found it.”

The next is a picture of the four of us sitting across the hill and the last one is the one when Greg told me to smile for the camera when we were getting off the lift.

"I love these," I say. And then look at the pictures again. Damn, I'm using that word a lot these days. "Thank you."

Greg grabs my shoulders. "You have the best time in Denver. I'll see you when you get back."

He gives me a hug. His shirt collar smells like fresh hung-outside-to-dry laundry. When he pushes me back, I keep my eyes quiet and maintain a steady smile because I can't tell if it was a *just-mates* hug. My stomach tightens as his face comes close. *He's going to kiss me*. Oh, my gosh. I can feel my eyes get round as I let my lips loosen. And he kisses me. On the forehead.

As my heart sinks into my boots, I force my face to remain cheery so he can't tell how disappointed I am. I'm such a dork. Why would he kiss-kiss me?

Mates. Just mates, runs through my head to ease my embarrassment. But wait. Would it have been a real kiss if Steph hadn't been right there? Maybe that's why it ended up a forehead kiss. It's possible, right? From now on, I dub forehead kisses as highly underrated and that gives me hope.

"Have a great time." He gives my arms a gentle squeeze. With a quick wink, he turns and walks away, waving over the top of his head, not looking back.

Steph and I watch him leave. My face is on broil. What the hell? Are we mates? Are we more than mates? What are we? Why

would he drive all the way to Calgary to give me these things? He could have waited until I got back.

“What was that all about?” Steph says as she continues to stare after him.

“Nothing.” I pull off my pack to get my ticket and avoid eye contact with her. “Nothing.” I repeat it to convince both of us. But nothing sure feels like something.

“That’s you and it’s on time.” Steph points to the arrival departure board. “Have fun. Send a few pictures and miss me a bit.” She hugs me.

“I will. Of course, I will.”

We hug for longer than normal.

“Okay, kid, get going.” She shooshes me away with her hands. “You don’t want me ugly crying here.”

I spin around cause my eyes burn and wave over my head at her.

As the door to security closes, I see her one more time as she wipes her hand across her eyes. Oh, Steph. I blink fast. She tries to be so tough and she’s not.

They say the firsts are the hardest and this will be our first without Oma or Opa. What will she do? The house is going to be so quiet. Tom won’t be around. Bucky is not a huge conversationalist and it’s not like Steph’s got tons of friends. She will be okay. Right? The line moves as people put their stuff in trays for the security scans.

This is going to be the longest ten days of my life.

After security I walk the long, Christmas lit hallway to my terminal. When they broadcast the Denver flight boarding announcement, I pick up my pace. Travellers hold out their tickets and ID for the flight attendant and I join the back of the line.

Go. Don't go. Go. Don't go. What the hell?

I tap my ticket against my palm. What am I doing? Its not like my dad's been all gaga about me coming to visit them. He came to town, talked, invited me for Christmas and rushed home. He's not exactly busting down doors to get to know me.

What's the difference if I meet them now or next summer? They might be disappointed if I don't show up or…maybe they'll all be relieved, and they can have the type of Christmas they're used to. I don't know. I hate myself for being insensitive to their feelings. It embarrasses me, and I check around to make sure no one can read my thoughts.

Reality is—I don't know them. I *know* Steph.

I snatch my boarding pass out of the attendants' hand and she jumps back like I hit her.

"Sorry, change of plans." I wave the ticket in the air as I jostle through the crowd to get out of the boarding line.

After I find a clear path, I grab my phone and punch in Steph's number. One ring, two rings. My pack thumps on my back as I hurry down the stairs. Three rings. Come on, Steph. Don't let me down. Four rings. She's probably trying to pull over, so she doesn't do the distracted driving thing.

Which way do I go? I read the signs and follow the exit arrows.

"Hello," Steph finally says.

"Come back and get me. I'm not going."

"What? What's wrong? What happened? Are you okay?" Her voice escalates with each question.

"I'm fine. I'm just not going. I want to stay here, with you."

Silence.

"Steph?"

"Yeah." Another pause. "Are you sure?" she says in a quiet voice.

"Yup. I'll figure out how to get my suitcase sent back and meet you out front where we came in."

"Jillian, have you thought this through? What about your dad and meeting his family?"

"I'll text him. Then call when we get home to explain."

"He'll be upset."

"If he's a decent guy he'll understand."

Silence.

"I've got to find an agent and deal with my suitcase. Meet you out front. Bye."

Then a quick text to Dale.

Sorry I'm not coming. I can't leave Steph alone. I will call later. Sorry.

***

When I find Steph at the entrance, her face breaks into a huge smile but she tones it down a notch when she sees me see her. We both power walk to each other. She grabs me and gives me the biggest hug ever complete with a kiss to the side of my head.

I made the right decision.

I keep my face pressed into her ski jacket and grin. Steph's getting soft on me. Who knew that was possible? As fast as the hug starts, it's over and we're marching out the doors to the truck.

As the lights of the airport fade, I turn to Steph. "Maybe we can do something for Christmas, start a new thing, you and me."

"Keep talking."

"We could decorate the house. There's no Christmas stuff out."

Steph snorts. "Sorry, I haven't really been in the mood for it."

"I know. Me either. But we can jazz it up. If it doesn't cheer us up, we'll fake it."

"Oma's got boxes of stuff in the attic."

I nod. “She loved Christmas and decorating and cooking and people.”

“But no ham and purple sauerkraut.” Steph fakes a gag. “I can’t do it again.”

“Gotcha.” I hate that I cringe at the thought of eating Oma’s Christmas Eve traditional purple kraut. I only ate it because it was Oma’s but really, it tastes like…well, there’s nothing really to describe the taste of purple sauerkraut.

Oma, I’m sorry. We all ate it because you put everything into making it and making it was your big tradition. And we love you. Look how easy the word keeps slipping out. I smile.

Did Oma and Opa meet up wherever you go when you die? Are they together? Or is that just every one’s way of making themselves feel better by pretending people you love meet again in the afterlife?

At least their boxes of ashes sit side by side in the living room. Steph even put Opa’s picture on his. I remember when I thought it was morbid when Oma’s box sat on the bookcase with her smiling face on the front. Now it’s kind of cute seeing them there together. Okay. I shudder. Now I’m the one being morbid.

“How about we do a Christmas Eve brunch?” I say. “Everyone probably already has dinner plans, but they might come for a brunch.

"Uh huh." Steph's head bobs up and down. "Keep going."

"We could invite Kyle and Mrs. Bronigan, Eddy and Barrett and Greg maybe. You know, if they're not busy already."

Steph glances at me but I face the front. She doesn't need to know about the tingle I feel when I think of Greg coming to say bye at the airport. It still bugs me wondering if he would have kissed me on the lips if she hadn't been there. He drove all the way to the airport to give me the manual and the pictures. That's got to mean something. Or else he's just the best friend ever. I have to be super careful figuring this out. I don't want to ruin 'just mate' status but if we can be more, how great would that be?

I exhale slowly, so I don't jump too far ahead. I will be cautious navigating this relationship status—that will be my motto. Cautious navigation.

"We can make fancy omelettes and bacon, make some cookies and stuff," I say. "Kyle likes pancakes with Nutella and ice cream. I could make Mickey Mouse ones for him."

"Yeah, that sounds good," Steph says. "A new tradition for us."

My grin hurts my face, so I let it relax.

"Hey," I pause and inhale a breath of courage. "With a new tradition maybe we could, you know, unload a bunch of shit we're holding onto and start fresh."

"What do you mean?"

"You know, I tell you stuff about stuff I should have told you about, and you can tell me what stuff you're keeping a secret."

"What happened? What didn't you tell me about?"

"Relax. It'll be a type of bonding experiment, you and me. Sharing secrets."

She turns and gives me squinty eyes. "I don't have any secrets."

"Oh, I think you might have one or two. We'll figure it out. And then we can both start the New Year with a clean slate. Easy peasy."

Steph lets out a long snort-sigh as headlights flash across the inside of the cab from the Christmas holiday traffic on the Trans Canada. I have ten days to just hang out. Maybe I can go boarding with everyone. And I'll study the manual and surprise Greg when I get my Learner's License.

Staying in Banff is going to be…what's the right word? Epic. Yup, it's going to be epic.

The End

Acknowledgements

Thank you to my family who are always a great source of ideas quickly followed by opinions and critiques. If you see your suggestion in my story, don't go taking all the credit. And if you recognize a character, be sure to keep their secrets.

A big thank you to long-time friend Dan Brunton who sent me a CBC Short Story Contest link so many years ago. How exciting to have Shelagh Rogers place my story in the top three. How disappointing to follow it up with a folder of rejections and the start of this roller coaster writing life.

Determined to improve my storytelling, I attended Writescape Workshops facilitated by the lovely Ruth Walker and Gwynn Scheltema. At the first session I sat next to Jack Livesley. It was the start of an invaluable mentorship that continued until his passing in 2018. His lessons on not being verbose and read it out loud sit on my shoulder when I write and often wake me up at night with a fright.

A huge thanks to my writing critique group: Andrea Adair-Tippins, Evelyn Pollock, Lisa Reynolds and Lyndi Allison. You gals are the best. Your suggestions,

comments and love helped the story grow to what it is today. Thanks to Brian Henry for the manuscript edit. Lisa Reynolds, Lyndi Allison and Sami Wackerle—you found the holes during the final review and I filled them. I appreciate all the time you spent with my story.

And thank you to Jude Pittman, Nancy Bell and all the great folk at BWL Publishing for making my dreams come true.

Not to be left last by any means, thank you Johnny Reid for always playing in the background and knowing just what music the muse needs.

Also published by BWL Publishing Inc.

Summer of Lies

Barbara Baker grew up in Banff, Alberta and spends her free time racing up and down the Rockies to keep up with an active family of outdoor enthusiasts. Her passions include writing, photography, exploring landscapes and time with her grandchildren. Many of her short stories are published in magazines and anthologies. Carousel Pictures made a mini film of her essay, Life Support, which played in the Toronto International Film Festival (fall 2019). You can contact her at bbaker.write@gmail.com and her author page at BWL Publishing https://www.bookswelove.com/baker-barba/

Manufactured by Amazon.ca
Acheson, AB

30215596R00186